A HISTORY OF AUGUSTAN FABLE

This book explores the tradition of fable across a wide variety of written and illustrative media, from its origins in classical antiquity to the end of the eighteenth century and beyond. It offers both a history and a poetics of the genre, presenting a body of evidence on the stable and transhistorical qualities of fable, while showing that many individual writers consciously employed these qualities in dynamic and witty ways highly responsive to their own historical and cultural moment. Tracing the impact of classical and European models on verse and moral fables of the eighteenth century, and the use of the fable by major writers – including Dryden, Pope, Mandeville, Swift, Gay, and Cowper – in their historical and literary contexts, Mark Loveridge offers the first full account of a significant form of English and European literature and suggests new ways of reading eighteenth-century literature.

Mark Loveridge is Lecturer in English at the University of Wales, Swansea, and author of *Laurence Sterne and the Argument about Design* (1982).

A HISTORY OF AUGUSTAN FABLE

MARK LOVERIDGE

PUBLISHED BY THE PRESS SYNDICATE OF THE UNIVERSITY OF CAMBRIDGE
The Pitt Building, Trumpington Street, Cambridge CB2 1RP

CAMBRIDGE UNIVERSITY PRESS
The Edinburgh Building, Cambridge CB2 2RU, United Kingdom
40 West 20th Street, New York, NY 10011–4211, USA
10 Stamford Road, Oakleigh, Melbourne 3166, Australia

First published 1998

Printed in Great Britain at the University Press, Cambridge

Typeset in Baskerville 10/12.5 (VN)

A catalogue record for this book is available from the British Library

Library of Congress cataloguing in publication data

Loveridge, Mark, 1951–
A history of Augustan fable / Mark Loveridge.
p. cm.
Includes bibliographical references and index.
ISBN 0 521 63062 2 (hardback)
1. Fables. English – History and criticism.
2. English literature – 18th century – History and criticism.
3. English literature – Early modern, 1500–1700 – History and criticism.
4. Didactic, literature, English – History and criticism.
5. English literature – Classical influences.
6. Moral, conditions in literature.
7. Animals in literature. 8. Ethics in literature.
9. Literary form. I. Title.
PR448.F34L68 1998
820.9'005–dc21 97–32207 CIP

ISBN 0 521 63062 2 hardback

For Kate

Contents

Illustrations

Illustrations by Randolph Caldecott from *Some of Aesop's Fables* (nos. 1, 3, and 5), by J. J. Grandville, from *Fables de La Fontaine* (Nos. 2 and 6), and from the Bayeux Tapestry (No. 4) are printed from copies in the author's possession. Illustrations from John Ogilby's *The Fables of Aesop* (Nos. 7, 8, 9, 10, 11), from his *Aesopics* (No. 12), and Thomas Chippendale's design for a *girandole* from *The Gentleman and Cabinet-Maker's Director* (No. 13) are all printed by permission of the Syndics of Cambridge University Library.

Preface and acknowledgements

This project has been under way for so long that acknowledging its debts is like the moment in *Waiting for Godot* when a stage direction instructs Gogo to gesture at the universe. Everyone knew something interesting about this kind of fable which I did not know: that was one of the things that so impressed me about the subject. Could anyone who has ever helped me please consider themselves thanked. However, I would like to single out for particular thanks my students and colleagues in the English department at Swansea, particularly Ian Bell, Andrew Varney, Sam Dawson, and Glyn Pursglove, and John Morgan in Classics; Howard Erskine-Hill, James Raven, and the students in the 'long eighteenth century' seminar at Cambridge; the staffs of libraries in London, Swansea, and Cambridge; R. P. Davies of the photographic unit at Swansea; Josie Dixon at Cambridge University Press, especially for her patience; and the Press's inscrutable but very sensible readers. Tomoko Hanazaki is due a public apology: he sent me a copy of his article which I promptly misplaced for two years.

The largest debt, though, apart from the one in the dedication, is to the writers of the several very good Ph.D theses on fable which, until about 1990, represented almost the whole of the work in this field. As far as I know, none of these apart from Thomas Noel's ever came to publication, presumably because the field was deemed not to exist. They deserved better. Things have changed a little since, but I am still conscious that part of my remit here is to *open* the subject as fully as possible.

One result of this consciousness is something for which I probably need to apologize to the reader. This is the use of a version of the 'author-date' reference system, which is not supposed to be viable in the Arts because of insuperable difficulties which I have tried to sidestep more or less elegantly, and which the reader may find distracting because unfamiliar. It became clear in the course of writing that the temptation to document the subject at all fully by adding footnotes and a bibliography was going to have to be resisted in the interests of presenting the outline of the case clearly. Author-date was the only way of forcing this discipline upon myself. The book might have been six times as large: there are more verse fables in the Augustan period than there are sonnets in the Renaissance, in English. What I wanted to stress was the persistence of the *generic tradition* across a variety of media, and so to describe a way of reading and writing – a manner of proceeding – which I think was inherent in the period but which has since been lost. To do this I have had to proceed somewhat on my own terms, and to keep scholarly interventions as light as possible. In those sections where large amounts of information are being passed at speed, I have usually indicated the source of the data elliptically by brief quotation. The most notable omission is probably Anne Finch, Countess Winchilsea: the reader is referred to Jayne Lewis's chapter on her.

The other apology is that I have not been able to make more of the material with which I concern myself directly visible to the reader. There is no anthology or collection of this literature: there is no widely available modern edition of Babrius and Phaedrus, apart from Perry's *Babrius and Phaedrus*, which dates from 1965. There is no accessible edition of Ogilby's fables apart from the Augustan Society reprint, also from 1965. How does one find out whether Smart's Story of a COCK and BULL and Hall-Stevenson's fables might really have something to do with *Tristram Shandy*? Whether generations of readers were wholly wrong to prefer Moore's *Fables for the Female Sex* to those of Gay? Why Croxall's was the most popular prose collection until well into the nineteenth century, why La Motte's fables were preferred in English to those of La Fontaine – and so on. For the moment, apart from the canonical writers whom I have treated at some length, the proof of the pudding must rest in the morsels provided herein. But, as Confucius says, *this too will change.*

Abbreviations

BNYPL	*Bulletin of the New York Public Library*
CR	*Critical Review; or, Annals of Literature*
EC	*Essays in Criticism*
ECS	*Eighteenth-Century Studies*
ELH	*Journal of English Literary History*
GJ	*The Gentleman's Journal*
GM	*The Gentleman's Magazine*
JEGP	*Journal of English and Germanic Philology*
JHI	*Journal of the History of Ideas*
MLN	*Modern Language Notes*
MLR	*Modern Language Review*
MP	*Modern Philology*
PMLA	*Publications of the Modern Language Society of America*
POAS	*Poems on Affairs of State: Augustan Satirical Verse, 1660–1714*
RES	*Review of English Studies*
SEL	*Studies in English Literature*
UTQ	*University of Toronto Quarterly*

Please note that in the text animals are given an initial capital letter when they are being discussed as the actors in fables, but a lower-case one where it is, or is more, a question of nature. The generic or general name of a fable – for example The Lion's Share – is designated by capitals without inverted commas. This form of reference has been extended, as a form of compliment, to one or two other works referred to in the text.

CHAPTER I

Introduction

> We emphasize . . . that we are not interested in the influence of separate individual authors, individual works, individual themes, ideas, images – what interests us is precisely the influence of the generic tradition itself which was transmitted through the individual authors . . . A genre is always the same and yet not the same, old and new simultaneously.
>
> (Bakhtin 1984: 159, 106)

> Examples are best Precepts . . .
>
> (Ogilby 1651: title-page)

This study will explore relationships between different aspects and manifestations of the term 'fable', in particular in the period between the English Civil Wars of the mid-seventeenth century and the start of the French revolutionary wars near the end of the eighteenth century. Its strategy is double. On the one hand, it puts forward a body of evidence which suggests that literary fable exhibits interesting stable, epochal, or transhistorical qualities as a genre – hence the first quotation above. On the other, it hopes to show that many of the individual writers of fable in English in this period were aware of these qualities, and employed them to develop a coherent but idiosyncratic literary mode, always highly responsive to its historical and cultural moment, which is as *considerable*, as dynamic, as witty, and capable of as much mischief as any other form of literary art in the period – hence the second quotation. The intention is, then, to present something between a history and a poetics of fable.

These are unusual contentions and procedures. Academic readers at large have not yet, despite several recent attempts, been provoked into admitting that fable in English is a viable literary mode. No current work on fable has enough confidence in its subject to venture more than a toe into the murky waters that lie post-1740: most stop with Gay, in either 1727 (his first series) or 1738 (his second). And the notion that the study of fable must involve interrelationships, which is the basic contention – indeed the crux – here, is a nut almost wholly resistant to critical teeth. Ask literary historians who deal with this culture what 'fable' is, and an informed reply will come in three quite separate parts.

There is firstly the verse fable, widespread, diverse, popular, and well-respected in its time, but now felt to be essentially minor. The two best general studies of the period's poetry, Eric Rothstein's *Restoration and Eighteenth-Century Poetry* (1981) and Margaret Doody's *The Daring Muse* (1985) virtually ignore verse fable, with very brief discussion of examples. Despite Vinton Dearing's description of a 'resurgence of scholarly interest' (Gay 1974: 2, 620) in Gay's *Fables*, a specialist volume of essays on Gay (Lewis and Wood 1988) could manage a total of only thirty-four lines on his two collections. When other major writers use verse fables, these are usually seen (to quote Rachel Trickett on Cowper) as 'insignificant in relation to their major works' (Trickett 1983: 480). But the idea that there could be any relation between Cowper's animal fables and his other modes, and that these relations might have been legible to readers even as late as the 1790s, is not canvassed.

The second element of the answer is that a fable, or moral fable, is a prose fiction; in particular, a non-realistic fiction with philosophical qualities, such as *Rasselas* or Voltaire's *Candide* – a *conte philosophique* or 'ouvrage qui dit plus qu'il ne semble dire' ('work which says more than it seems to say': Voltaire 1972: 61), as Voltaire has it in the dedicatory letter in *Zadig* (1748). Connections with verse fable are not felt to exist, beyond the broad point that each form works by using the representation of a specific action or set of events to convey a general 'truth' of some kind. Jayne Lewis's recent survey of many of the Aesopian aspects of fable in this period, *The English Fable*, mentions that there are such things as 'Aesopically inflected novels' in the 1740s, but chooses not to pursue this, perhaps restrained by Lewis's post-Watt view of the novel as subject to 'realist literary imperatives [which] robbed fictions as conspicuous and self-ironizing as Aesop's of much of their authority' (Lewis 1996: 19, 186). But even 'realistic' novels of the 1770s could use fable in a self-ironizing mode.

The third element is the meaning which might provide connections but apparently cannot. 'Fable' is the distressingly vague, notoriously hydra-headed technical term which, via a Latin translation of Aristotle's word *muthos* (henceforward: *mythos)* in the *Poetics*, can indicate the plot or narrative action of a tragedy or epic poem, and, by extension, plot in any form of narrative. Other meanings abound. Cicero divided narrative into three classes, Fabula, Historia, Argumentum, and defined Fabula as a non-realistic story. This usage and the previous one gave fable a life both as a genre in itself – non-realistic story – and a constituent part of many genres, plot. Sadly, this did not make for clarity of thought; and the problem was made worse by *fabula* being used more loosely in Latin to mean both 'story' and 'fable'. Another problem is that the English do not appear to *think*, or to have thought, about fable: the only book dealing exclusively with the theory of fable in the eighteenth century is Thomas Noel's *Theories of the Fable in the Eighteenth Century*, which demonstrates that to declare a bias towards the theory of fable in this period is to declare a strong bias towards the French and German manifestations of the topic. The English have virtually no native tradition of formal fable-theory. As late as 1761 Dodsley's 'Essay on Fable', 'the first and only attempt at a thorough study of the genre in England', (Noel 1975: 115) is still content to echo La Motte from forty years earlier, and La Motte has his roots in Le Bossu's work in the 1670s. As in other periods, the English like to make do with attitude and inventive practice rather than theory: examples over precepts.

Sometimes 'fable' has moral/narrative overtones – a 'moral fable' or apologue – but sometimes it is used to indicate specifically the part of a narrative which does not include the end-moral, the epimythium. In eighteenth-century models of literary probability, the fable (the story) should *conduce to* the moral, draw the reading mind towards it, but does not fully embody it. Or the fable – in a figure derived from La Fontaine's clever revision of the Aristotelian dictum that 'the *Fable* or *Plot* [is] the *Soul* of a *Tragedy*' (Rymer 1678: 4) – is the body of the story; the moral is the soul, as it is (ideally) invisible and immaterial. Fable, as Jayne Lewis points out before retreating to Aesopian ground, is 'polyvalent. It could signify a lie, any "feign'd or devis'd discourse", a plot, a hieroglyph, a parable, a myth' (Lewis 1996: 10). In the eighteenth century the word could also be used loosely to cover all of the period's fiction: in 1783 James Beattie managed to discuss virtually every canonical novel of the past eighty years under his siamese-twin headings of 'Fable' and 'Romance,' transferring himself quite unselfconsciously from discussion of Aesopian fables, via 'a more extensive field of fable', to the 'MODERN ROMANCE, or POETICAL PROSE FABLE' which is the fully-fledged novel (Beattie 1783: 511, 518). The period's technical literary terms lag behind its increasingly diverse practice, and the apparently naïve polytropism of 'fable' embarrasses and puzzles modern critics.

Such multifariousness can make browsing in 'fable' frustrating. Reading the Garland Press's *Fable Scholarship: An Annotated Bibliography* (ed. Pack Carnes 1985) conveys the moral that 'fable' is the province of folklorists: the secondary literature on modern literary fable is simply not present. Mythographers use 'fable' or 'classical fable' to mean something different again, the narrative mode of Greek, Latin, Scandinavian, and other myths about gods and supernatural heroes. Jane Chance can use the phrase *Classical Fable* in the subtitle of her collection of essays entitled *The Mythographic Art* (1990) but there is no indication in the volume that 'fable' might mean anything but 'myth'. And then, as Michel de Certeau points out in *The Mystic Fable*, the history of the 'spoken word [*parole*] . . . so closely bound to religious traditions' is often spoken of by 'its scientific "examiners" and "observers"' as 'fable' (de Certeau 1992: 12). French examiners, that is: the only English word to retain the proper sense of the verb *to fable* – from *fari* and *fabulari*, to talk, to hold discourse – into the modern period is *to confabulate*. Hence Cowper's charming subtranslational joke at the start of his fable 'Pairing Time Anticipated' (1792):

> I shall not ask Jean Jacques Rousseau
> If Birds confabulate or no:
> 'Tis clear that they were always able
> To hold discourse at least in fable. (Cowper 1980–95: 3, 51)

'This term [fable] originally referred to the stories whose task it was to symbolize a society' says de Certeau (1992: 12) with an airy inclusiveness, and apparently reverting to the written word. Epic (the other term for such stories), myth, fable, discourse as dialogue, all revolve together. But technically, to fable may mean to hold discourse, and hence may indicate the conversations of the 'two actors' themselves: what the Ant says to the Grasshopper, and *vice versa*.

Other studies quite properly become fascinated by the literary fable's closeness to and illumination of its social, historical, and political contexts. Annabel Patterson stresses the combative nature of seventeenth-century political fables in her *Fables of Power* (1991); Jayne Lewis's book is partly designed as a riposte, widening the area of interest to highlight fable's interests in the politics of representation, and focusing on fable's capacity for 'reactive mediation' (Lewis 1996: 3, 5, 12, etc.) between different political and representational positions. This kind of breadth is certainly necessary if the central grounds and functions of fable are to be properly understood, but there are as many problems inherent in arguments about the mediative powers of fable as there are in limiting fable's interests in power to the narrowly political.

Such multiple contexts and perspectives, taken together with the difficulties of definition and the large number of forms to which literary fable turns out to be related, make it difficult to study literary fable for its own sake. And although the fondness of English fable for attitude over theory, reactive example over precept, effectively constitutes a consistent character in itself, it also places a limitation on the aim of demonstrating that English fable is a coherent mode, in that it often necessitates inductive arguments from individual reaction in example and practice, or in a pattern of examples which adds up to a practice. It is best to retreat for the moment to noting that James Beattie does not seem to be puzzled by the term 'fable', and to revert to the main problem raised so far.

The two linked critical charges that can be made against fable have to do with status and coherence: the term cannot be interesting and valuable if it indicates merely a series of inchoate, discrete elements. A preliminary defence against such charges should firstly suggest that verse fable may have a coherent history of change through the period, and secondly should show that writers understood the various manifestations of fable – poetry, fiction, theory – to have some natural links and connections. This in turn might introduce the possibility that fable is not merely 'polyvalent', but is also a composite mode or strategy evolving from a common rootstock across different genres, and that this may be how Beattie apprehends it as late as 1783.

Verse fable in particular exhibits a peculiar flexibility, an ability to blend with and adapt to changing cultural surroundings. Rothstein and Doody both stress the movement of eighteenth-century poetry away from 'the idea of the poem as closed formal unit' (Doody 1985: 61) and towards more open forms and attitudes. When Rothstein attempts a 'diagrammatic statement' about the shifting focus of poetry, he defines it in terms of a drift away from 'a central theme – power – in the Restoration, to a central operating principle, that of interaction, corporateness, treatment of all themes in terms of social, intellectual, or moral composites' in the middle part of the period. After about 1735 this yields in turn to 'a controlling attitude . . . of sympathy, a call for fellow-feeling' (Rothstein 1981: 120).

The verse fable is well placed to reflect each of these shifts in emphasis, and hence to emerge as an aspect of the most adaptable of the period's literary modes. Power is its most fundamental interest or theme.

Aesop was traditionally a slave who spoke to his masters using the licence of indirection, and Aesopian fables often develop the Wolf-eat-Lamb morality of animal appetite, dominance, and natural hierarchy, in order to figure the worlds of social and political relationship. Seventeenth-century English fabulists employ the form as a way of expressing political tensions, and of exploring ideas about the limits of the heroic.

But its basic method or 'operating principle' is transformational and metaphorical: beasts, men, gods, inanimate objects, personifications of abstract qualities, all revolve together in a kaleidoscopic, sub-Ovidian universe, as do distinct political and philosophical positions. Intellectual and moral composites are entirely appropriate to the composite form of the fable-collection. And when the sympathetic mode is favoured, fabulists will develop the fable's innate stress on the kinship between human, animal, and lower and higher forms of life, and can shade the tone towards sympathetic humour and the self-mocking wit of fables which feature poets, oysters, and sensitive plants. This emphasizes the fable's more lyrical side, resulting in the greening of the form – *Fables of Flora, Fables of Flowers* – and also in the fable used as a mode for expressing post-pastoral alienation and discomfort in Cowper and others: sympathy denied.

But this does not mean that the fable simply followed fashions. Fabulists in the period are quite aware that in itself a fable is *si peu que rien*, and that *any* creative literary fable thus has to be conditioned or occasioned by, and adapted to, its context of use. Literary fable is always 'an active discursive intervention conditioned by precise social and historical circumstances' (Hirschkop 1986: 93), as Ken Hirschkop says of the Bakhtinian 'dialogical' condition.

The principle that a fable is intrinsically nothing is inherent in its history, the origins of which lie in Latin and Greek prose compilations of the orally transmitted Aesopian material. The materials of these collections were simple and neutral, but were designed to be available for use in giving flavour and zest to another medium, rhetorical discourse. Such collections acted as repositories of metaphorical, illustrative narrative devices: the 'morals' were originally attached to the fables as a means of codifying or indexing this inert 'raw material' (Perry 1965: xii). Prose fables were also used as a neutral educational medium for the teaching of language through late antiquity, and, in England and France, from the early Renaissance onwards. This provided a continuing reminder of the tradition of non-literary usage in the seventeenth and eighteenth centuries; and political fable as Patterson describes it continues the classical rhetorical tradition, appropriating fables *pro* and *con* particular positions. So any literary fabulist will be aware of fable as a 'genre' in the Bakhtinian sense – as an abstract or ideal construction, codified and centralized, somewhat akin to the '*langue*' in Saussurean models of linguistics – and aware of his or her own use of it as in tension between this fundamental aspect of fable and the availability of a potentially infinite number of revisions, adaptations, and original stresses – '*paroles*', individual voices. Here the fact that fable was the only modern literary genre to be invented in, or just after – one could almost say *by* – the English Civil Wars, at a point when the use of different styles of language was a central feature of religious and political division, must raise the intriguing possibility that English fable is one of the best examples of a fully dialogical form of literature. But as always with fable, it is wise to be cautious: if fable can (as we shall see) bear or carry any application, it can certainly bear or carry any *theory*, and eighteenth-century fable in particular often generates its own self-supporting and self-descriptive terminology, in figures of speech and phrasing. Again, we should retreat to examples.

If fable were a live and coherent subject through this period, very different writers should be capable of making idiosyncratic uses of their perception of such a basic and widely available principle as the tension between fable as a neutral, pre-literary mode and the embroiled nature of fabulist discourse as it is used and 'applied'. They might also then work to provide the second element of a preliminary defence of fable, demonstrable kinship between the various literary manifestations or aspects of the form. The two following examples, one from a dramatic prose satire of an extended verse fable of the 1680s and the other from a novel of the 1750s, show that the writers were in each case quite clear about the differences between the fable-in-itself and the energized literary fable. Crucially, they also show that they readily credited some of their readers with an equivalent capacity.

In 1687 Matthew Prior and Charles Montague travestied what they saw as the recent misuse of fable in Dryden's extraordinary Catholic-and-Protestant debate-fable *The Hind and the Panther*. They did this by picturing Dryden as Bayes, the 'author' of *The Hind and the Panther, Transvers'd to the Story of the* Country-Mouse *and the* City Mouse, and by throwing Bayes into conversation with Smith and Johnson (the pair of characters created by Buckingham to act as the sceptical audience in his earlier anti-Dryden dramatic travesty *The Rehearsal*). Near the start, Bayes is made to show off his grotesque misunderstanding of the relationship between pre-aesthetic and activated fable, by fulminating to Smith and Johnson about Horace's use of the story of The Country-Mouse and The City-Mouse in his Satire II, 6:

You remember in him the *Story* of the *Country-Mouse*, and the *City-Mouse*, what a plain simple thing it is, it has no more life and spirit in it, I'gad, than a Hobby-horse; and his *Mice* talk so meanly, such common stuff, so like *meer Mice*, that I wonder it has pleas'd the world so long. But I will now undeceive *Mankind*, and teach 'em to *heighten*, and *elevate a Fable* . . . whereas *Horace* keeps to the dry naked story, I have more copiousness than to do that, I'gad. (Prior 1959: I, 39)

The 'dry naked story' of the original neutral prose fable was in fact considerably elevated by Horace, in what was the fullest and most extended poeticization of an Aesopian fable prior to Babrius and Phaedrus. Horace's City-Mouse's appeal to his country friend to come home with him and enjoy the manifold fruits of the city manages to combine the awareness of being part of the animal creation with the full resonance of the humane *carpe diem* theme:

> Since all must dye, and must resign their Breath,
> Nor great, nor little is secure from Death;
> Then spend thy days in Pleasure, Mirth and Sport,
> And live like One, that Minds his Life is short. (Creech 1684: 477)

Bayes's misreading of Horace's fable acts as a tacit sign that his own fable would be doubly elevated, hyperbolical and absurd – '*Fable* upon *Fable*', as Bayes says later (Prior 1959: I, 53) – which was the charge generally levelled at Dryden's poem: constitutional 'absurdity' (Johnson 1905: I, 380). Neither Prior nor his bemused double-act of Smith-and-Johnson need say as much at this early point, though. The criticism, the 'moral', is unspoken, immaterial, as it should be in a genuine fable. Prior has already discharged it in general terms, in the discursive mode of the Preface:

Is it not as easie to imagine two Mice *bilking Coachmen, and supping at the* Devil; *as to suppose a* Hind *entertaining the* Panther *at a* Hermits Cell, *discussing the greatest Mysteries of Religion . . . What can be more improbable and contradictory to the Rules and Examples of all Fables . . .* ? (Prior 1959: I, 39)

But the dramatic display from Bayes carries the particular technical reason for the absurdity. Prior sociably assumes that his audience is conversant enough with this point about the proper levels of fable to be able to apply it for themselves, and then demonstrates the result.

Because Dryden's fable is absurd, Bayes's is too: Dryden's noble beasts become mice, though at first Prior retains the (falsely noble) sonority of Dryden's lines. Indeed, some of the lines of the travesty of the first Part are identical to those in the original, as for instance line three:

> *A milk-white* Mouse *immortal and unchang'd*
> *Fed on soft Cheese, and o're the* Dairy *rang'd;*
> *Without, unspotted; innocent within,*
> *She fear'd no danger, for she knew no Ginn.* (*ibid.*, 40)

Dryden might reply that to him 'fable' now meant something different. His preliminary address at the start of Part Three refers to 'two *Episodes*, or *Fables*' (Dryden 1956–92: 3, 122) inside the poem, bird-fables which the beasts rehearse to each other, as if a 'fable' were an illustrative sub-unit of narrative, as in Horace. Dryden observes decorum – beasts can make free with birds because they are (metaphorically) above them, as Volpone the Fox is above Corvino the Crow – but in terms of the purists' definition of fable implicit in Prior's Preface, his defence of fable as episode would merely admit the charge: fable within fable, '*Fable* upon *Fable*', is weirdly pleonastic. Dryden is well versed in the history of fable: it seems that he consciously chose to give the poem that marked his own conversion to Catholicism the quality of a monster, a 'creature of a double kind' (*ibid.*, 480), like the Anglican Panther rather than the Catholic Hind.

The second example of a writer making use of the distinction between the fable-in-itself and fable-in-action is from the long penultimate chapter of Charlotte Lennox's satirical novel *The Female Quixote* (1752), a chapter now convincingly attributed to Samuel Johnson rather than to Lennox (Margaret Doody sets out the evidence fully in Lennox 1989: 414–15). Arabella, the distracted heroine, is in conversation with a learned divine who plays the traditional literary 'moral doctor' or physician of the mind. This figure goes back as far as Lady Macbeth's doctor and, in Marlowe, Faustus's Old Man (though they have less promising material to work with), and may derive partly from fable's conceit of the philosopher-fabulist as 'Physitian . . . to the Frenzy-Times' (*Aesop* 1698[j]: 2). The doctor promises to cure Arabella of her naughty belief that the world of prose romance is real and actual. Arabella engages in a lucid discussion about other kinds of fiction, and fiction in general, demonstrating that apart from her foible about romance her mind is perfectly sound.

The argument then turns to the theme of absurdity *versus* truth, as the valiant Doctor tries to prove that romances are intrinsically absurd. He sets up two examples of kinds of literature in which, by contrast, 'Truth is not . . . injured by Fiction.' The first is Richardson's *Clarissa* (1747–8), which is said to convey 'the most solid Instructions, the noblest Sentiments, and the most exalted Piety', and the second is 'The Fables of Aesop', which 'though never I suppose believed, have been long considered as Lectures of moral and domestic Wisdom' (Lennox 1989: 377). This transition or conflation may seem curious – how is *Clarissa* like Aesop's fables? – but Richardson published his own *Aesop's Fables* in 1739 just before bringing out *Pamela* in 1740, and was fond of allowing his characters to use allusions to fables, sometimes to his own edition. Pamela's usual habit, especially early in the narrative, is to refer glancingly to Aesopian fables to illustrate her points or her own position.

Arabella is allowed to develop and refine the Doctor's point with such magisterial concision and elegance of expression as to suggest that she considers her opinion axiomatic – or that Johnson does:

> The Fables of *Aesop*, said *Arabella*, are among those of which the Absurdity discovers itself, and the Truth is comprised in the Application; but what can be said of those Tales which are told with the solemn Air of historical Truth, and if false convey no Instruction? (*ibid.*: 377)

This is not quite Prior's kind of absurdity, but a description which derives from stressing or recalling fable's transparently unrealistic nature and its lack of innate rhetorical colouring. The fable is felt to reveal, or 'discover', its own nature by not demanding the suspension of disbelief. It is 'never I suppose believed' that wolves and lambs talk; nor (if one then consciously doubles the absurdity, as fable often does) that if they could, Lambs would be quite so silly as to try to hold rational discourse with Wolves.

So pre-literary Aesopian fables are felt to be morally honest in themselves, rather than simply expressing 'morals'. Insofar as they disclaim or disavow the power to move the emotions, they disclaim 'those Arts of Deceiving wherein Men find Pleasure to be deceived' (Locke 1975: 508), in a pre-emptive deconstructive turn. This approach chooses to ignore their use in rhetorical practice, or to see fables as unwilling, innocent conscripts to arts of persuasion.

Romances, in contrast, deceive, ensnare the emotions, cover their tracks with a false but delightful patina of plausibly conjured truth. In

Defoe's *New Family Instructor*, a seriously minded brother explains to his sister that

> as the End and Use of every Fable was in the Moral; so a Fiction, or what they call'd a Romance, told only with Design to deceive the Reader, bring him to believe, that the Fact related was true, and so please and delight him with a Falshood instead of a History, must be . . . criminal and wicked, and *making a Lye*; being done with a Design to deceive. (Defoe 1732: 52)

Being *transparently* false, fables may express a Truth, not in themselves but 'in the Application', in the relationship between themselves and the wider significance towards which their specific action points. The Johnsonian reserve inherent in Arabella's definite article ('the Application' rather than 'their') allows the passage to suggest that the nature of this application, the Truth, is a more open question than being simply a 'Moral'. Arabella is being allowed actively to modify the Doctor's account rather than just agreeing, as well as presenting the point more vividly than does Defoe's well-drilled but slightly incoherent brother.

This suggestion of openness of application is particularly interesting if it comes from Johnson, who is only seven years away from re-applying the fable to the Eastern Tale and producing *Rasselas*. 'Application' is usually understood to mean the historical, political, and/or moral contexts towards which the figure of a fable is turned. In the late-seventeenth and eighteenth centuries, however, the fable was applied to so many new and different literary contexts as to make it clear that writers saw this as a form of 'use' in itself. Medieval and Renaissance fable had already built up its own distinctive set of relationships with what Mahlon Ellwood Smith refers to, in a seminal article, as its 'kindred forms' (Smith: 1915). By 1650 the fable had inherited relations with beast satire, beast epic, bestiary, allegory, emblem, parable, and political prophecy. Over the next 150 years the fable's kin changed and extended to include many of the favoured, newly ascendant, literary forms: satire, epic, narrative episode, history, *conte philosophique*, romance, drama, comedy; criticism; pastoral, mock-heroic, and burlesque (doggerel, the plodding or shuffling 'foûr-footed' line proper to the '*Four-foot Race*' (Swift 1957: 2, 607)). After 1730, the energies of fable dissolved outwards into the novel in general, philosophy, ethical teaching, nature-poem, sentimental elegy, hymn, lyric, epitaph, literature for children.

These relations will be touched on, in their place, in the following chapters. Many of them are surprising, and capable of surprising applications. To return to *The Female Quixote*: if Lennox had wanted to muddy the waters of the Johnsonian argument about fable and romance, she would have made Arabella point out that Aesop, as well as being a legendary fabulist, is a character in romance. To go to the most apposite example, Madeleine de Scudéry has him honour the Lydian court with his presence and fabulist wisdom in the later parts of *Artamène, ou le grand Cyrus* (1656), one of Arabella's six favourite French romances: de Scudéry is following or adapting the *Vita Aesopi*. But instead of rewriting the chapter and cheekily provoking the Doctor and the *mere English reader* with a point which, though it may now seem a little occult, would have been readily apparent to anyone who knew the French romances well, Lennox and Arabella cover their tracks with compliments, blushes, and silence in the face of the Doctor's 'proof', much as Smith and Johnson remain tactfully quiet about the *faux pas* of *their* dominant and equally loquacious male, Dryden/Bayes. That romance and fable are by no means the opposites the Doctor supposes them to be remains the knowledge only of those prepared, like James Beattie, to argue from the one to the other, or of those conversant with both forms.

This silent marginal or responsive comment *about* fable acts in each case *like* a fable. In itself it is nothing, invisible or encrypted in the main text of the novel and audible only in Smith-and-Johnson's gentlemanly reserve in the travesty. But in *The Female Quixote* its application, its relation to the wider structure of the episode, disturbs the moral of the ending and alters its textual/sexual politics radically. It shows that the Doctor's magisterial assumption that fable is simply a neutral medium, at its highest only a lecture of domestic wisdom, is as bad a mistake about the proper levels of fables (though in the opposite direction) as Bayes's misreading of Horace. Henry Brooke and Edward Moore had identified a specifically female audience of fable eight years earlier, in their *Fables for the Female Sex*, and women were of course notorious for reading romances when they should have been doing something sensible and useful, so one may presume many readers doubly expert in fable and romance to have been female. The articulated male ending of *The Female Quixote* is one in which the Doctor restores the heroine to common sense in the same way as (say) Henry Tilney is usually supposed to awaken Catherine Morland from the 'visions of romance' (Austen 1926: 199) at the climax of *Northanger Abbey* (1818). This kind of ending allows the dominant structure of *The Female Quixote* to remain secure. Conventional readers can happily accept the status quo, with Arabella restored to her proper place by men; the Doctor, and her consort, Granville. But the process of silent (female) marginal comment – Arabella, Lennox, Scudéry – about fable and romance disrupts the authority of this secure ending, helping to stimulate the slightly subversive and quite proper counter-reading of the ending, in which it is almost as sad that Arabella's spirit must be killed off by male 'sanity' and marriage as that Don Quixote must die at the end of his story.

It is difficult to ascribe such an indirect point to an 'author', though the refraction or diffusion of authority that comes with multiple authorship – real, as here, or supposed, as with Cervantes and Cid Hamet Ben Engeli – is one of the main features of a *Quixote.* Lennox (*via* Johnson) and Prior/Montague are clearly directing themselves to similar technical points about the levels of fable. Also they are using these points in the same way and for the same reason, to establish some silent counter-authority in the face of a dominant discourse which is felt to be absurd or open to criticism, whether this discourse be Dryden, romance, or Johnson. This second point extends ironically to Bayes, tactlessly straining to demolish Horace; even, indeed, to Dryden himself, who is answering the Anglican apologetics of his earlier *Religio Laici*, in *The Hind and the Panther.* The politics of fable seems to relate to voices and texts in multiple relation, more than to policies and polemics. These fabulists and counter-fabulists cover a very full range of genres or modes, despite this set of similarities: poetry, dramatic satire, burlesque, novel, argumentative discourse. Such forms of kinship are clearly more than isolated effects operating between a few texts, and seem rather to be part of a pattern of common interests and techniques. And if *The Female Quixote* is representative of a *continuing* pattern of usage of fable after 1740, this pattern is viable way past the point at which literary fable is conventionally supposed to have died the death – in the early or late 1730s, depending on how one sees the second series of Gay's *Fables.* That the ending of this particular novel is representative of such a pattern of use can now be made clear.

CHAPTER 2

Fables and novels

> Examples are best Precepts . . .
>
> . . . examples work quicker and stronger on the minds of men than precepts . . .
>
> (Fielding 1967[b]: II, 7)
>
> Didius, the great church lawyer, in his code de fartandi et illustrandi fallaciis, doth maintain and make fully appear, That an illustration is no argument,—nor do I maintain the wiping of a looking-glass clean, to be a syllogism,—but you all, may it please your worships, see the better for it—
>
> (Sterne 1978: I, 227)

This study originated, in part, in an attempt to account for an oddity in the fiction of Laurence Sterne and Henry Fielding. Both of these highly innovative and self-conscious novelists seemingly wished to claim very little awareness of the fiction, and the ideas about fiction, of their own times. Sterne wrote a major novel, *Tristram Shandy* (1759–67), in which virtually every other contemporary art and science comes under scrutiny, but he has next to nothing to say, inside his fiction or out, about any other English novelist or novel except *A Tale of A Tub* (1704: expanded 1710); not exactly recent, not exactly novelistic. In *A Sentimental Journey* (1768), Smollett puts in a brief pseudonymous appearance as a travel-writer. The word 'novel' was not in Sterne's written vocabulary.

When Austin Dobson unearthed the catalogue of sale of the whole of Fielding's library, he was surprised to see that the author appeared to possess hardly any English novels – just three, one of those a copy of *Jonathan Wild* (1743), out of a total of 653 volumes in the sale (Dobson 1896: the catalogue's contents are reprinted in Thornbury 1966: 168–89). In 1749 Fielding mentions 'Romances, Novels, Plays and Poems' on the second page of *Tom Jones* (Fielding 1974: I, 32), but in later chapters only once alludes to English novels in discussing his own fiction. In all other instances the comparison is with some aspect of drama, or with the novel as a 'Heroic, Historical, Prosaic Poem' (*ibid.*: 1, 152). All that is known is that he *rewrote* contemporary novels (his sister Sarah's, for instance) and that he read Richardson.

With Richardson the situation is much the same. In all the welter of literary allusion generated by his characters, no one would dream of lowering themselves by revealing that they had read an English prose fiction. In *Clarissa*, Mrs Sinclair's cook-maid reads 'the simple history of Dorastus and Faunia . . . when she should have been in bed' (Richardson: 1985: 273: the story is after Greene's prose romance *Pandosto*), and as a result sets fire to her curtains and is *found out*. Pamela remarks that her past story would 'furnish out a surprizing kind of Novel, if it was to be well told' (Richardson 1971: 213), so presumably her story as her author has wanted her to give it is something else. Although the most famous soporific–incendiary romance is the one read by the Lilliputian maid-of-honour (in *Gulliver's Travels* (1726) Book 1, chapter 5) who is responsible for the fire in the queen's apartments, Mrs. Sinclair's cook-maid is probably fashioned after the intriguing example of the sluttish mother in 'The Owl and the Nightingale', No. 13 of Moore's *Fables for the Female Sex*, whose vices are solitary reading and ardent spirits:

> When Miss comes in with boist'rous shout,
> And drops no curt'sey, going out,
> Depend upon't, mamma is one,
> Who reads, or drinks too much alone. (Moore 1749: 81)

Inflammatory prose fictions, presumably, rather than instructive fables that can be read in domestic communality and alluded to by a virtuous fifteen-year-old heroine in her letters and diary. Richardson himself had presumably read (*alone*?) the prose romance from which Pamela's name is derived, Sidney's *Arcadia*, but this derivation can only be alluded to in the morally murky atmosphere of the masquerade in *Pamela* II (1741). The conclusion from the examples of these writers is (as others have noticed) that whatever cultural status the novel enjoyed, it was mainly from relations with forms other than prose fiction *per se*: epic, romance, perhaps fable.

But the eighteenth-century English novel was not 'poetic' in the way that the nineteenth century's was: as John Speirs says, 'in the nineteenth century the poetic imagination enlarged and deepened the novel' (Speirs 1971: 332). By implication, nothing poetic could inform pre-Romantic fiction. Speirs does remark that all novels are poems in the

Aristotelian sense, but this is not a comment which, treated as a truism, can lead anywhere. These earlier novels are felt to reflect a sociable, discursive, reasonable culture which characteristically expressed itself in prose forms. However, Fielding's assertion in the Preface to *Joseph Andrews* (1742) that the 'comic romance' he is writing is a 'comic Epic-Poem in Prose' (Fielding 1970: 3) can be supported by Johnson's description in *Rambler* 4 (1750) of the 'comedy of romance' as being conducted 'nearly by the rules of comic poetry' (Johnson 1958–90: 3, 19) – even though Johnson said that he had never read *Joseph Andrews* – and by Beattie's later assertion that the case of the 'poetical prose fable' shows that 'Prose and Poetry may be consistent' (Beattie 1783: 518). A modern researcher in fable will be led quite naturally to treat 'the aims and methods of Augustan prose fiction in terms of those of Augustan poetry' (Kishler 1959: 52).

Beattie's 'fable' mediates as unselfconsciously between prose and other modes as does Fielding's 'Epic'. Both seem to do more work than a truism would. Beattie's is a very different use of 'fable' from those of moralistic eighteenth-century critics, and indeed from those of modern ones. Arnold Kettle, citing *Jonathan Wild* and other examples, might characterize the eighteenth-century novel as a 'moral fable' (Kettle 1967: 40–51 *passim*), but he only admires *Wild* halfheartedly under this heading, and the description of it and other novels as fable has an actively dampening effect. The moral fable seems to be understood as a form circumscribed by its moral function, unLucianic, unVoltairean, anal-retentive, unable to express itself fully. Surely *Sterne* can have nothing to do with this?

But Sterne's comments in the letter written in 1768 to Dr John Eustace, which talks of the 'true feeler' of humour bringing 'half the entertainment along with him' to the reading of a fiction, bear striking resemblance to Addison's remarks about fable in *Spectator* 512 (1712). Comments from Sterne about his philosophy as a writer are rare, and this gives his letter added interest. He goes on to say that the reader's 'own ideas are only call'd forth by what he reads, and the vibrations within, so entirely correspond with those excited, 'tis like reading *himself* and not the book' (Sterne 1935: 411). Whereas Addison says that

> if we look into human nature, we shall find that the mind is never so much pleased, as when she exerts herself in any action that gives her an idea of her own perfections and abilities. This natural pride and ambition of the soul is very much gratified in the reading of a fable; for in writings of this kind, the reader comes in for half the performance; every thing appears to him like a discovery

of his own; he is busied all the while in applying characters and circumstances, and is in this both a reader and a composer. (Addison 1965: 4, 316)

Addison is expanding his own argument about reading as the exercise of the mind, in *Tatler* 147 (March 16–18, 1709). This in turn is a discreet rejoinder to the aged emblematist Edmund Arwaker's rather condescending opinion in *Truth in Fiction* (1708), that fables are merely suitable instructive reading material for children, or for those whose minds 'are hinder'd from exerting themselves to Advantage by a mixture of Weakness and Infirmity' (Arwaker 1708: ii; compare Lennox/Johnson's 'lectures of moral and domestic wisdom' above).

There is less about exertion or exercise in Sterne's remarks, but the stress on the healthy, active mind of the good reader is very similar to Addison's, despite the difference between the 'ignorance' of 'the herd of the world' (Sterne 1935: 411) and Addison's typically urbane compliment of pretending to assume that all *Spectator* readers are intellectually vigorous. The sixty years between the two men are no bar to the notion of Sterne's being able to echo Addison casually: *Tristram Shandy* might be subtitled *'Tis Sixty Years Since* almost as appositely as is *Waverley*. When Sterne recalls, in a letter, old Lord Bathurst's compliment to him, of how much *Tristram Shandy* had reminded him of the Popes and Swifts he had entertained in his youth, Sterne's reciprocal list of the geniuses 'of the last century' is very revealing: 'Addison, Steele, Pope, Swift, Prior . . .' (*ibid.*: 305).

This attention to the active reading mind is not exclusive to Addison and Sterne: one may, for instance, also find Kames commenting on the related mode of allegory in his *Elements of Criticism*: 'we are pleased with the discovery because it is our own work' (Home 1762: 3, 112). The reading of another related form, history, was conventionally seen as involving this self-generated or self-motivated kind of mental activity in the audience (see below, chapter 6, p. 181–2). But fable might well have been in Sterne's mind in 1768, as he reflected retrospectively on his own fiction. What, then, of 1767, of the COCK and the BULL that end *Tristram Shandy*? –

L—d! said my mother, what is all this story about?—

A COCK and a BULL, said Yorick—And one of the best of its kind, I ever heard. (Sterne 1978: 2, 809)

Either a straightforwardly dismissive remark, say the scholars, or possibly an allusion to 'My Cousin's Tale of a Cock and a Bull' in the *Crazy Tales* (1762) of Sterne's crony, John Hall-Stevenson, the original of

Eugenius in *Tristram Shandy* and a fine verse fabulist when not writing prurient *Tales*. But there is just one verse fable seriously entitled 'A Story of a COCK and a BULL' (complete with capitals, as in *Tristram Shandy*). It is by Christopher Smart, and first appeared in the *Literary Magazine* for May/June 1756. Its occasion is the start of the Seven Years' War between England and France – the *Literary Magazine* prints it in the same number as a transcript of 'his Majesty's Declaration of War against the *French* King' (*Literary Magazine* 1 (15 May – 15 June 1756): 72) – and its purpose is to plead for 'a little more humanity' (Smart 1980–96: 4, 324) in mens' dealings with each other. The two beasts are given an unspoken but quite clear application by the historical context, the Cock as the Gallic Cockerel, the Bull as John Bull, so that the plea for humanity is given extra piquancy by being channelled through two beasts which are also national emblems. The Cock, who has been used for cockfighting, commiserates with the Bull on his return from being baited: the Bull has been reduced to this because, like Walter Shandy's bull, he is no longer 'equal to the department' (Sterne 1978: 2, 807) of serving the cows.

Toby Shandy is the other part of the 'application' of Smart's fable in *Tristram Shandy*. As with the two bulls, Toby's sexual status is dubious, in his case as a result of an injury sustained in service against the French in the War of the League of Augsburg, which, together with the War of the Spanish Succession, forms a historical analogy – from the 1690s and 1700s – with the contemporary Seven Years' War. In other words, the structural analogies of *Tristram Shandy* are modelled in part on those of a verse fable: much of volume 9 is concerned with exploring relationships between animals and 'HUMANITY' (*ibid.*: 2, 802). The historical analogy in particular acts exactly as it would, or should, in a fable, being completely silent yet absolutely fundamental. It must have been a strong presence in reading *Tristram Shandy* in the 1760s, yet it never emerges onto the surface of the book: readers are to *discover* the historical parallel, the kinship between their own reading time and the world of the novel, as they may *discover* the fable which points to that analogy at the end of the narrative. The 'reading' of the fable supports the 'reading' of history. One might apply Arabella's remark about absurdity and truth: it is one of those aspects of Sterne's novel which proves the relevance of the Formalist dictum that *Tristram Shandy* is, despite itself, a highly typical novel, yoking the eccentric and the normative. And one can say the same about Sterne's use of fable, because the use of the historical analogy has a close parallel in Hall-Stevenson's contemporary collection, *Fables for Grown Gentlemen* (1761). Fable 7, 'The Wild Ducks and the Water Spaniel', for instance, uses a 'complex and ingenious analogy which comments on France's attempts to persuade Charles II of Spain to enter the War of Spanish Succession, in the light of the Earl of Bute's efforts to arrange a peace with France, over the opposition of Pitt, who thought that Spain should be crushed before she could attack England' (Hartley 1971: 430–1). As Hartley shows, this analogy, though complex, is as tacit in the verse fable as it is in *Tristram Shandy*, being achieved simply by the use of two or three key words. Hall-Stevenson's fables have something of the same historical depth and wit as Sterne's fiction.

The fun becomes even more Shandean on examination of the other manifestation of interest in poetry in the final volume of *Tristram Shandy*, the curious parody of Pope's *Essay on Man* (1733–4) in which Tristram indulges at the start. Sterne, it transpires, allows Tristram to continue where the radical John Wilkes left off in *his* parody (or supposed at the time to be his) of Pope, the ingloriously obscene *Essay on Woman* (1763). Wilkes parodies the first ninety-four lines of Pope's poem; Tristram parodies, much more subtly, the next paragraph, lines 99–112. Wilkes was a political icon to Hall-Stevenson, who had ambitions to become Wilkes's verse propagandist after the death of Charles Churchill: Wilkes declined the offer. *Inter alia*, the *Essay on Woman* has an allusion to Europa and *her* Bull. So does Walter Shandy, in the final moments of Sterne's novel. William Kenrick rewrote the first few lines of Smart's fable in 1773 and printed the result, on the occasion of the election of Frederick Bull, a protégé of Wilkes's, to the office of Lord Mayor of London. More fables, more Cocks, more Bulls; Hall-Stevenson, Wilkes, Smart, Sterne: confusion upon confusion! – fable upon fable.

Smart's fable is eccentric but 'moral'. Sterne's engagement with it is equally eccentric, but forces it to perform one of the traditional functions of a fable, in directing the reader towards the wider world of possible political and historical application made clearer in Hall-Stevenson. So the ending of *Tristram Shandy* might be dismissive; or, perhaps, the 'peculiar intensity of allusive effect' could allow 'the COCK and BULL to form a sufficient *poetic* closure to the novel' (Loveridge 1992: 36).

This verges on a poetics: the connection with fable is clearly being used to some real structural effect, as part of a very complex sense of an ending. So is Lennox's, in *The Female Quixote*. And, lest the reader should think that this kind of use is only the property of zanies and burlesquers, so is *Pamela*'s. Not the exclamatory quiverings of the finale of the first part, but the second and final ending, which takes the form of a double, overlapping pair of fables: yet again, fable upon fable. The first moralizes on personified female types, Coquetilla, Prudiana, Profusiana, and Prudentia. The second is more in character for Pamela. It amplifies the insect imagery of the first (Coquetilla 'fluttered about the dangerous light, like some silly fly, [and] at last singed the wings of her reputation', and her lovers 'break through those few cobweb reserves, in which she had encircled her precarious virtue') into a fable of Prudentia/Pamela as 'the industrious bee [who] makes up her honey-hoard from every flower . . . every character is of use to her' (Richardson 1969: 2, 465, 470).

In other words, an imaginatively energized reworking of The Spider and the Bee. Richardson's habit when allowing characters to use fable for structural rather than simply allusive effect is to pick examples which have, or had, origins in the religiously sanctioned, related Renaissance form of emblem, but which then evolved into 'modern' fables. Peter Daly gives Whitney's sixteenth-century emblem of Spider and Bee, 'in which a flower gives honey to a bee and poison to a spider' (Daly 1993: 1, 141): Robert Borkat records the first evolution of this into fable, in which Bacon and his followers characterized themselves as the useful Bee and applied the Spider as 'medieval rationalist philosophers, originally the scholastic logicians' (Borkat 1976: 44), and also records Swift's equally original reversal of this in *The Battel of the Books* (1704), with the Spider there being applied by the commentating Aesop as the Moderns, and the Bee as the Ancients, the classics.

Pamela's final utterances justify her name and hence herself in terms of fable rather than of Arcadian romance. 'Pamela' seems to mean or suggest 'honeyed', *mel* being the stem of the Greek word for honey: *Melissa* is the honeybee, in Greek. It is important that she should find a positive association for her name: a *pam-child* was a knave-child in the eighteenth century, from the use of 'Pam' as the knave of clubs, the highest trump in the game of Loo. The romance connotations of the name become suspect in *Pamela* II, after they are exposed in the dubious context of the masquerade. But why is fable the natural ending of *Pamela*?

As Gillian Beer points out, *Pamela* II 'is, in large measure, an attempt to control the romance qualities' of *Pamela* I (Beer 1989: 36), with Pamela christianizing romance by her forgiving attitudes, and by rewriting the eclogues of romance into hymns. But as Beer also notices, other characters know that her name is really a pagan one; and the B.s' married life is far from 'an unfallen world' (*ibid.*: 25). To Richardson's credit, there are aspects of Pamela's character that resist being simply christianized in

Pamela II – wit, consciousness of her own merit, the capacity to play roles such as 'Lady Jenny', sullenness over not being able to nurse her own child, and the horribly uneasy jealous sulking over her 'rival' the Countess. It is this complex, if oddly realized, force of character that dictates a moralistic ending in the form of a fable whose associations lie between the Christian and the pagan, rather than of the merely Christian pieties of *Pamela* I.

The clue to what Pamela is doing with The Spider and the Bee lies in its most notable previous application, that in *The Battel of the Books*: indeed, this version seems to be the one with which Richardson is working, echoing Swift's diction very closely. Swift used it to characterize the furore of the current Ancients–Moderns controversy, with the 'wandring' Bee flying into the Spider's '*House*', his cobweb, and temporarily shattering it. The Bentleyan Spider swells up and berates the Bee for being a '*Vagabond without House or Home, without Stock or Inheritance*', and for the '*universal Plunder*' of his lifestyle, so different to the Spider's '*Native Stock within my self*', and '*large Castle*'. The Bee and Aesop then remonstrate in turn about the '*Dirt and Poison*' voided by the Spider, in contrast to the 'Sweetness *and* Light' of the products of the Bee: 'Honey *and* Wax' (Swift 1939–75: I, 148, 149, 151).

One of Pamela's constant worries is her lack of lineage. Mr B. is surrounded by relatives and property expressive of native stock and a depth of family history. Lady Davers writes to him: 'ours is no upstart Family; but is as ancient as the best in the Kingdom . . . ancient blood in your veins'. Satirical, vituperative, conscious of pedigree, she plays the Spider, claims Ancient status, and identifies Pamela as a mere Modern. Before her sudden implausible conversion to Pamelism she throws out much dirt and poison in her letters, both the word 'dirt' and abuse of character. Pamela is merely 'the Dirt you seem so fond of' (Richardson 1971: 221), and, later, 'painted Dirt' that will disgrace 'a Family, ancient and untainted' (*ibid.*: 328). 'Painted Dirt' sticks so hard in Pamela's mind that she repeats the phrase first to Mr B., and then to her parents, at the end of *Pamela* I. Aware that she has 'nothing at all!' (282), and that she is practically without a past, she is forced to concede glumly that 'in [Christian] Truth' (407) *dirt* is correct: '*Dirt to Dirt*' (350) is Lady Davers's triumphantly mocking version, quoting the burial service against the news that her brother and Pamela are married.

So in Christian mode Pamela no longer has any way of establishing a positive fictive identity for herself in an ending, especially since the romance is now also barred to her. But the 'Ancient' Bee provides her with control of the past. Pamela/Prudentia 'fortifies herself with the excellent examples of the past and present ages' ('*long Search, much Study*', in Swift) and so lays up her honey-hoard for futurity. The Bee also provides a correlative for her intellectual, moral, and social identities, being emblematic of her 'uniform judgment' ('*true Judgment, and Distinction of Things*', Swift), her 'sweet and unaffected' nature, which 'shines in all her actions and behaviour' ('Sweetness *and* Light'): her name 'smells sweet to every nostril' (Richardson,1969: 2, 470, 471; Swift 1939–75: 1, 150, 151). The dirt and poison of extravagant aristocratic temper such as Lady Davers's are answered by a relatively classless 'Ancient' identity which speaks of cleanness, control of temper, social use in the hive – and which marries Pamela's humility to her pride: Mrs Bee. The only important quality she does not manage to include is her 'Wit' (1971: 283, 293, etc.). This is a pity, since she could have; Swift's Bee, for instance, is 'disposed to drole' (148); but one had best not expect Richardson's surprisingly sympathetic reworking of Swift to extend to a complete temperamental affinity.

As well, then, as being a rewriting of Arcadia, the end of *Pamela* II is another rewriting of the heroine, via a subtle transformation of emblem-fable into novelistic fable, which circles back into the story in a manner similar to that of Sterne's COCK and BULL. As fable in *The Female Quixote* lies in a complex ground between romance, morality, and satire, and as Beattie uses fable to link romance and novel, so fable here partly solves the puzzle of the relationship between the discourses of romance-masquerade and Christian moral piety. But the downbeat spirit of the presentation is also similar to the apparently throwaway ending of *Tristram Shandy*. Her fable is merely one of Pamela's 'nursery tales', spoken to the children: just 'a woman's story' (Richardson 1969: 2, 471, 464). And the disguising of the fable is not dissimilar: most of its manifestations are dissolved into what appears to be Pamela's characteristically sententious mode. It says much more than it seems to say.

Again, fable is integral to Clarissa's story. William Rose Wray points out, for instance, that the initial action has a close parallel in the action and moral sentiment of the sixth fable of *Fables for the Female Sex*, 'The Wolf, the Sheep, and the Lamb', in which a greedy mother Sheep 'forces her poor defenceless lamb to marry a rich but murderous wolf' (the toadlike Solmes has the riches, Lovelace the rapacity): 'not only the parents but also the daughter should approve of the prospective husband' (Wray 1950: 139). But fable is also very much part of Clarissa's sense of an ending. The 'principal device' (Richardson 1985: 1305) which she stipulates for her coffin-lid is a serpent with its tail in its mouth. Belford glosses this device as the ring of eternity, which is at least as plausible as a Coleridgean gloss of the endless circle of narrative. But it is also a specific emblem, itself derived from Egyptian hieroglyphics for the world, or for time – Daly (1993: 2, 159) gives a harvest-wreath emblem by Paladin, in which the *ouroboros* is understood as an emblem of the year – the action of *Clarissa* covers a calendar year. And again, the emblem is associated with a well-known fable – a classical, Babrian, one, this time – La Fontaine has a version (VII, 16), as does Hall-Stevenson (1770, No. 13) – known as The Head and the Tail of the Snake, so once again a counter-reading becomes quietly available through fable. In one application, the venomous makes itself harmless by enclosing one poisonous end within the other. Fortunately this message, which Lovelace might find characteristically 'pert' from Clarissa if he were in any mental condition to try to read it, remains unspoken, apart from the text or application 'here the wicked cease from troubling' (Richardson 1985: 1306) beneath the hour-glass at the top of the coffin-lid. In the version that La Fontaine adapts, the Snake is drowned in a lake after the Tail insists on usurping the Head's right to go first: another mordant enough comment on Lovelace's reptile motives and argument-by-rape. Once again, the two-handled nature of a fable quietly critiques a discourse, a voice, as Pamela's doubled fable does that of Lady Davers and others.

Or a structural fable could be in the middle, rather than at the end. Goldsmith's novel *The Vicar of Wakefield* (1766) has an almost impossibly 'double' ending, with the Vicar's prison-sermonizing on the 'consolations of the wretched' (Goldsmith 1966: 162) replaced a few pages later by the 'unspeakable . . . pleasure' (*ibid.*: 184) of the conclusion. But the Vicar, Primrose, is given an allegorical fable in the centre (at the end of the fifteenth chapter of a total of thirty-two) on the subject of guilt and shame. At least, that is what the Vicar takes it to be about: its real subject is the *double reading* which is always promoted by Augustan fable.

A proposed trip to London for the Primrose girls has been suddenly and unexpectedly cancelled: Mr Burchell's letter-case has been found on the village green. Primrose has promptly 'broke open' both the letter-case and a note within, which advises the two visiting town ladies not to take the girls up to London with them, not to introduce 'infamy and vice into retreats where peace and innocence have hitherto resided'. The Vicar manages to notice that these abstractions are so general as to have two handles, that there is 'something applicable to both sides' (77) in the letter. 'Infamy and vice' could apply to London, in which case 'retreats' must be read metaphorically rather than geographically, as referring to the minds of the girls: or 'infamy and vice' could possibly apply to the moral character of Primrose's daughters, though this involves reading London as an innocent retreat. But the hint of the double reading is immediately dropped for the single, less flattering one. 'Reports of some malicious person' are deemed responsible for the slur cast on the girls' reputation, and Burchell is clearly 'the base informer' (76). When he turns up and has the effrontery to complain about the illegality of the Vicar's having criminally broken and entered his pocket-book, Primrose explodes – 'Ungrateful wretch, begone, and no longer pollute my dwelling with thy baseness' – which Burchell does, with a smile and the 'utmost composure' (80). From the moral high ground now occupied by Primrose comes the allegory, on the equally general subject of how the journeying pair, guilt and shame, parted company due to mutual inconveniences. Shame returned 'to keep company with virtue . . . Thus, my children, after men have travelled through a few stages in vice, shame foresakes them, and returns back to wait upon the few virtues they have still remaining' (81).

As used by Primrose this is a dry, naked story, a lecture of moral and domestic wisdom, simple and single in application, expressive of defensive moral security and self-belief. But Goldsmith is quietly holding out an invitation to a kind of reader who might know about the proper levels of fable, just as Prior and Montague held out an invitation to their constituency of presumed competent readers of fable. John Bender points out that the phrase on Goldsmith's title-page, 'a tale, supposed to be written by himself', casts a potential implied reader or narratee who knows that he or she is supposed to be 'doing the supposing' (Bender 1987: 183), and who is aware of the Vicar as an innocent abroad in a highly sophisticated narrative (and political) landscape. Such readers – one might perhaps call them Augustan readers as opposed to Victorian readers – are invited to make the proper, highly specific, application (that Burchell must feel amusement rather than shame because he knows that any guilt should be felt by the Vicar) and are hence invited to redirect and energize the allegory, make it double.

The best available evidence with which to work, given that we know nothing as yet about the moral character of the town ladies, and not much about the enigmatic Burchell, is the only thing that the narrating Vicar cannot use as evidence, his own character. In particular there is his chronic inability to accommodate himself to 'double' readings, whether of circumstance or character. If Ephraim Jenkinson, in the previous chapter, looks like a venerable religious gentleman, then he cannot be a sermonizing rascal. If the two ladies sound *almost* like fine ladies, there is no chance that they will be tarts up from London for a romp, despite the Vicar's outrageously funny naïve remark about Thornhill 'procuring my daughters the amusements of the town' (Goldsmith 1966: 81).

Primrose's allegory is a purely literary equivalent of Jenkinson. In Primrose's use, it is Jenkinson as seen from the outside, singly read. In Goldsmith's, it is Jenkinson in his full paradoxical complexity, a kind of literary deuterogamy to place ironically but not unreverently beside the Vicar's monogamous nature. Jenkinson, naturally enough, will eventually be instrumental in that happy ending, revealing to the Vicar that the wonderfully fantastical and improbable sequence of events and romance reversals was really the fruit of his, Jenkinson's, sense of 'the only probable means of freeing' (*ibid.*: 179) the Vicar from prison. Primrose, who as usual has been 'unable to form any probable conjecture' (178) about the course of events, unable to follow or guess Jenkinson's perverse *mythos*, accepts his assertion without a word. The distinction between the two uses of 'fable', the normative one of a probable (plausible) sequence of events delineating a single action and ending with an appropriate moral, and the unnerving *trompe l'oeil* effects and urge to critical retrospection inherent in actual fables, could hardly be clearer. Indeed, the lesson of Goldsmith's novel suggests that this second sort of fable may have as part of its agenda criticism of the more culturally dominant discourses of the first; that it stands in the same 'political' relation to them as Pamela stands to Lady Davers. Or, to put it another way, it allows Augustan readers to smile at the Victorian readers who are, Goldsmith seems to sense, likely to be the main purchasers and readership of such a narrative. A fundamental aspect of an Augustan fable is its fondness for working with, or between, imagined constituencies of readers who can and cannot read fables: Masters and Cockerels, to anticipate fable's own terminology.

The last and latest of this gallery of examples is Captain Mirvan's reworking of one of John Gay's fables in the final dramatic episode of Burney's *Evelina* (1778). As with all the other examples discussed, its presence has never been noticed before – Victorian habits of reading eighteenth-century novels persist through the twentieth century – even though it re-aligns the novel as effectively as do the rest.

The third volume of *Evelina* rises from the social comedy and satire of the first parts into the headier regions of family romance. Amazing discoveries abound. New 'real and . . . fictitious' (Burney 1982: 377) daughters, brothers, and sisters coruscate pleasingly through the text, with only the mildly sardonic voice of Mrs Selwyn allowing the narrative to keep one foot on the floor. Captain Mirvan then announces the final discovery to the assembled company. He has found the 'twin-brother' of the fop Lovel, and the gentleman is just at the door. Lovel expresses curiosity, obligingly disavowing knowledge of his own identity – 'really, I have not the least notion of what sort of person I am' (*ibid.*: 399) – which parodies Evelina's earlier sense of herself as '*Nobody*' (289, 235). But there will be no romance for him, as this is one of Mirvan's practical jokes. The brother is in fact 'a monkey! fully dressed, and extravagantly *à-la-mode*', with Mirvan protesting the close resemblance between Lovel and the animal. The incensed fop smacks the monkey, and in return is bitten on the ear, which makes him look, says Mirvan, as if he had been in the pillory and had his ear slit.

Mrs Selwyn is then allowed to give the silent clue to the origin of the fable, by telling Lovel that this 'may acquire you the credit of being an anti-ministerial writer' (400). An odd comment, for the late 1770s; but the allusion is not in fact to current politics or judicial punishments, but to Swift's poem '*Tim* and the *Fables*' (1728), which is in turn a reworking of Gay's 'The *Monkey*, who had seen the World', in which the Monkey appears as a beau, 'compleatly drest', just like Mirvan's animal. In Swift's reworking, Tim recognizes himself in the print of the Monkey in a copy of Gay's 1727 *Fables*, until he reads the fable and realizes it is about Monkeys, at which point – unable to grasp that the fable is not really about *Tims* – he begins to storm against the writer:

> *The cursed Villain! now I see*
> *This was a libel meant at me;*
> *These Scriblers grow so bold of late,*
> *Against us Ministers of State!* (Swift 1957: 3, 783)

But, protests Gay slyly in the second fable of his 1738 collection, 'I meddle with no state-affairs / But spare my jest to save my ears' (Gay 1974: 2, 384). Mrs Selwyn's joke is a good deal better than at first appears: she somehow manages to suggest that Lovel looks as though he has *written* a satirical fable (and been punished for it), rather than been the victim of one. The whole action of the chapter is probably similarly allusive, bearing resemblance as it does to Charles Johnstone's account in *Chrysal* (1760–5: Book 2, chs. 20–1) of the notorious episode at Medmenham Abbey in 1762 in which the ever-active Wilkes is said to have complacently introduced an irritated baboon dressed up as the devil into the perverse devotions of the Hell Fire Club.

Swift's fable involves an equally mixed relationship between writing and reading/application. To go back to Sterne and Addison, Tim is (unwittingly) 'reading himself and not the book', and so reverses the application. Application makes the Ass, or in this case the Monkey; though the poem is in fact a very active reworking of The Cockerel and the Pearl. In Burney the effects are similarly mixed, because the wider application of the fable as Mirvan reworks it is to burlesque the motifs of recognition and discovery that have been used in the novel's romance-story, and hence to suggest once again a sceptical or critical retrospective re-reading of the narrative. Mirvan's literary tastes are, given his bearishness, rather good: he admires Congreve's *Love for Love* and is not put off by its frank tone, as the Georgian gentlemen say they are. It is not implausible, nor unreasonable, that he would find the narrative of *Evelina* rather *outré*, and would wish to pass comment on what has become its tonally dominant discourse, the potentially absurd qualities of romance. The action also reworks the relationships between the sexes: in a story where violence is consistently offered to women by men, this is the first and only occasion on which the violence is, as it were, homosexual, Mirvan to Lovel.

When not part of an end or a middle, the fable may on occasion be part of a beginning, a submerged promythium. In Defoe's *Roxana* (1724), the heroine's first identifiable allusion is to the whistling of the brainless Cymon, the protagonist of the last of Dryden's *Fables* (1700). So is Clarissa's: unlikely sisters. Clarissa begins and ends her allusive career in fable. There is a teasing reference to Gay's fable of 'The *Hare* and Many *Friends*' in the first chapter of Austen's *Northanger Abbey*; the timorous Catherine will eventually learn the difference between a true and a designing friend. The fable begins a text full of critical engagement with the Gothic romance. At the end, Austen reflects briefly on her story and takes pains to disclaim all knowledge of its potentially paradoxical morals, as if the spirit of this kind of fable had infiltrated the narrative in the same way as it does in *The Vicar of Wakefield*.

Reflecting in turn more widely on these novelistic examples, the pattern of use becomes stronger and clearer. These fables confirm some of the conclusions suggested at the end of the first section, in that they both impart a sense of teleological security and finality to the works in which they appear, and suggest ways in which the works might be reviewed or re-engaged. Fables are supposed to conduce to conclusive morals, but these novels conduce to fables which both perform the conclusion and deny it: conclusions, in which nothing is concluded, to paraphrase another fable. In this way fable again becomes its own 'truth', rather than being an absurdity.

This structural use of fables is, it must be stressed again, *surprising*, to the point of being paradoxical, in reworking the reader's expectations of simple endings. Words such as 'usual', 'dominant', and 'normative' have cropped up parenthetically, but have not really conveyed the point that Johnson (if it be he, in *The Female Quixote*) may be found to be representative of the kind of contemporary literary–cultural understanding of 'fable' which would confine its use to the inculcation of educative social morals, to the literary structures of probability which allow writers plausibly to achieve this, and to glancing references which allow authors to convey the fact that the character in question has reached a certain level of literacy and socialization. This is, roughly speaking, the definition of 'fable' or 'moral fable' inherited by the twentieth century. In these kinds of use fables have, to quote Smith-and-Johnson, 'rules and examples' which must not be transgressed. A review of Dodsley's 1761 collection, for instance, insists that a fable 'ought to show, without equivocation, precisely and obviously what is intended . . . and the fable must be built, if not on truth, at least on probability' (*CR* 2 (Feb. 1761): 124). 'Moral fables' are lectures of moral and domestic wisdom, conveyed in probabilistic decorum. It might be argued that novels end with fables because many eighteenth-century magazine-articles end with illustrative fables (Bush 1965: 61ff., has a wide selection), and many novels were published in instalments in magazines and needed moralistic cliffhangers. But this is not how these fables are used. They give imaginative rather than merely moral sanction to the works in which they appear. They are all playful, or satirical, or are designed partly as a riposte or answer. Roxana and Clarissa use their confidential allusions (made to the reader and Anna Howe respectively) to Cymon to show their disdain for unattractive men, Roxana for her first husband and Clarissa the appalling Solmes, and to establish the sharp, vigorous side of their characters *at the expense of* conventional socialization. In each case the allusion to mindless masculine whistling picks up the sense of a sardonic reflection on a dominant or privileged discourse that is present in the other texts: there is some correlation between sexual and textual politics. Such reflections give more substance to the earlier assertion that a 'politics of discourse' may be integral to fable. When the sexual element is not present, the text comments silently on other kinds of discourse. The Vicar's fable or allegory works to ironize the moralistic discourse in which it is uttered, and ironizes the merely moralistic reader. The one example not so far reflected on is that in *Tristram Shandy*, where Sterne's allusion is made partly in the interests of trying to distinguish the later parts of the work from the earlier, and to 'answer' their drift (see Loveridge 1992: 48–9). Smart's fable answers the proudly nationalist note of the declaration of war against the French: the editors of the *Literary Magazine* must have included it understanding that this 'answering' was what a fable was for.

But there is also a sense of reticence, privacy, or secrecy about the presentation of the fable, which is often kept genuinely invisible or silent, to an unexpert reader. There is a characteristic double association, which includes elements of both powerlessness or incapacity and the realignment of authority. The COCK and BULL is really only a semi-private joke buried like a bone at the end of the novel, until dug out by the scholarly bloodhound: Smart's fable is not presented next to the declaration of war in the *Literary Magazine*, but at a discreet distance of a few pages. Clarissa's fable-from-the-grave emphasizes in another way that this association is with an authority that comes from being partly within and partly beyond the structure of the fiction, as is the 'moral doctor' in *The Female Quixote*. Clarissa's other fable, the panicky self-reflexive inversion of The Young Man and the Cat (rewritten to The Young Lady and the Tiger) which she writes when imprisoned by Lovelace and almost mentally unbalanced, is brought back into the story by being pieced together by him from scraps of paper voyeuristically rescued from underneath her writing-table. There is also a disquieting sense of unresolved or throwaway endings, age, dubious seniority, and long historical retrospect – the Seven Years' War seen against the wars of the 1690s, Swift and Gay seen from the 1770s, life seen from death, womens' stories, cock-and-bull stories. But these notions of 'doubling', of something that points paradoxically in two different directions at once, or that has the two *opposed* handles of the mottoes to the next section, have now become so pervasive that it is necessary to take a further step back, to give space to put forward and re-illustrate a general hypothesis which can then be accounted or searched for in historical terms in the following chapter and beyond.

CHAPTER 3

The Peachum position

> We may say of all human things, that they have two Handles, a right and a left: So we may with equal reason say of all the old Fables that they have an infinite number.
>
> ('de Witt' 1703: A2r)

> Every thing in this earthly world, my dear brother *Toby*, has two handles; – not always, quoth my uncle *Toby*.
>
> (Sterne 1978: I, 118)

> A Lawyer is an honest Employment, so is mine. Like me too, he acts in a double Capacity, both against Rogues, and for 'em; for 'tis but fitting that we should protect and encourage Cheats, since we live by them.
>
> (Gay 1973: 112)

We had best begin by separating one kind of doubleness from the other. Like Peachum in *The Beggar's Opera* (1728), some fables appear to act in a strange *double capacity*, at once for and against structures of power, inside them and out, whether these be structures mainly of persuasive narrative effect, of morality (*Truth in Fiction*), of political power, or of textual/sexual relationship. This is not an easy thing to do: fables have all the energy of paradox, just as Peachum's succinct lines trick the audience into accepting the analogy between the lawyer and himself, only to shade the analogy mockingly into 'protect and encourage cheats'. The paradox silently redoubles: Peachum acts for and against rogues, like (but/and also unlike) a lawyer. Fables are lawyers and cheats together. So this quality is not ambiguity, ambivalence, or mediation: Peachum is not that kind of fence.

Some fables, though, are not so paradoxical but relatively complaisant or compliant. In this period a twin tradition of fable evolves, one aspect of which is expressive of the values of voices which are more culturally dominant, and which use fables in a relatively unselfconscious manner. The other – 'double' fable, as above – is more eclectic, paradoxical, and witty, and is often in an anxious or provocative mood over questions of power.

The second tradition may be more interesting than the first, but often depends on it in some way. Patrick Delany may write a satirical fable of *A Pheasant and a Lark* (1730), but it will be his friend Jonathan Swift who promptly replies with the deviously double fable called *An Answer to Dr. Delany's Fable of the Pheasant and the Lark.* So the relationship is not between an infantine or pre-literary or simply rhetorical use of fable and a knowing, satirical use. If satire has become an aspect of the dominant poetic culture, the reaction can be against satire just as easily as it may be towards it. Swift and others such as Anne Finch can define verse fable as working against satire, but since Swift has as double-handed a grip of his pen as anyone, he can also use fables *as* satire (the 'double-handed' figure is borrowed from his 'Left-Handed' verse letter to Thomas Sheridan, where he apologizes for his poor handwriting by claiming that 'I was in great Haste, and the other Hand was employed at the same Time in writing some Letters of Business' (Swift 1957: 3, 968).

Double-handed fabulists, then, may also apparently react against themselves, against aspects of their own practice. Bernard Mandeville translated a selection of the fables of La Fontaine in 1703 under the title of *Some Fables After the Easie and Familiar Method of Monsieur de la Fontaine*, making it sound as though fables were something that the downmarket end of Pope's sociable 'Mob of Gentlemen who wrote with Ease' (Pope 1968: 639) might be writing. Mandeville's 1704 revision of this collection as *Aesop Dress'd* again stresses the socialized Aesop. But then, one year later, he began to publish what became (when applied more widely) the century's most fulminated against, subversive, *anti*social fable, *The Grumbling Hive; or, Knaves Turn'd Honest*, eventually known as *The Fable of the Bees* (1714–24). This Machiavellian or Reynardian procedure of helping to create a polite taste for a form which one then uses as a vehicle for shock tactics is perhaps more two-faced than double-handed.

A full answer to the question of how and why such a tradition of paradoxical or 'double' fable could evolve requires two complementary kinds of investigation. One of these is formal; the other is historical, and can be briefly anticipated here before being enlarged upon in the next chapter.

Writing about the political application of fables by Ogilby, L'Estrange, Croxall, and others, Annabel Patterson points out how clearly L'Estrange's Preface to his 1692 *Fables of Aesop* shows his awareness of two or more different traditions of fable, pedagogical, symbolic, and politically topical. From this she proceeds to a wider point, that 'the fable's literary history' is a pattern of 'moments in which fable tradition . . . is both galvanized and rendered introspective' (Patterson 1987: 277); made both self-aware and reactive. Historical considerations are felt to lie behind the seventeenth-century moments; the passing of power from Royalist and Stuart to Parliamentarian and Orange camps, and the marginalization of those who consequently felt that their traditional status had changed for the worse. The meanings of the basic fables become 'contestable' (Patterson 1991: 4) among political writers and speakers. Shifts of power generate inversions of fables, politically motivated reinterpretations and renewals. Literary fable follows this historical and political movement.

Patterson presents this as a quite natural extension of the dynamics of historical process and utterance into literary effects, but some aspects of this flowering of literary fable are paradoxical. In the western European tradition, secular literary fable and its kin are forms often associated with settled bourgeois cultures – the burghers of thirteenth- and fourteenth-century Picardy and Flanders favouring the later offspring of the *Reynard* cycle, for instance. The eighteenth century's frequent use of fables as mere 'social amenities and sentimental personifications' (Daniel 1982: 170) would point in the same direction. Samuel Croxall's Whiggish 1722 collection is the most popular prose edition of that century and beyond, but the notable fabulists between 1650 and 1700 – Ogilby, L'Estrange, and Dryden – are either Royalist/Jacobite, or Catholic, or Tory, or some combination of these, in their sympathies. To these can be added Anne Finch, Lady Winchilsea, writing fables from retirement at Eastwell after her husband had lost office after the Glorious Revolution in 1688; the initial 1690s 'Grub-street' Aesopian pamphlet *Aesop at Tunbridge* (1698), and many of the pamphlets which followed (Hanazaki 1993–4 has a fascinating close analysis of these); and Aphra Behn's cryptic 1687 contributions to Francis Barlow's widely known 'Catholic' collection. Edmund Arwaker was chaplain to the Jacobite Duke of Ormond, the dedicatee of Dryden's *Fables*. History had clearly conspired to put these writers suddenly into what they felt was a paradoxical position of opposition or subordination, and it is partly to this that they react. To put the point very broadly, they write as if they felt they had been *Aesopized*, strangely enslaved, by recent historical events; the Civil Wars, the Glorious Revolution.

Even Croxall, though Anglican and constitutionally Whiggish rather than Jacobite and Tory, can perhaps be included in this list, if belatedly. He grew disenchanted with the Whig administration in the late 1720s and delivered an outlandishly oppositional sermon to the seat of power, the House of Commons, in 1729, on the text of Proverbs 25, 5: 'take away the wicked from before the king, and his throne shall be established in righteousness'. Kings are advised that they should not 'screen wicked servants' – 'screen' being a key opposition codeword for Walpole after his protection of the ministers after the South Sea Bubble – and that by 'removing one obnoxious man [they] might oftentimes easily clear up every discontent'. 'This Sermon gave offence', says a handwritten note on the titlepage of the printed copy in Cambridge University Library, offering its own laconic little paradox, 'and was not desired to be printed, nor had the Dr. the thanks of the House' (Croxall 1730: 19, 20, titlepage).

So Patterson's word 'moments', the speed and force of historical process, is important. The emerging English literary fable does not belong to a natural order so much as to relatively sudden perceptions of the world-turned-upside-down, or as Patterson puts it, 'cultural instability' (1991: 142). Aesop may have been, in the biographical legend, a slave under masters and tyrants, but that legend also places him in a society settled and judicious enough to offer him his freedom on account of his agreeably subversive wit. English literary fable develops in a more combative atmosphere.

But there is a wider point. This study is concerned with 'moments', but also with an extended period of almost 150 years during which fable, it is claimed, undergoes a continuous process of change, reformation and extension. This is not likely to be possible if the causal factors lie solely in a relatively brief concatenation of historical circumstances; and the fact that fable becomes 'contestable' does not provide an adequate key to its strange ability to occupy double, rather than merely oppositional, positions. Perhaps the writers would have been able to see all their more paradoxical uses of fable as developments of the earlier history of the form, and hence to see their engagement with 'history' and with different readerships as a management of the relation of the timeless with the moment. There is after all Earl Miner's suggestive but teasing expression, 'discontinuous fable or allegory' (Dryden 1956–92: 3, 341) which he uses to describe the baroque qualities of Dryden's delightfully shifting, contradictory uses of fable. 'Discontinuous' is not as negative or neutral in cast as it may appear, because Miner knows he is dealing with a period in which such 'dark' allegories were often looked on with considerable suspicion. 'An Allegory, which is not clear, is a Riddle', complains John Hughes in his 1715 *Essay on Allegorical Poetry* (Durham 1915: 101): '*An* Emblem *without a* Key.*to't, is no more than a* Tale of a Tub', grumbles L'Estrange (1692: Preface). The word 'equivocation' is a particular bugbear of fable-theorists – 'an Image . . . must be just, that is, without Equivocation', insists La Motte (1721: 27) – and discontinuity often involves equivocation, the divided voice addressing an audience perceived as divided.

Miner refers this 'discontinuous' kind of fable to a noble and varied tradition which includes zoography, parabolic readings of scripture, and prosopopoeia, although the only clear resemblance to this mode of figuration that he finds is 'the glossing of Scripture into discontinuous figurative readings of various kinds', in particular the *moraliter* gloss, with its 'model of discontinuous tropology' (Dryden 1956–92: 3, 341). Engagements with scripture are less germane to other fabulists than to Dryden, but this mode of fable is in fact deeply ingrained in the tradition. Insofar as this is a historical question it must largely wait until the next chapter, but the seventeenth century was fond of paradoxes, and Miner provides the interesting clue that 'the Italian genre of the paradox' (*ibid.*) or *paradossa* played some part in the transmission of the philosophical cast of continental fable in the sixteenth and seventeenth centuries. We might now consider the question in terms more formal than historical. What general paradoxical qualities are inherent in fable?

'Fable is paradox', says H. J. Blackham. The fabulist is allowed 'to bamboozle and unsettle, to tease, to delay, to play all the tricks in, and not in, the book' (Blackham 1975: 178–9). This sounds promising. 'It lies, and it doesn't. It tells the truth, and it doesn't', says Rosalie Colie (Colie 1976: 6), characterizing paradox: but this is also the paradox of truth-in-fiction, lies that speak truth, already observed at the heart of fable. Swift's succinct 'And from a Fable form a Truth' (Swift 1957: 1, 252), describing the reader's possibly moralistic response to the lines comparing the financially speculating son to the soaring flight and watery death of Icarus, in his brilliant South-Sea poem *The Bubble* (1721), exhibits the classic double capacity of acting as both platitude and paradox. The poet-fabulist naturally induces a moral, an epimythium, through telling a plausible story, but a lie or *fabula* turns into an apparent 'truth'. Here the joke is that the conjuror Swift is both complacently moralizing the mythical episode *and* dazzling the reader with a 'fantastick Scene' (*ibid.*: 1, 251) akin to those perceived, in the poem, by the deluded eyes and minds of fever-stricken mariners and speculative investors. His moral at its widest is that readers must be both cool moral observers *and* sunstruck Icarean enthusiasts; lawyers and cheated. Working backwards from Swift's elegant and sardonic paradox, we may disentangle three which are native to the tradition, and which would have made fable of particular interest to the Augustans.

A social paradox, from which the historical sense of paradox evident in the English seventeenth-century fabulists, as mentioned above, partly derives. Aesop was not polite and respectable for most of his career, but a deformed slave who spoke to his masters under the cover of parabolic narratives which could themselves take paradoxical forms – speaking persuasively against eloquence, for example. But then he talked on equal terms to kings in their courts. Writers became as interested in these playful social and literary inversions of a slave/savant who could wittily and sometimes subversively educate his masters as they were, say, in a Beggar who could write an Opera, a shepherd who could sing more sweetly than a prince, or a gentle Yahoo.

This interest allowed other social paradoxes inherent in the form to receive emphasis. Gay's pastoral, or pastorally introduced, 1727 fables claim to hope to instruct the sophisticated cosmopolitan world of London and the court. Common readers are silently offered a choice between imagining themselves as a 'young PRINCE' being 'humbly' (Gay 1974: 2, 301, 299) addressed by a deferential fabulist, or as a witty post-pastoral fabulist addressing common readers with ideas above their station. *The Beggar's Opera* is concave-mirrored in 'The Prince's Fables'. The fables thus include the management of a complex figure similar to the 'Newgate pastoral' or Gay's favourite 'town eclogue', but in this case with the figure's oxymoron-like qualities detuned so that it may be contained within an outwardly decorous, moralistic, fable-world. Gay's introductory fable begins:

> Remote from citys liv'd a Swain,
> Unvex'd with all the cares of gain,
> His head was silver'd o'er with age . . . (*ibid.*: 2, 299)

This can be read as *like* a pastoral scene, but we also notice within three lines how conscious the poet is of cities, care, remoteness, vexation, age, and gain. Paradox and social inversion are in turn fundamental to English pastoral, which celebrates a state of innocence from the perspective of a decidedly fallen world, uses knowingly artificial forms to explore the ethical values of nature, and allows, or pretends to allow, aristocrats to play at being shepherds without dirtying their hands. Connections between fable and pastoral are natural: Anne Ferry remarks that 'the tradition of pastoral is the tradition of Hesperian fables' (Ferry 1962: 195), but eighteenth-century pastoral is often closer to the other, Augustan, kind of fable.

A spiritual paradox: fabulists often legitimized their form by pointing out that fables are like parables, and that Christ spoke in parables. L'Estrange's Preface to his 1692 *Fables of Aesop*, for example, invokes Christ's parables and Nathan's fable told to King David. When the Reverend Croxall illustrates 'The Stag Looking into the Water' with the example of a young lady looking into a mirror, the action of the fable is called a 'Parable' (Croxall 1766: 32: Randolph Caldecott's sketch makes exactly the same application 160 years later – the Stag will entangle the antlers he so admires in a thicket and be killed; the narcissistic lady's ruin is visible in Caldecott's inset frame, see plate 1). Also like parable, fable originates between spoken and written language. Christ spoke, Aesop told: *parole*.

But parables, as the word again half-suggests, have paradoxes of their own. 'The only kind of literature which has gospel authority is the parable, and parables are secular stories with no overt religious reference' (Auden 1963: 458). The spiritual content of parable – like the 'truth' of fable – lies only in the application, and in the character or authority of the speaker. Would the parable of the Good Samaritan be a parable if it were spoken by a Samaritan? 'Fable' also meant the lies of pagan religions, and 'parable' is the word mockingly used in some versions of the abominable *Reynard* – it is the seventh word in Caxton's translation of the text, for example (Sands 1960: 45) – for the tricks and blinds of illustrative narrative exampla as used by both characters and narrator. So fable is both like and unlike parable: holy and unholy: lawyer and cheat.

And behind these two lurks the fundamental paradox of fable. Fables, *si peu que rien*, are little and 'low', but, if they speak a truth, may be said to hold a treasure within them: the Pearl that the Cockerel finds in his farmyard dunghill (this in the fable which stands first, offered as promythium, in many collections of fables). It was Phaedrus, the begetter of literary fable, who originally made this fable reflexive, galvanized it, by adding at the end 'Hoc illis narro qui me non intellegunt' – 'This tale is for those who do not appreciate me' (Perry 1965: 278, 279): so the divided readership of fable begins with the original collection. Fables become an analogy of the new Christian treasure-of-the-humble – or perhaps *vice versa*: Phaedrus's figure predates Matthew's 'pearl of great

1 Randolph Caldecott, 'The Stag Looking Into the Water'

price' (13: 46) – but fables force the point by working so directly between vile bodies and high thoughts. The meek (poor) dunghill world of low animals and deformed slaves acquires a part of the literary and ethical world, and calls to its informed readers like a Grasshopper from a green spire.

But these are just ordinary paradoxes. 'Double', real, fables will force points even more. In the natural morality of fable, the Cock, in The Cock and the Pearl, will usually finish the fable by saying that he prefers corn to pearls, because he, a humble barnyard fowl, cannot eat pearls. So the treasure-of-the-humble moral can become doubly paradoxical and amusing, because the Cock, *speaking* the end of the fable, dismisses the p/Pearl, the (written moral) Truth. Grub first, then ethics! – the internal readership of the fable fails its intelligence test. Being only a hungry, noisy (illiterate) Cockerel, he cannot properly read the figure of his own fable – just as Tim, for instance, in Swift's revision of this fable in '*Tim* and the *Fables*', cannot read the figure of his. That function is left to 'intelligent Masters' (La Motte 1721: 16) who can read and write and make proper applications.

So the fable, as well as belonging to the dunghill world, belongs to those who would like to pick up and wear the Pearl, the Truth that comes with the social status of being able to read (fables). It is the paradox of pastoral, transferred consciously to the matter of *reading*. Only the blackest of slaves, the basest of Indians, would throw a precious, white, unreadable Pearl away, richer than all his tribe and proud of his own speech: but as his position as black slave now aligns him with Aesop, he may also be able to moralize on (read) this in his poignant self-reflexive epimythium.

In de Certeau's analysis of the historical relations between speech and the written word, the metaphors and morals of 'readership' which lie behind The Cock and the Pearl are, in effect, replicated in the process of the downgrading and loss of status of spoken language after the invention of printing. 'Although the "fable" [*parole*, the spoken word] speaks . . . it does not know what it is saying, and one must rely on the writer-interpreter to obtain the knowledge it expresses without knowing it' (Certeau 1992: 12). But de Certeau's writing itself acts as speech here, in the sense that he does not appear to know about the Phaedrian fable. The French tradition has generally taken fable rather seriously, and underplayed its jokes and perversities. The spirit of the alternative reaction is perhaps best encapsulated by two of the better-known illustrators of The Cock and the Pearl, Caldecott and Grandville – though one of these is French. Plates 2 and 3, two pointed illustrations from the nineteenth century, bear witness to a continuing tradition of knowledgeably witty treatments of fable which is largely missing from the canonical literature. Conversely, eighteenth-century illustrations tend to have been appropriated by the more genteel tradition: only after the age of Hogarth, Rowlandson, Gillray, and Cruickshank will great popular illustrators such as Tenniel and Grandville think fables a suitable subject for treatment. Caldecott and Grandville show clearly that although the

2 J. J. Grandville, 'The Cockerel and the Pearl'

paradoxes of fable may seem tough, they are widely available to an implied common readership, even as late as the Victorian period.

So the *natural* condition of literary fable is to exhibit a double capacity which both shatters and works with various dualisms of discourse and readership. Many fables, though, are content to work within those paradoxes which are assimilable to more straightforward or conventional purposes. In a more socially complaisant medieval Cock and Pearl fable such as those of Marie de France and Henryson, for instance, the Cock has a mental picture of the rich man who should own such a fine gem. Their morals play more on this, and are hence socially and ethically conservative rather than being developed into a reflexive joke. The fable is as witty as you wish it to be; or *as witty as you are.*

This argument began from the premise that in the eighteenth century there is a relationship between two different traditions, each with its own vitality. The beginning of this process is John Ogilby's sudden astonish-

3 Randolph Caldecott, 'The Cockerel and the Pearl'

ing transformation of the traditions existing in the first half of the seventeenth century, which is to say the use of Aesop as a straightforward school text or aid to rhetorical exercises, and the related (also rhetorical) politically engaged tradition of glancing spoken and written allusion, as documented by Patterson. What Ogilby did was astonishing because literary fable as a form had lapsed in England in the early sixteenth century, and in France before that: in literary terms, there was almost nothing to transform.

Then, late in the seventeenth century, the split between the normative or dominant and the more eclectic and subversive tradition widens, as English fable-culture very suddenly becomes more diverse and complex. Patterson's 'moment' again seems appropriate, as this process appears to begin from, or around, a single catalytic event or example, the publication of *The Hind and the Panther* in 1687. The gap between the traditions remains stable enough to allow the production of some remarkable hybrids and double agents until Gay's 1727 *Fables*, after which oppositional fable becomes a good deal more fluid as the conservative tradition expands and the energies of fable flow outwards into the novel and other forms.

Being complex, these processes need extended illustration, but one factor is perhaps crucial enough to be highlighted in advance. This is the support given to the normative or institutional uses of fable which was provided by English criticism's taking up ideas from French neoclassicism which credited Aesopian fable with all the dignity of a heroic classical form. Mainstream or hardline neoclassical criticism, as inherited from René Le Bossu and mediated by John Dennis and Blackmore to Addison and others, regarded Aesopian fable and Homeric epic as different aspects of the same form, a more generalized 'fable'. It then took the consistency provided by decorous and selfconsistent fable to be an essential moral and religious facet of narrative and poetic literature, without which works were thought to be technically 'corrupt', liable to disintegrate into their constituent elements. If the fable (*mythos*) is perverse, riddling, equivocal, or unnatural, it becomes a 'murmuring, as it were, at Providence' (Dennis 1939: I, 21, quoted by Patey 1984: 118; Dennis has been reading Leibniz's *Essais . . . sur la bonté de Dieu*). Douglas Lane Patey reincarnates this set of ideas and attitudes in his *Probability and Literary Form*, with this as the crux –

> If these fictions are indeed hierarchies of probable signs, their providential structure and interpretation follows logically from the very notion of literary form as the Augustans conceived it. Fable conduces to moral by virtue of its form, providential interventions to a superintendent deity. (Patey 1984: 207)

Dennis and Patey enlist fable on the side of providence, God, and by implication the dominant culture, dogmatic and religiose, which is happy to manipulate ideas about literary form to fit the shape of religious belief. More Providence than Wit, clearly, and perhaps closer to Whiggish (and American) myths and fables of progress, success, and happy morality than to the English Augustans. Faced with a quantity of evidence as impressive as Patey's, it is difficult to argue that eighteenth-century literary theory and practice did not embody such a view of the world – or at least that a 'right-handed' section of the audience would have liked it to. But the twentieth-century providentialist critics sometimes have an axe of their own to grind which is like that of the more moralistic neoclassicals themselves, and the model proposed has the drawback of being static where novelistic usage of such a paradigm is often pragmatic, innovative, and sceptical. Melvyn New's suspicions, in his essay '"The Grease of God": The Form of Eighteenth-Century English Fiction' (New 1976), that the period is in fact an extended moment of tension and conflict between providentialist and secular views of the world, seem highly relevant. Look for characters in *Tom Jones* who are prepared to say that they believe in something like the secret direction of providence, and you will find the evil Blifil (17, 2), the credulous Partridge (12, 8), Square's doctrines about the eternal fitness of things (of which he repents just in time), and, very briefly, the dupeable Allworthy (18, 7). Fielding keeps quiet about whether or how he expects the reader to 'believe' in the providentialist arrangements of the story.

An approach such as that of Patey and Dennis clearly raises the stakes enormously, although it also overloads *fables* (the argument originally was from fables (Aesopian and epic) to 'fable') with rather too much responsibility. It is also at odds with the paradoxical qualities of fable as indicated above: Ephraim Jenkinson's *mythos*, for example, is perverse enough, but contrives to cause a 'providentially' happy ending. And while one could assert that the fable-morality of hierarchies, natural orders, and things-in-their-place would be a perfectly suitable mode for conservative moralities, the conservative fable usually turns out to have been discreetly altered from a previous original, as with Marie's Cock and Pearl, which could be said to usurp the tradition. The 'natural' morality of fable is worldly, expedient, and prudential in a less-than-spiritual fashion: a hierarchy of wit and cunning, quite the opposite of a conductor towards a superintendent deity. And Augustan fables as employed by novelists and others clearly do not conduce to simple morals.

The more sceptical and pragmatic replies characteristic of the temper of English critics tend to bear this out – Addison describing fables as 'Pieces of Wit' in *Spectator* 183, for instance (Addison 1965: 2, 219), as if they were jocular, ingenious, and metaphorical, rather than vehicles for a higher morality. Much More Wit than Providence: 'piece of wit' is a phrase from Restoration stage comedy, used by libertines to describe an agreeably swift verbal riposte. But even as he is providing this definition,

Addison's other, more moralistic hand is dramatizing his own version of Plato's account, in the *Phaedo*, of Socrates's outlined fable on the interconnected nature of Pleasure and Pain.

This hand moralizes the topic by associating Pleasure with Virtue and Pain with Vice, and in so doing legitimizes an attitude developed by many later fabulists such as Hawkesworth, Moore, Brooke, and Langhorne, in which the hierarchy of wit of Aesopian fable is replaced by a hierarchy of virtue and moral sentiment. By the 1770s verse fables were *Moral and Sentimental* (the title of William Russell's *Fables* from 1772) rather than *Moral and Political*, as in the 1700s. Fables were used as vehicles for ethical and philosophical teaching, particularly in systems involving natural religion or a stress on the harmony of nature and virtue. The fable became 'a particularly fine medium for expressing a view of morality which coincided with that of the eighteenth century' (Bush 1965: 161). Do not disturb the natural (i.e. social) order. Work hard and watch your back, but Doasyouwouldbedoneby. 'Virtue makes our bliss below', to quote Hawkesworth's fable 'The Experimental Moralist' (*GM* XI (Nov. 1741): 602): 'not true', comments Fielding tersely in *Tom Jones* (1974: 2, 783) – there are different views of morality in the century. And for females, *one false step is ne'er retrieved*, or, as Moore's unbelievably near-the-knuckle line on this topic has it, 'the wounds of honour never close' (Moore 1749: 116). Partly gentrified by the earlier joint appeal to neoclassicism and Christianity, fables were now gentrified more thoroughly. Fable became almost as respectable a form as it did in France and Germany, though the English never had a whole polite periodical devoted to fables, as the Germans did – *Der Deutsche Aesop* – and English fable did not acquire the supporting and limiting intellectual framework of French and German critical theory.

Fables could now be used for the presentation of cultural heroes and norms in the 'ethical choice' tradition of fable. Particularly popular were those found in the emblematically derived 'twin streams' tradition, in which a calm stream represents Moderation or Temperance, and a more violent one Ambition or Indulgence. This tradition meanders or cascades from an example in Thomas Yalden's collection *Aesop at Court, or State Fables* in 1702 through to a scene or tableau in chapter 22 of Scott's *Waverley* (1814), in which the heroine, Flora, seats herself above a river which exhibits both moods, suggesting Waverley's impending choice between the romance of Scotland and the mundane world of England. Scott did not need to moralize the scene for his readers.

There were also many new versions of the several prominent fables about Hercules, and of the related mythical apologue of 'The Choice of Hercules'. This episode, familiar to a wide readership through its use as a school translation exercise from Greek, dramatizes the heroic nature of the Protestant work-ethic for the new middle-class audience in the story, originally from Prodicus, of Hercules's choice at a crossroads between two female figures, one voluptuous, one severe, who represent Pleasure and Virtue – or Luxury and Duty, or Idleness and Work. In the related fable known as Hercules and Pluto or Plutus, the opposition is between Fortune (Plutus being the son of Fortune) and Submission to Providence. The Choice of Hercules became an 'exemplum for the rise of the middle class under the impetus of mercantilism', a figure in which the 'equality between the labor of the hero and the labor of the private citizen' allows his example to 'show how, by labouring with one's own hands one may secure independence, and open for one's self many sources of health and amusement' (Owen 1969: 8, 33, and Beattie, 1783: 567, quoted by Owen, 8).

As Owen's phrase suggests, one definition of a fable is that it is an exemplum, an *example of a narrative* or an argument, as well as an illustration of a moral. A form which works through illustration and example will naturally be interested in characters who display the same quality of exemplarity; in particular in a famous and complex exemplar such as Hercules, who was potentially as varied and open in application as fable itself. Where the 'twin streams' tradition, being emblematic, is relatively conservative and stable, the representations of Hercules closely follow the general pattern of the history of English fable through the period in their twin traditions, which in this instance derive from very mixed classical and medieval origins. In these Hercules displays 'an extraordinarily wide, and often contradictory, range of features' (Economou 1990: 246). He performs heroic tasks, some socially useful, some less so, such as devirginating the fifty daughters of Thespius in a single night – his '*hardest* Task', says the dreadful L'Estrange (1692: 134). But he kills his friend Iphitus in a fit of rage, and is punished by being enslaved in the court of Queen Omphale; practises 'the vice of pederasty' (Wind 1938–9: 214) with almost as many underage boys as Thespius had daughters; suffers heroically in love and death. In the French tradition, which originates with Lucian's learned Celt in *Herakles*, Hercules is an exemplar of 'oral persuasion' (*ibid.*: 207) and eloquence.

Then, following a strong tradition of visual heroicizations of The Choice in European Renaissance art, Hercules was developed into a normative (bourgeois) ethical hero in English fable and iconography in the period shortly after 1700, after which he was promptly reclaimed by more satirical and sceptical reworkings of his complicated myth. Normative exemplar of heroic industry he may have been, but as Ronald Paulson points out in his cogent discussion of Hogarth's series of plates, *Industry and Idleness* (Paulson 1974), there is a competing poetic ethos in which Industry may translate as mere busyness and Idleness as valuable retreat or peace:

> How various his employments, whom the world
> Calls idle, and who justly in return
> Esteems that busy world an idler too! (Cowper 1980–95: 2, 171–2)

The satirical side of his English tradition will be illustrated more fully in incidental examples in the following chapters. The conservative eighteenth-century English myth originates with two writers whose treatments of Hercules are of considerable significance in the history of fable and narrative. Addison rehearses The Choice of Hercules in *Tatler* 97 (21 November 1709), and, more particularly, Anthony Ashley Cooper, third Earl of Shaftesbury, moralizes a Matthias illustration of 'that most familiar and quintessential of emblematic topoi' (Bath 1994: 256) in his 'Historical Draught or Tablature [tableau] of the Judgement of Hercules' (1713), which was included in later editions of the *Characteristicks*, a copy of which Fielding owned.

Shaftesbury claims the exemplary episode or emblem for a conservative discursive tradition by insisting that the representation must be so designed and executed that the characters all appear on the same heroic level. In particular, Pleasure must not appear as 'a mere scold', but is to have 'a middle character between the person of a Venus, and that of a Bacchinal nymph' (Shaftesbury 1914: 46, 43). Shaftesbury seems to be aware of the possibility of introducing grotesque or burlesque elements into the representation, as Dürer, for instance, had done in his probably parodic illustration of the episode (see Wind 1938–9). Joshua Reynolds would later paint David Garrick between Tragedy and Comedy, with Garrick clearly about to make the 'wrong' choice of the primrose path of dalliance with Comedy, and in a pose which David Mannings identifies (Mannings 1993–4) as closer to that of the drunken Silenus than the heroic Hercules. Such amusing interference would destroy the clarity of the meaning, the moral, and Shaftesbury is particularly concerned that this should be preserved.

To this end, his instructions to the painter about genre and style are couched in terms closely similar to those of contemporary fable-theory, and stress in particular that the piece must demand to be *singly read.* 'The piece must by no means be equivocal or dubious, but must with ease distinguish itself, as either historical and moral, or as perspective and merely natural'. Nothing 'of the emblematical or enigmatic kind [is to] be visibly and directly intermixed', because 'nothing can be more deformed than a confusion of many beauties . . . every grace must be sacrificed to the real beauty of this first and highest [historical and moral] order'. The painter must

> learn to reject those false ornaments of affected graces, exaggerated passions . . . be reserved, severe, and chaste, in this particular of his art; where luxury and libertinism are, by the power of fashion and the modern taste, become so universally established. (Shaftesbury 1914: 53, 55, 61)

In a variant of *ut pictura poesis*, painting is like society, as well as like other arts. Moral pictures must not bedeck themselves with the false ornaments of affectation, nor should an overlay of emblematic detail distract from the allegory of the whole: otherwise, as with Belinda's arraying her own image with the spoils of the world's luxury trades in *The Rape of the Lock* (just out in its two-canto form, in 1713) they will betray themselves to the dangers of perceived false and exaggerated emotional response. Shaftesbury links the dangerous Catholic overtones of self-iconizing and self-decoration such as Belinda's with those of 'false' painting elsewhere, exemplified by 'Egyptian hieroglyphics, magical, mystical, monkish and Gothic emblems' (*ibid.*: 62) – and hence, of course, with those of false narratives, such as Planudes's monkish romance, the *Life of Aesop* (*c.* 1300) or perverse fables. Similarly with reading: ambiguity, equivocation, is understood to be the sign or mode of Mandevillean moral duplicity and libertinism. As the great man Hercules chose the strait path of Virtue, so the reader of the picture should be able to choose the single, unparadoxical, heroically virtuous path – the *Primrose* path, if one wants a paradox – of direct meaning and truth. From the action or fable of the piece flows the moral, and this is what fables are for, not for crafty arguments in favour of luxury and of a vision of society as an amoral structure of power-relations and passions. Shaftesbury's reading of the episode resonates very widely.

Addison's version in the *Tatler*, like Shaftesbury's, carries a good deal of significance in the history of narrative. After giving an extended but straightforward version of the Choice, Addison drops back into his eccentric persona of 'Isaac Bickerstaffe' to pass the following remarks:

> I have translated this Allegory for the Benefit of the Youth of Great Britain; and particularly of those who are still in the deplorable State of Non-Existence, and

whom I most earnestly entreat to come into the World . . . I don't expect of them that, like the Hero in the foregoing Story, they should go about as soon as they are born, with a Club in their Hands, and a Lion's Skin on their Shoulders, to root out Monsters, and destroy Tyrants; but as the finest author of all antiquity has said upon this very Occasion. Though a Man has not the Abilities to distinguish himself in the most shining Parts of a great Character, he has certainly the Capacity of being just, faithful, modest, and temperate. (Steele 1987: 2, 340–1)

Everyman his own small hero, and the promise of allusive moral fiction for the unborn English tribes: fictions in which virtuous striving may turn out to be both heroic and interchangeable experience for the reader, defined by adherence to the codes of value in this fable and others. But the Bickerstaffean overtones of addressing an audience which is not merely juvenile but homunculean, or even less than a glint in their parents' eyes – there is obviously something Shandean about it, or something Bickerstaffean about Tristram – add a strange twist to the notion of fables as lectures of domestic wisdom. These are *very* young persons. Addison may moralize fable in such a way as to originate a conservative tradition, but, as before, there is an agreeable double-handedness about his approach.

So myth and fable did not, as some would have it, die out in the early eighteenth century. In the 1730s the Hercules-fables became available to the new novelists, at a point when satirical and conservative versions briefly enjoyed roughly equal status. The *Gentleman's Magazine* for 1738 extended its usual even-handed editorial policy – printing Cibber's footling laureate Birth-day odes to the monarch alongside a range of enthusiastic parodies of them every year, for instance – by printing two poems on Hercules. One is a straightforward poeticization of the Choice by Robert Lowth, Bishop of London (*GM* 8 (September 1738): 486; the conservative tradition now includes one Earl and one bishop), and the other is a doggerel jest, possibly by the juvenile William Collins, in which the poet offers to lend Jove his wife as a second Alcmena, to beget a necessary second Hercules to root out modern social and political monsters. But the poet will be cuckolded, and his horns will make Hercules think that *he* is a monster. So – 'Then lest I should share in the general drub, / Transform me, Oh *Jupiter*, into his — club' (*GM* 8 (January 1738): 45). The mocking conflation of the heroic implements of Hercules is a running joke in this side of the tradition.

Fielding thus develops his comic and satirical interests in exemplarity and in Hercules (Captain Hercules Vinegar; the hero's club (!) and the many other references in *Joseph Andrews*, and elsewhere) at a point where the figure of Hercules is available as cultural myth in the mixed ground between normative ethical tale, apologue, and reactive satire, just as the example of the Great Man himself is both rounded and shaded by recent political history. One might think that Hercules is a pointedly odd figure for Fielding to choose as an exemplar, an unrepresentative example of exemplarity. In terms of the popular tradition of straightforward pedagogical 'confidence in the power of human example' (Hunter 1990: 284) good and bad which G. K. Hunter dramatizes as lying behind and informing the early English novel (or some novels), he is; but this is by no means the only possible attitude to exemplarity. Timothy Hampton points out that as far back as the sixteenth century,

> humanist writing on exemplarity is seen as caught between a veneration of the timeless value of ancient models as patterns for action and a sharp awareness of the contingency that divides modern readers from ancient exemplars. (Hampton 1990: x)

So modern exemplarity may be difficult and problematical, even without the most immediate Great Man – Walpole – who is, both despite and because of his contemptible aspects, all the age has to offer as representative historical exemplar.

The contradictions inherent in the myth of Hercules make him a model of, or for, this divided response to example, which is everywhere in Fielding. When Fielding is wearing his magistrate's hat, and where a transparent 'belief' in the power of example might produce positive practical benefits, then he can 'believe', as he does in his right-handed collection of *Examples of the Interposition of Providence in the Detection and Punishment of Murder* (1752); but not in his fiction. If Abraham Adams venerates an exemplary ancient, Aeschylus, the body of his old friend – the manuscript – will first be used against him as evidence of theft. The exemplary text will then go up in smoke in the fire in the alehouse which Adams has entered to avoid a shower, while Fanny and Joseph experience their contingent re-uniting.

The most popular and influential Renaissance exemplars are such figures as Don Quixote, and Cervantes's novel 'narrates the impossibility of exemplarity' (*ibid.*: 293). *Joseph Andrews* is written 'in Imitation of the Manner of CERVANTES' (Fielding 1967[a]: 1), and similar problems to those involved in Adams's veneration of Aeschylus, or in the world's treatment of Don Quixote's admirable but bizarre visions, attend the presentation of Adams as modern exemplar. Quixote and Hercules are largely interchangeable, as far as the complexity of their exemplary functions is concerned: where a modern Hercules will comically go about to destroy social and political monsters, Don Quixote, in Fielding's play *Don Quixote in England* (1734), will find 'a plenteous stock of monsters' (Fielding 1967^{b}: 11, 67) as mad as he in the English country borough in which the action takes place.

Fielding's interests in what he sees as the necessarily Quixotic and Herculean powers of modern exemplarity originate in his early satirical plays, and flow from thence, via manifestations in his writing for the opposition periodical the *Champion* in the late 1730s and 1740, into the paraphernalia and introductions of his early fictions, giving them a fascinating mixed status somewhere between the modes of fable and history. It is, though, impossible to illustrate Fielding using *examples* of fable in the manner of the previous chapter (bar the intriguing use of The Cockerel and the Pearl, placed at the end of *Pasquin* (1736) – as so often, a piece critiquing a culture through modes of representation (here, tragedy and comedy) ends with a moral which is also a fable about interpretation or misinterpretation), because he is so fully exercised by the problem of the status of the text itself as an example or exemplar. The third of the many uses of the word 'great' and its kin in *Jonathan Wild* (1743) provocatively refers to the text itself as 'this great work'; and greatness is then promptly defined as 'bringing all manner of mischief on mankind' (Fielding 1982: 40). *Caveat lector!* – about to be bamboozled by the story, just as the great man Wild will try to dupe anything that moves.

The first of these manifestations of interest in exemplarity, Fielding's dedicatory letter to the opposition's new star, Chesterfield, prefaced to *Don Quixote in England*, begins to make it clear that it is the text or the dramatic representation itself that is to be thought of as exemplary in its double capacity (madly farcical but with moral/satirical powers; as opposed to, say, Adams's old-friend-but-roasted), as much or more so than the Quixote himself, and that exemplarity of this kind is itself oppositional in nature:

> The freedom of the stage is, perhaps, as well worth contending for as that of the press. It is the opinion of an author well known to your Lordship, that examples work quicker and stronger on the minds of men than precepts.
>
> This will, I believe, . . . be found truer with regard to politics than to ethics . . . a lively representation of the calamities brought on a country by general corruption might have a very sensible and useful effect on the spectators. (Fielding 1967^{b}: 11, 7)

The specifically political overtones of this, and the apparent faith in a unidirectional exemplarity embodied in a straightforwardly 'good text', are something of a red herring, as the very unFieldinglike air of 'perhaps' and the conditional tense near the end of the quotation imply. Especially after 1740, Fielding's texts can never be 'good' ones, because they are embroiled with the problem of responding to 'great' ones such as *Pamela*, which hold themselves up as exemplary by advertising their 'young Politician' (Fielding 1971: 313) of a heroine as an imitable pattern of virtue. When Fielding approaches exemplarity in the *Champion*, he appears to plump for a specific kind of example, the negative:

> we are much better and easier taught by the examples of what we are to shun, than by those which would instruct us what to pursue . . . we are more inclined to detest and loathe what is odious in others, than to admire what is laudable. (Fielding 1967[b]: 15, 330–1)

But this is used merely as an introduction to a denunciation of the disgraceful example of the Great Man himself, looked up to only by 'sycophants and slaves and sturdy beggars' – 'sturdy beggars' being transparent code for Walpole, after his notorious phrase for the crowds protesting against his Excise legislation in 1734, as the footnote about 'Roberdsmen' insists on revealing. 'Since then it is so wholesome a lesson', continues the essay, 'to show us what we ought not to do, or what we ought not to be, might we not instruct our youth much better by example than precept?' (*ibid.*: 332). This is an unexceptionable dictum – in the 1690s Vanbrugh said, almost without irony, that it was 'the Business of Comedy . . . to shew People what they shou'd do, by representing them upon the Stage, doing what they should not' (Vanbrugh 1927: 1, 206). But the sentiment is now tainted by the example of the 'great' negative exemplar, the encourager of political sycophancy and literary prostitution, just as the *example of the text* will be tainted by that of *Pamela* and other works such as Middleton's sycophantic *Life of Cicero*, which, in Fielding's subtly analogical and metaphorical mind, all train readers and young women in the political virtue and 'Wisdom of legal Prostitution for Hire' (Fielding: 1974: 2, 866). So, in the *Champion* essay, instructing our youth by negative example turns out to mean that schoolmasters should be enthusiastically thrashed to show the boys how much it hurts, and should be made to get drunk in public to show them the effects of intemperance. The precepts *about* example, in other words, do not survive the nature of the example itself, or himself, which has altered the status of the potentially 'exemplary' text and its advice.

From the *Champion*, Fielding next proceeds to an entirely double-handed apparent reversal of his apparent opinion about the efficacy of negative example, in the first sentence of *Joseph Andrews*: 'It is a trite but true Observation, that Examples work more forcibly on the Mind than Precepts: and if this be just in what is odious and blameable, it is more strongly so in what is amiable and praise-worthy' (Fielding 1967[a]: 1). Examples good and bad, trustworthy examples. But placing this magisterial sentence as initial moral or promythium effectively denatures its statement by offering it in the manner of a precept rather than an example, in an effect somewhat akin to that of the first sentence of *Pride and Prejudice*. So it is a quixotically bad example, heroically setting itself up only to be revealed by the windmills of the contingent world as absurd. The beautiful, praiseworthy examples in question – after a brief tour of Plutarch and Jack the Giant-Killer to prepare the new ground – turn out to be Cibber's derided *Apology* for his own life, and Pamela herself, the memory of the pattern of whose virtue is said to keep Joseph pure. Equal nonsense, of course: this is achieved by a combination of natural modesty, naïveté, superior physical strength, and anticipation of the charms of Fanny. But even 'the mere *English* Reader' (*ibid.*: 3) – Fielding's phrase for the incapable Cockerel-reader which all literary fables invent – should be able to interpret the book from these hints.

But showing that Fielding's interests in exemplarity are akin to the interests of fable is not quite the same thing as showing that Fielding works in a fabulist manner. To show that he does, and to begin to come to a redefinition of Kettle's 'moral fable', it may now be prudent to return briefly to the most difficult and persistent question involved in a study of this literature, which is in what sense it is proper to speak of it as having a political function. An expansive and inclusive approach to the literary history of this period such as the one proposed may seem perversely contrary or revisionist, in failing sufficiently to stress the engagement of its best poetry and fiction with the politics of discourse in the form of satire, critique of governments and policies, polemics. After all, as Mary Pritchard rightly says,

> the significant developments in the English fable collection came primarily in response to English political events, and each movement in that development can be understood as a response to the political and social milieu in which it was written. (Pritchard 1976: 4)

In other words, fable between Ogilby and Gay, and perhaps beyond, is properly understood, by readers, writers, and critics alike, as having a specifically political function, and one denies its nature by not stressing this as fully as possible. Yet Fielding (for example), though working in a manner which is clearly oppositional in a general sense, is only rarely oppositional in a specifically political sense. For every lampoon of Walpole that he writes, there is, before 1740 at least, a short comic poem asking him for patronage; and he may have allowed Walpole to buy off the publication of *Wild* in 1740. How can Fielding be, or be like, a political fabulist?

The point may best be addressed parabolically, or from a wider apparent digression answering the rather overdue question: why *Augustan* fable? The loosest definition, which is that it indicates some of the qualities of some of the major writers of the period 1650–1800, applies, but so do more specific ones, of which the first is germane.

The eighteenth-century 'Augustan' writers are sometimes so called from their complex but generally oppositional relationship with the most politically powerful figures of the period, who, for a variety of reasons, are associated with the tyrant/patron Roman emperor Augustus. English kings had been compared to Augustus since before the Civil Wars, at first in a relatively complimentary way, but later with a more ironical stress, especially after the arrival of crusty little George Augustus, George II, in 1727. Even Walpole himself played the role to some extent, driving Gay's and Fielding's plays off the stage but subscribing publicly to Gay's *Poems on Several Occasions* and Fielding's *Miscellanies*, giving Pope £200 for work on his translation of the *Odyssey*, and, according to one tradition, encoring one of the more equivocal songs when spotted attending a performance of *The Beggar's Opera*. But 'Augustus' was spoken for, so the Great Man's opponents and supporters had to choose other parallels.

Literary fable was originally Augustan in the precise sense of 'reflecting on Augustus'. Phaedrus records his own position as a freedman under Augustus in his subtitle, and the emperor occasionally figures obliquely as an 'actor' in the fables, as in the late fable (5, 7) about the flute-player called *Princeps*; Prince, who absurdly took the audience's applause for himself when the Chorus sang a line applauding the Princeps (emperor, in this case Augustus). Prince is laughed at for his presumption, and booted off the stage. Art should not overtly usurp the emperor or it will be treated roughly, would be one application. The fables also reflect more widely on political institutions and reprove tyrants, but such examples are usually discreetly distanced to historical Athens, as in the second fable of Book 1, The Frogs who Asked for a

King. Here Pisistratus is the original, tyrannical ('tyrannus') ruler – 'non quia crudelis ille / not that their ruler was unkind' (Perry 1965: 192, 193), says Phaedrus, delicately pretending to unsay what he has just said. Augustus would never boot an artist off the stage.

Phaedrus's collection is then full of wider, subtly ironical, understated relationships with masters of other kinds: with Ovid, for example, whose *Metamorphoses* collect and deploy fragments of myth in a fashion mimicked on a miniature scale in the next generation by Phaedrus's collection of the fabular-metaphorical particles of Aesop. Ovid had been exiled by Augustus for his poetry, booted off the stage as far as the Black Sea. Phaedrus was freed by Augustus for his, as Aesop was freed from slavery by his masters: a mordant double analogy.

Philosophical masters appear in the fables; Socrates, for example. And 'Phaedrus' is the name of one of Plato's Socratic dialogues, with the original character called Phaedrus obligingly setting up a critique of Platonist uses of language which Socrates then appears to demolish with his philosophical authority. So although 'Augustus' is used literally by the fabulist as a focus of power and political relationship, he is also part of a network of 'political' relationships which extends to the fables as poetry and as conceptual system. This would seem to argue towards an understanding of literary fable as being politically engaged – concerned with the relationship with 'masters' – on many fronts rather than one, in the way that has already been suggested.

So there may in turn be a connection between the politically and culturally oppositional character of the seventeenth-century fabulists and later 'Augustans', and the wider subversive or reactive aspect of literary fable used to transverse cultural positions, to answer the discourses of masters, or as reproof of tyrants. As many masters are obliquely addressed in *Shamela* (1741) as in Phaedrus – Middleton for his *Life of Cicero*; Cibber for his *Apology*; the shadowy figure who has written *Pamela*; Hervey; and the other shadowy figure who lies behind the usurped exemplary figure of Cicero – 'one of the contemporary criticisms of Middleton's book was that it falsified the life of Cicero to flatter Walpole's and Hervey's politics' (Rothstein 1968: 386). Middleton's compromised praise of 'the most famous *novus homo*, Cicero' (McKeon 1987: 138) illuminates the modern example from the footlights. Prostitute literary and historical writers form an amalgam with the sham virtue of Pamela; all employ a style 'whose naïve candor seems unquestionable . . . Cibber, like Pamela, writes with a wisdom that is above reflection, in a spontaneous style that is designed to disarm suspicion'

(Amory 1969: 241). All misuse style and exemplarity in order to bamboozle the unsuspecting – the *mere* – reader. Discourse, here as in *Pasquin*, as Eric Rothstein's article recently quoted argues, forms a composite culture of corruption, religious (the clerical Middleton), historical (Cibber's *Apology* also rewrites history by creating historical parallels favourable to Walpole), political, sexual, but always textual and *tonal* in its manifestations. The shadowy figure behind *Pamela* turned out to be the King's printer.

Historians have been known to complain that if *Shamela* is a critique of Walpole, he is nowhere directly visible. True, but his proxy voices are audible in the ventriloquial echoes that lie behind Fielding's comic insistence that prostitutes should be heard to speak like prostitutes; and it is to multiple voices, masters, texts, and readerships that English fable, from the Civil Wars to Gay and beyond, quixotically directs itself. But fable always did. Fielding is the inheritor of a long tradition.

Hugh Amory overstates his case slightly in calling *Shamela* an 'Aesopic Satire' because of its anonymity and its indirect oppositional quality. Arguing that 'Fielding aesopically implies . . . [that] the real author of *Pamela* . . . is no other than Sir Robert Walpole himself, the 'Magus' of the *Dunciad*, the 'Cicero' of the London Magazine, *fons et origo* of Ciceronian eloquence . . .' (*ibid.*: 241) is pushing Fielding's argument-by-analogy too far. Fielding's Walpole cannot rise to the status of *author*, only to that of literary pimp. Closer to the mark is Amory's reflection on C. B. Woods's observation (in *PQ* 25 (1946): 248–72) that 'Fielding's personal satire is often "double-barrelled" ':

> The ambiguity of Fielding's allusions in *Jonathan Wild* and in *Shamela* . . . seems to be a device for appealing beyond party personalities to a common political honesty on both sides. It is peculiarly aesopic, an ironic disclaimer that the satire has any personal application at all, except that 'if the cap fits', and the cap does fit an astounding variety of heads. (Amory 1969: 252)

This slightly staid perception or moral might in turn be extended or reinforced by McKeon's account of the 'double' quality of *Jonathan Wild*, critiquing both 'the idealizing, "romancing" method of traditional biographies' *and* 'the "new romance" of naïve empiricism and its modernized methods of imposing on the credulity of the reader' (McKeon 1987: 383) – compare Amory's comment about style used to 'disarm suspicion' above. This would give a proper sense of the trickiness and volatility of Fielding's fabulist method, its quality of seeming to satirize everything and nothing.

The main problem involved in trying to articulate the English tradition of fable is that the history of verse fable in particular suffers when seen in directly political terms. As Mary Pritchard says, apart from the grand exception of Dryden, who is both a great political poet with specific sympathies and an extraordinarily innovative fabulist, 'there is little evidence of any linear development of the skill with which fabulists were able to apply the fable collection to their respective political situations' (Pritchard 1976: 16). In other words, as Dryden did not technically write a *collection*, Ogilby is the best political verse fabulist in the language. This is an intriguing case, but one which, unless fable *is* 'political' in wider senses, makes it difficult to argue for a continuing integrity and validity that might make the tradition of interest to the new novelists.

There is also a more specific problem to do with transmission here, in that overtly politicized literary fable changed in nature and status in the eighteenth century. After Gay had responded to the fevered fable-culture of the late 1720s by turning his second series into 'The *Craftsman* in Fables' (Graham 1969), it was generally seen as desirable for collections of fables to at least appear to be, in the words of Richardson's 1739 subtitle, 'Abstracted from all Party Considerations'. After 1720, specifically political verse fable was almost entirely restricted to individual snipers in periodicals and broadsheets. Gay's second series bucks the trend, but even that had begun, with 'The *Dog* and the *Fox*', in the opposition *Craftsman* itself (No. 329 (June 1731): 231).

So if fable in the seventeenth-century mode is intrinsically political in only this narrower sense, there was a complete break in its history just at the point where this study wants to argue for ongoing coherence and evolution. That this is a crux, that seeing the form in this way makes it hard to take eighteenth-century fable seriously, is best demonstrated by Pritchard's reluctance to deal with Gay, and by the example of Patterson, who, near the end of *Fables of Power*, briefly approaches Gay's *Fables* from the viewpoint of an expert historian of seventeenth-century political literature. Disgust is not too strong a word. Gay's strategy, she finds, is simply to 'pretend that the political history of the genre had never existed'; the *Fables* appear to 'represent a reclamation of the genre . . . for what appears to be a transparent and indeed crystalline moralism of the most general kind, as appropriate, perhaps, for the instruction and amusement of an adolescent member of the royal family' (Patterson 1991: 149). Genteel, normative, complaisant, much in line with recent trends. Political interpreters of Gay's *Fables* typically come to this conclusion, though Patterson is perhaps forcing the point in the hope of being properly provocative. Bertrand Goldgar calls their political satire 'negligible' (Goldgar 1976: 45) in comparison with the contemporary lampoons against Walpole, with the unspoken corollary that the fables themselves are hardly worth discussing. Following and widening this opinion, S. H. Daniel asserts as received opinion that the tradition of English political fable was denatured and dissipated, 'primarily as a result of translations of the works of La Fontaine', that Gay's *Fables*, especially the first series, are 'noticeably apolitical', and that more or less the only use of fables in and after the 1730s was as a means of politely 'socializing individuals' (Daniel 1982: 158). Gay's 1727 *Fables* seem to disappear or become mute when read, as their context demands they should be, politically, just as Walpole seems to be invisible in *Shamela*. Politically aware and responsible literary fable in general disappeared.

However, it did not. John Hall-Stevenson's connections with John Wilkes, and Smart's assumption in 1756 that the fable is still available for the making of broad politico-philosophical points that stand against national policy and perhaps sentiment, are enough to indicate this. La Fontaine remained relatively little read *in English*, despite Addison's often-quoted but rather misleading remark in *Spectator* 183 about him having 'come more into Vogue than any other Writer of our Time' (Addison 1965: 2, 220). There is no complete English translation of his *Fables* (1668: 1678) before one in prose in Lyons (*La Fontaine's Fables now First Translated from the French by R. Thomson*) in 1806. The possible political overtones of publishing the work of a pacifist, anglophile French fabulist in English in his own nation, one year after that nation had been on the verge of invading England, are interesting. And fable certainly had a political life in the 1790s, when, for example, the author of *Aesop an Alarmist* (1794) used the Aesopian fable-collection to try to smooth and mollify his potentially revolutionary compatriots, using the conservative each-to-his-place morality of fable in a particularly unctuous manner. The collection concludes with a lengthy sermon against intemperance, in a homiletic variant of the more satirical anti-Jacobin spirit.

Even in a collection of *Sentimental Fables* such as Thomas Marryott's (1771) fable will be understood to have a political aspect. One of the fables (No. 26, 'The Turtle and the Epicure') is against Irish absentees; the collection was published in Belfast. Others engage in a very disturbing attempt to achieve a compromise between the radicalism of humanitarian attitudes towards animals such as those in Smart's 'Story of a COCK and a BULL' (and in volume 9 of *Tristram Shandy*), and the generally providentialist attitude of conservative fable. Fables such as 'The Oyster, the Eel, and the Lobster' – one of a long line of increasingly sentimental Oyster-fables eventually blown up by 'The Walrus and the Carpenter' – are used as a poetical humane killer:

> Canst thou without compassion look
> At the worm writhing on thy hook?
> What pangs convulsive must it share,
> What agonizing tortures bear;
> A thing that's vital in each part, –
> For thee to learn the fisher's art.
> But there are creatures, you will say,
> We must for our provision slay:
> Take then their lives, but let them feel
> As little pain as possible. (Marryott 1771: 76–7)

While this is not the Pythagorean vegetarianism that sometimes provides philosophical support for animal fabulists, it is important to remember that concern for the welfare of animals carries distinctly radical overtones at this point in history. Audrey Williamson says (Williamson 1974: 165–6) that Wilkes's attempt to secure better treatment of the animals in Smithfield anticipates Tom Paine's attitudes. But the other side of Marryott's coin appears most distinctly in No. 44, where a Colt convinces a Lamb that every creature's lot is fixed, and that the Lamb's destiny is to feed and clothe mankind. The Lamb, happy in his new vision of the cosmic economic order, 'smiles under the butcher's knife' (Marryott 1771: 276): sentimentalism reconciled with the abattoir. The Oyster, the Eel, and the Lobster are all boiled, by the end of the poem. Providentialist notions of fable seem tarnished, by 1770.

But Patterson and Daniel give genuine pause for thought. On the one hand, it has been realized for at least forty years that a political position of some kind lies behind Gay's second series in particular. This is a position with links to the opposition 'Country Persuasion' (Brooks 1984) and to the ideas that would later emerge in Bolingbroke's influential *Idea of a Patriot King* (1738, like the second series, but circulating in manuscript earlier). Anyone familiar with the *Fables* and their small secondary literature will find the opinions given above puzzlingly perverse. But the first series seems to lack the politically allusive diction, transparent or encoded, that is the usual sign of opposition satirical engagement – the list of nicknames for Walpole in *The Beggar's Opera*, for instance. This lack, together with their composed, slightly mandarin, initial style and relatively expensive production values, means that Gay's 1727 fables *look like* genteel fable, despite the potentially paradoxical qualities of Gay's practice briefly noted above. And of course they were supposedly written *for* the court: Gay at this point was hoping for preferment. But this does not mean that they are only genteel fable. Fables written for 'Augustus' (little William, to whom the collection is dedicated, was William Augustus) always place themselves in an equivocal position. There are many ways of creating a political relationship with the reader, making the reader a political subject; and one of these is to treat one kind of reader as an 'Augustus', a less-than-wholly-intelligent master.

A favourite strategy of the Augustans is, after all, to play with the responses of their readers by making their works appear to be like something else, whether it be Swift reading his 'Meditation upon a Broom-Stick' (*c.* 1702) to the Countess of Berkeley so piously as to make her believe it to be one of Robert Boyle's devotional exercises, or Sterne spending his own money to have the first volumes of *Tristram Shandy* identical in size, paper, and type to *Rasselas*. S. H. Daniel obligingly quotes the supposedly apolitical prudentialist cooings and warblings of the notoriously freethinking John Toland in his *Fables of Aesop* (1704), without noticing any of the little teeth behind Toland's gently smiling jaws:

> Prudence may justly be stil'd, the Guide of our Life, the Thread of our Labyrinths, and the Comforter under all Afflictions . . . the Capricios of Intemperance and Ambition (Toland 1704: 358)

may be avoided by the constant mind attuned to prudential concerns. The animal-world of fable thus provides a sufficient morality for all 'the complexities of human existence' (Daniel 1982: 163).

Even the Countess of Berkeley might not have been taken in by this trick. Anyone with the least sense of religion would have felt some concern at the suggestion that the natural morality of animals was adequate to cope with *all* the afflictions of the human condition, even without knowledge of the author's beliefs (the collection is technically anonymous). Or they would unless they had not noticed that Toland's discreet crystalline lure, which is deployed rather more tactfully than Daniel's blunt statement of the case would suggest, hides this subtly freethinking hook. What is subversive appears safe and polite: the fabulist attacks from within the gates, duping readers into accepting what they might usually scorn. Indeed, even Toland himself might well scorn it: six years earlier, wishing to give a sympathetic account of Milton in his *Life of John Milton*, he could report that the great man, although practising no form of Christianity in his later years, 'would say to his Friends, that the Divine Properties of Goodness, Justice, and Mercy, were the adequat Rule of human Actions' (Darbishire 1932: 194–5). In the light of this encomium, it seems unlikely that Toland would really think mere fable-prudence an adequate rule or sufficient morality for humanity.

Toland's collection purports to be a translation of the fables and 'Moral Reflexions of Monsieur Baudoin' – the august moral doctor, Jean Baudoin, under whose name appeared one of the two most prestigious mid-seventeenth-century French collections of prose 'teaching' fables (the collection was in fact made by Pierre de Boissat, the younger; Toland is working from an edition of 1701). But Toland's pose or disguise is, amusingly, punctured on many occasions by such charming anachronisms and naturalizations in the 'Reflexions' as references to 'Tyburn', 'the Fleet', 'the Wells, the Play, and the Park', 'Sir William Temple', 'Our late King William of Glorious Memory', and so on (Toland 1704: 131, 106, 105, 44–5, 45). Toland's prose, cultured, witty, agreeably vivacious, is clearly aimed at an audience that would like to think of itself as English ladies and gentlemen.

So the 'political' situation that Toland very cleverly creates is one in which the genteel, supposedly unpolitical, implied reader (the strategy is based on an assumption that such a readership of fable already exists in 1704, despite the plethora of 'political' *Aesops* in the 1690s) is made, by the text's disguise, to misapply or misread the fables in the way that Daniel does, to believe that the dangerous Pearl of freethinking is really just perfectly acceptable moralistic corn. The genteel reader, comically, becomes the dupe or slave of the fabulist, the Cock who cannot 'read' the fable. By spotting and admiring the method, such readers may emancipate themselves from their *mere* class-superiority to become the equals of the fabulist and intelligent masters of the situation; but such an awareness also entails a recognition that they have been politicized in the sense of being made to read culturally adversarial material with approval, and cunningly reclassed. Politics and authorial powerplay with reader-response are not different things.

This makes it all the more interesting that Gay's 1727 *Fables* have the power to make such an informed reader of seventeenth-century political literature read them in the way that Patterson does. Most contemporaries, and a little later Johnson, found Gay's first collection slightly disturbing rather than complaisant. If fable did evolve into a complex 'Augustan' mode, Gay may be playing off two kinds of fable against each other, and the politics of the text may lie in the relations established between text and audience, in something like Toland's manner. But not if 'political' fable can only mean fable in the narrower senses in which seventeenth-century fable is sometimes understood. Relations between text and audience are generated by all techniques and qualities of literary effect, and by the matrix of social, political, intellectual, moral and emotional interests that may lie behind these. The best Augustan poetry embodies such a matrix, and that is what Swift and Gay wrote in their fables – though this still remains to be proven.

'Augustan' is also used here less problematically, to point to something different from the other, mythic tradition of fable, which might, following Milton, be called Hesperian fable: something away in the west or elsewhere, rather than directly applicable to here-and-now. This other meaning was still current in the eighteenth century, but in English it was not the dominant one. Johnson's *Dictionary*, for instance, has five definitions of 'fable', of which only the third approximates to 'myth', and this is a phrase in which Dryden, seventy years earlier, was speaking jocularly about Hesperian fable. Johnson uses 'fable' to indicate 'fiction in general' rather than just myth. Milton, of course, cannot mention fables without a mordant glance at the truth/fiction paradox of Augustan fable (as already noted in Swift), even though he is invoking the other sort: the apples in Paradise, in Book 9 of *Paradise Lost* (1667) are 'Hesperian Fables true / If true, here onely, and of delicious taste' (Milton 1952: 79). Pagan apples, being merely fictional, have no taste. Christian apples are true, hence real, fruit, and hence delicious: so delicious as to be really tempting to a hungry Eve, who, as the serpent knows, has not yet had lunch. Only Christian apples can cause the Fall.

The frequent loose modern association between a more generalized 'fable' and myth, particularly classical myth, is an inheritance from one of the French neoclassical definitions, and from the unavailability of the word 'myth' itself in the eighteenth century. One finds 'mythic' occasionally and 'mythologist' quite often in English before 1700, and 'mythology'. But the native tradition never made the transition from *mythos* to the central noun, lapsing instead back to imitation of the French *fable.* Following Le Bossu, other critics were able to ignore all the obvious differences and to decide that Aesopian fable was simply a subspecies of epic myth, a procedure which English usage accepts more or less sceptically. 'Fable' thus does duty for very varied phenomena until the French invent *mythe* around 1818, the first recorded usage, 'doubtless . . . to escape the pejorative connotations of "fable" as Romantic interest in the "truth" of primitive culture increased' (Pearson 1993: 12). The imitative English usage of 'myth' begins around 1835, with the French 'e' retained on occasion until 1870.

But the history of the relations between these two traditions of English fable, Hesperian and Augustan, is still bedevilled by linguistic and conceptual uncertainty. This may account for the slightly depressing moment near the end of *The Honest Muse*, where Rachel Trickett assumes, like the eighteenth-century French, that fable means mythical narrative, and asserts that English poets after 1700 were 'deprived of the use of myth and fable' (Trickett 1967: 276: Trickett's only mention of fable). This is true in one sense but not in another. The problem arises because there has been so little airing of the subject of the general relations between fable, apologue, and other forms since Thomas Newbigging's suggestion, or assumption, in his *Fables and Fabulists* (1895) that the associations between Aesopian fable and narrative derived from the *fabella* rather than the *fabula*, which influenced the romance. According to Mary Lou Martin, the diminutive *fabella* indicates something akin to the Voltairean *conte*:

> a type of literature in which the imagination rather than superstition is given creative sway and in which the inventions of the author, while recognized as fictitious by the reader, may be viewed as true when applied to corresponding circumstances in human life. (Marie 1984: 19)

All that can safely be said is that mythical fable, like epic, tends to a structured inclusiveness, and towards conveying a sense of a secure collective identity in invoking a past with which the present has some link. Augustan fable tends to be brief, adroit, fragmentary or composite, a 'moment' or series of moments, after the manner of lyric, though not itself intrinsically lyrical. It addresses the present and the future as readily as it does the past, and is often political in general or specific senses. But this is not an absolute or fundamental opposition, because Augustan fable is capable of so many different manifestations. The Augustan mode can, for instance, happily pick up and play with both the manner and matter of mythical and heroic fable when it sees fit, as Fielding plays with Hercules: Swift in particular is adept at making Hesperian fables behave like Augustan ones. But Augustan fable has its own history.

CHAPTER 4

History, transmission, kindred

The history and transmission of fable are, in John Shea's academic understatement, 'almost incredibly complex' (Shea 1967: 5). The main concerns now, though, are *the generic tradition itself* and the emerging character of fable in English, rather than the details of fable's descent. One would not want to argue that all English Augustan writers were aware of this history or tradition in full, but the illustrative method here sometimes adopted, of glancing between examples from different historical periods, should suffice to show how pervasive was its influence.

In the first part of this chapter there is a tacit assumption that fable is a self-contained area or topic. This assumption will be gradually modified as related forms make their presence felt.

Fable begins in Greece. Here virtually all subsequent antique fables, such as those in Latin and in the classical Indian collections of myths and narratives such as the *Pañcatantra*, make their first appearance. Indian fable, though, has a quite separate transmissive history, in which many of the fables undergo minor changes: Indian fable is widely known and appreciated in the European Renaissance for its idiosyncrasies and exoticism. The 'Eastern Apologue' stimulated the eighteenth-century English taste for Persian or Oriental Tales, and forms a background to the Voltairean *conte* and the Johnsonian vision. A little sign of the Johnsonian presence in *The Female Quixote* is the Doctor's appeal to 'Locman the Wise' (Lennox 1989: 377), the fabulist-authority in Saadi's *Gulistan* (1258) as well as to Aesop.

Fable, in Greek *apologue*, – literally, 'off-speech' – is an idea which formalizes a '*façon de parler*' (Perry 1965: xxiii) or manner of proceeding which was inherent in many kinds of early-antique artistic material, verbal, iconographical, performative. The application of this idea or thought transforms such materials into an illustrative device, incorporating them into a system which, though ordered and codified, is also absorbent and permeable.

The two signs of this idea in antiquity are prose compilations of fables and a small scattering of references by historians and others to Aesop as a teller of tales. Suitable materials for inclusion in such collections are very varied; fairy-tales, aetiological nature-myths ('How the Crow got his Black Feathers'), stories telling of the cleverness or stupidity of animals, novellas, myths about gods and men, debates between rivals, or 'an exposition of the circumstances in which a sententious or a witty remark was made' (*ibid.*). Tie together a bundle or *fascis* of sticks, and you have a good visual image of political unity which may find its way into an Aesopian fable, which in turn may eventually be reapplied by Swift as 'The Faggot' (1713). In the twentieth century this image will be returned to something closer to its original use.

The first possible moment of definition of fable comes from the rhetorician Theon, in his *Progymnasmata* (*c.* AD 1–2). Theon takes Aesopian apologue as an example of the notion of *mythos*, and describes apologue as (variously translated) 'a fictitious story picturing a truth' (Perry 1965: xx) or 'an untrue discourse (*logos pseudēs*) . . . acting as a simile for truth' (Morgan 1993: 180). If Theon is, as he seems to be, making an equation or association between Aesopian apologue and Aristotelian *mythos* in general, then this is the extraordinary exemplary moment from which Le Bossu's conceptual framework, and hence all neoclassical ideas about this kind of fable, derives. Also, most of the extant classical literary work with fable – Phaedrus, Babrius, the *Vita Aesopi* – probably comes from the two or three generations following Theon, so his phrase merits close attention.

Story or *discourse* indicates a narrative or action, in a past tense: Theon suggests the accusative (third-person) case, the mode of narrative with 'external authority' (*ibid.*). *Fictitious* or *untrue* indicates falsity, or more precisely, the lack of probability or verisimilitude seen in the previous chapter; it stands pointedly opposite to the truth, so that a fable is both true and false; the quality called either 'absurd' or 'impossible', for example by Dryden in the Postscript to the *Notes . . . on the Empress of Morocco* (1674: Dryden 1958–92, 17, 183), where Dryden makes an analogy between impossible Aesopian fables and the wayward dramatic romance-fable of Settle's outlandish heroic play. A fable may be a 'vera fabella' (Phaedrus, 2, 5; Perry 1965: 240; compare Lucian's fabricated *Verae Historiae*), a 'true tale' or account of something that could have happened, but if it is, it is usually distanced by a preliminary remark about its intended application.

Picturing or *acting as a simile for* implies a metaphorical or figurative representation of a *truth*; so a fable is always either a metaphor, or like one. As the learned Hortensia says to the eponymous Aesop in Vanbrugh's play (1697):

HORT. Discourse without Figure, makes me Sick at my Soul;
O the Charms of a Metaphor . . .

AESOP Will you hear a Fable, Lady?

HORT. Willingly, Sir, the Apologue pleases me when the Application of it is just. (Vanbrugh, 1927, 2, 20)

So fable's wit is intrinsically metaphysical. This partly distinguishes it from the related form of allegory, in which the metaphor is more sustained and sequential, a parallel language or frame of reference.

Truth is a general proposition or position, sometimes understood to be moral or ethical, but not necessarily so. Theon is working with rhetoric, persuasion, rather than simply with narrative, and the *truth* (the moral) may be the case or argument which the speaker, perhaps a partisan lawyer or politician rather than a moralist – Menenius in *Coriolanus*, say – is trying to insinuate. So fable may be an entertaining or distracting joke in which the ethical content is 'anything or nothing' (Perry 1965: xxiv); or the story may naturally carry the double capacity of two or more completely different morals. The Fox who cannot reach the Grapes and so calls them green or sour may be a self-deluder, or, as in Caxton and La Fontaine, wise and prudent for rejecting the unattainable, and (like a fabulist) metaphysically and Foxily witty for transferring the sourness from himself to the Grapes. If one *truth* is well-known, part of the fable's wit may lie in reversing this, working with the form of paradox that involves foiling the listener's or reader's expectations. 'Exactly what the fables are to teach depends on the teller' says John McKendry (1964: 5), stressing the variety of possible applications in many fables as his first introductory point. Some of the morals of classical fable are perverse, and work by deliberately shocking the master-culture, exaggerating the physical basis of fable. Phaedrus's 'The Dogs Send an Embassy to Jupiter' (4, 19) turns out to be an aetiological myth explaining why dogs sniff each others' bottoms. And what exactly is the moral of 'The Man who Evacuated his own Wits'?

Xanthus [Aesop's master] said to him . . . 'Can you tell me why it is that when we defecate we look often at our own droppings?' Aesop: 'Because long ago there was a king's son, who, as a result of the looseness of his bowels and his loose way of living, sat there for a long time relieving himself – for so long that before he knew it he had passed his own wits. Ever since then, when men relieve themselves, they look down for fear that they, too, have passed their wits. But don't you worry about this. There's no danger of you passing your wits, for you don't have any.' (Perry 1965: 489)

The ebullient patchwork romance biography in Greek from late first-century Egypt known as the *Vita Aesopi* or *Life of Aesop* provides this beautiful little shaggy-dog story. Aesop teases his master with the prospect of a slave's moral about decadent living, but in the end the only clear application is 'ask a silly question, oh great one, and you'll get a silly answer'.

But possible general applications also lurk. Xanthus is a philosopher, and one with a pointedly 'ancient' name: Xanthus is also a river of Troy. The fable, indeed the *Life* in general, may express a reservation felt by first-century latinized Greeks about the famous philosophical cast of mind of their fourth- and fifth-century BC ancestors. So a fine fable, ingenious and open in its engagement with political and philosophical contexts, and one that the Aesopian tradition retained, in rewritings of the *Life*, until the Victorians finally disembowelled the tradition.

Aesop shimmers just above Homer on the horizon of historicality. Several early Greek historians mention him as a Thracian slave on the island of Samos in the sixth century BC, famous for recounting fables, and allowed his freedom on their account by his master. Then the legend transforms him to a Phrygian. Phrygia is remote, rural, central Turkey, a plausible place from which a slave might come, and the birthplace of Marsyas, 'on the analogy of' whom (Perry 1965: xl) the legend of Aesop was constructed. Both were the victims of Apollo's anger, both represent the universal Muses and 'a homely rural culture . . . coming into rivalry and conflict with the [aristocratic] Apolline culture' (*ibid.*: xli).

Emphasizing the ethos of the underdog, the legend makes him deformed, black ('for *Aesop* is the same with *Aethiop*' – L'Estrange 1692: 1), and horrifically ugly (Aes-opos = base face), so that he is confused with the beasts of which he speaks. The variety of possible origins builds up, in a conscious parody of the various Greek towns claiming to be Homer's birthplace which was still understood in the 1690s, when Aesop was to be found frequenting various English spas. As *Aesop at Tunbridge* has it: 'Seven wealthy Towns contend for HOMER Dead, / Through which the living HOMER begg'd his Bread' (*Aesop* 1698[a]: 16).

He is given picaresque adventures which translate him to the courts of kings, but which end with his unjust death at the hands of the

Delphic priests, abetted by Apollo. Yet another sarcastic association is developed between Aesop and a 'master', Socrates, who was also ugly and spoke rather than wrote, but who was proclaimed by the Delphic oracle to be the wisest of mortals. In Plato's *Phaedo*, Aesop is part of Socrates's sense of his own ending, his life rendered as art. Socrates spends his last days in prison under tyrants, composing a hymn to Apollo and translating fables of Aesop, the freed slave, into verse: a double obeisance.

Being a Greek slave, Aesop does not write: Phaedrus's 'Aesopus auctor' (Perry 1965: 190) means originator or source more than it means author or authority: something akin to Foucault's speaking of Freud and Marx as the begetters of ways of speaking. No fabulist is an 'author' in the traditional sense: catalogues almost always speak of collections of fables as merely 'translations' or 'paraphrases'. Yet all literary fabulists are authors. Problems of 'authority' and 'authorship' such as those raised by post-Barthes criticism are thus intrinsic to literary fable. Ian Bell begins his investigation into Fielding's problems as eighteenth-century 'author' by quoting the entry for the word in his 'Modern Glossary' – 'A laughing stock. It means likewise a poor Fellow, and in general an Object of Contempt' (Fielding 1988: 35; Bell 1994: 1) – which Bell takes as reflecting Fielding's sense of his contemporary position. It may well do; but if Fielding thinks of himself as a fabulist, it may also be a plain truth which is part of a similarly plain paradox about the slave who begets new discourses – as, of course, Fielding claims to be doing in his fiction.

So the point is not that the author is *dead*, but that the author is almost entirely a fiction. In the *Vita Aesopi*, the legend of Aesop's brute ugliness and illiteracy is forced further towards fable's paradox of the moral eloquence of the mute natural creation by making him dumb or barely articulate from birth. Isis (later, Diana) rewards him for his devotion by granting him clear speech. As in other Greek romances the presence of the cults is now strong, as is that of the 'dramatic and psychological paradoxes' (Heiserman 1977: 76) fundamental to antique romance. Jack Winkler plausibly relates the 'obscenity, and flouting of conventional decorum' (Winkler 1985: 276–91) of the *Life* to qualities of the *Golden Ass* of Apuleius, in which the protagonist is, in the *imbroglio*, similarly bestial, and similarly protected by Isis. Aesop becomes the 'champion of the common man's wisdom' (Perry 1965: xlv), the hero of antique plays and poems as well as of romance biography.

'Aesop's fables' acquire literary status at about the same time as his life, by being put into flexible Latin senarian (six-footed) verse by Phaedrus, around AD 30–55. His title, 'Phaedri Augusti Liberti Fabularum Aesopiarium' ('The Aesopic Fables of Phaedrus the Freedman of Augustus', *ibid.*: 190, 191), emphasizes the associations with liberation and servitude, the double-handed political overtones of Aesopian fable. It is a slave's medium, indirect and subversive, but it also strangely empowers the user, enabling him or her almost to join the culture that the fables address. Phaedrus reproves tyrants such as Sejanus, who had apparently prosecuted Phaedrus for his early fables, and points out that fables were invented for slaves to pass jesting critical comment on their masters. But he is polite about 'divo Augusto / deified Augustus' (274, 275) and says nothing at all about the later emperors under whom most of the fables were written. Many paradoxes revolve together. Fables critique power, but the slave almost joins the canon, becomes a classic, just as the socially marginal achieves cultural identity (though later Latin writers were as disdainful of Phaedrus, whom they largely ignored – *should* a slave write poetry? – as the modern critics have been). The low animal teaches from a moral world; the textually marginal moves towards the centre; the marginal or final fable comments on the body of the work, whether art (epimythium) or life (epitaph) or both. Queen Caroline knew this, promising Gay that he would be *taken up*, unlike the hunted Hare in 'The *Hare* and Many *Friends*', the final fable of the 1727 collection, into which Gay signs himself: the timorous (female) Hare 'comply'd with ev'ry thing, like *Gay*' (Gay 1974: 2, 369). Hunting may be a royal sport, but this court will not kill this fabulist. Indeed, Gay *was* taken up, being offered a £150 place – gentleman-usher to the two-year-old Princess Louisa – where the top court sinecure was worth £400 a year. But he chose to ignore Caroline's irony (Gay having dedicated the *Fables* to William, who was only three years older than Louisa) and to accept the fabulist's honourable death instead, or, in his case, comfortable exile with the Queensberrys.

If 'Freedman' may be less a biographical fact than a preliminary application pointing to Aesopian connotations, a reminder to the audience as to how to read fables, (nothing at all is known of Phaedrus except from his collection), so may 'Phaedrus'. The *Phaedrus* is the unusual Platonic dialogue in which the town-loving Socrates is led grumpily into the countryside by the young pastoralist Phaedrus. Socrates complains that 'the trees won't teach me anything, as the people in the town will' (Plato 1986: 27): the pastoral wisdom of fable can, of course, come from the trees themselves, as the later fabulist Phaedrus points out in the Prologue to Book I, with his 'arbores loquantur' (Perry 1965: 190). The duo sit down under a tree, and Phaedrus launches into voluble praise of Lysias, a contemporary charismatic orator. Socrates responds with what seems to be parody of either Phaedrus or Lysias. Then he manages to talk Phaedrus out of his belief in the power and value of rhetorical and metaphorical speech, and into or towards a belief in the need for rational dialectic in the service of truth, of which Rhetoric, in a codified system of 'divisions and collections' (Plato 1986: 103), should be merely the servant.

Phaedrus, uncoincidentally, is also the chosen name or pseudonym of Robert Pirsig's narrator/hero in his deconstructive fable *Zen and the Art of Motorcycle Maintenance* (1974), which has rather less to do with Zen than with traditional western philosophy. Pirsig's Phaedrus is even more unsure than his unreconstructed Platonic namesake about the value of dialectic, and is actively concerned to show that rhetoric is not a simple ordered system of parts. The motorcycle is greater than the list of components in the manual. Similarly, the fabulist Phaedrus draws attention to the distinction between the raw materials, 'materiam', and the gleaming finished form, 'polivi versibus / polished verses' (Perry 1965: 190).

What the first-century Phaedrus is doing is to attempt to remove fable from the service of utilitarian rhetoric, which was legal and political in colour and application (Theon) rather than philosophically neutral as Plato would claim. Phaedrus transmutes fable into an imaginatively energized and politically aware form, one which both flaunts and mocks its own status as 'persuasion'. Taken together with the anti-analytical nature of some parts of the *Life of Aesop*, this would suggest a first-century enterprise which might be characterized as historically or primally deconstructive, concerned with the relations between Rhetoric and Truth in its Platonic, fabulist, and utilitarian modes. Phaedrus can thus be felt to be subtly transversing two kinds of dominant position, political and philosophical.

About a third of Phaedrus's fables are from sources other than 'Aesop', a word that Phaedrus uses to describe both Aesop himself and a small book of fables in Greek prose, perhaps the one made by Demetrius of Phalerum in the fourth century BC, which is the only early example of which evidence remains. The prologue to Book I endows the form with the Horatian *utile dulci* or '*Profit* and *Delight*' (Creech 1684: 563); the full and proper function of literature:

duplex libelli dos est: quod risum movet,
et quod prudenti vitam consilio monet.

A double dowry comes with this, my little book; it moves
to laughter, and by wise counsels guides the conduct of life.
(Perry 1965: 190, 191)

This first doubleness is then, as one might expect, instantly redoubled by the laughing retraction that follows:

calumniari si quis autem voluerit,
quod arbores loquantur, non tantum ferae,
fictis iocari nos meminerit fabulis.

Should anyone choose to run it down, because trees too are
vocal, not wild beasts alone, let him remember that I speak
in jest of things that never happened. (*ibid.*)

Fables are empowered to move the passions and instruct to life, but are also merely impossible jests. The basic premises of truth-and-absurdity, literary power-and-powerlessness to match the fabulist's own, are elegantly revealed in five lines, and the rhetorical basis of the form demonstrated and exploded. Phaedrus is the only classical fabulist who can manipulate the form with such vigour, and it is quite possible that the development of fully literary fable depends, if not on his example, on his spirit. Rather than simple moral truths, paradox, absurdity, and provoking reflexive jokes in the service of a different truth lie at the heart of Phaedrian fable. The dark or 'discontinuous' nature of much seventeenth- and eighteenth-century fable in English is a combination of this quality with others provided by medieval and Renaissance habits of fabulist figuration.

There is one other classical verse fabulist of note, 'a hellenized Italian living in Syria, or somewhere near by' (*ibid.*: xlvii) known as Babrius, whose collection of Greek fables dates from the end of the first century. Babrius is more lyrical, less tough-minded than Phaedrus: his text was only rediscovered, on Mt Athos, in the 1840s, but Babrian fables done in prose and small fragments of the poetic text appeared frequently, and his historical existence was known.

Verse fable was then largely reabsorbed into the prose tradition, collectors using Babrius and Phaedrus without acknowledgement or indication that their source was poetic or other than 'Aesop'. The text of Phaedrus was recovered in 1596 and was disseminated swiftly and enthusiastically, though the first full English translation does not appear until 1705. Maximus Planudes's version of the *Life of Aesop* (*c.* 1300) ensured its transmission into the Renaissance, with the *Vita Aesopi* itself unknown until the early twentieth century. Planudes, perceived as a mysterious and arcane medieval monk, was generally supposed to be responsible for the apparently eccentric romance cast of the *Life* – hence Richard Bentley's scholarly fulminations about 'that Idiot of a Monk' (Bentley 1697: 147). Aesop's historical existence was known from the Greek historians, so it was supposed that Planudes had either invented his account or tampered with some sober historical document. This double view permitted much Renaissance and eighteenth-century speculation about the 'real' Aesop, especially given the desire of Protestant English writers to counter the often Catholic associations of seventeenth-century Aesopian fable (see Smith 1931 for the best survey of the history of the *Life*).

Literary fables percolated into medieval Europe from strikingly few sources: some prose and verse collections 'in the tradition of' Babrius and Phaedrus (Martin 1984: 21), together with an infusion of oriental material. Eventually a version of the famous 'Romulus' manuscript, reworking over eighty fables of Phaedrus and others, reached Dr Steinhowel of Ulm, who added another eighty from other sources, translated them into German prose, and printed them. A French translation of this was the source of Caxton's seminal *Book of the Subtyl Historyes and Fables of Esope* (1484). This remained in print until the seventeenth century, and was 'the main vehicle for preserving the medieval tradition' (Hale 1972: 122).

Fable also began to lead interesting lives in other English media, the first evidence of which is the representation of ten or more Aesopian fables in the decorative margins of the Bayeux Tapestry (?1080–1120). To date, interpretation of these and of their relation to the main panel has been almost exclusively in the hands of the victorious French. Given that the women of the workshop where the Tapestry was made were probably Anglo-Saxon while the overseers were probably Norman, this has resulted in a situation akin to The Lion's Share being interpreted only by descendants of the Lion.

Harold was in some sense a genuine usurper himself: he is the only English monarch not related to all the others. But the French have always vindicated William's invasion of England in 1066 by pointing to Harold's earlier hypocrisy in swearing an oath of fealty to William while in Bayeux. Harold, who had been knighted by William after a joint expedition to Brittany, then returned and assumed the English crown after Edward the Confessor's death, when he had originally, in 1064, been sent to Normandy by Edward to promise William the throne. This accusation of double-dealing may be *bel et bon*, but would hardly have seemed so to the native English after a decade or two of having their culture and society obliterated. As well as recording the great victory for propaganda purposes, one might expect 'indications that for the vanquished the Norman Conquest was a tragedy' (Anon. 1966: 14). Applying the power-relationships of Aesopian and Phaedrian fable would suggest an English counter-reading of the marginal fables of the Tapestry, in which tyrants are obliquely but strenuously reproved and the main or dominant text is commented on subversively and also, in this case, superversively. In other words a literary, Phaedrian–Peachum use of fable, polite but rude, making the Tapestry as a whole both for and against Normans.

A crucial example would be the two fables in the upper margin immediately after the swearing of the oath, the main event of the first part of the Tapestry (see plate 4a). The first pair of figures is clearly The Wolf and the Stork, with the Stork fishing the bone out of the Wolf's throat: this fable has already appeared once. The second pair is the third appearance of The Fox and the Crow, with the cheese mysteriously back in the Crow's beak – earlier it has been in the Fox's, and then in mid-air. Applying these two fables to the action would indicate firstly that Harold was in William's power when assisting on the expedition to Brittany and afterwards (and so could not have refused to swear the oath when asked), and secondly that it was William, who acquired the English cheese, who was akin to the (flattering and) false-speaking Fox, not the dispossessed English, who are figured in the Crow. William's knighting of Harold is thus seen as political manoeuvering or prospecting – which it may well have been – rather than an honour. So the marginal fabulist comment delicately unstitches and reverses the drift of the main panel, in which Harold simply swears an oath on holy relics.

Earlier parts of the Tapestry show fables which include tales of usurpation such as The Bitch and her Pups, who throw out the rightful occupant of a den by false-speaking, after having first been invited in (as William was invited by Edward, though the parallel is not perfect). The ultimate fable against tyrants, The Lion's Share, appears; fascinatingly, in the specifically Phaedrian and very odd version known as 'The Cow, the She-Goat, the Sheep, and the Lion' (1, 5) – the animals are particularly carefully designed (see plate 4b). The final moral in Phaedrus is that 'all the booty was carried off by ruthlessness alone' (Perry 1965: 199). In the early lower margin appears a beautiful scene of sowing and

4 'Wolf and Stork/Fox and Crow', 'The Lion's Share', 'The Swallow and Other Birds'

bird-scaring (see plate 4c) which, when read with the other fables, turns out to be The Swallow and Other Birds (see Henryson, Ogilby, and particularly Dryden): equally interestingly, not in its Phaedrian/Babrian version, in which the Swallow warns the other birds about the Mistletoe, which is used for bird-lime. This other, apparently western-European version involves the Swallow trying to warn the birds about the consequences of the sowing of the linseed or flax-seed – they will be trapped in nets made of 'line', *lin*, so the designs of the tyrant Man are to the fore. It is the main fable of the premonition of disaster; in the main panel, William's men appear for the first time.

After the oath, the fables become more difficult to assign and interpret: they are clearer while the action is more political than military. There are other iconographical techniques of subversive commentary in the Tapestry, so many in fact that one wonders whether the embroiderers (in both senses) of the episode got away with them. A main reason why the Tapestry survived for so long is that it was rolled up and put away for, apparently, some 400 years. The Normans perhaps grew a little sheepish about having taken possession of 'their' artefact. David Bernstein, in *The Mystery of the Bayeux Tapestry* (1986), provides a reading in which biblical images of Babylonian captivity and resistance in effect echo the reading suggested by the fables, or operate in tandem with these other images. If this is the case, the Tapestry is probably the only medieval occasion on which politically and culturally subversive fables are pressed into service alongside English biblical iconography. It is also difficult to think of another occasion on which the doubly dispossessed, Anglicized women soon after the Conquest, contrive to speak silent and eloquent political jests from within an artistic medium which celebrates their subjection and suppression. There are three women in the main panel. One is leaving a burning house with a child, one is being betrothed in public, one is nursing a man. Women, it seems, read and use fables at least as well as men, though they have fewer opportunities to show it.

Other lives of fable included their use as school texts for translation exercises in late antiquity, and again from the early sixteenth century. There are also at least two medieval oral traditions, one folkloric – some of Marie's fables appear to derive from folktales – the other aristocratic and politically charged. Lord Gray narrated the fable of The Mice Wishing to Bell the Cat to the conspirators against the favourites of the Scots King James III: Archibald, Earl of Angus, earned himself the nick-name of 'Bell-the-Cat' by offering to perform the task (Charles Montague was known as 'Mouse' after 1687 for his part in Prior's travesty of Dryden). Lady Alington wrote a letter to Margaret Roper, describing how Wolsey had merely recited fables to her when she went to him to intercede for Sir Thomas More. More, when he heard of this meeting from Margaret, replied that one of the fables that Lady Alington mentioned was a favourite with Wolsey, but did not apply to his own case (see Briggs 1970: 102). Henry VIII gave Anne Boleyn an *Aesop's Fables*, though which of the fables, if any, he underlined for her to apply to her situation is unclear: Wolf and Lamb, perhaps. These two uses – by rather than about 'Augustus' –

appear to apply themselves rather snidely to fable perceived as a feminine genre.

The limitation of written medieval fable is that, like the adaptation of classical bestiary and hieroglyph known as the *Physiologus*, it was moralized in the unequivocal sense of being taken into the custody of the Church, enlisted by the institutions of the dominant culture in a way that was to be echoed by the Christianized neoclassicism of the late seventeenth and early eighteenth centuries. Several early Christian writers had stood up for Aesop, most notably Augustine in the *Contra Mendacium*. Martin Luther almost completed a collection. Marie de France was probably abbess at Shaftesbury from 1181–1216: 'de France' (Marie 1984: 156) just means from France – she signs herself into her final fable, as Phaedrus personalized his ending, and as Gay will in 1727 – and her identity is not wholly clear. Other compilers of fable and related material are friars, priests, and bishops. Fables were collected, along with a wide range of other kinds of narrative and illustrative materials, to serve as *exempla* in sermons, returning the form to its preliterary origins in professional systems of persuasion.

This institutional bias meant that the 'essential independence of fable was not generally respected' (Blackham 1985: 82). Odo of Cheriton's fables may satirize the behaviour of clergymen and aristocrats, but they do so in terms of deviations from standards of social, ethical, and spiritual conduct which are pressed home repeatedly in the applications of his fables, which often allegorize the action neatly but oddly. Odo transforms the Stork and Fox, with their exchange of mutual inhospitality, to Bees and Beetles. The visiting Beetles are given honey to eat by the Bees, who are then offered dung when they dine *chez* Beetle. Honey 'is' the writings of the Church, dung 'is' the 'filthiness [and] foolish talking' (Ephesians 5: 4) of which Paul so vigorously disapproved. He exhorts men to 'refuse profane and old wives' fables' (1 Timothy 4: 7). Odo's action suffers in the analogy, of course: religious Bees should not offer secular Beetles honey from the same motives as Foxes serve Storks food in shallow dishes. Any reader or listener attentive to the parallel between Odo's fable and its origin would be puzzled.

There is an odd paradox behind the notion of a fable written against profane speech which may include fables, but, as we shall see, it took a more alert mind to make use of it. To some European minds, though, even this clerical use of fables was scandalous, the falsehoods of pagan fictions serving to distort the truth rather than to illuminate it. As late as 1528 the Council of Sens fulminated vigorously against the idea, and

Erasmus speaks deprecatingly in paragraph 45 of *The Praise of Folly* (1515) about preachers with a yen for enlivening their sermons with popular tales. Umberto Eco's *The Name of the Rose* (1980) has a compelling 'medieval' fictional dialogue about the use of absurd secular fictions and false images in sacred contexts, in the scene that takes place beneath the abbey's labyrinthine library near the end of the First Day. If the novel were rewritten to a medieval English setting it might be about the suppression of fables, rather than centring on the suppression and destruction of the only remaining copy of the second book of Aristotle's *Poetics*, the book concerned with comedy.

So fables could be understood to be good, assimilable to holy purposes, or to be profane and wicked, especially in continental Europe, where there was the example of the Reynard cycle to contend with. Of poets writing in Britain only four, Marie de France, John Lydgate, Chaucer, and, later, Robert Henryson, were even able to look towards the middle ground.

Marie, the first woman poet known to have written in any modern European vernacular, qualifies as English by residence, writing in Old French/Anglo-Norman for the entertainment of the late twelfth-century court. Hence she is, like Lydgate, in a position to straddle the divide between clerical and secular powers. Her *Fables*, for which, until the late eighteenth century, she was chiefly known, influenced or were the source of several other medieval collections. They are crisp, vigorous, and lively, of some importance for their 'innovations of character and style' (Marie 1984: 24), but at the same time socially conservative and straightforward. Her version of The Ass and the Lap-Dog, for example, is circumstantial and inward, concisely adding gesture, detail, feeling, and variable perspective to the original:

> En sun curage entendi bien
> que tuit li altre aiment le chien
> pur le seignur kil cherisseit
> e ki od lui se deduieit;
> suz sun mantel le fist muscier,
> si fist les altres abaier.
> Mult s'est li asnes purpensez . . .

In his heart the ass knew that everyone loved the dog because the master adored it and played with it. The master would hide the pup under his coat and make the other dogs bark. The ass often thought to himself . . .

(*ibid.*: 64, 65)

But the social context dictates the retraction, in a moral which justifies the beating of the Ass by retreating to a concise expression of the values of a hierarchical society where everyone knows their place: the Ass is simply 'the social climber, whom we have all seen at one time or another. . . . Many such people have met a fate similar to that of the ass who was beaten' (*ibid.*: 67).

This conservatism infiltrates Marie's conception of the function of the form. She recasts some Phaedrian fables in a manner which accentuates the oddness of the originals by revealing her own wish to tone it down and assimilate the fables to clear social purpose. In Phaedrus's version of The Lion's Share, all the animals that enter into partnership with the Lion are conspicuously herbivorous and timid: 'patiens ovis inuriae / a sheep, patient sufferer when wronged' (Perry 1965: 198, 199). This makes their attendance at the kill of a huge stag silly, and the Lion as odd as the rest for bothering to enter into such a partnership. Only he mentions his status as king of beasts, at the division of the spoils, and this is conspicuously more nominal than political: 'Ego primam tollo nomine hoc quia rex cluo / I take the first portion by virtue of my title, since I am addressed as king' (*ibid.*). Blurring the simple political application by adding absurdity, Phaedrus endows the fable with openness and potential – including different political applications, such as the possible folly of sheepishly accepting that a rather harebrained Lion is your ruler simply because he tells you he is – and so allows it to become one of the central fables in the continuing Aesopian tradition. Phaedrian absurdity is a very curious quality: it should act simply as an agent for psychic distancing, like irony, but in fact it always makes the fables more compelling and involving, because odder (see plate 5).

Marie, in contrast, gives the Lion's kingship legal status, and equips him with a seneschal (a wild Ox) and a provost (a Wolf) who acknowledge the Lion as lord and operate as members of a court. A wild Ox could not plausibly have much interest in the kill of a deer, but a seneschal could. The Phaedrian absurdity is glossed over, and the herbivores, who are placed in a second, shorter episode, seem socialized rather than odd. Rather than illustrating the perils or grotesqueness of living under tyrants, the fable seems to be happening in a disturbingly natural way inside a feudal system.

The post-Chaucerian John Lydgate also wrote between church and court. For sixty-six years he was a Benedictine monk at Bury St Edmunds, but much of his poetry was commissioned by noble patrons and is secular and courtly in nature. His status in the Renaissance was high,

5 Randolph Caldecott, 'The Lion's Share'

and in the eighteenth century he was compared favourably with Chaucer by Theophilus Cibber, Thomas Warton, and others.

His situation may be similar to Marie's, but his case is wholly different. Very early in his career – or so it appears to be – he translated six or seven fables, which have more potential and interest as fable than any others written between Phaedrus and Ogilby. Assuming that there were no more, it is a great pity that he did not – or could not – continue the fables into a full collection. Marie after all is practically French, Henryson practically Scots and a good deal later. The number of fully English medieval verse fables – excluding debate-poems on the grounds that they do not feature an 'action', though this is perhaps a little factitious – that have survived is, amazingly, less than a dozen, the majority of which come from Lydgate, in a small collection headed *Isopes Fabules.* This gives them a peculiar importance, as well as raising wider questions. They are dismissed by Lydgatians, who wave them away towards 'the favourite mediaeval tradition of the animal fable' (Renoir 1967: 50), which does not exist in English verse.

The fables have the main virtue of being fairly short, for Lydgate. The first six take up nine hundred lines, the seventh just twenty-eight. Lydgate's versification is competent and delicate, if a little downbeat when compared with his more ornate pieces. His Prologue stresses the intrinsically political nature of fables, and delicately develops the crucial association between their political function and the freedom that should be allowed in their wider interpretation and application, an association not to be met again until Ogilby. Aesop, he says, was 'poete laureate', and wrote to entertain the Roman senate: this may mean that he is conflating Aesop and Phaedrus. Aesop

> dyd hym occupy
> Whylom in Rome to plese the senate,
> Fonde out fables, that men myght hem apply
> To sondry matyrs, yche man for hys party,
> After theyr lust, to conclude in substaunce,
> Dyuerse moralytees set out to theyr pleasaunce. . .
> (Lydgate 1934: 567; subsequent references will be to this edition and will cite page numbers only)

Lydgate's early debate-poem *The Debate of the Horse, Goose, and Sheep* is much more explicit than this about the oppositional quality of fable, explaining, in the course of driving home the moral that poor people should not be despised by their neighbours, that ancient fabulists made fables

> Bi which ther wittis wer secretly apprevid,
> Vnder covert tyrantis eeke repreived
> Ther oppressiouns & malis to chastise. (563)

So Lydgate is well aware of the use of fable as reproof of tyrannical power – two of the fables are against tyranny – but chooses not to reflect on this in his promythium, the fables' Prologue. Crucially, if the fables can be applied in different ways, 'yche man for his party', this would indicate that Lydgate knows that each fable carries 'dyverse moralytees'. The other man will use the fable in another way: the lines posit a knowing audience, 'intelligent Masters', where fable's political functions are concerned. Tyrants may be reproved 'eeke', also, but this is just one part of their modes of application. Lydgate appears to be asserting the full, multiple function of Phaedrian fable, revealing the rhetorical basis of the form, a procedure which is completely at odds with the unequivocal clerical applications of medieval fable.

Beginning, as do Marie and Henryson, with a version of The Cock and the Pearl, here called 'The Cock and the Jacinth' (Jacinth = jacinthus, named in the 'Lenvoi' as the sapphire), Lydgate first restores and amplifies the fable's reflexive Phaedrian moral in his Prologue, which thus acts as an extended promythium to a fable which is itself usually a promythium to collections. Astutely, he develops the moral from the common English proverb that 'learning is better than house or land': 'Wisdom ys more in prise, than gold in cofers, / To hem, that haue sauour in lettrure' (566). He then continues and amplifies the gem/dunghill image into another of opposed colours, while retaining the domesticated quality which anticipates the setting of the fable. 'Orientall' means precious, as well as carrying an association with the east, light, stars:

> Perlys whyte, clere and orientall
> Ben oft founde in muscle shellys blake,
> And out of fables gret wisdom men may take. (567)

This doubling of the image produces a combination of subdued reflection and a gently lyrical quality which carries the moral onto the genuinely poetic level characteristic of several of the fables. The eastern association conveys the exoticism of the antique fable; the blackness of the mussel-shell recalls the blackness of the original fabulist. Other illustrative metaphors develop the same moral and the class-overtones of fable: 'Where syluer fayleth, in a pewter dyssh / Ryall dentees byn oft tymes seyne' (567). The metaphysics of fable are subtly insinuated in quiet English proverbs, domestic detail, and estuarine imagery.

Six of the seven fables are from Phaedrus, though they are all also found in the 'Romulus' manuscript, from which Lydgate is usually supposed to be working. It is possible that he had access to a direct prose paraphrase of Phaedrus which retained and appreciated his spirit, and that he briefly thought that spirit worth transmitting.

The most fascinating part of his fables is the envoys, the closing moral sentiments, which are a very distinctive mixture of the sacred and the secular. This mixing appears to grow naturally from the Prologue's assumption of the diversity of fable-morality. In the case of 'The Cock and the Jacinth', the prologue has proclaimed this multiplicity and then used, or used up, the Pearl-figure, so that the fable which follows is effectively freed from the reflexive moral which knowledgeable readers would have expected. This is why Lydgate retitles the fable itself, creating a feeling of suspense: how will he re-moralize the fable? If the 'Perle' is (as in *Pearl*) 'the meaning', what will the Jacinth be?

As the fable develops, the morals appear to be against idleness, deriving from the Cock's energetic nature and habits of regular early rising and 'diligent trauayle' (570) as dramatized in the story, and in his example of praising the Trinity with the 'treble laudes' (569) of his crowing. These natural allegorical morals are then tactfully expanded to include something close to what Chaucerian English would call 'buxumnesse', a religious submission to one's situation: 'suche as God sent, eche man take at gre' (574). Poorly handled, this would be simply a socially conservative tag such as Marie's, and rather ironical in its apparent opposition to the suggestion of freedom and openness in the promythium, but here the natural world has been so well realized that the moral resonates more persuasively and interestingly. Also, the Cock's ability to discourse on the appropriateness of corn to hens and precious stones to princes is itself expanded to include a philosophical sense of the naturalness of different choices to different situations, so that the moral returns partly to the initial premise of multiplicity:

> Of theyr nature as folke byn dysposyd,
> Diuersly they make eleccion.
> Double of vertu the saphyr in gold closyd.
> Yche man cheseth lyke hys opinion;
> On cheseth the best of wysdom and reson,
> And another (hys eyen byn so blynde)
> Cheseth the werst, the best he lyt behynde. (573)

The Cock gives the fable a double gloss, figured in the 'double of vertu'. Princes admire pearls and sapphires, wise and virtuous men like Pearls (and Jacinths), and Cocks like corn; things are as they should be. But vicious men choose badly where wise men choose well, each directed by their 'opinion', which is a much more unstable and casual quality than providential disposition. Some can see, some are 'blynde'. Wise men, says the Cock, may safely be shown holy relics: fools, who would scoff (as Cocks sometimes scoff at Pearls) may not.

So, like his moral, the complicated Cock clearly has 'natures twain' (see below, p. 93): he both eats the corn and possesses the Pearl. The

'Lenvoi' then re-moralizes yet again, with the sentiment now not just double but as threefold as the Cock's crow:

> Though thys fabyll be boysters & rurall,
> Ye may theryn consider thyngis thre:
> Howe that diligence in especiall
> Hathe agayn slouthe caught the souereynte,
> And, where fre choyse hath hys liberte,
> Cheseth the werst in ernest or in game,
> Who, but hymself, therof ys to blame?
>
> Who foloweth vertu, vyces doth eschew,
> He cheseth the best in myn opinion. . .
> Suche as God sent, eche man take at gre,
> Nat prowde with ryches nor groge with pouerte.
>
> The worldly man laboreth for rychesse,
> And on the worlde he set all hys intent.
> The vertuos man to auoyde all ydelnesse
> With suffisaunce hold hymself content.
> Eche man therfore with suche as God hath sent,
> Thanke the Lorde, in vertu kepe hem stable
> Whyche ys conclusioun of thys lytyll fable. (573–4)

Diligence, free choice, submission to God's disposing of things. Or rather, not submission, which would hardly square with the first two elements, but content, happiness. 'Gre' (or 'gree') is not an exact equivalent of 'buxumnesse', but a word which can mean both 'degree' and 'in good part, agreeably', or 'with good will'. Lydgate has used the phrase 'at gree' in the Prologue (568), asking the audience's indulgence, and that they receive the compilation freely and in good spirit, in the same manner ('lust' and 'pleasaunce') as the wise man takes the world ('content'). The marginal comment seems alert to this equivocation: 'The Tale of the Cok, that founde a precyous stone . . . that yche man shud take in gree suche as God sent' (566) could describe the taking of the moral, or of the fable. Take the fables as you will: it is my opinion that those who choose virtue choose well, but that is my opinion. Some choose corn, some Pearls: some are worldly, some are spiritual; all may choose well and be diligent and, in their own ways, virtuous. There *is* free choice and striving, but then there is something beyond that that is not free choice, with which we must be content. The Cock may have 'wyves' and be called 'Chaunceleer' (570), like the Reynard-cockerel, but this does not stop his song teaching us to praise God.

This is hardly monkish morality: Jacinths clearly have more facets than Pearls. In biblical terms, it seems to be partly a superior gloss of texts such as Matthew 6: 24, the verse about not serving two masters, God and Mammon. Fable, of course, has many masters to deal with. It is not surprising that the marginal comment in the manuscript ascribes the fables to Lydgate at Oxford rather than at Bury. Lydgate is notorious for being able to write on either side of a topic – against women when the context is religious, in praise of women when the context is courtly, for example – but in this rare instance there is a genuine and admirably mature attempt to give a sense of the whole coin rather than of just one side.

Three of the other fables have purely secular morals, as does 'The Wolf and the Lamb', except that the christianized Lamb is praised for his natural meekness as well as being equated with the poor. The long 'The Hownde and the Shepe' is against perjury and false witness: most of the morality is secular, but can expand to say forcefully and repeatedly that bearing false witness on Bible oath is treason against God. Remarkably, it can then expand once again – the effect in the first fable is not an isolated one – to deliver the supposed opinions of Aesop, the ultimate authority in this context, on the subject. Pagan authorities and Christian belief stand side by side, but Aesop is the last . . . best? . . . example.

Holy fables, a very few mixed ones; what of the wicked? The devil in this case assumes his traditional animal form, the Fox. Why the continental Reynard literature did not penetrate into English in any complete form before Caxton's translation of *The History of Reynard the Fox* in 1481 is a mystery. Two hypotheses are current. The first is social: the literate bourgeois English audience of fable and its kindred was less well-developed than the Dutch and Flemish middle-class which cultivated *Reynard*, and the courtly audience disdained a form of art that was not sanctioned by aristocratic or religious taste. The second, a *Name-of-the-Rose* hypothesis, is a little more sinister: zealous English monks working as librarians and scribes were quietly told to excise those kinds of fable that could not be enlisted by the church. Quietly, because it seems that fable is not actively written against very much in this period. Chaucer's Parson, for example, articulates strong anti-fable attitudes, but he speaks these. His sermon, which appears to be written, is devoid both of exempla and of reflections on their use (see Sands 1960: 35–6).

Both of these arguments are plausible, especially in combination, though the second is more interesting in its implication that the church recognized that some forms of fable were actively subversive of the first, orthodox, kind, and by implication of allegorical truths more widely. Perhaps this is why Lydgate has only six-and-a-half fables: he may have been warned off, and vernacular semi-secular fables arguing for political and interpretative liberty would not have attracted the protection of courtly patronage against church policy, as courtly-love material apparently could. It might also help to explain why Middle English is so 'surprisingly deficient in the beast story' (Wilson 1952: 134). Wilson finds only two pre-Caxton examples of works that approximate to this form, which is one of the fable's closer medieval kin (two popular literary genres, verse fable and beast-story, with only about fourteen examples in Middle English; and almost no *Reynard*; but then, there are also very few *fabliaux*). One example is the unique anonymous thirteenth-century manuscript of a beast-story called The Vox and the Wolf (two of the protagonists of *Reynard*, and they are given Reynardian names). The other is Chaucer's 'Nonne Preestes Tale', which was influenced by two Old French versions of *Reynard*, as well as by one of Marie's fables (Pratt 1972). Chaucer's Fox is called Russel: Rouseel is Reynard's eldest son in some of the later Dutch prose *Reynards*, so Chaucer seems widely knowledgeable. Taken together with the name of Lydgate's Cock, this would indicate a widespread English knowledge or awareness of an extended literary work of which there appears to be no direct textual evidence in the language until several generations later: there is 'no beast epic in English literature prior to 1481' (Sands 1960: 34)

Reynard, which was originally a series of poems known as the *Roman de Renart*, evolved from a mixture of the Aesopic tradition, European beast stories, and the French *fabliaux*. Reynard – a 'Germanic name made up of two elements meaning "very" and "hard"' (*ibid.*: 201) – as picaresque hero learns to outwit Isengrim the wolf, pillage the poultry (Chanticler, Pertilot), and dupe his lord, the empty-headed lion Noble. The popularity of these poems was such that the name Renard became the general French word for fox: *goupil*, the original, is still current but less often used. When, in *Romeo and Juliet*, Mercutio makes his laughing comments to the other lads about the Frenchified Tybalt as rat-catcher and prince of cats, he does so because he assumes Tybalt's name to be a variant of Tibert, the much-abused cat in *Reynard* [one has, by the way, seen a student who had not read the play render his name as Tibbles]. Shakespeare's use of the joke assumes that the late sixteenth-century English audience does not need this to be spelled out, so the story seems to have been widely absorbed once it was translated.

The spirit is violently witty, secular, and in its way as reductive of fable as the medieval clerical uses. Tibert has an eye smote out by the priest Martinet, and responds by ripping off the priest's 'right cullion or ballock stone'. Never mind, says Reynard piously, 'there is in this world many a chapel in which is rung but one bell' (*ibid.*: 68). The style and manner mock many favoured written and spoken dialects – dominant voices – from romance to the funeral service. Sustained allegory is practically absent, causality based on wit, power, and animal and authorial deceits. All courts from Rome to Paris teach 'Reynard's craft' (*ibid.*: 185).

So there were two distinct traditions of English medieval fable, one sanctioned, complaisant, exemplary, and usually unliterary, the other innovative, dangerous, and probably suppressed. There was very little possibility of critical relationship between the two. This throws a good deal of stress on to the only English poet, Chaucer, who tried to draw attention to the chasm as well as to bridge it. His works contain many vocal birds and beasts, but in three of the *Canterbury Tales* (*c.* 1370–95) the Nun's Priest's, the Maunciple's, and the Parson's, he engages with fable itself. The important work is done mainly through a sly, complex, and extended joke at the expense of St Paul, on the subject of biblical and medieval attitudes to fable.

This is a doubly important moment in the transmission of fable, given the later wide popularity of Chaucer and the reworking of the Nun's Priest's Tale by Dryden. Trebly, even, as it is used in such a way as to become one of the structural devices of the Tales. The discussion and use of fable is as intrinsic to the sense of an ending here as it will be in the eighteenth-century novels discussed above, and may even be as active a precedent as classical examples such as Horace's Country-Mouse and City-Mouse at the end of Satire, II, 6; Juvenal's use of The Father and Jupiter, and Hercules and Fortune or Plutus (fable-upon-fable) at the end of his Satire x; the death of Socrates in Plato; or the closure of Phaedrus's collection (see below, p. 96). Chaucer's expertize with fable is remarkable, as Jill Mann's selection of line 692 of the Wife of Bath's Prologue – the Wife's blink-of-an-eye, point-of-the-finger 'Who peyntede the leon, tel me who?' – as the motto for a chapter of her book on Chaucer testifies (Mann 1991: 48). Once again, fable is recognized as a female weapon.

The answer to the Wife's question is that it was the Man who painted the Lion: the Wife is addressing a group of (mainly) men. The Lion's point, in the epimythium of The Lion and the Man, the central fable of

6 J. J. Grandville, 'The Lion Humbled by Man'

the politics of representation, is that if Lions could paint, they would paint lions overcoming men, not the other way round as in the picture that the Man has shown the Lion to prove his own superiority. So if women could write, they would write women overcoming men, not the other way round as in Jankin's book of wicked wives. But of course if Lions can speak, perhaps they can paint too: an extra joke that only appears when the fable is sympathetically illustrated (see plate 6). It is, not surprisingly, a Phaedrian fable, though not in the poetic text as transmitted: Perry (1965: 479) notes a version of it in a prose paraphrase of Phaedrus.

Searching the Bible for an answer to the puzzle of whether fable is to be seen as a sanctioned (true) or a reprehensible (false) form of art, the medievals found a teasing double answer. There is a variegated positive side. The Bible contains parables which bear some relation to fables, and Christianity should not be unamenable to a metaphorical and sometimes paradoxical mode of utterance, being founded on some taxing metaphors and 'self-confirming paradoxes' (Colie 1976: Preface;

Ralph Venning's little 1647 book of 234 Christian paradoxes is called *Orthodoxe Paradoxes*: almost as bemusing as the Liar's Paradox). Nathan, hoping to remind a bullying and unremorseful King David about his rape of Bathsheba and murder of Uriah, tells him a parable about someone who stole a poor man's lamb, but then has to resort to pointing the finger when David simply begins to fulminate about such a despicable fellow. Ezekiel is instructed by God to deliver a long, perplexing, 'riddle'- 'parable'- fable (17: 2) about two eagles and a vine, but Ezekiel is not notably successful with figures of speech derived from fable. 'The fathers have eaten sour grapes, and the children's teeth are set on edge' (18: 2) – God, apparently quoting what Ezekiel has said, reproves him for this, which does seem a little severe, given that Ezekiel has only ever said what God told him to say. But it is interesting that God's proxy fabulist utterances take a more bizarre and riddling form than do those of men, in a century when riddles and unclear allegories are deemed by neoclassicists to be a 'murmuring . . . at Providence' (Dennis 1939: 1, 21; see above, p. 41). Providence though, cannot murmur at itself. Paul himself sometimes reworks fables: Belly and Members is transformed to Hands and Feet in 1 Corinthians 12.

Most clearly, there is Judges 9: 7–15, the fable of The Trees who Wanted a King, told by Jotham as a preliminary to his curse of Abimelech and the men of Shechem. The curse is effective and just: hence, fable must be a legitimate form. This fable seems to be original to Judges, but the Aesopic tradition, always interested in fables with a political slant, appropriated it later.

But as well as containing fables, the Bible also contains invective against a use of language usually rendered in English translations as 'fables'. This comes from Paul in 1 and 2 Timothy, and slightly in Titus. Chaucer renders this perplexing contradiction for his own purposes, by redoubling the double voice – pointing out, in fable, how Paul appears to speak against himself, both using and condemning fable.

The final flourish in the babel of moralities at the end of the 'Nonne Preestes Tale', Chaucer's version of the dangerous Reynardian episode of The Cock and the Fox, tells the reader to take the corn, the 'fruyt' (Chaucer 1973: 550; subsequent references are to this edition and will cite page numbers only) offered by the fable, and to leave the chaff behind. This is a metaphor which was often used to direct the piously-listening medieval audience of sermons to the moral sentence of fable-as-exemplum. Ignore the false fiction, take the true meaning: forget the fable, take the moral. Clerical exempla ignore the Pearl in the Cockerel's dungheap, fable's own equivalent metaphor. Chaucer's Pardoner, whose sermons are cynically tailored to the social range of his impressionable, unlettered audience, would probably tell us that such a metaphor would be too upmarket for illiterate peasants, though the Nun's Priest is talking to fellow professionals in his tale. Pretending to talk down, probably, with his preacherly chaff and corn, just as the Pardoner 'class-teases' the publican Harry Bailey by offering to let him buy pigs' bones as relics, at the end of his tale.

But the Nun's Priest's wit goes beyond this. In the context of a written fable about domestic poultry, the corn/chaff metaphor has the dizzyingly doubled effect of turning the reader or auditor into an analogue of the Cockerel Chanticleer, who, earlier in the tale, has been helping his wives to pick up grain in the yard; and animalized readers are the opposite of polite moralizing readers. Readers of fable who prefer corn to Pearls (rather than to chaff) would sell the precious text for a bag of corn – as in the Grandville illustration – and crucially, we are reading *fable*, not a sermon. It is a very dextrous, silent, sardonic Phaedrian jest, dependent simply on the implied reader's reading the proper fable into the action. Chanticleer's own moral sentence, his precious little Pearl, is, similarly, delightfully multiple. His quoting and immediate mistranslation or misreading of '*Mulier est hominis confusio*' as 'Womman is mannes joye and al his blis' (547) expresses both what he genuinely wishes to say to his beloved, soft-sided wife Pertilote and its opposites, his Cocky condescension at her lack of Latin and the proleptically ironical moral that will apply to his condition once his felt 'solas' in her has led him to reject his own premonitory dream about the Fox. As usual, the speaking Cockerel of fable cannot interpret, apply, read, what he says. So it seems that morals and fables are not true or false, as almost everywhere else in medieval England, but true, delightful, and false: grotesque and classical.

At the same time as the Nun's Priest is playing cat's-cradle with corn and 'moralitee' at the end of the Tale, St Paul is being jocularly invoked as legitimizing authority –

> ye that holden this tale a folye,
> As of a fox, or of a cok and hen,
> Taketh the moralitee, good men.
> For seint Paul seith, that al that writen is,
> To our doctrine it is y-write, y-wis. (550)

What, even *Reynardian* fables? Unlikely, but perhaps so. But is the moral against flattery, against being flattered and being foolishly trusting, against speaking when you should be silent, against being 'undiscreet of governaunce' (550), against the Cock for singing when the Fox flattered him, against the Fox for speaking at the wrong moment so that the Cock could escape from his mouth, or against the Fox for not realizing that the Cock was turning his own tactic of flattery against him? Hardly 'doctrine', whatever it be; but then, dubious piety ('taketh the moralitee, good men') is an authorial tactic in *Reynard*, as well as being used by the characters in the story.

Chaucer will repeat his reference to Paul, which casually conflates a verse in Romans 15: 4 with another in Timothy, in almost the same words just before his general retractions at the end of the 'Persones Tale', in the final paragraph of the *Tales*. So the final moral of the *Tales* – the 'Persones Tale' stands in the same relation to the *Tales* as a whole as the jesting moral of the 'Nonne Preestes Tale' stands to the tale – is itself double. Chaucer retracts his sinful works, and yet expresses a reservation about that retraction. Conclude the work: review the work.

In a spacious, almost cathedral-like Chaucerian irony, Paul's sentiment about the doctrineable nature of all writing, and hence even of Chaucer's reworking of a dangerous Reynardian fable, is demolished by the Parson in his Prologue, quoting who else but Paul on the subject of fable:

> Thou getest fable noon y-told fro me;
> For Paul, that wryteth unto Timothee,
> Repreveth hem that weyven soothfastnesse,
> And tellen fables and swich wrecchednesse.
> Why sholde I sowen draf out of my fest,
> When I may sowen whete, if that me lest? (674)

Fable-mongering preachers and secular fabulists sow chaff, not seed. The Parson's metaphor is designed to recall the corn and chaff at the end of the Nun's Priest's Tale, although in dramatic terms he is responding to the Maunciple's fable of Phebus and the Crow, which has just finished. The Pauline texts that have leapt into his affronted mind are 1 Timothy 4: 7, 'But refuse profane and old wives' fables', and 2 Timothy 4: 4, 'And they shall turn away their ears from the truth, and shall be turned unto fables'. Pagan fables and secular fictions, which are both covered by 'fable' in the Parson's speech and in the King James Bible, are false. Truth is Christian.

So Paul speaks against fable. But, of course, the uses at the ends of the

Parson's and Nun's Priest's Tales show Chaucer apparently using Paul to legitimize his own use of fable and of secular narrative. The first Pauline verse to which these uses refer says that 'whatsoever things were written aforetime were written for our learning, that we through patience and comfort of the scriptures might have hope' (Romans 15: 4). It comes at a point where Paul is stressing the powers of love, advocating tolerance to those whose beliefs are different from the orthodox, and asking that the strong, the true believers, should help the weak, the waverers, and perhaps the unbelievers. The verse is in key with this expansive and loving spirit, and seems to allow the possible legitimacy of kinds of writing other than the Christian.

It does, though, have the drawback of being in the past tense, whereas the Nun's Priest and Chaucer use the present in order that the sentiment should cover their own cases. Paul obligingly expresses the doctrineability of all writing in the present tense *just five verses* before the second of the Parson's anti-fable texts above, in 2 Timothy 3: 16: 'all scripture is given by inspiration of God, and is profitable for doctrine, for reproof, for correction, for instruction in righteousness'. This is close not only to Chaucer's 'doctrine', but also to a word often used about one function of fable, 'reproof', which has already been seen in Lydgate and will be seen again in Farquhar. But in this verse 'scripture' indicates only the holy scriptures: the context does not allow of any other interpretation. Saying practically the same thing as in Romans, Paul has said exactly the opposite: the verse excludes pagan fable quite as firmly as the Parson thinks it does. Chaucer's Reynardian trick involves bamboozling the audience – he assumes they know the Bible – with their memories of the other verse, so that they accept Paul as saying something that he has not quite said.

To complete the sinuous symmetry of Chaucer's elaborate jest, Paul is also casually written into the Prologue to the 'Nonne Preestes Tale', in Harry Bailey's oath 'by seint Poules belle' (542). St Paul, provokingly, says whatever one pleases, so that his words sound hollow. He may say *bong* in the bell at the start of the tale, but at the end he says *parp*.

One chapter earlier than the verse in 2 Timothy 3 which is the source for one of the Nun's Priest's texts, and only a little further distant from one of the Parson's texts against fable, Paul is in metaphorical mood concerning the wicked and the true believers, in 2 Timothy 2: 20. 'In a great house there are not only vessels of gold and of silver, but also of wood and of earth; and some to honour, and some to dishonour.' Paul appears to be trying to rework the well-known Babrian fable about a bronze Pot and a clay Pot floating down a river. The clay Pot, the weaker vessel, tells the bronze Pot, the stronger, to float further away, lest he himself be shattered. If Paul's earlier use of a figure about stronger and weaker vessels is to be coherent, the stronger should help the weaker: Romans 15, the source of the Nun's Priest's other text, begins 'we then that are strong ought to bear the infirmities of the weak'. But in 2 Timothy it seems that some vessels and men are sanctified, and some dishonourable, just as scripture is good and fable bad. Contradiction upon contradiction: literary practice undercuts doctrine, doubly so if Paul is reworking fable in the same book (2 Timothy) as contains his fulminations against it.

At the climax of the 'Nonne Preestes Tale' the vessels of metal and wood are sounding vessels, 'bemes', or trumpets, part of the cacophony with which the villagers pursue the Fox:

> They yelleden as feendes doon in helle; . . .
> Of bras they broghten bemes, and of box,
> Of horn, of boon, in whiche they blewe and pouped,
> And therewithal they shryked and they houped;
> It semed as that heven sholde falle. (550)

These lines are pointedly expanded from the bare 'sonent grailes et moineaux' of the equivalent moment in Branche II of the *Roman de Renart* (26, 573: Pratt 1972: 425). The cacophony of voices, to which the *silence* of fabulist application classically opposes itself, mirrors others at the climax of Chaucerian poems about birds and animals, but it also embodies the confusion Chaucer has found in the New Testament about the proper use of fiction. Vessels that speak a clear truth in pagan fiction speak not just darkly but confusedly in Holy Writ. The only biblical authority to speak about secular fiction contradicts both himself and Old Testament practice.

In short, the 'Nonne Preestes Tale' may be concerned with the provokingly confused and ill-thought-out nature of biblical and medieval attitudes to fable, as well as to secular narratives such as the *Canterbury Tales*. The Tale's full function is, as William E. Rogers puts it, to uncover 'paradoxes in the rhetorical stances of the other tales' in Fragment 7 of the *Tales* (Rogers 1986: 107), but it is also concerned with paradoxes in other, more dominant discourses, and through this with questions of language and belief even more widely.

The 'Maunciple's Tale' has two functions in the closure of the *Tales*. By revolving as many different aspects of fable as rapidly as possible, it prepares the ground for the Parson's affronted reactions in his Prologue and for Chaucer's final reversion to Paul in the envoy. At the same time, the relationships between the story, the 'iconographic originality' (Frese 1991: 108) of the 'two actors', and the wider structure, allow it to stand as the true end of the work. Fable becomes moral; the moral, the epimythium, of the *Tales* is – one might expect this by now – a fable.

Phebus is a god translated to earth, so the fable has a Hesperian element. The story is of Phebus's captive talking Crow with white feathers, which desires its liberty, and of his wife, whom he keeps as close as he does the bird. In good *fabliau* fashion, the wife does the natural deed with her illicit lover, while the Crow watches. It then sings 'cokkow! cokkow!' to Phebus, and tells him what has happened. Phebus kills his wife, repents, decides wrongly that the Crow has borne false witness, and punishes it by pulling out all its white feathers, turning it black, depriving it of its singing voice and power of speech, and slinging it out of the door: aetiological myth. But the Crow wanted its freedom above all else, so the story also tells of the cunning of the Crow and the stupidity of the god, who is also deprived of his singing as he breaks his musical instruments, as well as his weapons, in his mortification.

The remaining sixty lines present a variety of morals, some with Christian overtones, some secular and simple, some relevant to the story in one way, some in another. Presented with a fable and morality as mixed as this, the Parson retreats, via his bolt-hole of Pauline texts 'singly' read, to an extended prose sermon on Sin, Penitence, Confession, and Penance. The one paradox left to the poet is to make the Parson deliver his diatribe against fable and rhyme in rhyming couplets. Then, in poetic terms, the rest is silence.

Which is to say that the silence of the Crow and the god is mirrored in the silence of the poet, and the fable, the pilgrimage, and the text are complete. Phoebus Apollo is the patron of human music and poetry, and now has no voice. The martyrdom of the other patron of the poem, Thomas à Becket, is silently figured in the silence of the Crow. As Dolores Frese reminds us, 'bekit' is the old heraldic name for the crow: three black crows appear on the arms of Canterbury.

> The 'Tale of the Silenced Crow' is thus subsumed into the profoundly meditative silence engendered by the martyrdom of Becket, here merged to the equally profound and meditative silence attending the experience of aesthetic closure. (Frese 1991: 108)

The only noise is the faintest croak from Chaucer at the end of the

Parson's Tale, directing the reader back to the nature of the Pauline texts in the Nun's Priest's Tale. As in the Bayeux Tapestry and elsewhere, the small voice from the margin, the authorial equivalent of the mute eloquence of the animals (here, the bird), directs the reader back into the interpreting and reassessment of the main discourse, opening the possibility of discontinuity between one vision of the work and another.

Paul's words in Timothy were widely recognized as a crux by later writers exploring the relations between fiction good and bad, and may well have been so for earlier ones. The biblical background to Chaucer's covertly Phaedrian scenario of fable as simultaneously true, fictional, and false is replicated with startling neatness in Samuel Johnson's first three definitions of 'fable', in his *Dictionary*:

> 1 A feigned story intended to enforce some moral precept.
> Jotham's *fable* of the trees . . . Addison
>
> 2 A fiction in general.
> . . . all those *fable* makers . . . Dryden
>
> 3 A vitious or foolish fiction.
> But refuse profane and old wives *fables* 1 Timothy
>
> (Johnson 1755, 1756: 1, 'FABLE')

Johnson could not have allowed himself to approach this paradox in his poetry or works of criticism, which are much more sensitive to the demands of their personal Christian-neoclassical moralistic origins. Discussing Gay's fables, he insists that only the first definition is the correct one: 'a narrative . . . for the purpose of moral instruction' (Johnson 1905: 2, 283). It takes the freedom of lexicographical impersonality before Johnson can allow himself to imply that 'fable' (and by implication narrative in general) is essentially neutral, rather than moral, in its tendency.

When John Bunyan wrestles with the same problem in his 'Apology' for *The Pilgrim's Progress* (1678), hoping to legitimize his use of a semi-secular form of fiction for holy purposes, he produces not an endless circle but a deconstructive knot:

> *Sound words, I know,* Timothy *is to use;*
> *And old Wives' Fables he is to refuse;*
> *But yet grave* Paul *him nowhere doth forbid*
> *The use of Parables; in which lay hid*
> *That Gold, those Pearls, and precious stones that were*
> *Worth digging for; and that with greatest care.* (Bunyan 1967: 5)

It is unfortunate that the figure Bunyan chooses to represent the treasure within parable is so strongly suggestive of the crucial fable, The Cock and the Pearl: the metaphor silently explodes the argument, as with Paul's engagement with the vessels of fable in 2 Timothy.

Robert Henryson's late fifteenth-century collection of thirteen *Moral Fabillis*, written in Scotland in a form which was later to become Northumbrian English, and poorly Anglicized in the sixteenth century, presents a different problem. 'Nowhere in the history of fable is insistent instruction, spelled out so determinedly, yoked to amusing narrative' (Blackham 1985: 61). The stories are vivid, dramatic, demotic, and witty: five are amoral tales from the *Reynard* material, which was just becoming available. They present 'little pictures of society' (Henderson 1979: 170) with a Chaucerian realism and range. But the 'Moralitates' are thumped home with an exegetical force and bluntness which these days seems 'at best unpleasing and at worst desperately confusing' (Burrow 1975: 35). Some Moralitates are 'clear', some 'dark' (Powell 1983: 9): some of the fables exhibit a moral 'double vision' which is paralleled by the 'frequent tentativeness' (*ibid.*) of the morals.

The curious quality of Henryson's fables may have less to do with his vision of the form as such than with his familiarity with the free-ranging and multiple nature of medieval allegory. The Book of Nature does not give up its secrets easily, any more than the Bible yields its various levels of significance without exegesis. 'The fact', for instance, 'that an animal could have multiple and very opposite meanings was not considered confusing' (Rowland 1971: 4–5). Plural significance was a prerequisite of significance itself. The twelve creatures in Bishop Theobald's version of the *Physiologus* (written *c.* 1030; printed 1485), the first in English, all have double natures, and must thus be allegorized or moralized twice: 'Natures twain hath the Stag, and two with a mystical meaning. These nature's history tells teaching a lesson in each' (Theobald 1928: 26). Creatures of a double kind: double nature's single name. 'In Christ' also, explains Ralph Venning, 'there be two natures' (Venning 1647: 6). If natural metaphysics are to be understood as manifestations of the paradoxical metaphysics of Christianity worked by 'Nature, the vicaire of th'almyghty lorde', (Chaucer 1973: 106), they must tax human belief and demand faith in the same way as the Three in One, or the Word made Flesh. But Henryson's confusions are not deliberately worked in anything of the same way that Chaucer's are. Rather than controlling and provoking 'double vision', as many fables can, these seem at the mercy of a duality in the author's mind.

The one exception is his superbly integrated and very moving version of The Swallow and Other Birds, here called 'The Preiching of the Swallow', in which the relations between wit in its fullest sense, morality, the natural world, and religious feeling form a seamless web from the moment the fable starts. Not quite the Providence of Wit, more the Wit of Providence:

> The hie prudence, and wirking mervelous,
> The profound wit off God omnipotent,
> Is sa perfyte, and sa ingenious,
> Excellent ffar all mannis Jugement;
> For quy to him all thing is ay present,
> Rycht as it is, or ony tyme sall be,
> Befoir the sicht off his Divinitie
> God in all his werkis wittie is. (Henryson 1933: 57–8)

God's ultimate wit creates a beautiful, many-layered world, each level of which may be read in terms of another. The proverbial secondary wit of the Swallow is prudence or foresight, the delegated human and animal equivalent of providence; *promythian* or *promethean* wit. This allows the Swallow to predict the consequences of the fowler's sowing the flax that will eventually make nets to catch the other birds, and allows it to warn them. Diabolical wit fulfils the divine plan as apprehended by the Swallow: the fowler, the 'bludie Bowcheour', allegorized as the Devil sowing poison and catching souls in the flaxen net of sensuality, dispatches the 'wretches' (*ibid.*: 65) casually and graphically. The Swallow, the holy preacher (holy because, of course, it resurrects itself each year from river-mud), shares the morality with the poet. Human wit, a poor fourth, allows the poet to report humbly on these manifestations of an integrated universe. The tragic nature of the action accentuates the beauty and the wit. But 'The Preiching of the Swallow' is eighth, not first as it should have been, and its effect is, unfortunately, isolated.

If one takes the sign of literary fable to be the collection of vernacular verse fables, English fable suffered a complete dissolution at about the same time as that of the monasteries. There were no 'new collections of fables in English verse . . . published in the sixteenth century' (Hale 1972: 123), and only three low-grade ones before 1651. In France the situation was similar. When La Fontaine looks for earlier French verse fables, the only ones he finds are written in a language so different from his own that he must consider the authors 'comme Étrangers' (La Fontaine 1962: 6).

What makes this absence more striking is that Patterson, arguing from examples in Spenser, Sidney, Donne, Lyly, and others, identifies later sixteenth-century England as 'the time (and place) where the Aesopian fable entered early modern culture decisively' (Patterson 1991: 52). Which is to say, written culture, given the medieval oral traditions as noted above. So, depending on one's point of view, the period may be bereft of fable or full of it. The fable dissolved back into the marginal illustrative mode, available to a wide variety of literary and other writers and speakers, supported or balanced by the continuing use of Latin Aesops as second- or third-form grammar-school texts. Shakespeare's characters have above twenty glancing references to Aesopian fables (Baldwin 1944: 1, 610 ff.), as well as Menenius's fable early in *Coriolanus*: other dramatists' characters have a few. Hamlet bamboozles Claudius with the courtier-Cameleon who feeds upon 'air, promise-crammed' (3, 2) who can also be found in Gay, 'condemned to thinnest fare' (Gay 1974: 2, 305). Jonson's *Volpone* (1607) is a rare example of the form used as a continuous illustrative mode: essentially, the play is a Reynardian story with the poultry upgraded to carrion birds and the Fox's habits of disguise and deception made more secular – Reynard likes to dress as a monk in order to persuade the chickens of the purity of his intentions.

Why the dissolution of verse fable occurred when there was all this new related activity is not clear, though there was not much verse fable to dissolve. Part of the answer may lie in the new popularity, especially in the more socially developed parts of continental Europe, of prose collections with superb illustrations by craftsmen such as Maurice Gheeraerts: fable entered early modern culture in different ways in different places. The enlivening of fables by one form of art may have temporarily precluded their enlivening by another, and English printers, who could not match the quality of continental work, were often reluctant to compete. In 1586 Geffrey Whitney had to go to Leyden to find a competent printer for his *Choice of Emblemes and other Devises*, 'the first English emblem-book, properly speaking, to appear in print' (Bath 1994: 69). The emblem was briefly one of the fable's close kin, sharing some of its material with the Aesopic tradition. Whitney's emblem of 'Occasion', for example, is a reworking of Phaedrus's brief fable on 'Time' or Opportunity, which was in turn based on a related art, the famous statue by Lysippus which was interpreted allegorically as this emblem. Later fabulists occasionally attempted to renew the connection: Benjamin Harris's 1697 collection *Fables of Young Aesop*, for example, comprises emblem-pictures adorned with fables. By then, though, as the title indicates, emblems were drifting towards literature for children, especially among the Dissenters. Emblems are much less combative than fables, and as with 'Occasion' – the moral of which is, roughly, not to put off till tomorrow, etc. – tend to conservative thoughts, though the English tradition as represented by Quarles and others has a vigorous independence.

Phaedrus's version of this fable is, as one would expect, much more curious than this, and quite differently applied. The stress is on the bizarreness of the physical image – standing on a razor, wings on his heels, one lock of hair, and so on – and the moral is distanced by being attributed to 'the ancients' (Perry 1965: 267), whose habits of enthusiastic allegorization had led to what was quite probably only a statue of a youth at puberty being interpreted, read, in this fashion. The fable is also the second of four which form a reflexive close to Phaedrus's fifth and final Book which is, again as one might expect, proleptic of the eighteenth-century novelistic effects of closure. The first of these is the story of Prince, the flute-player, taking the applause that was directed to the emperor (Augustus: the ending of the collection adverts subtly to its subtitle). The last two feature a Bull being instructed by a Calf, and an Old Dog grown powerless with age. The collection finishes with one line from the Old Dog and one from the author:

> 'quod fulmus lauda, si iam damnas quod sumus'.
> Hoc cur, Philete, scripserim pulchre vides.
>
> 'praise me for what I was, if you condemn me now for what I am'.
> Why I have written this, Philetus, you can see very well. (*ibid.*: 369)

Time, in other words, is over; the Opportunity has gone. As so often, Phaedrian fable acquires its resonance by both saying and unsaying the bare moral, this time the one about procrastination. 'Occasionem rerum signicavit brevem / this figure represents the momentary nature of Opportunity' (367) *Vita brevis.* My work is finished, but if you look, you may see 'what I was'.

In the seventeenth century emblem became part of the culture that catered to popular literary-religious tastes, Francis Quarles's Protestantized collections of divine emblems-with-lyrics being particularly favoured. Emblem in general was the most popular of the fable's kindred: Daly (1979: 11) estimates that in Europe as a whole between 1586 and 1800 six hundred emblem-authors produced two thousand titles, some running up one hundred and seventy editions (one would have to read the bibliographies suggested at the head of the References, check through Pritchard's list of almost 1600 different named fables in English between 1650 and 1722 – Wolf and Lamb, etc., each recast many times – and remember that there are more editions of Gay's *Fables* than of *The Beggar's Opera* before one could grasp that fable was quite as popular as this, though its secondary literature is minute in comparison). Renaissance English fable thus developed against a context of a kindred form that had become expressive of new cultural values, in this case bourgeois tastes and morals combined with the sanction of religious feeling. Emblem was highly dynamic and vigorous in its response to these new values until the Restoration. Before 1600 it was religious in motive, very conservative in its political overtones, and allegorical and typological in mode. By the 1630s, in the hands of Quarles, 'secular and social factors came to play a larger part', and its artistic strategy had been adjusted from 'allegory and typology to narration and metaphor'. Quarles's pictures were 'capable of illustrating narratives, social comments, and political interpretations in the acompanying verse and prose' (Miner 1965: vii). In a brief introduction, Quarles places 'emblem' between Christian parable and 'darker' hieroglyphic – two of the forms perceived as fable's early kin: 'An Embleme is but a silent Parable . . . Before the knowledge of letters, GOD was known by Hieroglyphics . . .' (Quarles 1635: sig. A3).

The movement of the emblem towards narrative meant that it would be natural for fable to follow a similar track away from allegory later in the century, even before the arrival of the neoclassical definition of 'fable' as *mythos*. Bestiary, the other popular related form, had undergone a slower but similar transformation, with the intricate allegorical moralizations of the various versions of the *Physiologus* exchanged for a new openness and variety of approach. Topsell's spectacular *Historie of Four-Footed Beastes* (1607; expanded to *Beastes and Serpents* in 1658) initially defers to tradition – 'every living Beast being a word, every Kind being a sentence, and all of them together a large History' in God's natural chronicle (Topsell 1658: sig. A7r) – but not in the main text and illustrations, where the representations hover tantalizingly between natural zoography, fantasticality, and myths of various kinds. Like the animals of fable, animals could now carry meaning in many different ways.

But the main reason for the absence of literary fable in sixteenth-century England may lie in the formal prohibition, by Henry VIII and again by Elizabeth, of one of the fable's more dangerous domestic kin, the political prophecy. This venerable and exotic form, deriving from Geoffrey of Monmouth's twelfth-century *Book of Merlin*, frequently used animal and tree symbolism taken from heraldry and other sources to figure political persons and causes more or less darkly. Rupert Taylor quotes the case of the trial of the Duke of Norfolk in 1571. The Duke was accused of having in his possession a Latin prophecy forecasting his marriage with Mary Queen of Scots, and their childrens' inheritance of the English crown. At the trial this was translated and interpreted as

> At the exaltation of the moon (Percy of Northumberland) the lion (Elizabeth) shall be overthrown; then shall the lion (Norfolk) be joined with the lioness (Mary), and their whelps shall have the kingdom. (Taylor 1967: 107)

Clearly the Elizabethans had as little trouble as the medievals in allowing or even demanding, as in the *Physiologus*, that a single animal could represent two different things: the monarch, and whoever thought of himself as a possible monarch. Elizabeth, though, who had a very full understanding of the power of iconography and representational techniques as political propaganda, preferred that animals and emblems should not represent anything at all, unless they represented her in a wholly favourable light. She banned the political prophecy, but she and her loyal subjects appropriated the emblem-tradition: she particularly enjoyed the customary Oxonian welcome and jollification of a 'banket' and 'thousands of verses and emblematical poetries' (Nichols 1823: 3, 148) adorning the outer walls of (in this case) St John's.

But although the fable may be adapted towards panegyric as easily as towards anything else, it is hard to pay someone a compliment in a fable which both the fabulist and the recipient can be sure is straightforward in intention and effect. Practically the only sustained verse fables in the sixteenth century are Spenser's curious early poem *Mother Hubberd's Tale* and one of Philisides's songs in the middle of Sidney's *Old Arcadia.* Fulke Greville saw to it that the *Old Arcadia* was not published in the Renaissance, and unsold copies of Spenser's poem were 'apparently called in by the authorities' (Patterson 1991: 66).

In the sixteenth century, fables with any political overtones whatsoever, which is to say virtually all of them, would have been too close to the political prophecy for comfort. Indeed, the political prophecy was easily adapted in the later seventeenth century, by a simple change of tense from future to past, so as almost to converge with the new form of the literary fable. Rupert Taylor interestingly confuses James Howell's *Apologs, or Fables Mythologized* (1661) with the political prophecy, quoting (1967: 130) Howell's heraldicized, tidier version of the fable done more darkly by John Ogilby in 1651 as 'The Parliament of the Birds' – in

Howell's collection it is called 'The Great Council of the Birds'. Howell's version is not prophecy but recent history treated as myth, a figurative account of the events leading up to the death of Charles I. Ogilby's poem is a many-sided poetic commentary on the mood of contemporary events, though as these fables are both versions of The Swallow and Other Birds there is, perforce, also an air of looking to the future. Conversely, Patterson sees Howell's earlier *Dodona's Grove; or The Vocall Forest* (1640) and John Hepwith's riposte *The Calidonian Forrest* (1641) simply as fables, rather than as allegorical derivatives from the political prophecy (Patterson 1991: 82). It is unlikely that a royalist like Howell would have used the fable as such, before Ogilby had given it status and some royalist credentials in the 1650s. But one of the premises of fable is *arbores loquantur*, and Renaissance trees often have an air about them in which admonitory, premonitory, and other qualities are hard to disentangle, as in Brachiano's encouraging interpretation of Vittoria's fearful dream about the yew and the blackthorn, in Webster's *White Devil* (I, 2).

There is a close theatrical analogue to Howell's poem in Dryden's fantastical opera *Albion and Albanius* (1685), which, although not concerned with predicting disaster, provides a mythico-allegorical account of 'the double restoration of his Sacred Majesty' (Dryden 1956–92: 15, 11), the twenty-five years of the reign of Charles II, in an account of the liberation of Augusta (London) from the tyrants Democracy and Zelota, or Feigned Zeal. Charles, ever the gentleman, obligingly pointed the analogy between himself and Charles I by dying just before the first full production, thus enabling Dryden to write his apotheosis into the ending.

In his Preface, Dryden speaks of the relationship between the plot and the running political allegory of the 'double restoration' as that between a 'Fable' and a 'Moral' (*ibid.*); but the Epilogue speaks deprecatingly of the whole piece as '*our* Aesop's *Fable*' and reapplies the '*Moral of the Play*' more specifically as 'Plain Dealing' (54) between sovereign and people. This curious double-focus appears to be the result of Dryden's wishing both to point the analogy between the opera and Howell's mythologized English fable – the 'Aesop's *Fable*' – and, more widely, trying to establish an independent identity or genealogy of meaning for the word fable itself in the face of the new neoclassical sense of plot in general, *mythos*, which had recently come in from France. Much of the Preface is concerned with the problems of giving opera a specifically English identity – Dryden praises his French composer, Grabu, but looks forward to a day when an Englishman will be as competent – and there is a parallel, if fainter, concern with the naturalization of fable. Allegoresis is very much a part of the French use of fable, but Dryden's usage would link '*mere* apologue' and 'politically concerned allegory' rather more closely: and instead of providing a definition of fable, he keeps the question open by suggesting two definitions, without feeling any need to worry about whether these are complementary or in competition. Dryden, that is to say, provides a *double reading* or interpretation of fable, as if this were perfectly natural.

Whatever the causes, the effect of the absence of literary fable in the early seventeenth century is that there was little prescriptive precedent for the form, or burden of the recent past to cope with. English late-Renaissance culture could re-invent the fable largely in terms of its own immediate social, literary, and political concerns. Fable could be eclectic and original, decisively different from a closely related form like emblem, and yet consciously use and echo associations, tones, and traits already present in antique and medieval fable.

In intellectual terms the ground was quite ready, though not much tilled. In 1605, Francis Bacon had effectively accorded '*Allusive* or *Parabolical*' poetry one-ninth of the world of learning, and had instanced 'the fables of Aesop' as his prime example. Bacon's intellectual understanding of the functions and nature of fable is remarkable and rare for an Englishman before 1680, especially given that he has apparently no recent literary examples from which to work. He even engages sensibly, easily, and decisively with a question that was to become a crux in European fable-theory at the end of the century, of whether fables (and epics) have morals in them, or morals have fables which exist only to expound them. 'The fable was first' (Bacon 1915: 84), says Bacon firmly. He sees that fables are narrative in nature but make their effect through conceits and metaphors, and feels that they express 'the secrets and mysteries of religion, policy, or philosophy' while also serving to 'retire and obscure' (*ibid.*) those secrets, after the manner of hieroglyphic. This is an elegant and concise acknowledgement of the fact that seventeenth-century English fable inherited clarity and darkness, ease and discontinuity, in equal measure from its various backgrounds and contexts of use.

This varied and unique environment ensured that fable very quickly found a wide and receptive audience, one attuned to the form because familiar with its cousins, as well as with the non-literary histories. Practically non-existent before 1650, literary fable mushroomed after

1665, with collections published 'nearly every year . . . in uninterrupted succession' (Miner 1965: xii), momentum increasing rapidly in the late 1680s. The beast-fable was transformed from a marginal, barely literary genre to one which was 'looked upon as a chief representative of a number of kinds of figurative writing' (*ibid.*). This enables a wholly different current definition of fable, more open even than Dryden's, full of potential rather than technical and fixative. It is 'a Narrative applied only to express some special purpose or conceit' (Bacon 1915: 83); close to Voltaire's 'work which says more than it seems to say'. History, marginalizing the fabulists, was conspiring to place the fable closer to centre stage, in the hands of John Ogilby.

CHAPTER 5

The fable in the wars: Ogilby and after

The case to be made for John Ogilby is that his 1651 *Fables* have a claim to being considered as the defining literary work of the English interregnum, and that Ogilby was hence right to say that in composing this collection in particular he had effectively taken his 'degree amongst the minor Poets' (Ogilby 1670: Preface). There is then a second question, of his influence on later writers, or more precisely of his *example* as a fabulist.

The Fable in the Wars echoes the title of Edna Longley's book on twentieth-century war poetry: *Poetry in the Wars* (1986). Longley shows how seminal for later poets was the radical practice of even apparently unassuming poets who had been conditioned by the ambience of the First World War: Philip Larkin's appreciation for Edward Thomas would be a case in point. Ogilby invented a way of writing that reflected a nation at war with itself, and which was new not just in England but in Europe. For several decades he was acknowledged as the great original – *auctor* – of this new form, and his work presages many different uses and adaptations of fable into the eighteenth century. The influence of Ogilby on Dryden is already admitted, in the case of Dryden's use of fables from Ogilby in *The Hind and the Panther.* This chapter will seek to establish broader and more general connections between Ogilby's adaptations of fable in the 1651 collection, the 1668 *Aesopics*, and Dryden's habits of mind in some of his later works; not as influence, but as signs of two fabulists working in the same *generic tradition*, the classic mode of double-handed fable, and aware of fable's connections with other forms; heroic epic in particular.

There remains, of course, the teasing and so far unasked question of whether the great French original, La Fontaine, was influenced by Ogilby. Unasked, because the French much prefer their national cultural monuments (La Fontaine, the Bayeux Tapestry) to be *French.* The question is beyond the remit here, but: Marian Eames, Henrietta

Pritchard, and William Wray are, quite independently of each other, struck more by the similarities than the differences. There is La Fontaine's coy remark in the Preface to the *Fables* that there are modern verse fables 'chez les Étrangers' (La Fontaine 1962: 6) but not in French: he can only mean Ogilby. Davenant, who admired Ogilby, was in Paris in the 1640s. Saint-Èvremond, La Fontaine's friend, fled to England in 1657, and remained in correspondence with him: his 'Matrone d'Éphèse' was published in La Fontaine's *Contes* three years before Ogilby published his. La Fontaine is anglophile: several of his fables praise English culture and express hopes for peaceful relations between France and England. His 'Le Soleil et les Grenouilles' (1672), his only fable with a mildly bellicose drift and one which he did not publish in the *Fables*, is usually treated as an imitation of the 'Sol et Ranae' of Le Père Commis. In fact the tone (anti-Dutch) and the application (the Sun-King will dry up the Frogs' marshes if they become too presumptuous) are identical to those of Ogilby's version discussed below, which was published in 1668 and 1672. Only the king is different.

There are other verbal similarities; for instance, the same Virgilian flourish (from the *Aeneid*, 4, 445–6) at the end of 'Le Chêne et Le Roseau' / 'Of the Oke and the Reed'. Like Ogilby, La Fontaine uses a wide range of tones stretching from a combination of plainness and rhetorical force, through the conversational, to the resoundingly heroic; and his forms are quite as varied as Ogilby's. Most mix short and long lines after Ogilby's manner; sometimes they settle down to pentameter, sometimes they are poised and concise. His fables reflect the properties of his social environment as amply and precisely as Ogilby's reflect those of his. Ogilby's shifts of dialect are more boisterous, but one would expect this of a poet working within a conflict in which the subject of strife was in large part language itself, 'parliament' in the broadest sense. The Civil Wars were fought over the English language and its transmission quite as much as for control of other sources of power, and Ogilby's 'various languag'd Host' of different animals (1668[a]: 6) provides a running echo or motif of this arena of linguistic combativeness. La Fontaine's fables, on the other hand, reflect a society, or a class, at home with itself. But of such dangerous thoughts, no more.

'OGILBY THE GREAT'

One of the more interesting pieces of evidence of Ogilby's pre-eminence in verse fable before 1687 is the deference shown to his work in the

Preface to the 1673 collection called *Aesop Improv'd*. The writer stresses the usefulness and applicability of fables 'in these tumultuous times' – fables belong 'in the wars' – and defines his collection as a downmarket, cheap, unintellectual derivative of 'the famous Oglesby', whose readers are felt to need 'a better capacity, and more skill in Poetical phrases, and Fictions, than the generality of those who are willing to read Aesop's Fables are endowed with' (*Aesop* 1673: Preface). Fully adult and sophisticated readers, then; the savant audience of fable, not mere children or Cockerels, though *Aesop Improv'd* is an early example of fable being 'Abstracted from all Party Considerations, [and] Adapted To All Capacities' (Richardson 1739: titlepage). But not all of Ogilby's appreciative readers were so sophisticated.

When Alexander Pope was twelve years old, he wrote a play based on the *Iliad* and enlisted his school friends as actors. He took care to have them all costumed

> after the pictures in his favourite Ogilby . . . Ogilby's translation of Homer was one of the first large poems that ever Mr. Pope read, and he still spoke of the pleasure it then gave him, with a sort of rapture . . . 'It was that great edition with pictures. I was then about eight years old' (Spence 1966: 1, 14)

Readers are usually aware of Ogilby as brother to Dryden's Flecknoe, and often remember him as 'one of the Dunces in Pope's *Dunciad*'. The latter is not quite the case: 'Ogilby the great' is in the library of Pope's Hero as one of those books 'as fitted the shelves, or were . . . adorned with pictures' (Pope 1965: 727). Large poems, great editions, pictures: King Colley has the same tastes as the juvenile Pope, though not quite the same rapture.

The case is clearer with Dryden, who in public was keen to pillory and belittle the work of the most prestigious translator of the previous generation – probably in order to puff his own – but equally keen to pillage him in private. Both of the fables that the two animals rehearse to each other in Part 3 of *The Hind and the Panther* are derived from Ogilby, and there are many small echoes of the 1651 collection. The wider similarities between Dryden's *Fables* and Ogilby's are as fascinating as their many differences. In each case, the radical adaptation of fable allows the writer to link personal and public utterance, historical vision with private feeling, Ancient with Modern perceptions: more so than in any of either writer's other works.

Ogilby was born in Scotland in 1600, moving down to London when his father followed James VI and I south after 1603. His early trade was that of dancing-master: he was a talented enough dancer to perform in court masques. He became a theatrical manager and producer, rising in the 1630s to be Master of Revels in Ireland under Viscount Wentworth, later Earl of Strafford. As such, he ran the first theatre in Ireland, knew dramatists and poets: James Shirley and the ex-laureate William Davenant were to write introductory verses for *The Fables of Aesop Paraphrased in Verse* (1651).

This career came to a sudden end in the Irish rebellion of 1641. Arriving back in London with few resources, his employer having been adandoned by his monarch and executed, he set about rescuing his fortunes. He translated Virgil, then Aesop, more Virgil, then Homer. At the Restoration his royalist contacts and his theatrical and poetic talents secured him the task of composing the poetical parts of the London procession honouring Charles II. Restored to favour, he became Royal Cartographer and later Royal Cosmographer, printing and publishing huge folio atlases, upgrading his poetical productions to the same size, and returning to Aesop.

Printer, publisher, writer, entrepreneur: but his *Fables* were admired above all his other enterprises. Pepys and Aubrey speak highly of them; Edward Phillips devoted more space to Ogilby in his *Theatrum Poetarum* than he did to his own uncle, John Milton, with pride of place reserved for the *Fables*, 'as Compos'd propria Minerva' (Phillips 1675: 114). The 1651 collection went through at least five editions by 1675. But this distinction between the *Fables* and his other productions was lost, after Dryden's brief derogations in *Mac Flecknoe* and elsewhere.

Where his other translations stay close to the originals, the method in the *Fables* is 'Imitation' (Dryden 1956–92: 1, 114), the loosest possible form of translation. The main source is the barest, lowest, most common possible, the current school *Aesop*, but the *Fables* use classical and other mythologies, and exhibit a great variety of verse techniques: so, as later with Dryden, Fables Ancient and Modern. Contemporaries would have taken the point. Where literal translation was (following Horace's 'Ars Poetica') a 'servile' (*ibid.*: 1, 116) path, imitation was 'free', and 'the writers who claim most "freedom" for themselves are the royalist translators' (Potter 1989: 52). From this, and from Ogilby's history, one might infer that these are royalist fables, coded *samizdat* allegories of the destruction of the natural hierarchy by wolfish tyrants, written for supporters of the dead Lion. But this is Aesop, mediated by Phaedrus: Ogilby pointedly gives Phaedrus's version of the first fable, 'The Cock and the Jewel', in an early marginal note to the 1668 edition. The

Phaedrian/Lydgatean ideal, that fables should be capable of being interpreted 'yche man for his party', places the freedom of fable above simple loyalty to one side by allowing that the other man may write fables too. And it is unlikely that Ogilby himself felt wholeheartedly royalist after Charles's desertion of Strafford: the Civil Wars and interregnum mirror almost exactly the interlude of exclusion and loss of status in Ogilby's own life.

The problems go deeper. The admitted class-orientation of 'free' translation is at odds with the general perception of Aesop as transmitting the wisdom of the common man. The seventeenth-century notion of the superiority of free translation was 'based on a metaphor of class and competition: the imitator was an equal of the original author, and sought to excel him' (*ibid.*), and the translation does indeed surpass its main source. But why strive to *outclass* a slave or bondsman, Aesop or Phaedrus, whose fables made them free, when one's own class has just been diminished and excluded by civil war? Taking a third-form school text as one's source points up this socio-textual oddity. And, more widely, how does one reconcile the double-handed Phaedrian sense of fable with a historical present in which all political parties are at each others' throats, but where the large mass of English people, common and otherwise, are utterly weary of the madness and havoc of the distracted times?

Davenant's introductory verses make it clear that imitating Aesop is a special case:

> in thy Verse, methinks, I Aesop see
> Less bound than when his Master made him free:
> So well thou fit'st the measure of his mind.
> Which, though the slave, his body, were confind,
> Seem'd, as thy wit, still unconstrained and young,
> And like thy numbers easie and as strong. (Ogilby 1651: A5v)

Political and corporeal confinement is answered not by political emancipation but by the freedoms of the 'wit', the mind, which are in turn reflected in the 'free' style of imitation, easy and strong. This style liberates the Aesopian spirit in the sense that it matches and concurs with Aesop's mind, 'fitting' rather than striving to outdo or master it. The 'unconstrained and young' wits of Aesop and Ogilby hint wittily at other kinds of liberation: the 'body' of both Davenant and Ogilby is in its fifties at this point, and in Davenant's case is literally confined, constrained. His introductory poem is dated from the Tower of London, where he was incarcerated, 30 September 1651, less than four weeks after the final defeat of Charles Stuart and his Scots army at Worcester. Davenant was also suffering his period of exclusion, in his case from the laureateship.

Old; yet young: enslaved; yet free. The unconstrained spirit of Aesopian wit extends through more tacit analogies, especially between the confinements of Davenant and Socrates and the 'fit' nature of Aesopian translation. When Cebes asks Socrates (*Phaedo*, 60B) why he has chosen to versify Aesopian fables while in prison, Socrates assures him sarcastically that he is not attempting to imitate a professional poet and orator. Condemned philosophers and incarcerated laureates do not have that kind of status: fabulists are not *authors*. So while claiming equality for Ogilby with the free wit of the slave Aesop, claiming that Ogilby has not tried to 'master' him, Davenant can, paradoxically, also silently ally himself with the moral authority of the example of the philosophical master, the victim-fabulist Socrates. All this operates, in its historical context, as a sardonic comment on the immediate royalist plight: if the (political, royal) master cannot set us free from our chains, let us see what power a philosopher-slave's free wit has. We cannot be *translated*, but we may translate.

Ogilby's 1651 collection, at that date by far the most politically concerned ever written, is also one of the least politically restricted. The Lion in 'Of the Lion and the Forester' (No. 50), an ornamented version of The Lion and the Man, speaks the relevant Olympian sentence: '*From partial Pens, all Truth has been for ever shut*' (Ogilby 1668[a]: 123; subsequent references are to this edition and will cite page numbers only). This is usually a combative fable in favour of the unrepresented underdog, but here the Lion sees past 'his' moral – that if he could write or paint (or in this case, sculpt) he would do it very differently from the Man – to a wider perspective about all writing, all perspectives, all fables, which goes beyond even Ogilby's own inclusive epimythium. There is in this collection a fascinating tension between incorrigibility and corrigibility. Animals, and parts of the body such as Hands, can sometimes learn more than they would usually learn from their fable. Men, even authors, lost in their broils and dissensions, often cannot even learn as much.

Ogilby's achievement was to find, in the natural discontinuities of fable as he apprehended them, a suitable artistic form for the deeply felt discontinuities of contemporary English history. The fable collection's 'natural tendency to fragmentation becomes a mute witness to the state of England in 1651', though the fables themselves form a composite 'picture of life in England . . . which contained a wide-ranging and often ironic commentary on what he saw' (Pritchard 1976: 21). Ogilby's instinctive feeling for the temper of the times produces a subtle but pervasive effect which might best be rendered by Marvell's phrase in 'Upon Appleton House' (1681: written *c.* 1652), a 'Landskip drawen in Looking-Glass' (Marvell 1971: 1, 77). It is an Alice-world of forceful tragicomic resonances in which the scale is somehow both miniaturized and huge, the focuses disjointed yet strangely psychologically realistic: poems not for children or adults, slaves or masters, but, as with *Alice*, for readers now unsure of their size, in passage between worlds, in parenthesis.

Ogilby's instinctive feeling is matched by a sophisticated poetic strategy. English and European politics and history are put into perspective against wars in Heaven, the fall of the angels; epic themes, heroic and expansive contexts. But at the same time such events and trends are mocked and trivialized, by the animal-context, by lower aspects of the style, by the inclusion of Ogilby's exquisite version of the burlesque-epic poem called the *Batrachomuomachia*, 'The Battel of the Frog and Mouse', and by judicious uses of mythology. The much less heroic appetitive violences of epic, blood, guts, and unfeasibly large meals, are mimicked in a running stress on eating and gore: the Dog in No. 81 eats the Sheep, 'Sucks his warm Blood and eats his panting Heart' (206). Dimensions expand and contract with the same freedom as they do in 'Upon Appleton House', where the distant cows 'shrunk in the huge Pasture show / As Spots, so shap'd, on Faces do' (Marvell 1971: 1, 77). In Fable 54, 'Of the Tortoise and the Eagle', the Eagle holds the Tortoise aloft over (in the illustration, see plate 7) the globe, centred on Europe:

> Such was their Flight,
> They might
> See the dark Earth's contracted Face below,
> To cast forth sullen Beams, with Brazen Light,
> Like a huge Moon, and turning on her Poles
> Dark seas like Phoebe's Moles,
> Casting a dimmer Ray. (133)

The best introduction to this world is the cosmological start of Fable 40, 'The Parliament of the Birds', Ogilby's compelling version of The Swallow and Other Birds:

7 Wenceslaus Hollar, 'Of the Tortoise and the Eagle'

When Jove by impious Arms had Heaven possest
And old King *Saturn* setting in the West
Finish'd the Golden Dayes, A Silver Morn,
Pale with the Crimes success, did Earth adorn,
And gave its Name unto the second Age.
Then Skies first thunder'd, Seas with Tempests rage,
Four Seasons part the Year, Men Sow, and Plant,
(The Golden Times nor Labour knew nor Want)
Then Toyl found Ease by Art, Art by Deceits,
Then Civil War turn'd Kingdoms into States,
(For petty kings Rul'd first) then Birds and Beasts
Did with Republicks private interests
Begin to build; Eagles were vanquish'd then,
And Lyons worsted lost their Royal Den. (95)

Ogilby is rewriting the start of Ovid's *Metamorphoses*, where the horrific violence of the Age of Iron leads to a council of the gods rather than a Parliament of Birds. The historical present and recent past of interregnum and Civil Wars are very briefly set against what feels like an aureate Stuart past: Good King Charles (I)'s Golden Days. But two other correspondences are already at work. One is between the higher order of the Greek gods and the lower order of the beast-fable. Ovid's gods quietly metamorphose into beasts in the course of the paragraph, Heaven to a Den. The other is the continuing imaging of historical process in terms of the beasts and birds, of the original mythological framework, and of new ones. This begins as early as line 11, establishing a quite different perspective on golden Stuart days. Ogilby's republican birds, who have ejected their King and Lords, and are thus 'reduc'd' to a 'Popular State' (95), are full of the liberal arts, and are keen to drop mythological references, both pagan and Christian. Even the mistaken Linnet can rise to this pressured syntax and double reference:

May our good Angels those Coelestial Birds,
Who skreeking Eagles drove with flaming Swords
From this warm Paradise, our State defend,
'Gainst all dire Fowl, from Stygian floods ascend. (99)

So it is a three- or four-cornered fable, its mythologies multiple and disturbed. The usual natural hierarchy of beasts is linked with the upheavals of English history, with Christian imagery, and with the passional mythic world of energetic, shapechanging, pagan divinity. Jove, usually the highest power in fable, is revealed by the Ovidian framework as a usurper of the kingdom: his control dwindles from ultimate to secondbest, his higher world already a world upside-down.

Ogilby includes one of the fables which show him at his most powerless, 'Of the Eagle and the Beetle', where he proves unable to protect the Eagle's eggs against the vengeful little Beetle when so requested. In Fable 8, 'Of the Mountain in Labour', Fame predicts that the Mountain's issue will pull Jove from his 'Usurped Chair', and that the gods will 'sculk in several Shapes transform'd' (21). This is published at almost exactly the same moment as the Stuart prince is being hunted in the New Forest and is cowering up an oaktree. Royal beasts in the Fables are usually, as in 'Of the Lyon grown Old', 'Weak, Sick, and Lame', or otherwise powerless: live dogs are much better than dead or dying lions. The Carolean Lyon muses that "Twas no well-grounded Policy of State / By Arbitrary Power to purchase Hate' (57). Fables may be used for reproof of political mistakes as well as of tyrannical power, and a king or a prince may be as stupid as anyone else. Fables may also be elegaic, a lament for loss of power.

This could easily tend to burlesque, but Ogilby consistently avoids straightforward responses: to reprove and lament is not to mock. Even the extravagantly cheerful and boisterous 'Frog and Mouse' (see plate 8), nominally a burlesque or mock-heroic, is too lovingly and inventively detailed to be just that. Ogilby applies the spirit of the line from Book 4 of Virgil's *Georgics*, the Book about bees – 'A mighty Pomp, tho' made of little Things' (Dryden 1956–92: 2, 980) – which will later be of service to Pope at the start of *The Rape of the Lock*. Ogilby had, after all, just translated Virgil, and the *Fables* are full of miniaturized poetical heroic gestures. The Mousecovite King ('black Moustapha')

> Appear'd (may we great things compare with small)
> Like the World's Conqueror, though not so tall . . .
> Heroic Souls in narrow breasts confin'd! (13, 15)

> With mighty Souls in narrow Bodies prest
> (Dryden 1956–92: 2, 983)

The effect is rescued from burlesque into the sub-heroic or heroi-comical; spurious Homer transmitted through genuine Virgil. Dryden later used the battle of the bees' monarchs in the *Georgics* to figure the two English kings, the 'godlike . . . nobler' James, and William, who is figured in the less well-favoured bee, which looks like 'nature in disgrace' (*ibid.*). Georgic adapts well to the political innuendo of fable. Ogilby's interpretation is more open.

In *Paradise Lost* Milton uses many references to Hesperian fables in order to emphasize the superior dignity of his Christian epic, but the

8 Wenceslaus Hollar, 'Of the Frog and Mouse'

comparisons also suggest that his story is like the pagan myths, or at least capable of being measured against them. He casts himself as a more successful Eve, repeatedly tempting himself with pagan poetical titbits of extraordinary beauty, only to lay them by, sighingly but heroically, for the true fable of the Christian action and the sad task of telling it. Ogilby approaches the Hesperian from beneath rather than above, but to something of the same complex effect. In the description of the crayfish on which 'King Frogmoreton' (topically altered from 'Frogpadock' in the 1651 edition) is mounted in the 'Frog and Mouse', for instance:

> Although the many-footed could not run
> With the great Crab, which yearly feasts the Sun;
> Nor with the golden Scorpion could set forth
> And measure daily the Tun-bellied Earth;
> Yet such his speed, he ne'er was overtook
> By any shel-back'd Monster of the Brook. (11)

Not supernaturally heroic, but naturally so, as well as comically diminutive.

In 'The Parliament of Birds' there is a more violent flux of scale and perspective. At first Jove the usurper seems to be like Cromwell, who is thus momentarily placed in a heroic setting. But the reference dissolves as Jove dwindles rapidly from the presiding force to a mere parenthetical reference from the Swallow: 'Then said the Swallow, fearing future Fates, / Whom Jove will ruin, he infatuates' (99). As well as following the heroic structure suggested by the Ovidian opening, the poem follows the image of sowing and planting in the sixth line. Its fable is that of the foresighted Swallow who tries to warn the other Birds about the results of the future flax crop; linseed, the food of the Linnet, whose 'Private Interests' dictate arguments against interference with it, but also 'line' or linen to make nets to catch all the Birds.

So from supernatural origins the fable subsides to natural consequences, and the tones and eventual moral are gradually subdued to match: the poem works from big to little. In the middle parts the Birds drop their guard and the level of their diction to banter with nature and history. The Linnet accuses the Swallow of having 'drest up scar-Crow doubts', and accuses the other Birds of nursing 'Malignants', a scathing Parliamentarian term for the royalists: but the Swallow insists that the flax must be pulled up 'Branch and Root' (97, 98). By the end, of course, the presiding power is the new destroyer, Man: even the foresighted Birds are captive, overthrown, decoyed by their 'dearest Friends',

> And Man e'r since did rule the Earth alone.
> When this sad Ditty silver'd o'r with Age
> A Captive Stare sung in his woful Cage;
> When Civil War hath brought great Nations low,
> Destruction comes oft with a Forein Foe. (100)

So the end-frame expands timidly, to Earth, Civil War, and Europe: several of the other fables are similarly concerned to suggest the parallel between the possible destiny of England and the fate of the smaller continental nations which had been swallowed up by others in the Thirty Years War, and the Anglo-Dutch naval war over trade was to break out the following year. But the epimythium is even further subdued, being merely about private interests and perverse advice, and relating only to the Linnet. Indeed, Ogilby's morals are often so subdued that they seem inappropriate to the fables, until this is sensed as a wider movement of mood. The energy drains from the poetry: the fable enacts or mimes loss of power, reduction, poetically, at the same time as presenting images of captivity which mimic the state of its historical friends. Syntax drops quietly into lines: the metallic imagery (Ogilby's world is full of hard objects, the debris of the Age of Iron) dwindles from the cosmic to the cage. Heroic tones degenerate to a dismal ditty, the god to a parenthesis; epic becomes history.

It is easy to miss, or to overlook, this poetic coherence, when the frames of reference appear so disjointed and incongruous. The analogies of fable are being developed into something closer to the charged, multiple changes of poetic symbol and imaginative energy. But no one expects – or expected – a mere translator of Aesop to be able to do this.

'The Parliament of the Birds' is in many ways a microcosm of the *Fables* more widely, particularly as concerns the movements of mood, tone, and scale. Most of the epimythia are very quiet. One, at the end of No. 65, 'Of the Sun and Wind', even vocalizes and then applies the mood, in the distinction between 'quiet' and 'ranting'. The Wind has been blowing noisily away, failing to win the wager with the Sun over which of them can remove the traveller's cloak. The Sun quietly remonstrates:

> *Great Actions are not carried on by Noyse*;
> What Ranters nor loud Blustring can obtain,
> A Fancy, or facetious jest may gain.

Including, that is, the indirect, sometimes silent, jests of fable, which may succeed where a larger and noisier work would not. The moral picks up the hint about Ranters and twists it in a surprising direction:

> *Loud threatnings make men stubborn, but kind Words*
> *Pierce gentle Breasts sooner than sharpest Swords.*
> *To Rant and mouth is not so neer a way*
> *To Cheat your Brother, as by Yea, and Nay.* (166)

The Yea and Nay Men were the group surrounding George Fox who, following Justice Bennet's quip to Fox in 1650, were about to become known as the Quakers. They justified their contentious refusal to swear oaths by quoting James 5:12, 'swear not . . . but let your yea be yea; and your nea, nea', and Matthew 5:37, 'let your communication be Yea, yea; Nay, nay'. 'Children of light' was their earliest name for themselves (John 12:36, Ephesians 5:8, 1 Thessalonians 5:5), so the Sun is as perfect a figure for them as the Wind is for the flamboyant style of the Ranters. Unlikely heroes for a royalist, but then, as is often the case, Ogilby's attitude is complex and devious. A quiet religious sect is superior to a noisy one, not because it is morally superior but because it is more effective, more likely to succeed: the semi-mystical charismatic persuasion known as the Ranters had just been dissolved by the effects of the Blasphemy Act of 1650. The dialogue of the two actors, the Sun and Wind, thus figures a disturbed moment of dialogue, a historical reversal or shift of power, between two immediately contemporary voices, attitudes to language. Somehow the silence of the dispossessed Royalists, the reticence (*let your words be few*) of the persecuted Quakers – Fox was in prison in Derby, in 1651 – and the virtual silence of the fable's application are made to mirror each other. As with the Carolean Lyon, contempt and respect seem to lie next to each other in Ogilby's mind, but the dominant note is one of sour admiration. The hierarchy of these fables is, after all, not a hierarchy of virtue but the classic one of wit, energy, and expediency, in which a noisy but idle rustic can receive a disconcerting reply when he prays to Hercules for aid in extricating his cart from a rut: 'We help the active, though they wicked are; / *The Gods ne'er did, nor will, hear Idle Prayer*' (102). Put your shoulder quietly to the wheel and the gods will be with you, whether you deserve it or not: the work-ethic, minus the ethics. Not quite the message one might expect from a heroic exemplar such as Hercules, but messages from or about Hercules, especially those in fable, are rarely straightforward.

Where most end quietly, most of Ogilby's fables begin vigorously and grandly; No. 3, 'Of the Lion and Other Beasts', most vigorously of all:

> When troops of Beams led by the grey-eyed Dawn
> From Eastern Ports rush'd with recruited light,
> And beat up all the quarters of the Night . . . (5)

Omar Khayyam is quite restrained in comparison. In the same mode, replicating the movement of historical mood over the previous ten years, No. 27, 'Of The File and the Viper', begins by universalizing

English history against the fall of the angels, with the File ('strong *Iron-Sides*' – Ironsides being the most approving epithet for Cromwell) described as wearing a skin

> . . . so hard and rough,
> As that infernal coat of Buff
> The *Luciferian* General had on
> In the first grand Rebellion:
> Which no Coelestial arm
> Could harm,
> Or pierce,
> But His, who guids the Stars, and Rules the Universe. (65)

As Mary Pritchard points out, the 'coat of Buff' recalls the buff leather jerkins worn as battle-dress by the cavalry of the New Model Army, so that the '*Luciferian* General' appears to wear the coat of the regular troops. '*Iron-Sides*', the File, thus suggests both Cromwell and the power of the army. In No. 8, the Mountain's issue will 'Crack 'twixt his nail, Ironside *Leviathan*' – 'a complex image indeed, and one that is highly ambiguous, for it suggests an absolute government headed by the army' (Pritchard 1976: 62). The tone used of Lucifer in No. 27 is curiously admiring, in the hyperbole of the final line, yet the stanza also contains bathetic constructions ('had on'), so that the little and grand are held in stylistic relationship, in a subtle management of fable's paradoxes of relative size which is echoed by the Lilliputian/Brobdingnagian lines.

Given the possibilities raised by the opening image, the fable as it develops is complicated but uncommitted in attitude. The 'Artist' has been using the File to 'polish' a piece of metal statuary or decoration, 'The Snakes which Periwig the Gorgon's Head', which is seen, in the illustration (see plate 9), lying on the floor. This is the motive for the Viper's fruitless attack on the File: it thinks the Artist is attacking the snakes. So where the File suggests Roundhead military gear, the Gorgon's head suggests the fashions of a higher civilian class: and the doubly deposed head (chopped off, and knocked off the stand by the 'speckled Mail / Which shining arm'd th'old Dragon's Tail', (66) on the Dragon on which the Artist is also working) that of a Stuart monarch. Now Cromwell seems to be both File and Dragon, and the Dragon like Lucifer, or Sin. But the Dragon is just another hard, mute, semi-animate object, suggestive but shorn of emblematic status. In this curious looking-glass landscape there is usually, by the end of the fable, an implicit admiration for power, even amoral or usurping and destructive power, which is again reminiscent of some of Marvell's political poems of the

9 Wenceslaus Hollar, 'Of the File and the Viper'

1650s, in particular of the 'Horatian Ode' (written 1650). 'What's won by Arms, by Force he must maintain', (*ibid.*: 110) reflects the Hart at the end of a stanza of No. 45: Marvell's poem closes with the detached moral to Cromwell: 'The same *Arts* that did gain / A *Pow'r* must it *maintain*' (Marvell 1971: 1, 94). Many aspects of that poem, its sub-emblematic objects, semi-cosmological historical framework, and brief but variously measured lines, are echoed or reflected in Ogilby's technique.

Being a composite or multiple image, Ogilby's passive File may plausibly speak a general moral about war to the angry Viper, before the more remote epimythium:

> When thou begin'st a War, not only know
> Thy own, but Forces of the Foe . . .
> *He is not wise with his own Strength himself o'ercomes.* (66)

This could be a moral to Charles-as-loser, now as toothless as the Viper; a wider moral about the dangers of a powerful but divided army; or an aspect of the widest moral of the *Fables*, the hope of leniency and better times that emerges most strongly in the moral of the tree-fable 'Of the Oke and the Reed' (No. 67), the nearest Ogilby could come to a political prophecy:

> *Though Strong, Resist not a too Potent Foe;*
> *Madmen against a violent Torrent row.*
> *Thou mayst hereafter serve the Common-weal;*
> *Then yield till Time shall later Acts repeal.* (170)

In late 1651 the Royalists were much in agreement with such morals. They retreated, submitted, became quiet; lived at home, if their estates had not been sequestrated. All visible and audible fidelity to the king was extinguished for several years.

The arts in general had already mirrored this retreat from the public domain. There was practically no theatre. It was difficult to get large books printed, and even the ambitious Ogilby had to bring out his productions in quarto until 1660. Music had also become smaller in scale, domestic. As Roger North, also a Royalist, later remembered, 'when most other good arts languished Musick held up her head, not at Court . . . but in private society, for many chose rather to fidle at home, than to goe out, and be knockt on the head abroad' (North 1959: 294). In such a mood, eighty-one fables expanded to two hundred pages of varied lines, with just a few in pentameter, and broken up by the same number of illustrations, made a moderate enough classical author. The retreats of tone and scale, from cosmic to cage, exuberant to sad, also mirror this cultural ebb tide, and many of Ogilby's animals are glad to live quietly at home. The Tortoise, in 'Of the Tortoise and the Frogs' (No. 53), envies the Frogs their freedom and ease of movement and laments his own 'Adamantine Skin', until he sees the Frogs being devoured by eels:

> The Tortoise did begin,
> To find
> His mind
> Contented with his Inn!
> And thought the Gods now kind
> To grant him such a Fort,
> Over whose Roof one drove a Loaden Cart;
> Better to bear his Castle on his back,
> Though it should crack,
> Than to be made a prey
> While he abroad did play,
> To every Grig, and Jack.
> Then thus aloud his Error he confest:
> I live in Walls impregnable, at Rest,
> While all my Friends with Tyrants are opprest. (132)

Again, like Davenant, constrained in body but free in mind: the Tortoise, as in stanza 2 of 'Upon Appleton House', represents the self-contained man, as it also did in the emblem-tradition. But in the next, No. 54, 'Of the Tortoise and the Eagle', the Tortoise's castle will be shattered as the Eagle drops him from a vast height. Frogs and Mice live in ponds and holes, and the Ants in No. 33 in caves, while the despised vagabond Fly makes temporary residence in palaces. Men live in houses, if they are lucky. A quarter of the 1651 illustrations are of interiors or have a house in the background; that to the Frog and Mouse features a ruined castle (mysteriously rebuilt in the revised 1668 plate) which may remind the reader that the Eagle Cromwell has just destroyed Raglan and others. Ogilby selects fables – or, more properly, selects more fables, as the collection is based around the first forty-five of the school *Aesop* – which portray common people, only occasionally gentry or professionals: Husbandman (4), Traveller, Forester (2), Rustic, Artist, Master, Young Man, *Egyptian* King, Dancing-Master (Ogilby signs himself in), Thief, Shepherd. Forty per cent of the illustrations

10 Wenceslaus Hollar, 'Of Cupid and Death'

have one or more human figures. A middle ground of something close to realism thus emerges, to link the range of varied tones and figures. In this ambience even a semi-emblematic fable such as 'Of Cupid and Death' may also be resonant of current historical conditions (see plate 10). Cupid and Death accidentally exchange arrows, so that the young people are slain while the old folk, 'their House clear'd', marry each other, or romp with 'one Leg . . . in Wanton Sheets, the other in the Grave' (94). This civil-war 'Tragicomedy' is another figuring of the world-upside-down, this time a touchingly sad and ludicrous one, an oblique expression of what must be one of the most common profound emotions of a country where men do not have to go away to fight: 'a land where parents bury their children', as Yitzhak Rabin said of Israel/Palestine (BBC Radio 4, 5:35 p.m., 13/9/93). There are very few examples of this in English literature.

Paralleling this tempering of the fantastical and heroic elements of the fables is the use of coded language, words which might have been designed to convey esoteric or hidden political messages, after the manner of so much writing in the Wars. Our enemies will not understand us if we speak like this amongst ourselves. But Ogilby, whose phrasing ranges from the heroic to the proverbial, uses only terms in common parlance among a wide, politically literate readership: Branch and Root, Ironsides, Malignants, Saints, Yea and Nea Men, Roses and Thistles, Master Speaker, Sequestration. Perhaps the best example of this ironically pointed but widely current politically allusive diction comes in No. 12. Lamenting the death of good king 'Frogmoreton' from No. 10 (one of Ogilby's innovations is to endow the fables with small narrative links, or to follow animals through a sequence, as with the Tortoise), the Frogs who Desire a King – until Jove sends them the predatory Stork – plead with the god to 'withdraw / *That cruel prince that made his Will a Law*' (32). The old proverb that 'the laws follow still the prince's will' – which Teresa Panza quotes in Part 2, chapter 5 of *Don Quixote* (1615), for instance – had suffered a recent sly shift in its English meaning. 'Those whose wills are laws' had meant primarily the parliamentary leaders since at least 1645, when the royalist musician William Lawes was killed at the siege of Chester, engendering the anonymous pun: Will Lawes was slain by those whose Wills were Laws. Marvell uses a subdued, maliciously tactful version of the joke in his skilfully managed almost-panegyric 'The First Anniversary of the Government under O.C'. (written 1655), in the course of his rewriting of Jotham's fable of the Olive, Bramble and Cedar / The Trees who Wanted a King.

Cromwell's 'climbing Flame' threatens a general conflagration of the whole forest:

> Therefore first growing to thy self a Law,
> Th'ambitious Shrubs thou in just time didst aw . . .
> And the large Vale lay subject to thy Will,
> Which thou but as an Husbandman wouldst Till
>
> (Marvell 1971: I, 115, 116)

But rather than planting the vine of liberty, as in Marvell's next line, Ogilby's 1651 Husbandman in the equivalent fable chops down the lot, the Cedar, Elmy Peers, Ash, Fir, Pine, and sacred Oak that speaks Dodon's oracles. 'Husbandman' in Marvell becomes even more dubious in the light of Ogilby's illustrations to the four fables that include this figure: in three he is wielding an axe with destructive intent, in the fourth he is killing the Birds he has caught in his net. Anything more disturbingly different from the original seventeenth-century point of reference of the word, John 15:1 – 'I am the true vine, and my father is the husbandman' – is hard to imagine.

The phrase later became a cliché for the proud usurper. 'His Will is Law', reflects the none-too-bright Atrides bluntly in Dryden's version of *Iliad* I, 'this proud Man [Achilles] affects Imperial Sway' (Dryden 1956–92: 4, 1594). Davenant, also aware of the joke, gracefully returns and complicates Ogilby's allusion in his own introductory verses, in the interests of claiming the moral and poetical high ground for the author:

> Laws doe in vain with force our wils invade;
> Since you can Conquer when you but Perswade.
>
> (Ogilby 1651: A5v)

The disavowal of a direct rhetorical strategy inherent in Ogilby's choice of fable as a mode (*fictis iocari nos meminerit fabulis*; see p. 69) leads to yet another silent semi-comical analogy, this time with the archetypal legislator – probably Moses, whose supposed access to the purity of primal language meant that he was capable, according to Rousseau and others, of 'constraining without violence and persuading without convincing' (Rousseau 1973: 216; *convince* is from *vincere*, to conquer). Aesop, with his 'translation' of the primeval language of animals, is metaphorically credited with a similar access.

This is, ostensibly, high ground with a royalist bias. But for Ogilby to cast Charles I implicitly as 'King Log', the first of the two monarchs in 'The Frogs desiring a King', is even less complimentary than casting Cromwell as the second, the rapacious Stork, even though the next fable, 'Of the Frog and Ox', apologetically transforms the log to the 'gracious Soveraign, mild King *Log*' (33). Once again, the Stuart monarch as wooden block has a vivid parallel in Marvell, anticipating his 1655 lines

> one Thing never was by one King don . . .
> Nor more contribute to the state of Things,
> Than wooden Heads unto the Viols strings.
>
> (Marvell 1971: 1, 109)

At this point in history both 'Royalist' and 'Parliamentarian' (Marvell was tutor to the daughter of Fairfax, the ex-parliamentarian general, from 1650, and M.P. for Hull after 1660) are sceptical and reserved in their attitudes, and their similar *paroles* and moods sometimes reflect this. But the two poets, though they are each bound to the moment and to a particular constituency, also manage to appeal tacitly to a readership beyond the immediate political fracas. There may also be closer connections: Marvell is responding to Davenant's *Gondibert* (1650) in 'Upon Appleton House', for instance.

It is not a question, though, of Ogilby being able to appeal either directly or indirectly for reconciliation, mediation, and redemptive wholeness, because such figures and messages had a provocative royalist bias where translators were concerned, just as Dryden's appeals for moderation in the late 1680s will be understood as provocative by Swift. Potter quotes the royalist Charles Cotton's proto-Eliotic poem, also from 1651, on Edward Prestwich's version of *Hippolytus*, 'where he imagines the translator, like Aesculapius with Hippolytus himself, breathing life into a dismembered corpse' (Potter 1989: 52).

> Hippolytus that erst was set upon
> By all, mangled by misconstruction,
> Dis-member'd by misprision, now by thee
> And thy ingenious chirurgerie
> Is re-united to his limbs, and grown
> Stronger as thine, than when great Theseus' son.
>
> (Cotton 1923: 402)

The body of the hero/text has been mangled by the competing voices of interpretation, the literary equivalent of the ranting and caterwauling brethren and their opponents. Now it is restored – 'translated' – to its exemplary condition, the king's child. But in Ogilby, whose history is more fractured and perhaps more representative than Cotton's, the double political voice of fable, at once slave and master, is extended to a deeply troubled and paradoxical scepticism over the value of distinct political and linguistic positions. There is no middle ground to occupy, no cool space of language in which lost children may be restored: Ogilby's response to the Quakers' reserved linguistic practices in 'Of the Sun and Wind' may look perverse, but it is in fact perfectly representative of the aggressive contemporary reactions to their desire to use a form of language which might be common to all men. When the Quaker Thomas Ellwood, Milton's amanuensis and the editor of Fox's *Journal*, put off the use of 'false titles' and addressed his father in the second person singular, the reply was equally strong: 'Sirrah, if ever I hear you say 'thou' or 'thee' to me again, I'll strike your teeth down your throat' (Ellwood 1900: 37–8).

Ogilby's pragmatism is at its most devious in the fable that he added to the end of the collection, to act as epimythium, in the folio edition of 1668: 'Of the Frogs Fearing the Sun Would Marry', the most startlingly doubled fable that he wrote.

The Frogs are Dutch, and the poem ostensibly a typical Restoration anti-Dutch satire. Ogilby dramatizes the recent phenomenal rise of the Dutch merchant marine:

> Are they with Force not able to invade?
> No matter; They'l undo the World by Trade:
> Four Frogs, two Tod-poles, and one greasy Toad
> Deep-freighted Bottoms bear from Road to Road. (207)

The Frogs gather in front of their smart new Stat-house to hear the dreadful news that the Sun will marry. Consternation! – a family of Suns will burn up their trade routes and boil away their bogs, but the statue of Neptune, visible in the illustration (see plate 11), comes to life at the end to tell them that their fears are foolish:

> Suspect no Conflagrations from the East;
> But a new Sun now rising in the West.
> His Flames beware, make Peace, or Arm with speed . . .
> He threatens my large Arms to bind in Chains,
> And now at Home a second Neptune Raigns;
> Who Three great Nations Swaies, and two fair Isles,
> His People Ruler of the Ocean stiles. (210)

In 1668 this should be a panegyrical compliment to Charles II, Ogilby's royal employer, after the manner of Dryden's heroicization of English naval power in the second Anglo-Dutch war in his *Annus Mirabilis* the

11 Wenceslaus Hollar, 'Of the Frogs Fearing the Sun Would Marry'

previous year. But a year makes a lot of difference. In June 1667 the Dutch had effectively brought this war to a close by sailing up the Medway and breaking the boom at Chatham harbour, where many ships lay unmanned for want of money to pay the crews. Four warships were burnt out, and the Dutch compounded the ignominy by pointedly sailing away with the *Royal Charles*, the ship that had brought Charles to Dover in 1660.

Far from being matter for panegyric, this fiasco was the central action described in Marvell's virulent anti-Stuart satire *Last Instructions to a Painter* (written 1667). And far from continuing in the heroic vein, Ogilby's enigmatic moral is couched as a rebuke or reproof to a 'Prince' whose notorious poverty had been partly responsible for the enforced inactivity of the British fleet in 1667, and whose ministers had been forced to make several concessions to the Dutch in the treaty of Breda:

> *Princes beware to Aid a Growing State.*
> *Lest they be first that give you the Check-Mate.*
> *Wealth and Success turns Humbleness to Pride:*
> *Beggars on Hors-Back to the Devil ride.* (211)

The supposed compliment to Charles becomes more curious still given that the *Royal Charles* was originally the *Naseby*, one of forty specialist warships built by Cromwell between 1649 and 1651, and named after his famous victory of 1645. His programme had effectively doubled the navy's strength, enabling it to win the first Anglo-Dutch War two years after the 1651 *Fables*. In other words, Ogilby's compliment was originally addressed not to Charles but *to Cromwell*: the reference to three nations and two islands is very pointedly about Cromwell's Irish campaign of 1649–50 and his overwhelming victory at Dunbar in September 1650. It seems that this is one of those not infrequent occasions when a poet plays a game of double-bluff with Charles, offering criticism disguised as panegyric – not exactly mock-panegyric, but 'praise that mocks praise, the sententiousness which mocks itself as satire' (Nokes 1995: 383), as Nokes says of one of Gay's fables – while at the same time flattering any reader, including Charles, witty enough to penetrate the design.

So the fable was written in 1651 but kept back from publication, and then revised for application in 1668, when it was allowed to stand, as final fable, as epimythium to the collection. At this point Neptune's compliment to Charles has a very disconcerting double face, one panegyrical, the other ironical: just enough trace of its origin is left visible to ensure that the fable sits warily in a middle ground which is even more complicated than that of the rest of the collection.

It is too quiet an effect to be active satire. Four years later, in 1672, when the balance of naval power was more even, the fable could be safely republished on its own as *The Holland Nightingale*, and be understood as a straightforwardly patriotic anti-Dutch piece: the single, or single-handed reading. But in the 1668 edition, the punctuative or structural effect of this final fable is akin to those of Phaedrus's collection and the closing fables of eighteenth-century novels. Like them, it expresses a double-edged combination of elements, secure and resolved finality (claptrap patriotism, in this case) together with a teasing hint that the reader might review the collection, or the novel, in a quite different frame of mind. Standing both inside and against the structure, it operates paradoxically both for the author as master-contriver of the work, the favourite of the King (Cosmographer Royal) and premier fabulist of the day, and for the author as slave-subversive, the disillusioned sceptic, satirist, and mere fabulist. Again, fable as lawyer; fable as cheat.

OGILBY TO DRYDEN, 1651–1687

Until the explosive events of 1687, the development of English literary fable is confined to a slow proliferation of minor verse collections, several of which defer to Ogilby, who remains the main English voice. This throws a good deal of stress on to his extensions of the function and scope of fable in his second collection, the 1668 *Aesopics*, which he published together with the revised *Fables*.

In the *Aesopics*, the subtle mood of sub-heroic lament and disquiet in the 1651 collection is immediately replaced by the establishment of a transparent politico-mythological framework, adjusted in line with the post-Restoration feeling of confidence and celebration characteristic of the early and mid-1660s. Jove is no longer a criminal usurper of Heaven, but is instead 'crown'd in Starrie Robes' and in due process, after 'the summon'd Gods a Council held' – 'Old *Saturn* fain, cov'nanting Gyants slain, / Government chang'd, began your Silver Raign' (Ogilby 1668[b]: 2; subsequent references to the *Aesopics* will be to this edition and will cite page numbers only). At the same time, there is the strong reservation in 'Silver', to any reader who remembers the opening lines of 'The Parliament of Birds'. The subtle but direct hint that history may be capable of repeating itself, that the natural consequence of another Silver Age is another Age of Iron, adds the note of caution or suspicion that was becoming characteristic of responses to Charles II and his policies in the later 1660s. This hint becomes more pointed when one learns from Howard Erskine-Hill (1983: 216) that the line from Virgil, 'Redeunt Saturnia Regna', which had appeared on one of the triumphal arches at James I's 1603 coronation procession, had been similarly used by Ogilby in 1661 for Charles's procession. The motto praises the king directly as Saturn, the original ruler of the Golden Age. Yet again the fabulist answers one of his other voices in fable.

It is a very shrewd and sardonic rewriting, but for the moment the note of confidence holds. Cromwell can now be named and characterized directly as the 'cursed curr' in 'Of the Oxe and Dog in the Manger' (4). Fables which speak poorly of royal beasts are pointedly recast, so that The Lion's Share (in its non-Phaedrian version) becomes 'Leopard, Fox and Ass', with the Leopard as 'Master of the Royal Game'. The confident and expansive tones of the openings of the 1651 *Fables* are now sustained throughout: the Leopard warns the Ass, at the end, 'But he who e're to this fat Buck pretends / Had better, *Dam Me*, eat his Trotters ends' (7). A difficult notion, until one sees that the fables have absorbed some of the dramatic gestures that go with the vivid new style of Restoration stage comedy. The Leopard is asking potential 'pretenders' to mimic the putting of four fingers in the mouth nails upward, expressive of fear – or rather, he is asking an Ass to mimic a theatrical gesture which would mimic the emotion of fear. Animals, actors, human beings, is the natural hierarchy. ' 'Tis dangerous to deal with Hect'ring Lords', warns the moral of the next (8), but the fables themselves are all in jocular, slightly overbearing pentameter rather than the teasingly varied lines of the *Fables*. Even the little Crab in 'Of the Crab and Her Mother' has the face to quote her own author shrilly to her Mother, so keen is she to acquire the social grace of genteel ambulation: 'Examples are best Precepts, Talk's but talk: / Leave finding fault, and Shew me how to Walk' (20). But alas, the Crab family is, to quote L'Estrange's version, 'just in from the Shires' (L'Estrange, 1692; 221) and even Mother's style of walking is a trifle oblique and rustic. Like mother, like daughter, is the moral, with the rider that the conventional exemplarity of fable may on occasion be its satiric target.

The mythological framework and epic themes of the first collection are then quickly replaced by a vivid account of the professions, entertainments, and changing fashions and fortunes of London after 'The King's happy Restauration' (50). Peacocks wear livery; we hear of Mincing-Lane, the Strand, Whitehall, the rebuilding of St Paul's after the great fire, the Puritan Calves-Head Club. The entertainments are often literary or theatrical: Ogilby's Fox wheedles the cheese from the Crow's mouth by flattering her that she is beautiful enough to sing before the King and be his 'White Crow': 'I thought you Black, when in a Mourning Gown / And Vizard-mask you lately came to Town' (18).

12 Wenceslaus Hollar, 'Of the Swan and Stork'

White Crows can sing, as we know from Chaucer. Fashion becomes costume; the action of fable, acting, or talking about acting, or duplicity. 'Nell' herself appears in No. 8, 'Of the Swan and Stork', the *tour de force* of the collection. The ex-Republican Stork is now doing better than the Royalist Swan under the new régime, and obligingly explains to him how it is done: 'Then said the Stork, Birds of my Coat and Feather, / Like Steeple-Cocks, turn round with wind and weather' (12). And indeed his coat is now at least as beautiful as the Swan's, and more modish (see plate 12). In his new garb he visits theatres and buys fine literature, all of which he is keen to discuss at length. But the Swan, now shabby-genteel and almost as thin as the Puritan Ox, 'Praise-Jove Bare-bones', in 'Of the Ox and Steer', is not impressed with the state of affairs that has occasioned this reversal, and expresses the residual satirical function of the fable in a plaintive, *dégagé* tone. The fault lies at the top: 'King's Chambers open lye', so that 'Daws, Rooks, and Owls' (13) are now admitted among the noble birds. A remonstrance to Charles's promiscuous ennoblings of his favourites and mistresses: the King may be genuinely Jovial as well as Ogilby's patron, but this does not exempt the more notorious of his policies and habits from becoming targets. The thin Ox is rewarded for his Puritan austerity by seeing the predatory, sarcastic Wolf and Fox, the 'Lion's Purveyors', snatch the plump, bantering, upper-crust Steer rather than himself, so this is a world where there are dangers in getting above yourself, and Puritanism is not necessarily to be disdained, even by the Royal Cosmographer.

However, the most significant aspect of the *Aesopics* is its movement away from the early semi-satirical mode, through the socialized fables, to the two long, digressive verse narratives, 'Androcleus, or the Roman Slave' – an extended version of the tale usually known as Androcles and the Lion – and 'The Ephesian Matron; or Widow's Tears'. The Ephesian Matron is the story of the notoriously virtuous noble widow who watches and fasts over her beloved husband's corpse in a sepulchre, in great distress. She is then consoled by the company, food, and what Sterne would call *some other things* of a soldier who is put to guard another corpse. So effectively is she consoled that when someone steals the corpse for which he is responsible she allows him to replace it with her husband's body, in order that he should escape being hanged for dereliction of duty while doing his consoling.

These two stories occupy the final third of the *Aesopics.* They are generally supposed to have originated in narrative episodes by Aulus Gellius and in Petronius's *Satyricon* respectively, but both are Phaedrian fables. The first appears in a collection of Phaedrian paraphrases, the second in the text known as 'Perotti's Appendix', which contains some thirty-three fables and fragments transcribed by a humanist scholar from a defective manuscript of Phaedrus, now lost, in the early Renaissance. Caxton printed both of them as fables, and they were then retold many times in different forms.

Their importance in the *Aesopics* and for the later track of fable is multiple, and begins with Ogilby's selection and treatment of what are, in terms of the rest of the collection, two very odd stories. Neither is set in a recognizably social world like that of the previous fables, neither is English in application, neither is, as given, satirical. Each, in fact, has an element of the sentimental ethos of some eighteenth-century fables. William Cowper later subtitled his version of Androcles 'Reciprocal Kindness the Primary Law of Nature'. The Ephesian Matron may be told in such a way as to imply satirical comment on the fickleness of virtuous women – La Fontaine's sardonic moral in 1682 is 'Mieux vaut Goujat debout qu'Empereur enterré' (La Fontaine 1991: 513) – better a live oaf than a dead emperor – but Ogilby's story concentrates on the recuperative powers of human nature in distress, and on the paradoxical effects of the harmonizing of extreme and self-destructive emotions, as does 'Androcleus'.

More important is their form, and the suggestion of kinship between fable and narrative, particularly fable and epic, at a point in time where such relations were about to be discussed with some seriousness. Ogilby is not a critic, but in a form that works under the motto of 'Examples are best Precepts', practice will carry its own point. His 'Androcleus' is an episodic, semi-Ovidian, semi-Reynardian beast-epic, and in its treatment of the passions, almost a mini-beast-*Iliad.* The Ephesian Matron is, beside this extraordinary performance, a more straightforward narrative.

The traditional fable of Androcles and the Lion occupies only the final three of Ogilby's thirty-one narrative units or episodes, which tell the story of Androcleus and the speaking animals among which he finds himself. The Lion was once a man, a ruler with a family and a menagerie, and he rehearses the story of his transformation. He killed his wife's lover, who had drugged him and sewn him up in a lion's skin, with such horrific violence that he was changed into the animal shape of his passion. In this form he escaped, was captured, tamed, and taught to play genteelly on stage with his master, imitating Hesperian fables such as Mars and Venus. In an intriguing and quite deliberate reworking of the paradoxes of fable and romance, the slave-animal gains a kind of power that the master-human lacked, and a reflexive consciousness of his curious thespian passional expression and self-control (*paradoxe du comédien*) through which to speak the paradox: 'Thus I my Passions rul'd, commanding more / Than when I Govern'd Men or Beasts before' (161). So the story, like 'The Ephesian Matron', modulates between the strange violence of destructive natural passions and the even stranger forms that the harmonization of such passions can take. Any moral lies somewhere in this ebb and flow, rather than being specified at any point; an effect amplified by the story's episodic nature.

This is also a good description of some of Dryden's central interests and structural procedures, in his 1700 *Fables*. The clearest example of the 'Madness' of the passions being curiously controlled by art would be 'Alexander's Feast', that of the bizarre sociable transformations of love, the bearish 'man-beast' Cymon licked into shape by the mere sight of the beauty of Iphigenia: 'More fam'd for Sense, for courtly Carriage more, / Than for his brutal Folly known before' (Dryden 1962: 821). Whenever possible, Dryden aggravates the negative emotions of his protagonists so as to stress their uncontrollable and elemental nature. The nobility of the wrath and grief of the Homeric gods at the start of the *Iliad*, for instance, is shifted towards a reiterated 'Fury' or 'Turbulence of Mind' which can also approach, via personification, the level of an abstraction. Achilles, whose

> . . . Heart, impetuous in his Bosom boil'd,
> And justled by two Tides of equal sway,
> Stood, for a while, suspended in his way,
> Betwixt his Reason, and his Rage untam'd;
> One whisper'd soft, and one aloud reclaim'd. (*ibid*.: 667)

Pallas, sent by Juno, tries but fails to 'calm' his mind: the only effective mental control in the poem now belongs to the poet, twining together elemental forces, emotions, and personified abstractions in a subtle braid of metamorphosis.

This coincidence of mode and theme derives from common interests in epic and political philosophy, together with Dryden's professional concerns in criticism. Ogilby had translated the *Iliad* and the *Odyssey* earlier in the 1660s, and the first book of the *Iliad* features, as above, amongst Dryden's *Fables*. It was originally intended, according to a comment in the Preface, as 'an Essay to the whole Work' (520) that is, to a full translation of the *Iliad*. Neoclassical critics from the 1670s on became embarrassed by the roughness and casual violence of epic, particularly the Homeric poems. One reaction was to expose them to burlesque; another was to try to dignify them for a politer audience by arguing that they were allegorical in form and intention, and hence moral. Fulgentius had already provided a model for this, allegorizing the first half of the *Æneid* as the mind acquiring moral wisdom and control over its passional impulses. It was widely felt that the general moral of epic must be the need for the good government of the passions and the will, as an analogue to or metaphor of the necessity for moderation and consensus in political affairs both national and international. This moral Dryden partly articulates in the 1697 'Dedication to the *Æneis*' (1956–92: 3, 1011), though he does not refer to it again in the Preface to the *Fables*, which contain parts of the *Iliad*, probably being aware that emollient morals about moderation and consensus from those in opposition to William were now widely interpreted as a form of surreptitious political manoeuvering. Swift, in his early satires, is particularly irritated by Dryden and L'Estrange, and refuses to allow that those 'who having spent their Lives in Faction, and Apostacies' (Swift 1958[a]: 3), can offer such disingenuous statements of neutrality and semi-retired disengagement and be taken at face value.

Read in terms of this supposed general moral, Book I of the *Iliad* acts as a double or treble promythium to the fable of the whole work, so that Dryden's reference to Book I as an 'Essay' might also indicate 'key' or 'plan'. First, Pallas calls to Achilles for calm; then Nestor's longsighted admonitory speech to Achilles and Atrides talks of the 'youthful Passions' and 'private Int'rest' of the heroes' quarrel wrecking the Greeks' corporate war-effort (Dryden 1962: 669). By itself this is just a homily, but at the end of Book I Hephaestus makes a parallel point in the equally strife-torn world of the gods, telling Juno that she has both private and social reasons not to provoke Jove, who at this point is tired and emotional, and on a short fuse:

> Not only you provoke him to your Cost,
> But Mirth is marr'd, and the good Chear is lost.
> . . . one submissive Word, which you let fall,
> Will make him in good Humour with us All. (*ibid.*: 679)

This paralleling suggests an unspoken running metaphor or structural analogy between the higher and lower worlds of the *Iliad*, a figure alluringly close to fable's analogical correspondences between man and beast, man and gods, and also between the microcosms of the stories and the macrocosms of social and political applications. So epic and fable might be in the same relationship as Olympus and the Trojan plain: and if epic is like fable it must *be* moral, rather than just containing morals.

This conclusion of kinship between the two forms can be reached by systematic reasoning of this kind, and by then supposing that allegoresis is the proper method of enquiry in interpreting epic narrative. But it can also be reached more simply and directly by recalling the example of 'The Parliament of Birds', No. 40 in Ogilby's 1651 collection, which was one of the pair that Dryden adapted in *The Hind and the Panther*. Ogilby was probably reasonably well versed in the connections between allegory and epic which had been developed through the Renaissance, but he applies the supposed *moral of epic* quite naturally in some of his fables, as part of his sense of possible reconciliation and of the dangers of faction. As with Achilles and Atrides, it is the 'private Interest' of the Linnet that leads to the destruction of the commonwealth of Birds, as the epimythium reminds the reader: 'private Interest blinds / The wisest, and betraies the Noblest, Minds' (Ogilby 1668[a]: 100). Several of the fables that follow continue this stress. The Bear in No. 44, 'Of the Bear and Bees', who is stung by 'a too waspish Bee' (*ibid.*: 107), beseiges the 'Waxen Cities' of the hives in search of revenge but is overcome, and ends by reflecting on the folly of 'Making a Private Quarrel National' (107, 108). At the end of No. 47, 'Of the Rebellion of the Hands and Feet', the Hands moralize to the dying Feet about the effects of the choleric insurrection of the members, the 'Levellers', against the Belly, now that Reason 'once King', is 'Depos'd, and dead'. 'All that are Members in a Common-Wealth, / Should, more than Private, aim at Publick Health' (114, 116) – a more grown-up socialist sentiment than one might find even in most twentieth-century British socialism, let alone seventeenth-century, though Ogilby is also approaching Paul's reworking of this fable in 1 Corinthians 12: 'there should be no schism in the body; but that the members should have the same care one for another'.

As so often, Ogilby's phrasing and topic here are also adapted from current political philosophy and debate. Hobbes, to use the example most pertinent to this fable, argues in *Leviathan* 2, 19 that 'in Monarchy, the private interest is the same with the publique', but that a ruler of lesser stature will 'for the most part, if the publique interest chance to cross the private, [prefer] the private: for the Passions of men, are more commonly more potent than their Reason' (Hobbes 1973: 98). But the heroic elements of Ogilby's style, and the stress in both Nos. 40 and 47 on the factiousness of minor powers, help to suggest the epic context. Such transference between forms feels quite unselfconscious and appropriate, so that fable and epic are brought together much more delicately and suggestively than will be the case with the later neoclassical critics. As they are also, if in a different way, in 'Androcleus'. It is of course very interesting that the 'monarchist' Ogilby pointedly rewrites the phrasing of Hobbes's rather blunt 1650 argument for absolute power in such a way as to argue for a case that has such a different tone to it. In Ogilby's world, although men like the Husbandman may be ruled by their passions, a moralistic member like the Hand can, with the benefit of experience, argue against private, factional passions and for a fair social ideal.

Dryden was far too skilled in the cunning and plausible use of structural figures ever to credit that epic could be reduced to allegory, and he is always concerned that his readers have to ask themselves questions about the ways in which his *Fables* 'signify'. Rather than applying simple allegorical techniques, he contents himself with repeatedly tweaking the reader's nose with small verbal suggestions that his material may bear this or that moral or political application, or with allowing the contemporary context of thought to affect the application silently, as Ogilby does with Hobbes. The effect of Hephaestus's words to Juno, for instance, is conditioned to some extent by late seventeenth-century proto-feminist applications of the recent Whig arguments about the legitimacy of resistance to tyrannical rulers: such applications of political argument to family relationships were, briefly, taken quite seriously. It is an amusingly reflexive moment, as what Hephaestus is, in effect, pointing out is that emollient professions of domestic moderation and agreement may be a form of surreptitious political manoeuvering: the gods defuse the possible charge against Dryden by applying the moral in the semi-comic context of coping with a drunken leader. As with Ogilby's narrative fables, the *Iliad* becomes just another narrative in which tumultuous passions are activated, in part managed, and commented on in a discontinuous, highly responsive, Ovidian system of changing shapes and forces. More like a fable than an epic, in other words.

The multifunctional nature of Augustan fable is succinctly illustrated by the history of the only other verse collection of note before the appearance of the *Aesopics* in 1668. This was the polyglot English, French, and Latin *Aesop's Fables* originally published by Francis Barlow in 1666, and adorned with 112 of his 'sculptures' or decorative illustrations. Barlow's intention was to upgrade the basic pedagogic fable-collections, in order to appeal to the private, newly prosperous audience beyond the schools, which were now suffering from 'widespread degeneration . . . and lack of trust in them' (Noel 1975: 6). For the first time, fables were used to further the study of another vernacular. The text is weighted towards

French, with each verso page having the fable, and a lengthy account of the fable's moral and possible applications, in French prose. Latin prose and brief English verse versions of the fable lie under the illustration on each facing page. The format and production values, particularly the amount of space devoted to the prose morals, are strikingly akin to those of the classic pedagogical French editions of Aesop, 'Baudoin's' *Fables d'Ésope phrygien traduites et moralisées* (1631), and Audin's *Fables héroïques comprenant les véritables maximes de la politique chrétienne et de la morale* (1648). Barlow's collection is the first penetration of the more dignified, respectable ethos of French teaching fable into English culture.

It might be expected that a reworking of pedagogical French *Aesops*, with their sonorous and detached morals, for primarily linguistic purposes would be politically neutral, but French, with its associations with the upper class, the court, and Catholicism, had a particular resonance which was soon exploited. Some of the English fables in Barlow's revised edition of 1687 are attributed to the loyal Aphra Behn, who was given the remit of shortening the fables to six lines each, two couplets for the fable and one for the moral. In several cases the moral is given a very specific political slant, designed to reconcile opinion to, or to moralize on, the failure and bloody aftermath of Monmouth's recent rebellion, and by implication to warn against any future mutiny against James II – the collection was printed by the king's printer, Henry Hills: Judith Sloman, pressing the point, refers to it as the 'Catholic Aesop' (Sloman 1985: 159). Monmouth is the Dog in No. 80 who sees in a stream the reflection of the meat he is carrying in his mouth, and

> To catch the shadow lets the substance fall.
>
> So fancy'd crownes led the young warriour on
> Till loosing all he found himself undone. (Barlow 1703: 161)

Dryden's Hind uses the same fable more wittily, perhaps too wittily, in the course of her defence to the Panther of the Catholic belief in the bodily and literal, rather than figurative, presence of Christ in the Eucharist – James's religion as well as Dryden's:

> For *real*, as you now the Word expound,
> From solid substance dwindles to a sound.
> Methinks an *Aesop's* fable you repeat,
> You know who took the shadow for the meat.
> (Dryden 1956–92: 2, 486)

An argument against figuration delivered in highly figurative language: a piece of wit from the mother Church which alludes to the body of Christ as 'meat'. The fact that the shadow/substance opposition, which comes so pat in a discussion of transubstantiation, is shared with a fable in the 'Catholic Aesop' seems to be the only justification for the Hind's amazing lapse of taste. Both these fables derive from 'Of the Dog and Shadow' in Ogilby, where 'The Shadow and the Substance, like a Dream / Vanished' (Ogilby 1668[a]: 3). It is further testimony to Ogilby's continuing authority as fabulist that all of Behn's anti-Monmouth fables are also found among the eighty-one of Ogilby's 1651 collection. There are many other echoes and similarities of application – Behn's Bear, in No. 86, 'The Bear and Bee-Hives', 'grieves, his private fewd prov'd nationall' (Barlow 1703: 173), just as did Ogilby's. Co-opting a major fabulist for narrowly political ends because of his general political reputation quickly became standard practice, as the cases of Dryden and L'Estrange will make clear. In Behn's version of Ogilby's 'Battle of the Frog and Mouse', Monmouth is figured in the bird's two victims: 'The fond aspiring youth who empire sought / By dire ambition was to ruine brought' (Barlow 1703: 71). He is also the 'late pittyed president' (*ibid.*: 49) of No. 24 – possible popular feeling in 1686 is briefly acknowledged – as well as the Snake killed by the Countryman in No. 50, with its wider implacable moral: 'Mercy extended to ungratefull men / Does but impower em to rebell agen' (*ibid.*: 101). He is even the girl transformed back into her natural shape of Cat, in The Young Man and His Cat: 'Ill principles no mercy can reclaime, / And once a Rebell still will be the same' (*ibid.*: 143). This is even more disconcerting than finding such stark political morals insinuated into a 'teaching' *Aesop*, or disconcerting in a different way, because the fable does not fit the case, and the fond youth, who has elsewhere (*ibid.*: 71) represented Monmouth, is not part of the figure as he should be. But Behn is as little concerned about discontinuity as is the other 'Catholic' fabulist, Dryden: her version of 'The Two Potts', for example, manages to suggest two applications in six lines:

> Two Potts (of Earth and Brass) at distance swim,
> The first of lighter burden cuts the stream,
> The Brass entreats her stay, but she reply'd
> No, thines too rough to touch my tender side.
>
> Mix not with those whose wealth for thines too great
> To keep an equal pace with them thou't break. (169)

This was all too much for Charles Montague, especially as 'brass' and 'brazen' were two epithets commonly applied to the notoriously obdurate and notoriously Catholic James II by his antagonists. In early 1688 Montague retaliated by in turn co-opting Behn's fable for his innovative 'Story of the Pot and the Kettle', the first of the new breed of incidental or occasional political verse fables (there are none in *POAS* before this, and Bush (1965: 21) finds none in the periodicals before 1692). Montague's poem is very witty in its subtle use of inversions of social tone and poetical wording for political ends. His upper-class brass Kettle is threatened with inundation in a boisterous river – a good metaphor for the situation, and also proleptically ironic, as James would be sneaking away to escape to France just a few months later, flinging the Great Seal of England into the Thames as he went, in a fit of pique. The Kettle addresses the lower-class earthen Pot (Colonel Titus and the Dissenters: James had just invited Titus, a Presbyterian, to join the Privy Council) with open patrician vowels but duplicitous professions of social equality:

> Come, brother, why should we divided lose
> The strength of union and ourselves expose
> To the insults of this poor, paltry stream . . .
>
> (Lord 1963–75: 4, 234)

But the less rhetorical Pot retorts with forceful consonants, a neat social inversion or paradox of its own which echoes Behn's fable as part of its irony, and a charming pun on constitutions physical and political: 'Such different natures never will agree; / Your constitution is too rough for me' (*ibid.*). It also translates the 'paltry stream' back into 'waves', 'billows', and 'tide': the Kettle has been underplaying the potential dangers, as well as 'slyly' appealing to the Pot as a class-equal. The moral, to the Whigs, is to forego the proffered alliance: 'For know that you are clay, and they are brass' (*ibid.*). Outside fable this would be a toffee-nosed insult: here, it points out that where James may well be sinking rapidly, the lighter Whigs are quite capable of swimming on their own, so that the jest modulates cheekily between effrontery and flattery. As political satire in the 1680s it is remarkably couth and even-handed, as a reading of the previous seventy or so pages of *POAS* 4, with their unremitting obscenity, violences of tone, and naming of bodily parts, would confirm. As such it operates as a remonstrance in literary as well as political terms, in much the same way as Montague's joint effort with Prior against Dryden does. Its suave and jocular continuity contrasts with Behn's vivacious but fractured version, and its classic restraint and double-handedness mock the sourness of her blunt polemical morals. Really it is not satire at all but a self-contained illustrative episode or rhetorical persuasion which elegantly borrows satirical attitude from the wider social context, in the silent 'application' of a common epithet for James.

Barlow's collection was then sufficiently popular in the more genteel English fable-culture of the eighteenth century to act as an influence on the furniture-makers Thomas Johnson and Thomas Chippendale, when mid-century taste turned towards the ornamental French mode. French decorative arts, porcelain, delft, tapestry, and ornamental sculpture, had been using Aesopian motifs since the mid-seventeenth century: the labyrinth in the gardens at Versailles was adorned with fountains in the form of Aesopian motifs, for instance. Louis clearly wanted to appropriate the political iconography of fable in the same way that Elizabeth and her loyal subjects had appropriated emblem. English designers now took these motifs to be natural companions for *chinoiserie* and mythical scenes. Both Johnson and Chippendale used Aesopian decorations in their designs for that least utilitarian or morally justifiable of ornamental objects, the *girandole* (see plate 13). Chippendale's designs for these are so fanciful and delicate that very few were actually made. Johnson, for example, transposes Barlow's illustration of 'The Fox and the Cat' 'from two dimensions into three to form the underframing of a console table' (Gloag 1968: 362).

The history of Barlow's collection thus illustrates in miniature several of the characteristic stages of development of the English verse fable. Its origins in the school *Aesop* are plain, but its format reflects the *gravitas* and cultural elevation of the French teaching collections. Behn's repointing of the English verses, and the silent alignment of the fables with Ogilby's, illustrates the reactive quality of the narrowly political English fable. Montague's reaction in turn illustrates the combination of oppositional qualities, tonal even-handedness, and jocular manipulation of social paradox characteristic of fable in its fullest development. Significantly, it is the only poem of any quality generated by the collection, a high-class artefact directed against the highest class. Then its later history takes the collection more straightforwardly to the heights of fashion, ornament and gentility.

In the 1690s and 1700s, though, the adaptation of French fables, whether from the 'teaching' *Aesops* as with Behn and John Toland, or from La Fontaine as with John Dennis and Mandeville, always has a combative edge to it which reflects the embattled English fable-culture

13 Thomas Chippendale, design for a *girandole*, featuring Fox and Grapes

of the period. That two little French 'teaching' fables pass from pedagogical solemnity in Barlow to Montague's quicksilver political wit and Dryden's extraordinarily provoking exposition of Catholic doctrine in a couple of years is a good illustration of a much wider process. English fable defines itself against the French; what was neutral or 'easy' in French is converted into an oblique exposition of freethinking principles in Toland, or into using the 'Easie and Familiar' (Mandeville 1703: titlepage, and 1714: Preface) Fontainean style for preparing the ground for *The Grumbling Hive.*

In particular, La Fontaine's mode was never translated directly and transparently into English. Throughout the period his fables were conventionally seen as 'Inimitable' (*GJ* January 1691–2: 23, and Lockman 1744: 2, for example), a double-edged adjective for any translator hoping for even the freest form of translation. The problems involved in the translation of La Fontaine are at their clearest in John Hall-Stevenson's interrogation of his own mode in 1762, bantering his English readers and fellow-fabulists with their perennial inability to accommodate the verse, moral, and social freedoms of his model:

> I very readily excuse
> Your want of complaisance
> To my strange Muse,
> Dress'd in the careless dress of France
> À la Fontaine
> A slattern, but quite plain.
>
> According to your notions,
> You must dislike the flimsy wench.
> Her dress and all her motions
> Are so intolerably French;
> A graceless copy of a graceless hobbler,
> Just like a gouty shoe made by a cobbler.
>
> (Hall-Stevenson 1762: 45)

The primary model of polite French fable after 1720 is not La Fontaine but La Motte, whose conservative but highly attractive verse fables took just two years to be translated into English prose in their entirety by the excellent Robert Samber, whereas it took La Fontaine's a hundred and twenty to be translated, in France, by a very indifferent hand. S. H. Daniel's assertion that L'Estrange and Croxall were the focal figures in an English attempt to combine the literary grace of fable-writing, 'as found, for example, in the works of La Fontaine . . . with a popular and often political appeal' (Daniel 1982: 153) is bizarre partly for its ascription of semi-Fontainean grace to the gruff, buttonholing prose of L'Estrange. It also underestimates the exent to which translation from the French had, especially between 1690 and 1720, a natural, silent, political resonance which is still audible in a historically aware fabulist such as Hall-Stevenson. The meaning of 'translation' is often – as with Ogilby and Cotton – translateable in turn, in this century: to continue the French connection of the 1760s, the chapter of Sterne's *A Sentimental Journey* which is headed 'The Translation' is concerned partly with supposed cultural differences between England and France, but also with translating the hieroglyphs of gesture into language. Conspicuously, it does not translate French into English. So as usual, fable's 'politics' involve responses to modes of discourse, voices, *paroles*, not just policies; and such resonances and responses can now be explored in parts of the following chapter.

CHAPTER 6

Transitions: Dryden to Mandeville

Before 1687, only a few extended verse narratives such as those in Ogilby's *Aesopics* had picked up the hints of possible connections between apologue, episodic narrative, and illustrative digression already offered by more theoretical writers such as Bacon. In *The Tragedies of the Last Age* (1678) Thomas Rymer echoed Ben Jonson's description at the end of his *Timber* (1641) of the competing neoclassical notion that 'fable' could also mean *mythos*, the single unified action of the plot, but clearly Rymer was also still thinking in the same derogatory English way about the term as Dryden did four years earlier when faced with *The Empress of Morocco*. 'Now if you call this a Fable', he says when dealing with the vagaries of *Rollo, Duke of Normandy*, 'give me one of old *Aesop's*' (Rymer 1678: 19). Fable also meant fiction in general, and myth, and a lie. So there were many competing definitions of fable, but relatively little application of them.

After and even during 1687, everything changed. Fable was suddenly a live issue, and so it was to remain through fifteen years of political and cultural change which diversified the form rapidly, transmitting it to the eighteenth century as an activity with several different potential audiences and areas of application. Fable in general quickly developed into a mode which, as in Ogilby, links art of different kinds, high and low, verse and narrative, heroic and scurrilous. At the end of the century, in the middle of the battle between the Ancients and Moderns in which Aesop figured as one of the main bones of contention, fable was redefined in the light of all these developments by Dryden, in his extremely popular and influential *Fables Ancient and Modern*. One of the aims of this chapter is to provide a context in which this work can be briefly discussed with a critical fiction of transparency, as a natural product of a poet whose working life coincides almost exactly with the history of modern English literary fable to date. The three most important stages in this process are the changes in Dryden's use of fable between *The Hind and the Panther* and the 1700 *Fables*; Roger L'Estrange's collection in prose of 1692; and the series of English reactions to French fable.

THE HIND AND THE PANTHER AND ITS AFTERMATH

The Hind and the Panther was read widely, with three London editions in 1687, and one each in Dublin and Edinburgh – this last printed under James II's aegis at Holyrood, at the press set up by L'Estrange in 1686 in order to persuade the Scottish Parliament to repeal the Tests. This connection reinforced the more recent royalist associations of fable established by Hills's printing of Barlow. But the universal public reaction was enthusiastic derision. Dryden had published a poetic defence of his Anglicanism only five years earlier, in *Religio Laici*, but now he was writing an outlandish apology for his new Catholic faith, and defending the increasingly indefensible James II, just one year before James's ignominious departure for France. Responses were various; in a very few years the culture of English fable included parody of Dryden; reactive occasional fables such as Montague's 'The Pot and the Kettle'; small-scale verse collections of satirical, political fables; large politically oriented collections in prose and verse; episodic narrative, in L'Estrange's *Fables and Storyes Moraliz'd* (1699), and indeed in Dryden's *Fables Ancient and Modern*; and discussions of what fable was, or should be. Dryden in 1687 is a main catalyst in the creation of modern English fable, in both its narrower and wider manifestations.

The literary vehicle of *The Hind and the Panther* is a tissue of absorbing discontinuities which appear to mimic its concerns in political and religious controversy. Paradoxes of Christian faith and Catholic doctrine are discussed in the paradoxes and metamorphoses of fable, with speaking animals debating such topics as the incarnate godhead, the Three in One, and the 'dumb Scripture', the Catholic belief in the superiority of oral tradition to the written books of the Bible. Such concerns and beliefs are, as was seen briefly with de Certeau in chapter 1 above, remarkably close to some of the concerns and metaphors of fable. Christ, who teaches 'not as the scribes' (Matthew 7:29), speaks his pastoral paradoxes from the Mount – 'Blessed are the meek: for they shall inherit the earth' (Matthew 5:5) – as the unlettered Aesop and his low animals speak theirs from the fields and forests. To a newly converted poet accustomed to fable, it would seem natural to embody doctrinal matters through the conversation of its creatures, especially through two that are also among the standard dozen of the *Physiologus*. But anyone who thought that 'fable' meant the lies of pagan religions, and/or a 'single unified action', would have been horrified.

Like Chaucer's 'Maunciple's Tale', Dryden's poem suggests a bewilderingly wide range of possible definitions of fable, mixing extended narrative, beast-debate, prosopopoeia, illustrative interpolated anecdote or episode, malicious satire, mysterious truth, personal feeling, doctrinal argument, political prophecy, allegory, apologue for brief witty reference within the poem, apologue for glancing allusion by the poet. Provokingly, the new neoclassical meaning is the only one that does not apply. Dryden seems able to forget that some uses of fable were laughably oldfashioned, some perennially respectable, some novel. Spenser's bizarre and outdated 'mother Hubbard' (Dryden 1956–92: 3, 504; references to Dryden, other than to the *Fables*, are to this edition and will cite volume and page number) can be invoked as unselfconsciously as can Aesop. Literary time blurs: the historical moment is addressed through literary techniques some of which are, like the material of the religious discord that presses upon the present, '*as old . . . as the Times of* Boccace *and* Chawcer *on the one side, and as those of the Reformation on the other*' (3, 470).

In one sense there is, again, a simple rationale behind this procedure, but the effect is extremely unsettling, with the timeless and the moment, the abstract, the historical, and the personal, uneasily dissolved into each other. For example, near the start of Part 3, the final section of the poem, Dryden reminds his readers of the reasons why the Catholic Hind need not fear her 'dangerous guest', the Anglican Panther:

> Let those remember that she cannot dye
> Till rolling time is lost in round eternity;
> Nor need she fear the Panther, though untam'd,
> Because the Lyon's peace was now proclam'd. (504)

This moment anticipates a wider structural movement from the relatively Olympian doctrinal debates of the earlier sections to the historically conditioned and embroiled present and future tenses of the part to come. The beasts are to take on personae and moods that can express the contemporary tensions and anxieties of political life in 1687, and express also some of Dryden's own fears and hopes for the future – 'the two inset fables offer pessimistic alternative visions of the future, even though this is a Roman Catholic poem in a Roman Catholic reign' (Erskine-Hill 1995: 61). But passing from the sublime to the ridiculous in the manner of these four lines is a very odd way of anticipating a poetic change of this kind. A sonorous reminder of the Hind's timeless immortality is followed by a claim implying that Catholics have nothing to fear from Anglicans because in early April 1687 James II, the royal Lion, has issued a declaration of indulgence granting liberty of worship in public and suspending the tests which kept Catholics from holding office.

Nor was this the untroubling leonine *fiat* suggested by Dryden's flat emblematic method. James had issued the indulgence without parliament, whom he had prorogued eighteen months earlier, and was visibly and unsuccessfully trying to stitch together another more compliant parliament which would pass his measures into law. Public opinion against Catholics was already simmering at the heavy-handed policies of the king and his inner group of extremist advisers, and was to come to boiling-point the following year. Moderate Catholics (of which Dryden claims to be one) were, not surprisingly, much perturbed by the developing situation, and would have been puzzled by the implicit call for insouciant trust in the royal policy. Dryden's message in the fables that the beasts exchange in Part 3 is much the same. The Hind easily reads the Panther's fable as expressing 'the people's rage' against her Catholic sons, but can apparently calm her adversary simply by telling a fable in which James 'makes all Birds of ev'ry Sect / Free of his Farm' (3, 535). There were no public Catholic expressions of support for the poem.

Wider aspects of the poem are as unstable as the moment in the lines quoted. The figuration shifts silently. As Miner points out, one common practice is that typology, analogy with Christian referents, often mixes unselfconsciously with 'other sources' (3, 344), so that Dryden's post-Reynardian Chanticleer can somehow call the Catholic faithful to their devotions, in the Hind's fable, as easily as Lydgate's can praise the Trinity with his crowing. A medieval technique for the most modern of moments, but meshed into a distinctive wider method. Poor King James is not even allowed to retain his figurative identity as Lion, but must become also the 'Plain good Man' (3, 526) of the Hind's fable near the end of Part 3, the owner of the farm on which the loyal Catholic poultry and the wayward Anglican Doves or Pigeons are at loggerheads. The original cast-list of beasts representing the English sects is replaced by birds: bird-fable is added to beast-fable, the Hind's fable is added to the Panther's. The Buzzard in the Hind's fable is either William of Orange, or Gilbert Burnet, or partly both: 'it is as if we couldn't decide whether Achitophel were meant to depict Monmouth or Shaftesbury' (Zwicker 1984: 57): or (in the gloss provided by the commentary in the Traquair

House manuscript of the poem in *c.* 1689) the Buzzard is partly Burnet and partly a 'Presbyter', which Burnet was not (see Erskine-Hill 1995: 71). And so on. Whatever might have appeared to be clear and single must be subtly mystified and made double, paralleling in an occult way the authority of the Catholic church, which is said to lie not in one place but two, the verbal pronouncements of 'Pope and gen'ral councils' (3, 487). Paralleling also the Christian mystery of the escape from the tomb, during which (in Part 1) 'one single place two bodies did contain' (3, 472), the rock, and the body of Christ. Through this occult process of submerged structural metaphor the poem becomes a 'mysterious writ' (3, 503), as 'darkly writ' (493) as the Pauline texts. It asks blind leaps of literary faith, and a juggling of literary and religious categories, beliefs, and disbeliefs which tests the paradoxes of fable almost to destruction. Davenant thought that Aesop had illuminated the 'clouded Text' of ancient wisdom with the audiovisual hieroglyphics of fable – 'blest be *Aesop*, whom the wise adore / Who this dark science did to light restore' (Ogilby 1651: Preface) – but Dryden effectively reverses this emphasis.

The mysteries of Christianity are thus re-absorbed by, or into, the metaphorical techniques of secular and pagan poetry. 'What more could fright my faith, than Three in One?' (3, 472) asks Dryden rhetorically in an early moment. For almost all readers, the answer was that a figurative technique in which James was to be apprehended on three, or even four or five, different levels was designed to frighten literary belief just as much as Dryden's religious faith could be tested by doctrine. Dryden's James is a king; a symbol or emblem of kingship which is also an animal, the Lion; an analogue of Jove, equipped with 'rowling thunder-bolts' (3, 510); and a plain good man – who happens to own a farm stocked with emblematic birds. The anonymous author of *The Revolter* exactly caught the strangely multiple, shifting spirit of the piece by saying that Dryden deserved 'to be reckon'd in the number of the Heathen Gods; For he has . . . made new Metamorphoses's to make a second *Ovid* more work' (Anon. 1687: A2). The passions of the god, acting as the motive to metamorphosis, seem to have outrun the control of the poet. The appetency of religious *conversion*, the primary change of state, has inadvertently transferred itself into poetic method, which becomes proto-Ovidian rather than Christian: metamorphoses without the Ovidian control.

Contemporary critical reactions were sometimes very astute and incisive, the products of minds which were clearly fully engaged with this endlessly provoking and fascinating poem. The most plausible modern explanation of Dryden's difficulties with structural metaphor and figurative language effectively (if less sarcastically) concurs with *The Revolter* in identifying them as in large part the result of Dryden's conversion to Catholicism. Donald Benson identifies transubstantiation as the central issue in the poem – 'the main question' (3, 485), as the Hind says. Denial of transubstantiation in the Eucharist was a crucial part of the Test Act: Catholicism insists on 'the bodily interpretation of the Eucharistic presence' in the face of the 'essentially figurative' (Benson 1982: 201, 200) Anglican doctrine of Real Presence. The Catholic wafer *is* the body and blood of Christ: meat rather than shadow, in the Hind's typically unsettling Aesopian phrase. This anti-figurative emphasis of Catholic doctrine is accompanied in the poem by the Hind's account of the 'dumb Scripture', the denial of the power of the written word in scripture. Taken together, such beliefs 'about substance and language carry profound implications for poetry' and imply a 'decline of faith . . . in the power of figurative language' (*ibid.*: 207), the effects of which have been observed by many commentators in Dryden's poetry of the late 1680s. Conversion to Catholicism is accompanied by scepticism about metaphor. This scepticism or anxiety affects the fabling, the figurative structuring, which becomes dislocated and discontinuous, or, rather, more discontinuous than Dryden had probably intended – the criticism of *The Revolter* is, in the end, too sweeping, given that there are genuine principles behind some of the figurative strategy.

Dryden's extraordinary manner of proceeding leads to many figurative effects that are apparently contrary to the poem's main drift. The immaculate Hind has numerous young: it is the Anglican Panther who does not breed, because she is a hybrid monster, a compromise, living like the Minotaur 'in her own labyrinth', the English maze of Anglican error. This makes her a 'creature of a double kind' (3, 480), duplicitous, where the Hind, the one truth, should be single: Duessa and Una.

But in the English tradition of sacred zoography, *both* creatures have double natures. 'Natures twain hath the Stag . . .' (Theobald 1928: 26), and so of course does the Panther, who is usually understood to represent duplicitous friendship hiding 'natural rapacity' (Kinsley 1953: 334). The Panther's 'fam'd' (3, 490) sweet breath is, as the Hind appreciates, a source of danger. But in the contrary *Physiologus*-tradition, she (or in this case he: bestiary-animals are male, fable-Panthers usually female, like Dryden's) is not duplicitous but simply a beautiful wild animal which is also an analogue or type of Christ because of his beauty and his breath. After feeding, he goes to sleep in a cave for three days. When he wakes he roars a slightly synaesthetic sweet roar, at which the animals draw near; but the dragons, to whom Panthers' breath is poison, run away at the sound:

> Christ in a mystical sense is said to resemble the Panther . . .
> . . . for a time He lay in a sleep, when by death he redeemed us,
> To all the world He sent forth a sound . . .
> Whom all the tribes of the earth, if they truly believe in Him follow,
> Only one flies and lies hid . . .
> That deadly serpent of old . . . (Theobald 1928: 45)

This tradition is strong enough for the black panther to be available to James Joyce as a natural 'image of suffering Christ' (Joyce 1992: 943) in *Ulysses* (1922). Fable-panthers are similarly not duplicitous. The Phaedrian Panther who falls into a pit (Perry 1965: 260–1) and is stoned by shepherds but fed by other people, kills the shepherds and their sheep when she escapes, but tells the fearful others not to worry: deeds are paid in kind. Good people, like good animals in the *Physiologus*, have nothing to fear from the judicious Panther.

Even without this odd interference from traditions of figurative language, Dryden's genuinely 'double' Panther seems closer to the metamorphosing mysteries of the poem and of faith than does the Hind, more at home in the poem's English labyrinth, which can come to seem like a garden of forking tongues rather than forking paths. Then again, the Hind has doublenesses of her own: her sword is, as the Panther comments at one point, 'double edg'd' (3, 508). The Catholic Hind accuses the Anglican Panther of equivocation in her doctrine of Real Presence in the Eucharist (3, 486), but admits in the same breath that the most notable equivocators are the Jesuits: an extraordinarily doubled set of double-speakers. When the Hind maliciously alludes to the Panther's barrenness at the end of a long vituperative passage against the 'dodging tricks' (3, 491) of the Panther's authors, she bizarrely concludes her remarks and the paragraph by appearing to admit that the abhorred Anglicans are to be preferred to the other sects, and by implication also to the Catholics:

> For sects that are extremes, abhor a middle way. (492)

Anglicanism can only be a *middle way* between radical Protestantism and Catholicism, the other 'extreme'. Presumably searching for a figure that expresses the degenerate Anglican compromise or 'mix' (491) of church-authority and private spirit, Dryden has instead found one that comes close to expressing the golden mean, the reasonable way. No wonder

Thomas Heyrick accused him of having 'plaid booty' (Heyrick 1687: 'To the Reader'), which is what a jockey does when accepting a bribe to lose a race. It is not a question of Dryden having tried to defend Catholicism and failed, but a question of him having written a poem which appears to suffer subconsciously from divided loyalties, or double agency, the one thing that the audience in such divided times could not stomach.

Which is to say that the poem often expresses the classic 'double-handed' capacity integral to fable, acting (to adapt Peachum) both against Catholics and for 'em, but is most unwilling to acknowledge fully that it is doing so. Paradoxically, Dryden is quite aware that it *should* be doing so: intellectually, he knows as well as Ogilby that a fable should dramatize and work between extremes represented by different voices. In the preliminary address he can even announce this as his conscious programme, betraying a puzzling split between the temper of his poetic and critical discourses. He twice identifies the poem as a '*Satyr*', but insists that it is only directed against '*the refractory and disobedient on either side*' (3, 467). The interpolated fables in Part 3 are both said to contain '*the Common-Places of* Satyr . . . *which are urg'd by the Members of the one Church against the other*' (3, 469): again, admirably even-handed, and as if Dryden expected his readers not to respond to delegated satirical technique as satire. He is willing to acknowledge the virulence of current Anglican feeling against the Catholics and James, and expresses the hope that the symptoms will soon '*have abated*' and the disease '*worn out*' its '*Malignity*' (467), just as the Panther merely yawns and goes to sleep – providing another echo of the *Physiologus*-Panther – at the end of the poem, instead of baring her teeth at the ending of the Hind's fable. In terms of Dryden's wider 'fable', the unspoken moral here is that a fable told with less 'malice' (3, 520) than the Panther's was will mollify the opposing church and result in a peaceful conclusion. Moderate courses will prevail; fable points to the cool linguistic and political space that was denied to Ogilby.

But this reconciliatory programme is presented in a violently skewed way. At the end of the poem, for example, the early image of abatement of malignity and loss of virulence is represented not only in the Panther's weariness and loss of energy, but also in the Hind's closing description of the likely destiny of the Anglican Pigeons of her fable:

> . . . sunk in Credit, they decreas'd in Pow'r.
> Like Snows in warmth that mildly pass away,
> Dissolving in the silence of decay. (3, 536)

No one persecutes the Pigeons, they simply fade away, as the disease will abate if left alone. But the last line is far too poetically charged to convey this moral. It is the most lyrically forceful moment in the whole vast poem, passing in an instant from abstraction to melodious landscape to sibilant physical corruption. Dryden habitually reserves physical present participles ('rolling time' / 'rowling thunder-bolts') for moments which convey a sense of great energy or emotional power. The effect here is to create as powerful a sense of figurative gloating over the corpse of the enemy as did the Panther's account of the death of the Catholic Martyn, and the energy is clearly the poet's, not the Hind's. The sentiment may technically express mildness and a natural, unforced waning of power, but it does so with such barely concealed animus that it cannot be other than a retaliation against the Panther and her fable. Even the '*Choughs* and *Daws*, and such Republick Birds' (3, 535) are now largely exempt from this animus, which is perceptible in many other overcharged phrases and passages directed against the Panther. No wonder caveats cloud the poem's ending: the Panther's yawnings are 'affected', her desire for rest accompanied by a 'seem'd' (3, 536).

The moment that identifies Dryden's difficulties most tellingly comes in Part 2, in the speech from the Hind at lines 228–96. In the latter part of this she lapses into scornful paraphrase of the arguments of the dissenters against the established church, the compromise of the 'middle way'. Why should the 'lawful tyranny' of Catholicism be replaced by the 'bastard' authority of Anglican episcopacy? 'Either be wholly slaves or wholly free' (3, 492). As before, the Hind gives the game away. In the poem's terms it is not the Catholics who are in the natural paradoxical position of the fabulist dramatized, for example, in Davenant's verses before Ogilby's *Fables* – enslaved but/and free – it is the Anglican church, the duplicitous Panther. Dryden is forced, in the end, to admit that for him Catholicism is the dominant discourse, the true guide, the lawful power: but *emperors* cannot write fables, merely appropriate them. Or print them, as James did.

Montague and Prior were first to react, with their urbane and extremely clever mock, the preface to which takes Dryden to task for breaking the natural rules of fable: probability, consistency, decorum of style. But instead of showing any interest in such intellectual questions as where these 'natural' generic rules might have come from, the criticism proceeds through an equation made between literary qualities and social and religious ones. Smith and Johnson hail their friend Bayes as a social equal, but his recent conversion to Catholicism has inexplicably metamorphosed him into an aggressively noisy and bombastic lower-class embarrassment, whose spoken and written idiolect has been converted to match. As in *The Revolter*, one change is felt to have led to another; the converted voice. Ears become '*Lugs*' (Prior 1959: 1, 42) – shades of Atrides's teeth as 'Grinders' (4, 1593) thirteen years later – his own body a 'Carkass', and his favourite poetic diction is now such aureate nouns as 'Bag', 'Pot', and '*Stum*' (Prior 1959: 1, 55, 45, 55). In other words, he writes as he talks. Swearing repeatedly, he grows excited and outlandishly loquacious. His audience ask a few bemused questions, comically appear (like the Panther!) to go to sleep, treat him with amused condescension, politely refuse to be drawn into debate (Englishmen supposedly do not discuss politics until after the third bottle, religion not until after the fourth; and *great actions are not carried on by noise*), and then take their leave.

The understated moral of this brilliantly comic performance is thus made pointedly the same as Dryden's, if more direct. If you do not provoke your antagonist, social decorum may yet be preserved. If Dryden's fable preaches a moral which it does not perform, this one performs it without preaching, as a fable should. Low comedy carries high ironies. This stress may be simply a general tacit remonstrance, or may also refer to the moment at the end of Part 1 of Dryden's poem where the Hind, ludicrously, is said to consider the Panther to be 'a well-bred civil beast' (3, 484), when Dryden has just spent several hundred lines assiduously casting aspersions on the Panther's genealogy.

That the riposte is cast in dramatic form carries yet another unspoken comic point. Smith and Johnson have not read Bayes's poem – goodness knows how many bottles English gentlemen would have to drink before they discussed their *reading* in public, or how many rough seas they would have to sail before they articulated anything so *infra dig* as a plain-dealing Manly (rather than gentlemanly) moral. They merely listen and respond as Bayes reads the piece out, the ensemble providing a brief oral mock-tradition of interpretation which neatly undermines the poem's Catholic stress on church oral tradition. The poet is voluble, but his poem is dumb. *The Hind and the Panther* may be, in part, a dialogue, but it is conspicuously *written*.

So *The Hind and the Panther Transvers'd* is both a work with a moral or application about social harmony and decorum *and* a violently polemical burlesque: another double-handed fable. This emphasizes the difficulty of producing, in the late seventeenth century, works of literature which are genuinely mediative or moderate in tone and effect. This difficulty is often underestimated: Ralph Cohen, for instance, musing 'On the Interrelations of Eighteenth-Century Literary Forms', reflects that

> the aftermath of the Civil War brought with it a body of controversial literature – in both poetry and prose – as well as appeals to subdue controversy. One solution was for literature to appeal to as many groups as possible, seeking to satisfy each. The premise of social, political, and natural variety had as its basis God's plenitude and the implicit harmony underlying the universe. (Cohen 1974: 41)

This is broadly true, but much too quick and sweeping. Even the *Spectator*, one of Cohen's main examples of a mixed form which 'served to foster a sense of interrelation of interests of readers' (*ibid.*: 73), could be treated polemically by a writer like Mandeville. Claims of moderation, as with the Trimmers or *The Hind and the Panther*, were either intended or perceived as duplicitous. The reasonable tones sometimes referred to as 'ease' retained very distinct class-overtones until well into the next century, and needed modification with words such as 'familiar' if these were to be avoided. The mode of fable, with its stress on shock, paradox, and privacy or silence of application, is one which stresses mediation only through combativeness. It may appeal to a varied audience, but not directly and transparently: the implied *full* reader is, to repeat, both split or double – Cockerel, *Tim*, slave, Bayes, speaker: intelligent master, free, philosopher, reader – and possessed of an ironic perspective on the paradoxes of this doubleness.

Other more-or-less immediate replies to Dryden included Heyrick's *New Atlantis* and the anonymous *Revolter*, which ingeniously transforms Dryden into an analogue of the 'two actors' of fable. Mr D. the Romanist duels it out with Mr D. the Protestant, who wins all the arguments. This procedure implies that *Religio Laici* and *The Hind and the Panther* could be, and indeed were, seen as two components or episodes of a composite meta-fable, with the second designed to have a character as conspicuously antithetical to the first as does the Grasshopper to the Ant's 'Plain *Truths*' (1, 321). This in turn argues a sophisticated understanding of how fable in general might operate, but also hints at the new suspicion, in some quarters, of the old paradoxes and doublenesses overtly displayed. Prior and Montague were Dryden's juniors by thirty-four years: the opinion of *The Revolter* was that his poem was 'altogether Antiquated' (Anon. 1687: 2).

After the 1688 Revolution, parody of the poem and its author quickly became a politically correct literary sport after the manner of the usually Whig *Absalom and Achitophels*. In 1690 Tom Brown revised his 1688 pamphlet *The Reasons of Mr. Bays changing his Religion* as *The Late Converts Exposed*, an imitation of Prior and Montague's piece which concludes with a version of 'The Fable of the Bat and the Birds'. This was cheeky and doubly apposite: in Ogilby's 1651 *Fables*, Dryden's immediate source for the two fables in Part 3, this fable figures as 'Of Birds and Beasts' (No. 29), and the Hind refers ironically to the Catholic cockerel as a 'Beast of a Bird' (2, 529) for disturbing the Anglican Pigeons' beauty-sleep. In Brown's mock, the traditionally turncoat Bat (Bays) is neither bird nor animal but favours whichever party is uppermost. Found at last on the losing side, he is ostracized and mocked.

Then the circle widened: if one turncoat could be mocked in fable so could another. Again in 1690, the egregious William Sherlock, Dean of St Paul's, disavowed his nonjuring principles in the interests of reconciling himself with the new Williamite regime. Tom Durfey took his change of heart to task in the domestic animal-satire *The Weesils* (1691), in which Sherlock's wife is deemed responsible for his defection, as Dryden's wife had, supposedly, been for his conversion. The tradition of fable-collections was now reinvigorated and repoliticized: also in 1691, Robert or Richard Burton (writing as 'Nathaniel Crouch', and author, in 1693, of a *History of the House of Orange*) produced forty-two *Delightful Fables in Prose and Verse* which redressed a perceived imbalance by defending the Revolution, arguing against the recall of James, and admonishing the excesses of Restoration courts. In this atmosphere Roger L'Estrange, now out of office after a long career as censor and licenser of the press to the Stuarts, published his five hundred prose *Fables of Aesop and other Eminent Mythologists* (1692). This was later to become a totem for political causes even more than was Dryden's poem, which was to achieve a curious posthumous rehabilitation.

When the little 'Grub-street' Aesopian pamphlets began to appear in the later 1690s, *The Hind and the Panther* and *The Hind and the Panther Transvers'd* were still available as models. But 'parody' now began not simply to attack Dryden, but also to attack the character and policies of the original parodists. The Tory *Aesop in Spain* (1701) contains an attack on Montague, now Earl of Halifax and a very senior Whig financier and politician who had only just escaped impeachment for his role in the management of the Partition Treaty, which had promised Spanish Italy to France:

A Milkwhite Rogue, Immortal and unhang'd,
By Fate and Parliaments severely bang'd,
Without a Saint, a Devil was within;
He sought all Dangers, for he knew all Sin. (*Aesop* 1701: 14)

And when the High Tory and Jacobite William Pittis – 'drunken Pittis' as he liked to be known (Newton 1936: 284, quoting the 1705 Tory *Dunton's Whipping Post*, 26) – was expanding his 1708 *Aesop at Oxford* as *Bickerstaffe's Aesop* in 1709, the connection between Tory positions and parody of Dryden was still being made. Pittis's attack on the universities in 'Aesop's Thanks' begins with

Two Milk-White Hinds, with Age and Honour crown'd,
Had long for an Alliance been renown'd,
While they, without Contention, sep'rate fed . . .
(*Aesop* 1709: 12)

Dryden and L'Estrange were now the twin godfathers of Tory and Jacobite fable, co-opted to become dominant voices susceptible to a single reading – in each case probably most strenuously by Pittis, according to Theodore Newton's plausible ascriptions – as firmly as Aphra Behn had co-opted Ogilby's fables for hers in 1687. On the other side, republican fable-collections also now needed to be given famous godfathers, adequate moral doctors. The translator of the collection of Dutch fables known in English as *Fables, Moral and Political* (1703) was happy to let himself be thought of as translating the fables of the patrician Dutch republican John or Johan de Witt, who had been tutor to the father of William III. This collection is almost always ascribed to de Witt, but Aphra Behn's character Dullman's line in *The Widow Ranter* (1690) – 'the Rabble swore they would *De-Wit* me' (Behn 1990: 249) – assumes that the London audience knew that de Witt had been shot by political opponents, and then dismembered and partly eaten by a mob, in The Hague in 1672. Bolingbroke refers to this episode as a 'dreadful and well-known Tragedy' in an exercise in historical parallel in the *Craftsman* in 1729: the analogy in the *Fables* seems to be between Aesop's unjust political death in the legend and the death of an '*able* and *honest Minister*, who was sacrificed to the Rage of *popular* Resentment' (Varey 1982: 87, 83). Fabulists now began to assert dominance by claiming, seriously or more-or-less comically, kinship with such totemic figureheads, rather as Fielding and the fabulists will use Hercules later. Sometimes they also reproved and remonstrated about such uses: the unpartisan *Aesop Return'd from Tunbridge*, one of the replies to the notoriously Tory/Jacobite pamphlet *Aesop at Tunbridge*, complains about Aesop being presented as '*the* Bully of Tunbridge' (*Aesop* 1698[e]: 1): not for his social behaviour but for his aggressive satirical-political persona. The original legendary bully-orator, the exemplar whose words are as forceful as his deeds, is of course Hercules, as in the Host's appeal to Falstaff as 'bully Hector' and 'bully Hercules' *in The Merry Wives of Windsor* (1, 3), and later in Ogilby's fable, 'The Rustic and Hercules'.

L'ESTRANGE AND THE 'GRUB-STREET' AESOPS

Since 1677, Sir Roger L'Estrange – 'Towser', to his opponents – had been filling in the gaps in his work for the Stuart press by spying for the government, and by translating from the classics and from French and Spanish. Seneca and Tully rub shoulders with Erasmus and appealing volumes of 'curious indecency' (Kitchin 1913: 377) such as *The Spanish Polecat*. After the Revolution brought his public career to an end, he became as senior and influential in the realm of prose translation as Dryden was in the poetic. His translations gave him a reputation as a model of prose style which lasted until the *Spectator* (No. 135) took him to task for making free with English spelling. Thereafter his political reputation, the directness of his style in the fables themselves, and his inveterate fondness for the risqué – 'a Fellow had got a Wench in a Corner, and very Earnest they were upon the Text of Encrease and Multiply' (L'Estrange 1692: 472) – lost him favour.

Late in 1688 three booksellers approached him with a proposal for a prose *Aesop*. Given his previous political history, and the recent history of fable and fabulists, they must have looked forward to a very pointed performance, and the eighteenth century thought that that was what they had got. Croxall and others reviled his 'pernicious principles' (Croxall 1766: Preface), and, like Richardson, altered the fables to express the British 'principles of LIBERTY' (Richardson 1739: xii). But L'Estrange insisted in the Preface to his 1699 collection of *Fables and Storyes Moraliz'd* that the earlier collection had been written

> without Streyning any Thing all This while, beyond the Strictest *Equity* of a *Fair*, and an *Innocent Meaning*; or making a Spiteful Use of *Wire-drawn Inferences*... [I] made a Scruple of keeping close to my Text, without Lashing out into *any Extravagant Excesses*, of what sort soever, either *Personal*, or *Publick*. (L'Estrange 1699: Preface)

It is tempting to almost believe him. A Pearl may of course be very small, which makes it hard to argue from the balance of a collection. But of his five hundred 1692 fables, just fifteen have a 'strong . . . political bias' (Hornbeak 1937: 35) in the sense of being screwed up past the prevalent conservative tone to L'Estrange's Filmerite pitch, and there is no overt anti-William sentiment. Historical 'Reflexions' are distanced to the Civil Wars, 'our Broils of Famous Memory' (L'Estrange 1692: 21) – L'Estrange was seventy-six – and 'the Troubles of King Charles the First' (*ibid.*: 328). It is true that audiences would have made immediate historical applications of the parallel between broils in the 1640s and broils in the 1680s, and that the almost pathological force of his declarations for Divine Right is pointedly directed towards irritating those currently attempting to establish a viable limited monarchy with William, but the Morals and Reflexions are often couched in the general and plural. '*Kings are from God*', says the Reflexion to No. 19, 'The Frogs Chuse a King', 'and . . . it is a Sin, a Folly, and a Madness, to struggle with his Appointments' (*ibid.*: 21). The bluntness of this gives it, potentially, a double application: it was wrong to struggle with James: it is wrong to struggle with William. ' 'Tis a Great Unhappiness to lye at the Mercy of a Raging Lion', says No. 412, 'but it is a Christian Duty nevertheless to suffer patiently under the Justice of such a Judgment' (*ibid.*: 388). Subjects should be stoical about tyrants. The audience knows L'Estrange to be Jacobite (and, if they had read his *Seneca*, stoical): hence one application is that Jacobites should be stoical about William. But as with Dryden, a hint of double agency was something that the audience would resist like a temptation of the Devil – or rather, there are no readings of L'Estrange which comment on this quality, because if the audience could tolerate his politics they contented themselves with admiring his style or adding to his morals, as in the 'Remarks on Sir Roger L'Estrange's Edition of Aesop's Fables' which were incorporated into the 1701 edition.

L'Estrange's *Aesop* is remarkably multi-handled. Fully Lockean prefatory declarations of pedagogical purpose rub shoulders with ribald and paradoxical fables such as 'The Sick Hermit', where the chaste and holy young man, on being put to bed with a young woman for cure, complains eloquently about his previous good health. The massive folio was probably intended for fathers, patriarchs, to read to their children if and as they saw fit, rather than for the children directly (there are pictures in the 1699 volume, though – Hornbeak says (1937: 48) that they were sometimes coloured in by young artists). Richardson, not understanding this, was bemused by the inclusion of items such as 'The Sick

Hermit' and 'The Priest and the Pears', where a cocky cleric, on his way to officiate and eat well at a wedding, pisses mockingly on some Pears he finds lying on the ground, only to be prevented from reaching the wedding by a swollen river. Returning, he is happy to eat the Pears. The moral is that hunger is the best sauce (!) – but tell this fable to a juvenile, and you will be asked why the Priest did not have the wit to wash his Pears in the river.

L'Estrange's Morals and Reflexions are almost always plural in the sense of being multiple, and are often alert to the absurdities inherent in the fable. His version of The Lion's Share ('Lyon, Ass and Fox', No. 206, one of Hornbeak's fifteen) is first moralized bluntly as 'There must be no Sharers in Sovereignty', but the moral then continues by moralizing the Fox, not the Lyon, and moralizing on relative rather than absolute values: 'Court-Conscience is Policy. The Folly of One Man makes Another Man Wise', and so on. In other words, the first moral becomes the moral of the *Lyon*, rather than of the fable in its entirety.

The fable has finished with the Lyon thrashing the Ass for presuming to divide the spoils equally, and with the Fox then reserving a small piece of the dead deer to himself and presenting the Lyon with all the rest. When the Lyon asks him who taught him to carve, the Fox replies that he 'had an Ass to my Master; and it was his Folly made me Wise'. The Reflexion then applauds the survivalist wit of the Fox, who has 'enough for himself', and the stupidity of the Ass, without reflecting on the sovereignty of the Lyon. L'Estrange finishes by reflecting again on the curious status of the Ass's part in the fable, noting mordantly that '*Asses* are No great *Venson Eaters*' (L'Estrange 1692: 177). So the 'sovereignty' of the fable has effectively passed from the Lyon, via the 'Policy' which serves for 'Conscience' in a court, to the Aesopian wit of the Fox which allows him to read the situation and accommodate himself to tyrannical power where the Ass cannot. The fable may have absolute power as its premise, but its story is about how the boisterous mobile, or a fabulist wit, might learn to cope with antagonistic power as a problem. Or how a child might cope with a very strict father, which throws an interesting light on to L'Estrange's political patriarchism.

But those who wanted to give the *Fables* a 'single' reading did so from the start, and this was generally, as with De la Crose in his *Works of the Learned*, an enthusiastic anti-Trimmer reading. This is not surprising: L'Estrange had been pursuing 'Mr Trimmer' in his newspaper the *Observator* through the mid-1680s. 'Mr Trimmer' was the popular name for the inscrutable and opportunistic George Savile, Earl of Halifax, and for the increasingly influential grouping of moderate Whigs, Baxterian dissenters, and uneasy Church of England men which was associated with him. 'Trimming' meant (to the Trimmers) balancing, trimming the Ship of State by shifting political position as circumstances dictated. To Jacobites, and, supposedly, to L'Estrange, it meant, by 1688, a despicably subtle upsetting of the Stuart applecart. What is surprising about these single readings, from which all subsequent secondary ones devolve, is that they pass over the three prominent linked fables, Nos. 39, 40, and 41, which are specifically concerned with '*Trimming*' (*ibid.*: 43) – in two, in the shape of the Bat, which was already a symbol of political opportunism in the shape of Tom Brown's fable against Dryden. Here, surely, was a chance for revenge. Surely L'Estrange will not feel he can accomodate himself to Trimming, the most provoking example of double capacity, duplicitous pretended moderation. Croxall, rewriting the fable in 1722 and supposedly countering L'Estrange's pernicious and extreme principles, simply regards the Bat or turncoat as 'notoriously low and vile' (Croxall 1766: 213). But L'Estrange's fables are quite different.

The three fables are Bat and Weazle; Bat, Birds, and Beasts; and the Estriche or ostrich, which like the Bat was supposed to be half bird, half beast. In the first, the Bat escapes twice by claiming to be whichever kind of animal the Weazle is not at that moment pursuing, and is then praised for 'Playing the Trimmer' (L'Estrange 1692: 42). In the second, the Bat who repeatedly deserts his party is castigated as a '*Time-Serving Trimmer*' (*ibid.*: 43). The case of the exotic Estriche, an oriental fable-creature imported by the well-read L'Estrange (he also has Tigers) apparently because of his fascination with the idea of Trimming, replicates that of the Bat in the first. The collective Moral says that

> *Trimming* in some Cases, is Foul, and Dishonest; in Others, Laudable; and in some again, not only Honest, but Necessary. The Nicety lies in skill of Distinguishing upon Cases, Times, and Degrees. (*ibid.*)

One should, it seems, shift position as circumstances dictate. Recent politics are outreached, in a continuation of the drift away from simple satire and invective in the *Observators* of the 1680s towards a more balanced and open relationship between its dialoguists, Trimmer and Observator. Violet Jourdain notes how much more closely these later numbers approach the condition of mixed Socratic dialogue than do the earlier ones, with Trimmer now allowed to develop a satirical attitude of his own to the stylistic and emotional oddities of his opponent, 'even patronizing him with the nickname "Nobs"' (L'Estrange 1970: vii). Trimmer may be a subtle hypocrite, but the power of the snarling Nobs/Towser is pointedly inadequate to deal with the watchfully Foxy Trimmer. This openness of reaction is continued into the 1699 *Fables and Storyes Moraliz'd*, where the fable called 'A Trimming Mechanique' contrives to mock the conventional Augustan/Antonine opposition by telling the story of a mechanical who, in the war between Antony and Augustus, teaches one parrot to cry 'long live Antonius' and the other 'long live Augustus . . . so that whether soever got the better of it, one of the Birds would be sure to be on the Stronger Side' (L'Estrange 1699: 199).

But the most determined 'single' reading of L'Estrange, amounting to the kind of paradoxically supportive travesty that was observed with *The Hind and the Panther*, comes – again, probably from 'drunken' Pittis – in the shape of the 1711 pamphlet called *Aesop at the Bell-Tavern in Westminster, or, A Present from the October-Club. In a few Select Fables from Sir Roger L'Estrange.* Thirteen of its seventeen fables are recycled from the earlier *Bickerstaffe's Aesop*, itself recycled from *Aesop at Oxford*, and from the 1701 *Canterbury Tales Rendred into Familiar Verse* – 'Canterbury Tale' had, both in this period and earlier ones, derogatory overtones similar to those of 'Aesop's Fable' as Dryden uses it in *Albion and Albanius*: and 'satirical pamphlets alluding to Chaucer . . . had been published since the civil wars' (Hanazaki 1993–4: 245).

Where L'Estrange merely borrowed Dryden's phrase about the '*Choughs* and *Daws*, and such Republick Birds' for his parenthetical jibe about the '*Republican Daw*, that *Kaw'd* for Liberty' (L'Estrange 1692: 152) in 'The Daw with a String at 's Foot', the *Bell-Tavern*'s equivalent fable advertises itself stridently as 'The Republican', and forces the analogy throughout. L'Estrange's 'Kite, Hawk, and Pigeons', which has a carefully crafted Cromwell/William moral, that it is a '*Dangerous Thing for People to call in a Powerful and an Ambitious Man for their Protector*' (*ibid.*: 21), becomes 'The Revolution' and features Pigeons, Kite, and Vulture, with the Vulture recalling William's notorious hook nose:

> One of the *Vulture's* Grasps will do
> More harm and Execution
> Than any Kite with Ten Times Two,
> I'm for another *Revolution*. (*Aesop* 1711: 10)

L'Estrange's innocuously moralized fable of 'A Hedge-Hog and a Snake', in which the Hedgehog forces the Snake out of its hole by refusing to leave and prickling the Snake's sides, is transformed into 'The Naturalizing Act', against the recent influx of largely Huguenot French immigrants. And No. 6, 'A Trick Worth Two', comically features 'Roger' himself (the name is a conventional epithet for a rustic, but one can hear the man) in characteristic voice, learning to grasp the Nettle, an action which will be allegorized as encouraging Dissenters to use the liturgy by fining them:

> Was ever such a Damn'd ill-natur'd Puss,
> To serve her very Landlord thus?
> Said Roger by a Nettle stung . . . (*ibid.*: 14)

These fable-pamphlets sprang up partly for political reasons, but also because of a new desire for 'single' or simplified readings of fable. The playfulness and paradox of the form often had to be played down as it became popular with a new audience which, if it did feel a connection between morality and metaphysical wit, tended to reserve this for the disconcertingly exuberant preachings of some of the Nonconformists, with their enthusiastic spiritualizing of natural phenomena. But L'Estrange's *Aesop* is important not so much for the work itself as for the short-term reactions, the longer transmission through the reactions of Croxall and Richardson, and the change in emphasis between 1692 and 1699, the second collection, *Fables and Stories Moraliz'd.* This is of interest for its lack of conventional fables: it consists almost entirely of jests from Boccaccio and other tellers of tales, and small narrative episodes which verge on the status of *conte* – this last coming closer to Dryden's 1700 collection. A moral fable is now a story that can be *Moraliz'd* upon. *Moraliz'd* recalls Baudoin's 1660 title, *fables traduites et moralisées.* It becomes clear that if the fable has to be moralized in the sense of being commented upon by the teaching fabulist as 'moral doctor', the status of its morality will depend entirely on the persona of the fabulist, whether actual or perceived. If the fabulist wishes to be eccentric or multi-handled, or is perceived as politically partisan, then so will the collection: everyone may now be their own Aesop.

One of the corollaries of the intellectual cast of French fable (outlined below) is that the connotations of the phrase 'moral fable' around 1700 are quite different from those of the phrase as used in twentieth-century English. The felt overtones of 'moral fable' as used now properly belong to much later in the eighteenth century; *Moral Tales for Young People*, to quote the title of Maria Edgeworth's 1801 collection. Baudoin's categorization of fable, 'a standard one' (Noel 1975: 17) through much of the eighteenth century, divides fables into several categories, the 'Raisonnable, Morale, et Mêlée, ou Propre, ou très-propre' (Baudoin 1631: 'Au Lecteur'). 'Morale' is described as the kind which aims to 'imiter la façon de vivre des Créatures raisonnables' (*ibid.*): fables about beasts that stand for people. The adjective approaches the English 'manners' at least as closely as it does 'moral' – the translation of Le Bossu's adaptation of this category says that such fables 'derive their name of Moratae from the Human Manners, which are attributed to them' (Le Bossu 1697: 13). This shades the meaning of phrases such as *morales et politiques* in the titles of the collections – this one from Osmont's 1630 collection, *Les Fables d'Ésope ou Instructions morales et politiques* (Paris, 1630). *Social* and political would be just as good a translation. The phrase 'moral and political', much used in the titles of English collections from the 1690s and 1700s, can mean either that the collection aims for the French *gravitas*; as in the case of Walter Pope's *Moral and Political Fables, Ancient and Modern* (1698), or that it is politically partisan but anxious to appear philosophical, as in the case of the 'de Witt' *Fables, Moral and Political* of 1703, which argue a fully co-ordinated Dutch republican philosophy, augmented by anti-Cartesianism and quite a lot besides.

If one approaches Addison for a definition of a fable in the early eighteenth century, one does not find statements about morality. Rather, there are firstly the double-handed procedures noted in earlier chapters, and secondly, the charming, circumstantial, illustrative story in *Spectator* 512, the fable-within-a-fable (borrowed from Tonson's *Turkish Tales* of 1708) told to the warlike and tyrannical Sultan Mahmoud by his Vizier, who claims to have learnt the language of birds. Returning from hunting, the inquisitive Sultan asks the Vizier to tell him what the two owls he sees perched in a tree are saying to each other. The Vizier at first claims that the owls' conversation is such that he cannot possibly repeat it, but at last reports that they are discussing the dowry of the first owl's daughter, who is to marry the other owl's son. The second owl is demanding fifty ruined villages – owls are fond of ruins – as his daughter-in-law's portion. The first replies that he will settle five hundred on her 'if you please. God grant a long life to Sultan Mahmoud! whilst he reigns over us we shall never want ruined villages' (Addison 1965: 4, 319).

Sultan Mahmoud is so touched that he immediately rebuilds all the towns and villages that have been destroyed in his wars, and becomes a benevolent ruler. Framing Addison's piece of 'oriental extravagance' are a 'ridiculous piece of natural magic' from Democritus about how mixing the blood of various birds produces a serpent which transforms anyone who eats it into an adept in bird-speak, and some remarks about how the mind is 'pleased ... amused ... [and] highly delighted' with the imperceptibly insinuated morals of fables (*ibid.*: 318, 319). As Addison's attitude thus proscribes the drawing of simple moral and political morals ('the reader comes in for half the performance', etc.), his performance had best speak for itself.

HOW TO TAKE LIBERTIES WITH FRENCH FABLE

Dryden's Preface to *Albion and Albanius*, with its emphasis on the naturalizing of a continental form, opera, also marks the beginning of a search for a stress on fable which was consciously different from the French. This reactive stress became stronger when, in the 1690s, English fable became widely aware of French fable as a dominant cultural voice. Three important representative reactions, across a variety of media, are John Vanbrugh's very popular adaptation of Boursault's play *Les Fables d'Ésope* (1693) as *Aesop* (1697), John Dennis's 'translation' of ten of La Fontaine's fables into Hudibrastic burlesque verse in his *Miscellanies* (1693), and George Farquhar's engagement, in his 'Discourse Upon Comedy' (1702), with René Le Bossu's ideas about fable in his *Traité du Poème Épique* (1675, translated 1697).

La Fontaine is a monument of French poetry, Boursault's play an elegant socio-moral comedy in verse, Le Bossu's treatise the most influential of all neoclassical works on the theory of fable and its kin. But in the 1690s English writers were much more cautious than they had been a generation earlier about importing the higher modes of French culture. A more socially diverse literary public was beginning to demand a review of moral values and technical practices. The French were seen as less 'free' in political terms than the post-Revolution English, and England and France were at war for most of the decade. In this ambience, English fabulists were very concerned that French practice should be vigorously adapted to domestic conditions, and that Aesop, if he was important, should be liberated and given an English character: *Aesop Naturaliz'd*, as a seminal 1697 collection expressed it.

The differences between English and French attitudes to fable at this point and later are largely the result of differences in context and background. Through the late Renaissance, the most characteristic English usage of the word 'fable' carried derogatory or sardonic overtones. It indicated something feigned, odd, old-wifeish or mythological:

not-necessarily-to-be-believed, except by someone else. Many of Dryden's uses of the word carry this counter-meaning, even inside the *Fables* themselves: 'Fables of a World, that never was!' (Dryden 1962: 798). In the Epilogue to *Albion and Albanius*, Dryden's slighting description of his piece as a mere 'Aesop's *Fable*' continues where the self-mocking and audience-mocking Prologue left off, with its references to the degenerate tastes of the day. Satire will not work on, nor wit strike on, such dense blocks as this audience. But a little bit of Frenchified operatic 'show', complete with 'confus'd' dances, several 'very large, and . . . very glorious' machines, and an outrageous emblematical drawing of the diabolical Shaftesbury, complete with 'Fiends Wings and Snakes' and 'Phanatical Rebellious Heads' which suck poison from a 'Tap in his Side' – Shaftesbury had been fitted with a silver pipe to drain a running discharge after a coach accident – is guaranteed to 'bubble' the servile (royalist!) English audience just as easily as the tyrannical Democracy and Zeal have bubbled Augusta (London), with her 'servile fear', in the opera itself (Dryden 1956–92: 15, 54, 14, 47, 51, 53, 23). The *writer-speaker* dramatist comments on the *listening and watching* (rather than speaking) Cockerel-audience, which is thus forced to observe its own divisions. As so often, panegyric of Charles is double-edged – if this piece of transparently duplicitous, double-handed, rococo (royalist!) nonsense, which could be safely and conspiratorially described as an 'Aesop's *Fable*', has any edges.

As well as these other meanings, 'fable' could also mean simply 'apologue', but these were still mostly either safe school translation exercises for twelve-year-olds or illustrative verse stories with odd political overtones. There was, apart from Bacon's earlier comments, little sense that fable might be philosophically justified.

As Georges Couton says while tussling with the background to La Fontaine, 'la préhistoire des fables garde bien ses secrets' (La Fontaine 1962: xiv): the evolution of modern literary fable is studied as little in France as it is in England. But the difference in emphasis is clear. The French pedagogic tradition of fable was very strong, with the corpus having been augmented by original fables from sixteenth-century continental humanists. Fables were deemed suitable material for instruction in the universities as well as throughout the school curriculum, which contrasts markedly with the drift of the English educational collections. These had begun to direct themselves more towards the home tutorial market, but still operated as fairly elementary exercises. Barlow's collection is one such, but the most striking example is John Locke's *Aesop's*

Fables, in English and Latin, Interlineary (1703). The English philosopher philosophizes even less about fables than he did in his brief comments in *Some Thoughts Concerning Education* (1693). Simply remarking that *Aesop* is 'the only Book almost that I know fit for Children' (Locke 1989: 242), he publishes what was originally just a useful compilation written for the son of a family friend. L'Estrange's collection has more Lockean overtones than does Locke's.

But in French Jesuit and Oratorian colleges, pupils, as well as translating and commenting on grammar, were required to echo classical pedagogic practice by becoming active practitioners, amplifying Latin prose fables, adding circumstantial detail, figures of speech, and stylistic colour. Associations were thus developed between fable and narrative method, and between fable and 'l'idée de style'. A fable 'pouvait passer du style "simple" ou "rude" au style "orné, soigné, fleuri" ' (La Fontaine 1962: vi). There were apparently no French seventeenth-century verse fables before La Fontaine, but the educational form was effectively already operating as a halfway house between rhetoric and literature.

La Fontaine says that his aim in his 1668 *Fables* is to enliven, 'égayer' (*ibid.*: 7), Phaedrus, his main source: to add charm and an agreeable gaiety. In so saying he is able both to appeal to the tradition of pedagogic stylistic decorum and to signal his desire to transcend it, to create a coherent world of social and poetic tone. He also endows his collection with a Preface which dignifies fable by mentioning most of the important classical associations: Socrates, Plato, Aristotle, Avienus, Quintilian on style. Again, this dignity was already a feature of the French 'teaching' *Aesops*: Audin prefaced his collection with an 'Apologie en faveur des fables', Baudoin his with an analytical, categorizing, 'Au Lecteur, Sur le Sujet des Fables'. Both weight the text towards morals and applications, with the fables themselves kept very brief.

In La Fontaine's main text this emphasis is reversed, but the poems themselves cultivate a thoughtful, often gently philosophical mood, flattering readers with the assumption that they will respond to material of weight as well as to humour and teasing. Sometimes this philosophical cast is more than mood. Fontainean fable has, for instance, an anti-Cartesian drift, fully articulated in the 'Discours à Madame de la Sablière' appended to Book 9 of the *Fables*. This is a facet of his fables which drew Mandeville, who quickly came to react against his own Cartesian medical education, to La Fontaine and then to fable more widely. The Cartesians, who believed that animals were a kind of machine, were enthusiastic vivisectors, and were wont to hold public demonstrations of their art. These offended the politer echelons of society which comprised La Fontaine's audience. So a fabulist working with a classical author (Phaedrus) who implied that animals had some moral status of their own was effectively engaged in an Ancients-and-Moderns skirmish. In La Fontaine's Snake and File (see Ogilby) the File belongs to a clockmaker, and the fable is addressed to the spirits of the Modern age who try to dent the works of antiquity. But as La Fontaine is a Phaedrian fabulist, he can also assert quite happily in the Preface to the 1668 *Fables* that he is a Modern, which in many respects he is. Twentieth-century French criticism, not understanding the double-handed politics of fable as well as their author does, sometimes takes this to be a misprint. But a polite anti-Cartesianism does not jar the relations between academe, professional criticism, and the new literary fable, which remain as affable as do the relations between writer and reader in the *Fables* themselves. The polite audience returns the compliment, and canonizes La Fontaine, bar the *Contes*. It would take several more decades before English poetry could bring itself systematically to imitate, even in the loose sense, high fables produced in such decorous circumstances.

THE FABLE DRAMATIC: BOURSAULT AND VANBRUGH

John Vanbrugh's revision of Edmé Boursault's stylish and varied comedy in rhyming couplets *Ésope à la Ville* (played 1690: published as *Les Fables d'Ésope*, 1693) as the racier prose-with-songs *Aesop: a Comedy* in January 1697, with the great Cibber as Aesop, had the important effect of offering a wide English audience an example of an Aesop with a stage-character derived from the French, but 'naturalized' and expressing himself in demotic English. *Aesop* was performed at Drury Lane 'nearly every year until 1720' (Vanbrugh 1927: 2, 7), so Vanbrugh's play would have formed a vivid introduction to the literary fabulist – an *example* of a literary Aesop, crucial if teaching in fable is by example, and if the fable depended, as with L'Estrange, on the character of the fabulist – for many more people than did the few partial translations of La Fontaine or the expensive folio of L'Estrange. The Grubean sages, always alert to the moment, responded in late 1697 and 1698 by inventing the form of journalistic–poetical entertainment which consisted of small pamphlets chronicling Aesop's travels to various English spas and, later, as 'political temperatures rose in the wake of the treaty of Ryswick' (Pritchard 1976: 178), European towns. Mary Pritchard has a detailed and thorough account of this craze in her excellent thesis, and points out that they form a precedent for the later occasional fables done as individual political broadsides in newspapers and magazines. Some of these pamphlets, like Pittis's and the first politicized collection, *Aesop at Tunbridge*, are Tory, and, after 1701, derive largely from L'Estrange; some, like *Aesop at Bathe*, . . . *Whitehal*, and . . . *Amsterdam*, are Whig ripostes to *Tunbridge*. Some are apolitical, like the chatty *Aesop Naturaliz'd*, the scatty *Aesop at Islington*, and the more socialized *Aesop at Richmond*, which, after an introductory jibe: 'Since *Aesop* stroles from Place to Place / Like banish'd Tory in disgrace' (*Aesop* 1698[j]: 1), decides that he 'No longer is a Polititian' and has given up polemic and 'Treason' (*ibid.*: 2), and presents instead a gallery of spa-characters in the mode of the 'Wells' poems of the 1690s such as the charming anonymous *Islington-Wells; or, The Threepenny Academy* (1691). This and *Aesop at Richmond* are not unlike Christopher Anstey's *New Bath Guide* seventy years later. Pritchard, Sloman, Patterson, and Hanazaki quite properly point to contributory proximate causes for this efflorescence of *Aesop*-pamphlets, such as the lapsing of the Licensing Act in 1695, the new Triennial Act, and the effects of the policies of the fabulist Montague. But as so often, English fabulists seem to be working directly from the nature, or the perceived nature, of specific examples: L'Estrange, and, in particular, Vanbrugh, who is himself working from the example of Boursault.

In both plays, Aesop's function is to appear to mediate both technically and stylistically between the romantic plot of the upper-class characters and the bevy of lower-class characters who come to him hoping for various kinds of preferment or favour from Croesus and Learchus, to whom Aesop is acting as adviser. This being Vanbrugh, his adaptation slants the play away from the upper-class group and towards the lower, dispensing with Learchus's son and daughter, transforming the two old deputies of Syzicus into country tradesmen, and identifying the hypocritical mother of a daughter who has eloped rather more precisely as a 'Lewd Mother', in the Dramatis Personae. Where Boursault's old men come complaining about the wealth of Learchus and Croesus and are told the fable of the Belly and the Members in this generalized context, Vanbrugh's 'Ordinary Trademen' also complain about the more pressing and topical topic of taxes. Aesop easily talks them out of this complaint –

> If the King had no money, there cou'd be no Army; and if there were no Army, your Enemies would be amongst you: one Day's Pillage woul'd be worse than Twenty Years Taxes.
>
> (Vanbrugh 1927: 2, 27)

This emollient moral also engages smoothly with the many satirical responses to William III's standing army (a sitting duck as far as satire was concerned) as well as with other recent semi-fabulist English poems on the subject of the new taxes, such as Henry Hall's 'Ballad on the Times' from 1696:

> We are all like the dog in the fable, betrayed,
> To let go the substance and snap at the shade . . .
> We pay for our newborn, and we pay for our dead,
> We pay if we're single, we pay if we wed . . . (Lord 1963–75: 5, 499, 500)

The functions of both Vanbrugh's and Boursault's Aesop are the populist but conservative ones of talking to everyone on their own level, moralizing the romantic couple and Learchus into a happy ending, and thus reconciling what might have been antagonistic elements of society through indirect and inoffensive satirical banter. Fables told in easy and familiar verse are the one form of discourse appropriate to all levels of society, governor, and bumpkin. Tonally, this seems a quite different use of fable from the factionally politicized *Aesops* which the play helped to generate or provoke; but, again, what in English appears to be moderation (and in French perhaps was) is also written to a highly specific agenda. Vanbrugh's Aesop operates as a more discreet and successful Menenius, bantering folk out of their grievances by disguising compliant patrician attitudes to Williamite taxes as folktales and comedy. That the first response was the satirically oppositional Tory *Aesop at Tunbridge* is no surprise.

THE FABLE POETIC: DENNIS AND LA FONTAINE

Not many snooks are more pointed than the one that John Dennis cocked at La Fontaine in his outrageous Hudibrastic revision of ten of his fables in 1693, the first English translation of any of the *Fables*. As John Ozell says in the Dedication to his translation of Boileau's *Le Lutrin*, Hudibrastic burlesque is a form 'where great Events are made Ridiculous by the Meanness of the Character, and the Oddness of the Numbers' (Ozell 1708: *3r–*3v). But there are no great events in animal fables, which themselves mimic and reduce the world's great events. Dennis is effectively burlesquing La Fontaine himself, his high French author, while his Preface exalts Butler, who is much the stronger influence. The effect, seen against the magical quality of the originals, is, in John Shea's apposite phrase, that of 'a bull in a china shop' (Mandeville 1966: iii). Dennis's treatment of 'Le Cochon, La Chèvre et Le Mouton' can act as a representative example.

La Fontaine's 'Dom porceau' squeals horribly as he is being taken to market, and is rebuked by the driver of the cart: why can't he be quiet like the wise Sheep? The Pig stops squealing and elucidates feelingly. The Sheep and the Goat could perhaps be right in thinking that they are going to market just to be milked and shorn, but he is a pig, and who wears pig's wool or drinks pig's milk?

> Ils pensent qu'on les veut seulement décharger,
> La Chèvre de son lait, le Mouton de sa laine.
> Je ne sais pas s'ils ont raison;
> Mais quant à moi, qui ne suis bon
> Qu'à manger, ma mort est certaine.
> Adieu mon toit et ma maison. (La Fontaine 1962: 219–20)

They think that all anyone wants from them is the Goat's milk and the Sheep's wool. I don't know if they're right; but when it comes to me, I'm only fit to eat, so I'm bound to die. Farewell, my roof and my house.

A Pig suddenly and fully humanized in his inferences from his knowledge of his own unfortunate natural and cultural differences from others; in his plausible – if optimistic, as we know from mordant authorial comments earlier in the fable – reserving of judgement about their destiny; in his inferential conjuring of their thoughts from their silence (the Sheep and Goat have said nothing); and in the plangency of his lament. Intelligence and soul: a complicated Pig, a Pig we wish we had met. But the wholly original moral that follows ironizes and reverses this carefully established hierarchy:

> Dom porceau raisonnait en subtil personnage:
> Mais que lui servait-il? Quand le mal est certain,
> La plainte ni la peur ne changent le destin;
> Et le moins prévoyant est toujours le plus sage. (*ibid.*: 220)

Master Pig proved an elegant reasoner; but what good did it do him? When disaster is certain, neither fear nor fulmination will alter destiny; and the shortest-sighted is always the wisest.

Where ignorance is bliss, wisdom is the capacity to be regardless of one's fate; a perpetual possession of being well deceived. This is as pointedly insouciant about the expedient, contingent morality of fable as it is about the reader's carefully cultivated feelings for the Pig. Fables usually operate inside a prudentialist, or, at the highest, providentialist framework, so foresight is good; the wisdom of the Swallow, or the Ant. But here, to be able to foresee one's fate yet be powerless against it smacks of tragedy. And the reader, having yielded to the fiction, can foresee the poem's ending, the moral, much less clearly than the poor Pig foresees his: so in the moral's terms, the reader is wise. La Fontaine engages in the bantering kind of paradox which consists of the reversal of expectations and categories. One should of course expect a twist in the tail in a fable about a Pig, but still, God does not seem to have arranged things for the best in placing this Pig in that cart. The moral leaves a suspicious taste in the mouth, but this is accepted as an aspect of the extraordinarily high wit.

In contrast, Dennis's Pig is simply aggressive in his diction, his sentiments, and his social orientation. Faced with his fate, he proclaims that he is a beast

> Whom Wastcoateer has made a Fat Pig,
> For some Cits ravenous Spouse, with Brat big.
> 'Tis for her maw I'm grown this Squab bit;
> May the Jade choak with the first gobbet. (Dennis 1693: 26)

Monosyllabic slang, mock-rhyme and -rhythm, and a very basic power-structure: all the playfulness and paradox that La Fontaine has inherited from Phaedrus vanish. The 'translation' is as scathing about the pretentions of its original as the Pig is about the lady.

This is not merely casual violence against La Fontaine and the French: it is part of an attitude taken from the French more widely, and so forms part of yet another double-handed enterprise. Dennis is also making a point about decorum, which is that animals and other 'low' creatures properly belong on the lowest rung of the linguistic ladder. Dogs and other animals should speak doggerel, and doggerel is the mode of burlesque: so burlesque must be the proper form for animal fable, verse apologue. This point is itself based on an association commonly made in this period, between the linguistic and social properties of burlesque. For example the author (possibly Tom Durfey) of the Hudibrastic satire on L'Estrange called *Pendragon; or the Carpet Knight His Kalendar* (1698) charmingly explains in his Advertisement that the shambling four-beat doggerel line is like 'Four Feet', but that

> those Four Feet are . . . by no means obliged to be but Eight Syllables . . . in place of the last, it is a part of its Excellency some times to have Two, Three, or

Four Syllables (like so many Claws) crowded into the time of One Foot . . . [Burlesque's] Nature is to Ridicule, Flatter, Huff, and Banter, by turns; to Scratch and Claw now, and anon to Grin and Bite like a Satyr. ([Durfey] 1698: A2r–A2v)

Bitcherel, he says, would be doggerel written by a woman: and where mock-heroic is like a graceful lady, burlesque is like an ungainly chambermaid.

In fable, animals speak; doggerel is 'low' like an animal: so animal fable is a 'low' form, and should be written in burlesque. Mandeville agrees, in essence; the '*strict Numbers*' of his 'Familiar Verse' (Mandeville 1703: Preface and titlepage) are also octosyllables, though purged of Dennis's sub-Hudibrastic lurchings. Octosyllabic couplets were, as Calvin Yost puts it, the 'orthodox form' (Yost 1936: 101) of the verse fable thenceforwards, especially in the periodicals: anyone choosing a more flexible form, such as Hall-Stevenson, was innovating – or imitating La Fontaine.

Dennis's remonstrance springs from a genuine feeling that La Fontaine is guilty of breaking this decorum of literary forms. Fable has natural rules, after all, of consistency and decorum, and must not get above itself: Prior and Montague would agree, in a gentlemanly way. But Dennis's point is made from the full rigour of a neoclassical mind nourished by French critics such as Le Bossu and by the 'teaching' Aesops that lie behind La Fontaine. With the form returned to its proper 'low' state, almost as low as the little fables of Audin and Baudoin, Dennis added voluminous abstract Morals and Moral Reflections, again after the French mode but now in 'high' heroic couplets. The fundamental paradox of the form, that fables may be both low (dunghill, fiction, false) and high (Pearl, moral, true) is carefully separated out and denatured in the split between the fables and their application. The dignity of fable is now merely the dignity of the academy and the critic: this is what Dennis really wants from the French. That a French fabulist suffers does not matter: Butler is the *appropriate* master, and English. In his Preface, Dennis says that he would be 'ravished to see that we out did the *French* in Arts, at the same time that we contend for Empire with them' (Dennis 1939: 10): the competitive ethos of translation so carefully disdained by Davenant and Ogilby. The high Arts are criticism and moral reflection: these deserve high poetic style. Criticism deals seriously with fable, but fable has high and low forms: the proper stylistic level for a low form is not '*égayé*', but '*rude*'.

Dennis's later veneration for the Christianized, neoclassical French vision of fable made him one of the main transmitters of this attitude to that new, pious, bourgeois part of the eighteenth-century English audience which needed to be talked gently into a trust in imaginative literature. His admiration is not for verse apologues, but for the supposedly moral tendency of a very generalized 'fable'. For example, in *The Stage Defended* (1726), a reply to an attack on the stage by William Law, Dennis argues that 'Every true Dramatick Poem is a Fable as much as any one of Aesop's: it has . . . a direct Tendency to teach moral Virtue' (Dennis 1943: 308). He goes on quite logically to justify the drama by justifying 'fable'. He mentions Jotham, and Christ:

> Jesus Christ, who best knew the nature of man, made use of Fables or Parables, as most proper at the same Time, both to please, and to instruct, and Perswade. For a Fable is a Discourse most aptly contrived to Form the Manners of men by Instructions disguised under the Allegory of an Action. . . . a play is a Fable, that is, a Composition of Truth and Fiction . . . the Action is feigned and the Moral true, and can therefore never be contrary to a Christian temper and spirit. (*ibid.*: 308, 312)

This is a man who believes what he is saying. It is clearly very odd as argument, cutting a number of knots in a sweeping, sentimental fashion. What is perhaps most remarkable is the suggestion that because a play is a fable, it cannot be immoral. When Dryden and Rymer compared a play to an Aesopian fable half a generation earlier, the intention was to mock, not to purify. But from where do Dennis's convictions come?

THE FABLE CRITICAL: LE BOSSU AND FARQUHAR

More than two generations after René Le Bossu published his *Traité du Poème Épique* (1675, trans. 1697 as *A Treatise of the Epic Poem*), Fielding's Parson Adams is still able to impress an audience with a passionate defence of Homer which, as Stuart Curran points out, is partly mediated through 'the French critic' (Le Bossu 1970: xi). Curran also points out that Fielding praises Le Bossu in *Tom Jones*, Book 11, chapter 1, as one 'of those noble Critics, to whose Labours the learned World are so greatly indebted' (Fielding 1974: 2, 569), though this may not be quite the conscious affirmation that Curran takes it to be: Fielding is none too fond of critics, and is well aware that current English theory on epic and fable still amounts to not much more than reworkings of Le Bossu. Nor is Adams' audience impressed in the way he might have intended: his host, Wilson, is convinced that he has 'a Bishop in his House' (Fielding 1967: 199). Fielding's lightly ironized reverential attitude is shared by

Pope, who often 'believes' Le Bossu in his translations, but then uses 'Martinus Scriblerus' to implicate Bossu in the conception and plan of *The Dunciad Variorum* (1728–9): finally 'Ricardus Aristarchus' (i.e. Bentley as parodied by Warburton) works scathing remarks about the 'putid conceit!' of this 'Gallic critic' (Pope 1968: 711) into the prologemena to *The Dunciad* (1742–3), but then refers to him as a standard authority. But by far the most creative and remarkable use of Le Bossu is that of George Farquhar in his 'Discourse Upon Comedy' from 1702: remarkable because it exposes Dennis's post-Le Bossu arguments from fable about the morality of drama to ridicule, a full generation before Dennis used them. But to begin at the beginning:

Fable, according to Le Bossu's widely-repeated dictum, is 'un discours inventé pour former les moeurs par des instructions déguisées sous les allégories d'une action' (Le Bossu 1675: 12). Dennis's sentence above translates this accurately, pointedly adapting the 1697 translation of 'W. J'. which gives 'moeurs' as 'Morals' (Le Bossu 1697: 7). Reworking Baudoin's scheme, which 'regards fable as encompassing narrative literature in general' (Noel 1975: 17), and in which Aesopian fable is thus seen as a subsection of a wider kind, Le Bossu is able to include epic under the heading of fable: fable is the nature of epic. He will not even distinguish immediately between Homer and Aesop on grounds of scale: both are engaged in the same enterprise:

> First then I say, that the *Moral Truth and Instruction is apparently the same in both. Aesop* and *Homer* would have us learn, *that a misunderstanding between those of the same Party exposes them to . . . their own Ruin: and that Concord preserves and renders them Victorious.*
>
> The Fiction is likewise the same. Both have feigned a Confederacy of several Persons together, for the Maintenance and Defence of their Interest against a Common Enemy. Again, both have feign'd some disturbance that happen'd at first in this Union; and that those who quarrell'd met with an equal share of misfortune. Lastly, both have restor'd to the Party of these United Persons, the Concord and Victory which was the consequence of their Re-union.
>
> There's nothing remains now but to give Names to those fęign'd Persons. As for the Nature of the *Fable*, it matters little whether the Names of *Beasts* or of *Men* be made use of. Homer has made choice of these last; and has given the Quality of Kings to his Personages. He has call'd them *Achilles, Agamemnon, Hector, Patroclus*, and has expressed by the name of *Grecians*, that Interest which the Confederates were obliged to maintain. Æsop in his way, has given the Names of *Beasts* to all his Personages: the *Dogs* are the Confederates, the *Wolf* is their Enemy, and he has called the *Sheep*, what the Poet has term'd the *Grecians*. (Le Bossu 1697: 21)

It is not possible to suspect Le Bossu of irony, though one may suspect partiality: *bossu* is French for hunchbacked or deformed, which Aesop traditionally was. Strictly speaking, all that Le Bossu is doing is developing a few passages in Horace which speak of Homeric heroes as if their characters were allegorical of qualities such as Anger and Wisdom, and zealously conflating 'fable' in Aristotelian theory with fable in Aesopian practice; possibly that of La Fontaine, though no examples are mentioned. Using the 'sister arts' notion, he proves that the moral takes precedence over the fable: do not artists and sculptors sketch the design, outline, or plan, and then find suitable materials with which to work? Le Bossu's processes of argument are extremely careful and plausible, and he soon modifies his bald conflation, so it is easy to see why others found such statements credible – Pope and Fielding admire him because he is relentlessly analytical, rather than judgemental in the English manner. But the effect is, as Jane Austen might say, dreadfully derogatory of an hero's dignity, and the suggestion that epic energies are closer to the animal than the divine is dangerous for epic itself.

Ralph Cohen points out that in the eighteenth century, 'poetic kinds were identified in terms of a hierarchy' stretching between the lowly epigram and epic, and that a feature of this hierarchy was 'the inclusion of lower forms into higher' (Cohen 1974: 35). Le Bossu's argument, which proceeds partly by paradox in identifying what is highest in poetry directly with what is lowest – Aesopian fable is a kind of epigram – disturbs even such an interrelated hierarchy radically, in its almost literal insistence on fable's figure for itself as both Dunghill and Pearl, an equivalent of the Christian treasure-of-the-humble (Le Bossu is *Le Père* Bossu).

Dryden puts three parenthetical complimentary references to Le Bossu into the Dedication to the 1697 *Aeneis*, none of which demonstrates that he has read the *Traité*, and one of which, that Spenser would have been a better poet if he had read Le Bossu, is actively absurd. He then ignores him completely in the Preface to the *Fables*, where he has almost nothing to say about the morals of his own epic fables, which tend to work through clouded analogies rather than through the allegories of an action. And he could never take such a straightforward conflation of epic and fable as Le Bossu's seriously: Ogilby, though the morals of his fables are, as was seen in the previous chapter, sometimes akin to the perceived morals of epic, printed a *burlesque* of an epic (the Frog and Mouse) as a fable. But it must be pleasing to have a scholarly and unworldly Frenchman dignify one's subject-matter, especially given the very broad historical irony involved in his arguing, in the late 1690s, that confederate states should stick together in order to defeat tyrannical opponents.

Farquhar's 'Discourse Upon Comedy, in Reference to the English Stage, in a Letter to a Friend' (published in Farquhar's *Love and Business* in 1702) is his elegant contribution to the wide argument engendered by the Societies for the Reformation of Manners, and in particular by Jeremy Collier, who argued that the effects of the Restoration stage were so immoral that plays should be censored or perhaps banned. The 'Discourse' takes the form of a close parody of Le Bossu's 'moral' method and argument. Farquhar's strategy is to play off one kind of felt absurdity against another, answering two complementary discourses, moral and critical, which he feels are in danger of becoming dominant. He argues first for the independence and Englishness of stage comedy, but then appears to change his mind and to conflate drama with Aesopian fable, where Le Bossu worked between epic and Aesop. The mode is a brilliantly plausible Horatian lucidity, which is even extended into paradoxical or burlesque arguments such as the position that if dramatists make plays moral (boring), the London audience will grow restive and take to making assignations for after the performance, ensuring that the most moral of plays will promote 'more Lewdness in the Consequence' than the most immoral. From within this banter he insinuates his comparison, as carefully and tactfully as Le Bossu developed his:

there is something in the Nature of Comedy, even in its present Circumstances, that bears so great a Resemblance to the Philosophical *Mythology* of the Ancients, that old *Aesop* must wear the Bays as the first and original Author; and whatever Alterations or Improvements farther Application may have subjoin'd, his *Fables* gave the first Rise and Occasion.

Comedy is no more at present than *a well-formed Tale handsomly told, as an agreeable Vehicle for Counsel or Reproof.* This is all we can say for the Credit of its Institution; and is the Stress of its Charter for Liberty and Toleration. Then where should we seek for a Foundation, but in Aesop's symbolical way of moralizing upon Tales and Fables, with this difference, That his Stories were shorter than ours: He had his tyrant *Lyon*, his Statesman *Fox*, his beau *Magpy*, his Coward *Hare*, his Bravo *Ass*, and his Buffoon *Ape*, with all the Characters that crowd our Stage every Day, with this Distinction nevertheless, that Aesop made his Beasts speak good Greek, and our Heroes sometimes can't talk English. (Farquhar 1988: 2, 368, 377)

Having demonstrated the parallel, he then uses it mockingly against Collier and the Societies:

for ought I know it might prove a good means to mollify the Rigour of the Persecution, to inform the Inquisitors, that the great *Aesop* was the first inventor of these poor Comedies that they are pursuing with so much Eagerness and Fury, that the first *Laureat* was as just, as prudent, as pious, as reforming, and as ugly as any of themselves. . . . We shou'd inform them besides, that those very Tales and Fables which they apprehend as obstacles to Reformation, were the main Instruments and Machines us'd by the wise *Aesop* for its Propogation; and as he would improve Men by the Policy of Beasts, so we would endeavour to reform Brutes by the Examples of Men. (*ibid.*: 377–8)

Examples follow, and then the *coup de grâce*. Where Le Bossu merely assumes the parallel between fable and 'Parables divinely invented' (Le Bossu 1697: 40), Farquhar flourishes it in Collier's face:

if these Pagan Authorities give Offence to their Scrupulous Consciences, let them but consult the Tales and Parables of our *Saviour* in Holy Writ, and they may find this way of Instruction to be much more *Christian* than they imagine. (Farquhar 1988: 2, 378)

The extension of 'Tales and Fables' to 'Tales and Parables' is the final piece of cheek – the *tales* of Jesus Christ, the divine raconteur! – and parallels the surreptitious work with the word 'reforming'. The critics, unused to banter based on paradox, were suitably affronted, though Collier himself did not respond. But Farquhar was not the only writer to use fable to answer false masters in the form of Collier and the Societies: Dryden and Mandeville did too. So *The Fable of the Bees* is part of an English *tradition* of Augustan fable.

DRYDEN'S *FABLES ANCIENT AND MODERN*

Literary history first derided *The Hind and the Panther* as absurd and antiquated, and then reduced it to a figurehead for or against political causes. The collection or miscellany of narrative, lyric, discursive, and sermon-like episodes ranging from Homer to himself in the form of a 'highly episodic verse novel' (Miner 1972: 263) that Dryden called *Fables* was read with almost unqualified enthusiasm and respect throughout the next century, and was admired by the Romantics: Wordsworth, Scott, Byron, Godwin, and others. Horace Walpole used them as a source for *The Castle of Otranto* (1764): Roxana and Clarissa have both read them, and use them. So the collection faces forwards in time as successfully as it faces backwards, channelling varied material towards equally varied audiences: it is an important transitional work between the Renaissance and the Romantics. The Dryden critics, over the past thirty years, have been similarly appreciative.

What had Dryden learnt to do with fable in just thirteen years, to persuade such audiences to treat his collection so sympathetically? And why did he call it *Fables*, which was doubtless one of the gambits that attracted later readers? To put it more strongly: given the reception accorded to *The Hind and the Panther*, why did he choose to justify himself by way of fable *twice*? In a letter to Charles Montague, with whom he was now largely reconciled, he referred to one of the original poems in the collection, 'To my Honour'd Kinsman, JOHN DRIDEN', as 'a Memorial of my own Principles to all Posterity' (Dryden 1942: 120). *The Hind and the Panther* had been a memorial of his principles, but that poem, as Dryden foresaw, was also a tombstone-inscription to his public career: the Hind's self-reflexive triplet-apostrophe in Part 3, like other parts of the poem, is written with a plangency which argues a good deal of authorial feeling behind the lines:

> Down then thou rebell, never more to rise,
> And what thou didst, and do'st so dearly prize,
> That fame, that darling fame, make that thy sacrifice.
>
> (Dryden 1956–92, 3, 510)

Montague and Prior were yielding to a natural temptation when they retaliated by making the application personal, remarking that Dryden seemed to have been commanded by the Hind to 'Sacrifice *his* darling Fame' as an act of religious penance or mortification (Prior 1959: 1, 36). The poem becomes a personal myth of exclusion and dis-integration. Why should Dryden work with 'fable' again, to the extent of telling Montague about his own principles?

A key to a brief answer may lie in a combination of Eric Rothstein's perception of the broad movement of English poetry in this period as one away from the theme of power and towards an interest in the principles of interaction, relationship, and synthesis, with Judith Sloman's comment that 'the multiple meanings of "fable" allow Dryden to cut across the hierarchy of genres once again, since fable can describe so many aspects of literature' (Sloman 1985: 168). In other words Dryden uses 'fable' here for something of the same reason as he subtitled *Absalom and Achitophel* simply *A Poem*, in order to achieve a 'carefully induced generic confusion' (Zwicker, 1984: 89) which will allow his complex synthetic effects to remain uncramped by the political overtones inherent in a choice of a specific genre.

It would of course be equally correct to argue the opposite – that fables in 1700 are laden with potential Catholic and Jacobite overtones after *Aesop at Tunbridge*, L'Estrange, Barlow, etc. – but Dryden coolly takes advantage of the range of his material to place himself just to one side of this position by entitling his collection *Fables Ancient and Modern.* This echoes the less provocative part of the subtitle of the French *Aesops*, *histoires tant anciennes que modernes* (Audin), rather than the *Moral and Political* that the more partisan collections were prone to import. It is also a tacit remonstrance to the temper of the current *querelle* between the Ancients and the Moderns. Dryden mixes time up: his three pieces from Boccaccio parallel parts of the *Aeneis*; at the end of an original (Modern) poem, 'Alexander's Feast', Alexander is led away 'with Zeal to destroy' the Persian city by Thaïs, who 'like another *Hellen*, fir'd another *Troy*' (Dryden 1962: 508; subsequent references in this chapter are to this edition, and page numbers only will be given). So Dryden modulates between fixed positions, Ancient and Modern (as Theseus will mediate beween the rivals Palamon and Arcite, and as Dryden's cousin, John Driden, will 'steer betwixt the Country and the Court' (608) parties) via fable; rather as Swift will in *The Battel of the Books*.

In other words, the title performs a moral silently, as fables should. Opposites, and the fixed positions represented by oppositions such as Ancient and Modern, are fascinating, but require an idiosyncratic synthesis which suggests that Modern poems may take their place beside others; and fable, with its understanding of the handles of fixed positions, is the proper mode for this, even though the fables themselves may be pieces of myth or narrative episodes.

The *Fables* bear out Rothstein's thesis in many ways, of which perhaps the most central is that they allow Dryden to synthesize personal feeling – 'inner multiplicity' (Sloman 1985: 50) – with as public an utterance as he wished to make, and at the same time to establish the exceptionally dynamic relationship with readers which is a fundamental quality of Augustan fable. Where the multiplicity of *The Hind and the Panther* consistently suggests strain and a writer relatively unsure of his relations with the audience, the *Fables* sublimate these tensions: where the earlier poem is darkly writ, this is an alluring kaleidoscope of perspectives:

> I will sing of mighty Mysteries,
> Of Truths conceal'd before, from human Eyes,
> Dark Oracles unveil, and open all the Skies. (798)

The dark science is, as with Davenant's Aesop in 1651, restored to varied light. As opposites such as personal and public are fascinating, we can begin with the more private aspects of the collection.

A 'Memorial . . . to all Posterity': in other words, an epitaph of himself, a personal statement of summation made at what he sensed was the end of his life. In the Preface, Dryden makes it clear that he intends the 'Memorial' quality to apply – or be applied – more widely. He several times talks briefly and quietly of his advanced age and bodily infirmities, and begins by contrasting the 'House' he has constructed in the *Fables* with the incomplete palace left by a nobleman who 'never lived to finish' his 'Palace' – echoing the heirless ducal 'House' of Ormond in the Dedication (520, 515, 520). The sense is of a familial version of the contrast between a well-wrought urn and half-acre tombs: the personal shades into the professional. As elsewhere, the fable of life conduces to the moral, the epitaph, itself couched as fable. Socrates composed hymns to Apollo and versified Aesop: high and low culture. Dryden writes fables Ancient-and-Modern, synthesizing the heroics of epic fable with the anti-heroism of the fable-pamphlets and the scabrous burlesques of epic of the 1690s. In the *Fables* Dryden was able to integrate the Christian and political elements of his 'Principles' more fully into his Ovidian or Pythagorean poetic medium of flux and metamorphosis. This integration is, in its own way, *Moral and Political*, as well as partly historical in method, but also highly personal and peculiar, as may best be seen by the effects made in the ending of this ending.

The ending is not a moral, but a bizarre and, in its place, extremely shocking fable, Boccaccio's unnerving story of 'Cymon and Iphigenia'. Before it, there is what looks like an ending: Dryden first adapts Chaucer's eulogy of his final pilgrim, the Parson, in 'The Character of a Good Parson', and then doubles the Christian ending by writing an 'Epitaph', in this case 'On a Fair Maiden Lady', whose spirituality is idealized gently and delicately. One male, one female, 'of a double Kind, / Varying the Sexes' in alternate poems: like the Hyena in 'Of the Pythagorean Philosophy', who is male one year and female the next. This idealized pair, Parson and Lady, stand, as final exemplars, next to the venerated Duke and Duchess of Ormond, from the Dedication and the first poem, apparently completing a pattern.

Here doubleness, the 'double Kind', is at last a natural condition and also a 'Wonder' (808) rather than a sign of Panther-like duplicity, but must still be outreached or redoubled. As the Vicar of Wakefield's prison-sermon will come before the real ending, so the conclusion of the 'Epitaph' concludes nothing. 'Cymon and Iphigenia' is the opposite of a eulogy or epitaph: it is full of casual violences, double rape, massacre, and unanswered self-justifications by naked power. 'My Love disdains the Laws / And like a King by Conquest gains his Cause' (823) says Cymon. 'Right have I none', says Cymon's double, the jealous and besotted magistrate Lysymachus ('The cause and crime the same'), before massacring the 'double Bridegroom' and his fellow-Rhodians; ' 'Tis Force . . . must justify the Deed' (827–9). It seems that it does: at the end, Cymon and Lysymachus are 'happy each at Home', in married bliss, where the usual poetic fate of Dryden's warlike adventurers is to be 'wreck'd at home' (831, 349). And the ravishers' war ends in a truce, and in peace: private vices, public benefits. The fable could be either a deconstruction *or* a secularized demonstration of William Sherlock's odious dictum that 'God, when he sees fit, and can better serve the end of his Providence by it, sets up Kings without any regard to Legal Right, or Humane Laws' (Sherlock 1690: 33). Sherlock is the 'flatt'ring Priest' whose 'senseless Plea of Right by Providence' (814), which merely 'justifies the next who comes in play' (in this case, William III), is derided near the end of 'The Character of a Good Parson': the poem seems absolutely sure of its ground at this point. But Cymon's unanswered appeal over the head of Rights and Laws can be read as an 'example' of successful opportunism in the service of Love just as easily as it can be read as a negative example of what right-by-conquest looks like in practice: the gloss to the anonymous 1620 prose translation of this tale, the version from which Dryden was working, says simply 'Love (oftentimes) maketh a man, both wise and valiant' (Boccaccio 1620: sig. Hh2^{v}).

By themselves these final reversals and paradoxes seem akin to the paradoxical wonders of the romance-tradition from which Boccaccio's novellas partly descend, but this fable's functions are also classically circular, returning the reader to many of Dryden's recurrent themes and interests, including the topic of armies *versus* navies, and to the interests in Homeric and Virgilian epic. As Sloman points out, Boccaccio's story 'contains [ironic] parallels both to Virgil and to Homer, since much of its action involves a sea journey and its conclusion is the rape of a city for the sake of abducting two women' (Sloman 1985: 144). More widely, Dryden's myth finally returns, as a myth should, to its houses or homes, literary, political, and moral, and considers them together. But the houses are also the houses of masters. These are the family or genealogy of poets which forms the foundations of the 'House' of Dryden-as-writer; the ducal house of Ormond, the dedicatees and hence the political 'masters' of the collection; and the house of artistic morality, fable-morality, that contrasts with the new narrowly moral voice of Jeremy Collier and the Societies for the Reformation of Manners. Where the Ormonds are addressed in the first poem, the final paragraphs of the Preface address themselves to Collier, an address which is completed at the end, in 'Cymon and Iphigenia'. Dryden here chooses fable to answer Collier and the Societies, as Farquhar and Mandeville will, and in doing so defines himself through meditating on his own artistic ground.

As Phaedrus began his ending by recalling the master addressed in his title, Augustus, in the fable of the flute-player called Princeps, so Dryden begins his by recalling two 'masters', Collier and the Ormonds, in the *poeta loquitur* at the start of 'Cymon and Iphigenia'. The optimistic moral here proposed to the Duchess, and to the 'Fame' of 'all the Fair', is 'When Beauty fires the Blood, how Love exalts the Mind' (816), a moral which the fable first embodies and then reverses. If there may be a 'Man within' (809) the beast, in 'Of the Pythagorean Philosophy', there may still be a beast within the man. Iphigenia is a fit foil for her hero: 'impotent of Mind', she hugs her ravisher and forgives him. 'Sex to the last' (825) comments Dryden: so much for *that* moral, and so much for the Fame of the Fair. The poem began from the premise that the 'Pow'r of Beauty' still inspires Dryden's 'Wit' where it once 'inflam'd [his] Soul' (815), but the wit seems to transform the morality, where Love and Beauty transform Cymon.

The dedicatees, the pointedly heirless Duke and Duchess – 'You owe Your Ormond nothing but a Son' (543) – are curiously mirrored in Cymon's father, who is similarly 'wanting in a worthy Heir' (817). The Duchess is as pointedly beautiful as Iphigenia – 'that Angel-Face' / 'her celestial Face' (540, 820) – but how does this help? What on earth will become of any Ormond *fils*, given these parallels? Analogies which are to be felt as parallels are deliberately made important at the start of the collection: the opening poem compares the Duchess to Chaucer's Emily in the next poem, 'Palamon and Arcite', and the historical parallel is then extended to a comparison between Ormond being sent to Ireland by William, and Palamon to Thebes by 'Conqu'ring *Theseus*' (*ibid.*: 540). In a period when the historical parallel is a form of argument in itself the educated reading mind is forced to make connections via analogy, and Dryden sees to it that the *Fables* operate in this way. In this sense, the discourse of fable is felt to lie next to the written discourse of history, a point which John Wallace, quoting Virgilio Malvezzi's *Discourses on Cornelius Tacitus* (trans. 1641), may explain or illustrate:

> The drawing of necessary consequences depended on the skill with which the historian had gathered and marshalled his facts, but, above all, on the astuteness of his learned audience, deducing and applying the precepts therein implied. 'A man delights in Tacitus' cunning', said Malvezzi, 'because by it he discovers his owne.' (Wallace 1969: 272)

History, like fable, is conventionally seen as philosophy teaching by example, but of course examples are also precepts, or can become so when they are applied. History and fable thus make their Morals in the same way, silently activating and heating the reading mind to read hidden clues and to sense attitude and pattern from these. The resemblance between Malvezzi on Tacitus, and Addison, Kames, and Sterne on fable and allegory (chapter 2, pp. 16–17) is striking, and perhaps helps to explain Sterne's readiness to engage silently with Smart's historical fable. The discourse of history clearly supports or lies behind the later examples.

Dryden's strategy, which centres on a few historical parallels and on just two expository statements of political position, one in the second half of the 'Kinsman' poem, and one in 'The Character of a Good Parson' (lines 106–20, which include a historical parallel), is to give the reading mind hints in parallels, analogies, and echoes which it then feels the urge to apply more widely. The various procedures above, the deducing of an attitude from hints in the title, the deducing of a more general personal quality in the collection from hints in the Preface, and the finding of a pattern in the ending which is like the reflexive or circling pattern of other fable-endings, are examples of the mind of a reader conversant with 'fable' being played on and made to work through hints and analogy, though not historical analogy.

The various hints of the historical world may even stimulate the reading mind to provide a single reading in which the engagement with the post-1688 world expands to fill the whole frame, as for example in Rachel Miller's fascinating thesis. Allusions to contemporary issues such as 'succession, abdication, and vacancy; allegiance and passive obedience; *de facto* and *de jure* rule; usurpation . . . just conquest and providential appointment . . . William's foreign and domestic policies, particularly his continuation of the wars and his reliance on standing armies, land grants and foreign advisors' (Miller 1984: 14) allow for a mode of almost continuous application to the immediate political scene.

But, again, the references in the text are unsettled, or pass teasing duplex messages. There seems to be a form of authorial detachment behind the political allusions which, like the Lady's soul in the 'Epitaph', lies next to passionate involvement but can only be curled, ruffled, by it, without being stirred. In 'Sigismonda and Guiscardo', Tancred may have a palace guard which in peacetime is 'Fit only to maintain Despotick Pow'r' (636), and the Williamite 'Standing Army of the Sky' (593) may laugh appreciatively when Jove usurps Heaven in 'Palamon and Arcite', but a passage (lines 399–404) in 'Cymon and Iphigenia' is equally scathing about the country militia, 'an alternative form of defence sometimes preferred by William's opponents because it would be comped of local men, not mercenaries answerable to the king' (Sloman 1985: 155). Dryden would prefer to see the nation rely on naval power, but the final victoriows navy belongs not to the just, but to the assassinating 'Ravishers' (831) Cymon and Lysyimachus: as in other things, the final tale seems to ironize what might have been a straightforward moral. No fixed position is settled on. The other subversive, burlesquing tale, 'The Cock and the Fox', acts in the same way in making comedy of what has elsewhere been a positive, and creating just the kind of paradox or reversal that the Nun's Priest achieved in Chaucer's version:

> At one point, Partlet's unwilling submission to Chanticleer's feathering is likened to passive obedience . . . which is one of the good parson's virtues . . . the reference is brief, serving more to echo or undercut other tales than to discuss contemporary events. (Reverand 1988: 159)

Many parallels lead nowhere, or pass contradictory messages, as the rest of the poems often do – Theseus's enthusiastic praise of the married state at the end of 'Palamon and Arcite' comes just before Dryden envying Driden his condition, 'Lord of your self, uncumber'd with a Wife' (606), for instance – or they become embroiled with other hints and parallels. The Duchess is like Emily, but also like Iphigenia: as so often in fable, what was panegyric shades towards satire, so that the collection ends rather less deferentially than it began.

Pointing out that 'Cymon and Iphigenia' promises a clear moral which it then denies the reader brings the discussion (at last) back to the other part of the double reference, *Moral* and Political, in the *poeta loquitur* – to the 'severe Divine' (815), Jeremy Collier. Collier's 'ungovern'd Zeal' against Dryden's house parallels Alexander's 'Zeal to destroy' the 'Persian Abodes' (816, 508) – 'Zeal' is the word Dryden initially uses about Collier in the Preface, though he then decides that his motive may have been simple muckraking in 'the Rubbish of Ancient and modern Plays' (538). Collier is disparaged in the *poeta loquitur* for his unpriestly 'witty . . . Railing', but most pointedly for his heated, single, 'too plain' reading of 'the double Meanings of the Stage', double meanings which Dryden then proceeds to transform into the strange double-handed morals of (Boccaccio's) fable. But not immediately: the moral proposed to Collier, given that 'Love's the Subject of the Comick Muse', is that Love is not

> always of a vicious Kind,
> But oft to virtuous Acts inflames the Mind.
> Awakes the sleepy Vigour of the Soul,
> And, brushing o'er, adds motion to the Pool.

Love, through the musical 'Chime' of the poetry which it 'invented . . . Soften'd the Fierce, and made the Coward Bold' (816). But lurking echoes of the music of 'Alexander's Feast' – 'Sooth'd with the Sound the King grew vain' (506) – already provide a silent counter-application of this line, as 'inflames' does to its line. The *Fables* are, as already noted, quite obsessed with amplifying the imagery of fire in the service of dramatizing various kinds of heroic but destructive 'turbulence of Mind' in the characters. All the fables examine and develop the post-Ogilby 'moral of epic', dramatizing the relations between ordered and disordered minds. The skilful politician Ulysses manages the private passions of Ajax for his own benefit, only indirectly for the common good. But the authorial obsession with fire-imagery sometimes seems a kind of turbulence in itself, as does the curious energy of the reading mind pulled from the relaxation of the narratives into the vertiginous vortices of parallels, analogies, and echoing images. And the 'brushing' image in the moral to Collier produces such a pull, for it is an echo of 'The Flower and the Leaf': 'Sea's wou'd be Pools, without the brushing Air, / To curl the Waves' (726), and also a reprise of the lines on the page just before 'Cymon and Iphigenia', in the 'Epitaph' to the Lady who had 'A Soul so calm, it knew not Ebbs or Flows, / Which Passion cou'd but curl; oot discompose' (815). But the pool in the *poeta loquitur is* discomposed, set in motion, made turbid, turbulent, as Cymon's mind will be, as the reader's is. Analogy and parallel work in different ways in the *Fables*, sometimes historical and intellectual, sometimes directly through poetic metaphor and echo, the double strategy providing two contrasting handles for the reading mind – as fables do. The elemental world of some of these metaphors emphasizes other 'gothic' aspects of the technique, distance, sublimity, transitions to higher and lower states. The present reading obviously yields a little to the disordering heat of this more lyrical or metaphysical procedure (usually signalled by words such as 'as' and 'like' in the paragraphs above and below), as this is a very fetching quality in the *Fables* which is much less often stressed than the cooler historical analogies.

So 'Cymon and Iphigenia' acts as a provocation to thought about the nature of artistic morality, and raises the question of morality in the collection at large in the context of an address to a contemporary public exemplar of morality, Collier. If they promise morals which they do not perform, to what kind of moral do the *Fables* conduce, given that the moral in the title seemed to be about the falsity of fixed positions and the need for synthesis?

The moral for the reader is a performative rather than preceptual one, about reading, particularly about heated 'single' readings or applications in the Collier mode or any other. Where *The Hind and the Panther* focused on the topic of language in writing and speech, the *Fables* are more about writing and the perennial topic of fable, the nature of reading; the reader's reading of Dryden, and Dryden's own reading. As *The Hind and the Panther* completed a meta-fable involving *Religio Laici*, so the *Fables* complete another.

In the Preface, Dryden promises that the morals of the individual poems will 'leap foremost into sight, without the Reader's Trouble of looking after them' (523), as if these morals were little animals that the moral hunter-reader might pursue with the same directional vigour and ease as the hunter-kings will zealously pursue the 'Boar' in 'Meleager and Atalanta' that 'sprung amain / Like Lightning sudden, on the Warriour-Train', or with the same wisdom as 'the Wise', the 'sagacious Hounds' (613, 700) in the next poem, 'The Cock and the Fox', follow the Fox in their burlesque hunt. Hunting, sex, storms, and war form the Virgilian epic nexus for the life of the passions. Dryden invites the moral reader to mount in quest of parallels and analogies, to apply the example, to moralize the 'secret meaning of this moral Show' (741), and this appeal is impossible to resist.

But, as with the historical parallels and the other messages, the morals cannot, in the end, be hunted down. Sometimes there is a clear moral, as in 'The Flower and the Leaf', with its cool homily about the laurel leaves outlasting the daisy, but even this is both trite and mordant given that Dryden's professional laurels had been removed twelve years earlier. Sometimes the moral is the opposite of a moral, as the 1620 translator's gloss of 'Theodore and Honoria' makes clear: 'adventure oftentimes bringeth such matters to pass, as wit and cunning in man can never comprehend' (Boccaccio 1620: sig. M14ᵛ). 'Adventure' is sheer luck, mixed perhaps with activity and face: not the stuff of any kind of moral morality. And Dryden provides his own subtle reworking of Chaucer's fable-morals in the Nun's Priest's Tale. The end of 'The Cock and the Fox' faces us with that least plausible of characters, an honest Dryden who has written a 'plain Fable' about 'Negligence . . . Credulity . . . [and] Flatt'rers', and who cites the parables of Christ as evidence of the easy paradox that 'The Truth is moral, though the Tale a Lie'. But then

> in a Heathen Author we may find,
> That Pleasure with Instruction should be join'd:
> So take the Corn, and leave the Chaff behind. (701)

The 'joining' in one line is neatly contradicted by the winnowing, separating image in the next: the momentarily pious author opines that what Horace has joined, God and the reader may pull asunder.

But if reading is not to be *only* like the heat of hunting, what is it to be like? The other use of the reading/hunting metaphor in the Preface comes when Dryden describes his experience of the *Canterbury Tales* as that of 'a Variety of Game springing up before me'. Not moral reading, but simply *reading*: and rather than pursuing, Dryden is 'distracted in my Choice, and know not which to follow' (531). In particular, reading Homer makes Dryden read like one of his own heroic characters, with distracted passion. 'You never cool while you read *Homer*', he tells us: Homer is the greatest spirit among the classical authors. But there is only one piece of Homer in the collection, and the 'Agitation of the Spirits' that is occasioned in Dryden by Homer's admirable temper, 'violent, impetuous, and full of Fire', results in a 'Weakening of any Constitution . . . and many Pauses are required for Refreshment betwixt the Heats' (525, 524). A plunge in a cool, still pool, perhaps: reading is as physical or passional a process for Dryden as he intends it should be for the reader, and heat is life and energy as well as turbuence, zeal, and railing. Hot and cool, single and double, impetuous and reflective: the cycles or circles of experience, with the minds of writer and reader gradually coming to terms with the processes. Reading is life.

It is important, given the circling effects of the narrative ending in 'Cymon and Iphigenia', that Dryden's animal-emblem for human life in the *Fables* is neither quarry nor hunter, but the endless circles of

> The Hare . . .
> Emblem of Humane Life, who runs the Round;
> And after all his wand'ring Ways are done,
> His Circle fills, and ends where he begun,
> Just as the Setting meets the Rising Sun. (607)

Prey it may be, but the circling Hare is also an image of the hunter-Kinsman himself, John Driden, now returning in his old age to the favourite pursuits of his youth. So in another circle of wit, the Hare is both prey *and* hunter, and thus a symbol not only for the circles of human life but for the doublenesses of the *Fables* as a whole, which begin with the same sun-image, used of Theseus:

> A Chief, who more in Feats of Arms excell'd
> The Rising nor the Setting Sun beheld. (544)

And as the hot circles of the sun rising and setting create the circles of passional human life and the circles of the *Fables*, so the cool stars which circle in the 'Platonick Year' and 'at certain Periods . . . resume their Place' (540) create the Duchess of Ormond as another Emily and another Iphigenia. Poetic and narrative technique is embodied in analogy, symbol, element, temperature: the reading mind is again given hints, taught to apply characters (including Dryden's) and circumstances, to experience the buffeting of different states and cycles, and so to experience and reflect on the conclusions in which nothing can be concluded, embodied finally in the many buffeting and circling effects of 'Cymon and Iphigenia'.

This is the nexus of qualities, unique to the *Fables*, that speaks so powerfully to Dryden's appreciative audiences: the poeticizing of the Life and its ending; the combination of historicality with gothic qualities of distance and sublimity, and with elemental and epochal metaphors and parallels; the obliquely treated epic interests in the flux of the passions and the minds of both characters and readers; and a subtle stress on an artistic morality which goes so far beyond that of Collier and the Reformers. Almost all of these qualities are developed from classic and permanent qualities of Augustan fable, though Dryden's awesome synthesis is, admittedly, unique.

In particular, it seems to be the doubly embodied theme of the mind's experiencing ordering and disordering energies which so fascinates the eighteenth century. Miner's definition of the collection as a kind of 'verse novel' is extremely suggestive: the probabilistic ethos of the novel in this period derives its special emphasis on character from a more discursive and more directly moralistic kind of reflection on the stability ('temper') or instability of the mind, in fable derived from epic and heroic story. One might adduce the villainous Schedoni's cool lessons for the hero Vivaldi at the end of Ann Radcliffe's *The Italian* (1797), about how he has been able to play upon Vivaldi's 'ardent imagination', with its eagerness to 'experience its own peculiar delights' and soar 'after new wonders into a world of its own!' (Radcliffe 1968: 397, 398). It is as though Dryden's readers were required to become their own cool, reflective, sardonic Schedoni, as well as the heated, passionate Vivaldi, just as (if great with small we may compare) the reader of Swift's 'The Bubble' is asked to be both detached moral observer and sunstruck Icarean projector. Fable becomes novel. The *Fables* are indeed fable, though fable used in extraordinarily original ways: where Swift can transform Hesperian fable into Augustan, Dryden transforms almost everything available to him. So fable must *now* be a mode which can carry such a nexus of interests and qualities.

CHAPTER 7

High Augustan fable: Mandeville, Swift and Gay

Discussing the contexts of English literature in the 1720s, Ian Bell says of the Augustans' literary uses of indirection, irony, and code that such qualities often

> worked . . . to consolidate an oppositional community of readers who shared a body of attitudes and commitments, and could present themselves as the rightful custodians of authority, while at the same time recognizing their exclusion from power. (Bell 1994: 159)

Bell here puts his finger on the cultural position that might make the fable a natural mode of expression for Gay and Swift, both of whom are associated with the emerging political opposition to Walpole. But the most notable 'oppositional' use of fable in the early part of the century was Mandeville's, in *The Fable of the Bees*, and Mandeville, though also a notable ironist, is not politically oppositional – except in the sense that his politics and cultural orientation are in turn almost the opposite of those of Swift and Gay. So there is an intended polemical edge to the procedure of suggesting that the three writers who, taken together with Dryden, represent English 'Augustan' fable in its highest form of development, may have common interests and strategies in fable, and that Gay might be read against Mandeville in a comparative rather than combative sense – as Ogilby may be read against Marvell, say – where fables are concerned.

Such oppositional communities, and writing for and from them, may have been more various than is sometimes assumed, and even the politically oppositional mode seems to have been flexible and permeable rather than exclusive. When Samuel Croxall decided to shift political position in 1729 and to deliver his oppositional sermon using one of the key ironic anti-Walpole codewords, 'screen', (see chapter 3, p. 33), he delivered it directly to the very audience he wished to oppose, not with ironic intent to the opposition audience. The superior indirection of irony becomes the plain man's statement. Rather than being an exclusive or esoteric jargon, such coded diction seems to have operated as a common resource for writers and journalists who wished to drop into or out of a particular position, and it often originated with the commonly perceived words or actions of the political administration or its friends. If, say, the *London Magazine* creates an innuendo or flattering parallel between Walpole and the eloquence of Cicero, then 'Cicero' will quickly become a widely available ironic codeword, ready for silent application by Fielding in the paraphernalia of *Shamela*. Croxall, whose fables and collections of short fictions and *Lives* gave him a very wide audience, does not seem to have been a natural politician, nor a natural 'Augustan' any more than Mandeville, and he did not have to give up his broad constituency of readers as a result of his sermon.

One should remember that 'oppositional' uses of fable at the start of the eighteenth century take one of three forms. There are collections such as the 'de Witt' *Fables, Moral and Political*, which articulate very broad political and cultural reactions: more narrowly political reactions such as those of Pittis; and examples of the answering of the discourse of what are perceived as newly dominant false moralists, as in Farquhar, perhaps Toland, and Dryden. Only the third of these traditions employs the indirection of full irony, and Mandeville's *Fable*, though never yet discussed as such, is the most prominent example of the development of this part of the tradition. Swift and Gay write fables which are sometimes clearly a sublimated version of, or development from, the political context of discourse in the 1720s, but they treat this discourse and others in a highly sceptical and playful manner which is more reminiscent of Mandeville than of either of the political traditions.

As before, though, this is not a case about influence, to be argued, but of demonstrable kinship of method and manner; again, the *generic tradition*. The only necessary preliminary assumption is that the verse fables of Gay and Swift and *The Fable of the Bees* do not direct themselves *primarily* to political events and causes as such – Bell remarks on the Augustans' writing characteristically revealing 'an inability to exert influence over events' (Bell 1994: 159) – but to 'political' uses of language, dialects, voices: as with Walpole in *Shamela*, the opponent is not visible but audible by implication. Manner of discourse is a main target of fable, and the manner and conditions of discourse were specifically political topics in the 1720s.

The first task is to suggest an answer to a basic question about Mandeville's *Fable* which has never been answered satisfactorily, if at all.

Why was it initially conceived as fable, and why did Mandeville insist that it should continue to be seen as such, by retaining the title in each subsequent expansion after 1714, and by including the original verse fable, unaltered, in every expansion but the last, in 1729? In what sense is *The Fable* a fable, and in what sense is Mandeville a fabulist, rather than, say, a satirist or a social philosopher?

DR MANDEVILLE'S PRESCRIPTION: *THE FABLE OF THE BEES*

Bernard Mandeville emigrated from Holland to England in the 1690s, when he was in his twenties. English was his fourth language, counting the academic Latin of his medical education. This education was Cartesian, but he was also familiar with recent continental traditions of sceptical and empirical enquiry into physiology and the human passions which derived classical support from the writings of Lucretius and Epicurus, and he quickly reacted against his early systematic training. His temper, sceptical and alert, together with his love of irony and paradox and his sensitivity to the curious tones in which the English characteristically expressed themselves, impart to his work a remarkable effect, which Philip Pinkus nicely terms 'stupefaction' (Pinkus 1975: 205).

Mandeville's engagement with the dialects of English moralism and moral philosophy began in 1705, with his verse fable *The Grumbling Hive: or, Knaves Turn'd Honest.* This poem, which contains almost the whole of *The Fable* in miniature but largely without the rhetorical tricks of the later prose essays, is the story of the flourishing and 'Spacious Hive . . . That liv'd in Luxury and Ease' (Mandeville 1924: I, 17; subsequent references will be to this edition and will cite volume and page numbers only). The Hive, great rather than good, mimics English society in little, with 'all Trades and Places' behaving in a manner which in most other poets would call for satire. The lawyers, for example,

> . . . kept off Hearings wilfully,
> To finger the refreshing Fee;
> And to defend a wicked cause,
> Examin'd and survey'd the Laws,
> As Burglars Shops and Houses do,
> To find out where they'd best break through. (I, 20)

Little Peachums-in-reverse: but the cooing rhymes reassure the reader that all is more or less as it should be, the 'Easy' style mirroring the 'Ease' of the Hive. Multifarious paradoxes saunter easily and familiarly through the lines. Vices serve virtues, virtue makes friends with vice, luxury employs millions of the temperate, vanity is a minister of industry; what was well done last year is a crime the next. As the universal harmony reconciles discords, so 'the State's Craft' ensures that although 'every Part was full of Vice, / Yet the whole Mass [was] a Paradise' (I, 24).

Each brazen Bee then has the effrontery to engage in ridiculous moral discourse, complaining about the universal frauds of his fellow-workers and lamenting the lack of '*Honesty*!' in the Hive. Jove, momentarily invoked to provide a satirist's comically redundant indignation and anger at this hypocrisy – there are no satirical personae in Mandeville, only the genially unmoral moral doctor and the odd 'Sermonizing Rascal' (I, 27) – transforms them all to honest Bees. The suddenly moral Hive is promptly reduced to the level of a Spartan economy, its individuals valiant but without the capacity to pay professional soldiers to fight in its defence – a sobering thought, two years after Blenheim. Eventually, though, this moral heroism pays its own dividends. The Bees drive their enemies off, and, leaving the small remnant of their Hive still remaining to them, return themselves to the state of Nature proper to a fable:

> to avoid Extravagance,
> They flew into a hollow Tree,
> Blest with Content and Honesty. (I, 35)

So 'leave Complaints', is the moral: 'Fools only strive / To make the Great an Honest Hive' (I, 36). Complaining, moralistic grumbling, indignant Jovian swearing: whatever does not express itself in the reasonable, unrhetorical tones of Mandevillean paradox is reprehended. But the noisy discourses themselves, the positions that the poem appears to be answering, are never directly audible or specified in the poem, but are instead sublimated into a composite background buzzing.

The paradox of *The Fable*'s many paradoxes is that the more disconcerting they seem, the closer they approach to the truth which no one else can express except the pastorally detached but power-attuned fabulist. A standard work of historical reference vindicates *The Fable*'s view of its age:

> government itself, from the pensioned peer to the bribed elector, was corrupt ... There were scandals, more often exposed than corrected, in every executive department. There was scarcely a man in high place who was above suspicion

... Yet, in spite of everything, the liberty, good and bad, was less remarkable than the success, the tremendous achievements, of the British state. There was misery and confusion, but there was victory. Contemporaries did not give themselves the trouble of inquiring into this paradox. They explained it by the ... general superiority of everything that was British to everything that was foreign ... (Clark 1965: 259–60)

It would perhaps be fairer to say that the paradox was inscrutable because it was so novel. British society had recently passed through a series of revolutions in its financial, constitutional, and mercantile nature that had effectively turned it into the first fully modern state, but the tones and values of its social philosophy were largely still those of classical civic humanism or the patrician meliorism of the emerging Moral Sense school. 'Urban capitalism with all of its ambiguities was becoming the dominating mode of life, but its implications had yet to penetrate fully into the consciousnesses of Mandeville's contemporaries' (Hopkins 1975: 169). Mandeville is well in advance of his time in many respects.

Beginning a chapter on 'High Augustan' fable with *The Fable of the Bees* involves what Mandeville would term a 'seeming Paradox' (1, 100). Although the literary tactics of the essays of the *Fable* bear resemblance to the oppositional disguises of the Augustans, the *Fable*'s social frame of reference derives from robustly new-Whiggish premises which would have disconcerted writers such as Gay, Swift, and Pope, whose politics gravitated towards the more traditional ground of the 'Country Persuasion' (Brooks 1984). These premises were, firstly, that the new English culture of portable money and government finance through taxes was to be applauded for its effects of creating wealth, vigorous social mobility, and luxury or conspicuous consumption, and through this creating the capacity to support the modern professional army that was capable of resisting the aggrandizing ambitions of Mandeville's *bête noire*, Louis XIV. And secondly, that what most English moralists in the civic-humanist or Christian traditions regarded as vices – profligacy, indulgence, frivolous fashion, aggressive economic individualism – well, Defoe puts it most clearly: 'Luxury, however it may be a Vice in Morals, may at the same time be a Virtue in Trade . . . by degrees we have brought Vice and Extravagance to be absolutely necessary to Trade' (Defoe, *Review* 3, 66, 7 Feb. 1706 and 3, 42–3, 24 Jan. 1706, quoted by Moore 1975: 124, 123).

That an ambiguity which can appear as a sobering truism in Defoe appears as provoking paradoxes in Mandeville would argue that this fabulist, like others, is more interested in provoking than in the exposition of sober truths. There are two difficulties involved in reading *The Grumbling Hive.* The first is that the deliberately indeterminate nature of the complaining and grumbling voices makes it hard to hear exactly who is being provoked or targeted by the fabulist, and the full reading of a combative public fable usually involves having a reasonably clear sense of who or what, among the posited audience, one is *not* supposed to be. Listening to Menenius's fable in *Coriolanus*, for example, one is not supposed to be a grumbling plebian, but someone listening in a different mood or class.

The second difficulty is that the freewheeling originality of *The Grumbling Hive* also detaches it from specific targets. This originality is extreme, particularly in literary terms. In fable, the Hive is usually either 'a symbol of the orderliness of absolute monarchies', or representative of 'Dutch [i.e. republican] frugality, discipline and commercial success' (Hundert 1994: 27). This one is neither; Mandeville's Bees are busy but wayward, and live under a limited monarchy. When Hundert engages with the other possible Dutch connection, the 'de Witt' *Fables, Moral and Political*, all he can say is that it 'is impossible to tell . . . whether Mandeville . . . responded directly to' them (*ibid.*). As with other creatures in the plural, fable-Bees are usually engaged in a *querelle* or battle of some sort, and tend to be burlesque rather than post-Virgilian – Ogilby's Bear and Bees; Frogs and Mice, Cranes and Pygmies, Rats and Weasels. But these Bees are allegorical of English society and moral voices, and the style is de-Hudibrasticated. The only feature of fable that Mandeville emphasizes rather than contradicts is the central and traditional one of answering the discourse of 'masters', in the shape of false moralists.

Strikingly, this answering is *understood* to be the function of fable. The wider moral should not be spelled out (see, for example, Prior's Smith-and-Johnson) but may be left almost tacit, as the other discourse is here left implicit in the 'Grumbling'. The fabulist, as usual genuinely if paradoxically socialized rather than partisan and factional, does not provoke by imitating the satirical or aggressive power-tones of his antagonists/masters, merely by waving them away. The fabulist-Bee (to reverse the figure, as in *The Battel of the Books*) does not imitate the poisonous dirt of the Spider: '*great Actions are not carried on by Noyse*' (Ogilby 1668[a]: 166). To redirect one of Mandeville's central figures of speech, the fabulist becomes a '*skilful Politician*' (1, 412) who can subtly control, temper, and manage the passions and perverse discourses of his antagonists, just as real politicians manage the pride and self-love of individual members of the wayward multitude for the common good.

'The Slave was to manage the Master's Pride' remarks La Motte of Aesop's function, in a strikingly Mandevillean set of phrases; 'Self love is managed by Instruction' (La Motte 1721: 15, 14). The vocabulary of the management of the passions descends to Mandeville partly from the French tradition, La Rochefoucauld and Pascal, and it descends also to later French fabulists. But Mandeville, unlike La Motte, would not go so far as to make this point outright: politicians and fabulists must seem to be your friend, not your slave-ringmaster, manager, or tamer. The work in which it is clearest that a narrator is managing the passions of the audience in this way is Mandeville's *The Virgin Unmask'd* (1709), where Lucinda manipulates the younger Antonia's taste for and expectations of romance-stories (and Mandeville manipulates the reader's taste for pornographic works with titles like *The Virgin Unmask'd*) in such a way as to educate her into the ways of the real world and the superior merits of novelistic rather than romance narratives.

Given Mandeville's originality, and given his refusal to specify particular targets in *The Grumbling Hive*, one is left only with Isaac Kramnick's suggestion in *Bolingbroke and his Circle*, since repeated by others. This is that Mandeville was defending the financial revolution against the verse pamphlets of the 1690s and 1700s which attacked 'the corruption of English society by money' (Hopkins 1975: 169), and which form a background to parts of Pope's *Moral Essays* (1731–5): 'Blest paper-credit! last and best supply! / That lends Corruption lighter wings to fly!' (Pope 1968: 574). Kramnick's argument is clearly plausible, though there are one or two problems. Money as such is not a central topic in *The Grumbling Hive*, with its stress on activity, work, and discourse; and the pamphlet-war in question was characterized by a rhetorical extravagance of tone (the chameleonic Pope mimics it in the space of a couplet) which Mandeville chooses to answer by simply disengaging himself from it. Some anti-money satires were highly personal in their mode of attack, and when not personally, generally aggressive. Robert Gould, for instance, fulminates so heatedly against the supposedly aphrodisiac female drinking of chocolate that his metaphysical linking of the luxury of these twin appetites with the urge after money becomes slightly incoherent:

> Vain *Sex*! at once both *Foolish* and *Unjust*!
> To Think they need *Provocatives* to *Lust*:
> Were all their Lives to be *one Nuptial Night*,
> Their *Stock* would never be *exhausted* quite;
> Then, on their Natural *Fund* they might rely,
> And not so lavishly take on *Supply*. (Gould 1693: 14)

The '*Stock*' is women's own lust, but the 'Natural *Fund*' (fund = money, but also bottom, both of people and ships, as '*Supply*' = both provision and 'supplementaries', or the filling of vacant spaces) appears to be that of their husbands, who are thus urged to heroic labours. Presumably mutual marital chocolate would do the trick and balance the accounts, but Gould either overlooks this or assumes that men are immune to its effects.

Another problem is that several of these pamphlets are from the early 1690s or earlier, whereas Kramnick says that they were a 'reaction to' (Kramnick 1968: 201) the birth of the Bank of England in 1694. Gould's *The Corruption of the Times by Money* is from 1693. Ned Ward's *The Miracles Performed by Money* is 1692, not 1695 as Kramnick gives it, and Ward hardly *disapproved* of money. His poem, which was preceded by *The Poet's Ramble After Riches* (1691), is only a satire in the sense that Volpone's initial mock-panegyric at the start of his play is satirical:

> Mony what Wonders can it not effect?
> Who ever faild that had it, of Respect? . . .
> 'Twill make an *old Man* have a youthful Skin,
> And *Beldams*, old as *Aldgate*, not Sixteen;
> Make *Cowards* Valiant, and make *Blockheads* Wise,
> And from low Dunghills make th'ignoble Rise . . .
> But ah! what Pen its *Miracles* can tell,
> Which *Heaven* purchases and saves from *Hell*? (Ward 1692: 20)

For a full understanding of *The Grumbling Hive* one is better directed to Ward's *The London Spy* (1703), which, as well as having a 'Character' of a stockjobber among its many satirical portraits, has an interesting picture of that other modern phenomenon, the London 'REFORMING CONSTABLE . . . the wicked servant to a pious society' (Ward 1955: 276, 277), whose virtuous but profitable zeal against lowly tavern-whores is quite as hypocritical and self-serving as is that of the Reformers for their Charity-Schools, in *The Fable*. 'The Saints', as Vanbrugh put it in the Preface to *The Relapse*, 'have too much Zeal to have any Charity' (1927: 1, 11). Moral reform was a very *fashionable* crusade in London in the 1700s, after the Queen's patronage of the Society for the Reformation of Manners from its inception in 1692; after Collier; after William's proclamation against vice and impiety in 1703; and after the Lord Mayor's attempt to close Bartholomew Fair in 1700. To put it more widely, and in post-Bakhtin mode, 'self-exclusion from the sites of popular festivity . . . was a major symbolic project for the emergent professional classes' (Stallybrass and White 1986: 83, 112). *We* are polite (and so is, or should be, our culture), *you* are not.

All that Mandeville does in *The Grumbling Hive* is to point out that, as so often in the bizarre English social system, the pot is calling the kettle black – or rather vice versa, because Kettles are upper-class and Pots lower-class (namely Montague's fable of 1688). He pointedly extends his critique to 'All Trades and Places', refuses to indulge in name-calling, and invents a low fable which, while disdaining and quietly inverting or de-sublimating the high-horse rhetorical tones of contemporary moralists into grumbling, complaining and swearing, also disdains the depths of Hudibrastic slumming.

The Grumbling Hive is, in stylistic terms, close to Vanbrugh's popular stage-Aesop (who is also for the new taxes) in its capacity to talk familiarly to a wide social audience in relaxed syntax and a bantering idiolect which ranges easily between, in Mandeville's case, 'Cabbage' and 'Mutability', 'Dice' and 'EUTOPIA' (1, 21, 25, 18, 36). The brief passage on the class-nature of Justice in London is one of the few places where Mandeville allows the subtle class-nature of the moral critique as a whole to become clear:

> Yet, it was thought, the Sword she bore
> Check'd but the Desp'rate and the Poor,
> That, urg'd by meer Necessity,
> Were ty'd up to the wretched Tree
> For Crimes, which not deserv'd that Fate,
> But to secure the Rich and Great. (1, 23–4)

Elsewhere the fabulist's work is done indirectly, left implicit in the quietness and *déclassé* quality of the tone. So the poem is not merely a remonstrance against a particular, minor, discourse, although it probably is that as well (Gould certainly *buzzes,* in a fashion which is hardly 'polite'). It is a remonstrance against something much more deeply ingrained and more permanently English, the quality in the 'polite' audience which will not allow Gay's Beggar, in the epimythium to his Opera, to have a variant of the same point about class and justice stand as the moral to the whole piece. The 'lower sort of People', as the Beggar says, 'have their Vices in a Degree as well as the rich', and are punished for them where those in high life are not. But the Beggar has forgotten that Macheath is bound to be saved by the English audience: partly because Macheath is an opera-Hero, and partly because of the pseudo-pastoral principle mockingly embodied in Mrs Peachum's line 'The Youth in his Cart hath the Air of a Lord' (Gay 1973: 112, 54).

Mandeville could leave this lesson barely audible, coolly tacit in the fabulist manner, because the peculiarly class-ridden nature of English social morality had been a butt of the other English culture from which *The Fable* is invisibly derived – stage comedy (Mandeville plays the 'Truewit', raising a silent speaking eyebrow at the loud Witwouds and the false pretenders to virtue) – since at least as early as the exchange of complex words between Medley and the Shoemaker, in Act I of Etherege's *The Man of Mode* (1676):

MEDLEY Whoring and swearing are vices too genteel for a shoemaker.

SHOEMAKER 'Zbud, I think you men of quality will . . . engross the sins o'the nation. Poor folks can no sooner be wicked but they're railed at by their betters. (Etherege 1979: 20)

This derivation from and engagement with various representative and enduring English 'voices' is what gives the poem its continuing importance in subsequent expansions of *The Fable*. The most unnerving quality of *The Grumbling Hive* in particular is the prescience of Mandeville's thought, its seeming to engage with English voices which are themselves not yet fully audible, and even of appearing to create the objects of its satire. Where Swift's *Tale of A Tub* is effectively a 'burlesque of the novel . . . twenty years before the first novel was written' (Josipovici 1979: 154), Mandeville's fable is designed to provoke, call forth, the moral voices that he answers: catalysis by irritation.

Taking fable as an example of such a voice or discourse, one might plausibly say that *The Fable of the Bees* teaches the lesson that literary fables should not try to reform society through polite ethical instruction and genteel appeals to taste and a 'moral sense', because society, like fable, is primarily managed through power-relations in which wit, appetite ('passions'), and cunning are the dominant forces. To insist that either fable or society is actively governed by moral criteria is moral hypocrisy, and usually involves imposing one's own moral criteria on everyone else in the interests of retaining a dominant position in the discourse and the social structure. But the kind of literary fable which argues a polite *moral*-social case of this sort systematically, which popularizes the philosophy of Mandeville's subsequent satirical targets, Addison and Shaftesbury, does not yet exist, because it will be invented or developed, partly as a response to Mandeville, in the 1730s and 1740s. There are other examples: the flourishing of the Moral Sense school derives some of its vigour from its urge to make sure that *the principles of . . . Shaftesbury are defended against . . . the Fable of the Bees*, to quote the subtitle of Francis Hutcheson's *Enquiry into the Origin of our Ideas of Beauty and Virtue* (1725). Everyone took Mandeville seriously; virtually every major eighteenth-century writer on political, ethical, and economic topics had to define their position in relation to him.

Eventually he even began to take himself seriously, and to direct himself to a more straightforward delivery of his programme of arguments about the nature of society. From the perspective of the twentieth century, *The Fable* in its later manifestations contains a proleptic statement of the scientific principles behind the modern discourses of sociology, but even here the prolepsis often has an ironic flavour. Thorstein Veblen, author of *The Theory of the Leisure Class* (1899), would surely not have been best pleased when F. B. Kaye published in his edition of *The Fable* the letter he had received from A. O. Lovejoy, in which the authoritative Lovejoy opined that nearly all of the ideas in Veblen's impressive tome, which was 'regarded, when it appeared, as a very important and original contribution to economic theory and social psychology – may be found in Mandeville's "*Remark M*", and elsewhere in his prose appendices' (2, 452). Remark M's ten breezy pages conclude with a high-spirited and jocular comparison between 'virtuous Ladies' who *do not* drive as hard a bargain as they can, nor pay for their goods as late as possible, and similarly minded cats which, 'instead of killing Rats and Mice . . . feed them, and go about the House to suckle and nurse their young ones' (1, 134).

Mandeville's preoccupation between 1705 and 1729 was the po-faced deconstruction of what he perceived to be the false, hypocritical, and mystifying discourses of genteel English moralism as they engaged, or failed to engage, with shifting economic and social circumstances. The method of his subsequent essays in *The Fable* is to critique and partly demystify those discourses by adapting them and 'exposing their rhetorical strategies' (Hundert 1994: 92). This method gives *The Fable* a dynamic transmissive quality, in that it anticipates later uses of fable in writers such as the appreciative Voltaire, whose *Contes* are also, as Roger Pearson says, 'instruments of demythification, of "defabulation,"' which substitute 'the authentic fable of reason' for 'the "fables" by which men have sought to explain and govern the lives of others' (Pearson 1993: 34, 36, 243). True fable answers false; the Nun's Priests reply to the Parsons.

While this is close to Mandeville's general purpose, the crucial difference between Mandevillean and Voltairean fable is the quality of disguise or deception in Mandeville. The method in *The Fable* after 1705 is often too close for comfort to *imitation*. As in the recent examples provided by writers such as Farquhar, Toland (who, as well as writing a semi-subversive *Aesop*, was the Englishman most closely associated with Lucretius, the classical stimulus to the sceptical doctrines behind Mandeville (see Hundert 1994: 47)) and Dryden, the answer to false prophets is not to be achieved by mere opposition, but through a strategy which begins by adopting some of the 'colours' of the targeted discourse, its stylistic or argumentative premises, as a cloak of disguise. Where the clerically dressed Fox Reynard would contrive to persuade a pious and trusting chicken that he was 'a cloisterer or a closed recluse become' (Sands 1960: 52), Mandeville will open 'An Essay on Charity, and Charity-Schools', one of the essays added to *The Fable* in 1723, with a definition of the 'pure and unmix'd' virtue of charity which is so idealized as to be quite beyond social manifestation. His then admitting 'the Rigour of this Definition' (I, 253) insinuates to the pious and trusting reader that he must be a rigorous moralist, and hence trustworthy. At the same time it creates a great deal of Foxy rhetorical space in which to prove that charity defined not as an abstract moral concept, but as a quality mediated by 'the Esteem of the World' (*ibid.*) – the crucial phrase slipped into the Essay's first paragraph – is really not charity at all, but a species of self-interest, even, or especially, when it involves a pet 'charitable' scheme of the English middle-classes for their inferiors: the charity-schools.

Even his favourite method of paradox is part of this disguise, bamboozlement by apparent gentrification, because it is so cleverly suggestive of the sanctioned if slightly old-fashioned paradoxes of Christianity. Spiritual truth may be cleared by the explosive 'seeming Contradictions' (Venning 1647: 41) of Christian paradox, which raise the mind above mundane life to a state of metaphysical faith receptive to higher truths. Venning's collection of spiritual paradoxes was still current in the early eighteenth century, but reduced to six pages of '*Pious Contradictions*' (Dunton 1707: 39) in John Dunton's *Athenian Sport*, where it shares space with satires against Honour – a Mandevillean form – and '*a Paradox in praise of* Farting' (*ibid.*: 114). Mandeville's secular truths or mock-truths are achieved by a method of 'seeming Paradox' which, by keeping the reader continually in suspense as to whether the thought is really paradoxical or not, distracts the mind from the shadier processes of the argument and produces a disturbing suspension of disbelief, a sensation of *apparent faith* in conclusions which seem at once perverse and incontestable.

For example: 'Chastity may be supported by Incontinence, and the best of Virtues want the Assistance of the worst of Vices' (1, 100). But how so, good Dr Mandeville? We know that Montaigne quotes Tertullian's dictum that 'incontinence is necessary for the sake of continence' (Montaigne 1958: 652), but he is speaking of a time and place in which it was the practice to keep boys and girls in churches, in order that the congregation could assuage its lusts properly before divine worship. This is not current Anglican practice: how is it of relevance to such unpriapic Christians as we?

In one of Mandeville's many decorously managed but highly Reynardian 'parables', as Philip Harth calls them (Mandeville 1989: 10; compare chapter 3, p. 36, though Harth does not seem to know about *Reynard*), seven thousand distinctly contemporary Dutch sailors, their need strong upon them, return simultaneously to Amsterdam and prowl the streets. Thank God there are 'Harlots to be had at reasonable Prices'! (1, 96) – if there were not, 'the Chastity of Women of Honour' (1, 99) who are at large upon wholly respectable business would be at the mercy of these fearsome appetites. The female world suffers an absolute, but perfectly conventional, division: everyone knows that women are either virtuous or they are not (*one false step is ne'er retrieved*, etc.). Male sexual powers are dangerous and easily stirred, and the sailors had perhaps had chocolate in their cargo. And from the necessity of dexterously managing such appetites in a manner akin to the [wholly fictitious!] practice of the English universities, of giving the Fellows a monthly allowance '*ad expurgandos Renes*' (1, 99) – the comically double euphemism, the medical Latin and the less medical 'Renes', kidneys, used for the unmentionable parts, lends mock-decorum and plausibility

from this necessity flows the social necessity for properly managed licensed brothels, as expanded upon in the subsequent *Modest Defence of Publick Stews* (1724). So 'Extremes in Nature', as Pope has it in the *Essay on Man*, 'equal ends produce, / In Man they join to some mysterious use'. Vice may serve virtue mysteriously, and the corrupt passions of fallen man may be so managed as to produce a 'Whole' in which, seen under

'HEAV'N's great view', one cannot tell 'Where ends the Virtue, or begins the Vice' (Pope 1968: 522, 523). *Quod erat demonstrandum.*

Such dualistic divisions as Mandeville's in his initial gambit here, between 'Principle and Appetite', chastity and chocolate, set 'the terms of all philosophical discussion of the nature of morality throughout the century' (Harrison 1993–4: 154). In this intellectual and moral climate such an argument is unanswerable, because it works by forcing morally normative presuppositions to natural, if comically grotesque, conclusions. The fact that women are treated at one moment as if they were merely suppliers of manual labour at reasonable prices, and at another as if they were merely vessels of abstract moral qualities, is somehow elided; just as the style, no longer pseudo-mediative as in the *Hive*, oscillates bewilderingly between that of the genteel moralist and that of the habitual observer of sailors and harlots in Amsterdam streets, of nasty over-grown sows eating little babies, of family squabbles about curtseys, of *décolletage*, or of whatever distractingly vivid exemplum is required.

As F. B. Kaye points out, Mandeville's discourse usually achieves its effects by eliding or juxtaposing contradictory systems of value, for example judging 'the public results of private actions according to utilitarian standards' but judging private 'conduct . . . by the motive which gave it rise. The paradox that private vices are public benefits is merely a statement of the paradoxical mixing of moral criteria that runs through the book' (I, xlviii, xlix). But, again, it is very hard for the normal eighteenth-century mind to grasp that this is happening, because paradoxes which work between partial or private evil and the greater good are so irritatingly close to the distracting legitimate paradox that bad examples may become 'good' ones, capable of warning others from the same path, if seen *sub specie aeternitatis* – under Heaven's great view – or with the right aesthetic distance: 'All partial Evil, universal Good', to quote Pope again (1968: 515). Pope went so far as to write a couplet on private vices and public benefits into the *Essay on Man*, but then thought better of it. But he did include Arbuthnot's startling epitaph on Francis Chartres among the footnotes to the *Moral Essays*. Chartres's character was of the very worst. He had raped his servants, amassed a huge, barely legal fortune 'by a constant attention to the vices, wants, and follies of mankind', and was 'infamous for all manner of vices'. He was prosecuted, imprisoned, and fined, but he was never punished for the worst of his crimes. Arbuthnot's epitaph acknowledges this, but –

Oh Indignant Reader!
Think not his Life useless to Mankind !
PROVIDENCE conniv'd at his execrable Designs,
To give to After-ages
A conspicuous PROOF and EXAMPLE,
Of how small Estimation is EXORBITANT WEALTH
in the Sight of GOD,
By his bestowing it on the most UNWORTHY of
ALL MORTALS. (*ibid.*: 571–2)

This literary or rhetorical example of private vices becoming public benefits was quite acceptable, where Mandeville's examples were not, because it shelters more fully in the shade of Christian paradox. But the presence of such paradoxes meant that it was impossible for eighteenth-century reactions to be as analytical as Kaye's remark above: for one thing, if Chartres could be a valuable negative exemplar in this way, Mandeville could too: the vice of the *Fable* might warn the public from its path in the same way that Fielding's tippling schoolmasters, in the essay in the *Champion*, could warn the boys of the perils of drink. Partial evil, universal good; private vices, public benefits.

SWIFT AND THE *FABLES*

Jonathan Swift's engagements with Aesopian and Ovidian fable are scattered across the thirty-five years between 1698 and 1733 (it seems that he wrote no fables after the death of his friend John Gay in late 1732) and are embodied in prose works and some twenty poems, most of which appear to shade towards what Richard H. Rodino identifies as the 'inclusive and conciliatory' pattern or impulse common to that side of Swift's poetry which does not 'work defensively, by exclusion and rejection' (Rodino 1981: 91). In other words, Swift senses that readers do not think of fable as a natural form for the display of *saeva indignatio*, but as something closer to a '*well framed Tale handsomly told, as an agreeable vehicle for Counsel and Reproof*' (Farquhar 1988: 2, 377). Although this inclusiveness becomes deeply duplicitous in some of his later examples, his satirical fables contain neither the violent *parti pris* of collections like Pittis's, nor the low-slung tones of Dennis, being much closer to the 'easy and familiar' of Mandeville and other fabulists of 1697–1704, the period when Swift was evolving his own version of the flexible octosyllabic medium characteristic of this mode.

This is true of all his uses of fable before 1712, and of some after. That year marks the beginning of a disruption in Swift's treatments of fable, containing the first of his three straightforwardly satirical verse fables, one against the repeal of the Test Acts, two against Marlborough, which date from 1712–15. After this he disengages from fable almost totally for a decade. When he renews his interests, it is to very different ends.

From the relatively straightforward examples of his earlier fables, Swift scholars decide that Swift is a straightforward fabulist, that he 'accepted the basic assumptions of the "orthodox" English fable, articulated by John Dennis: limited and unequivocal application: precedence of moral over story' (Rodino 1981: 94). This is too sweeping in its identification of an 'orthodox' English fable – Dennis's sources are French, not English, where the theory of fable is concerned, and such attitudes only become 'orthodox' in the late 1720s, after La Motte – and tends to mask the more idiosyncratic patterns of fable in Swift's *oeuvre*. In 1712 Swift also produced a much more typical fable, 'Atlas', the first of the series of poems that he addressed to Robert Harley, later Earl of Oxford. The fable of Hercules relieving the heroic but weary Atlas of his burden, the globe, is applied to Robert Harley's situation in late 1712, after the attack by Guiscard and deaths in his family. The depressed Harley was considering giving up political power, and the fable is a tactful, sympathetic and witty suggestion that he might reasonably do so without loss of dignity and respect.

Atlas, who 'bore the Skyes upon his Back / Just as a Porter does his Pack', is a '*premier* Minister of State', the sub-porting Hercules (as one would expect from this side of the tradition) 'not so strong', and a politician 'of second Rate' (Swift 1957: 1, 160; subsequent references will be to this edition and will cite volume and page numbers only): Bolingbroke, presumably, though the tact extends to not naming names. The poem works deftly between the treble illustration, mythical hero, second-rate hero, and common porter, and dramatizes the stresses of high politics and loss of power and personal energy in Harley. Readers will now easily recognize this as the natural ground of fable, sardonically debating power and its loss or lack: Hesperian fable is, as often in Swift, made to perform as if it were Augustan. And it is fascinating to see big men and little men, heroes and porter, at play in Swiftian fable fifteen years before *Gulliver's Travels*.

Other early fables also approach this ground, and begin to develop a characteristic pattern. The only satirical element of the Ovidian 'Baucis and Philemon' (1706: expanded 1709), for instance, is that the old couple are, if anything, less pious after their transformation from mere 'Yeoman' rustics to the 'furbish'd up' parson and his 'Prim' wife (I, 111, 115, 116) than they were before. This element is largely subsumed into one of the two wider interests of Swift's fables, the comic dissonance between higher and lower classes of various kinds – hero and porter, premier hero and substitute hero, parson and rustic, gem and dung, gold and brass, apple and horse-turd, polite illustration and monkey, Houyhnhnm and Yahoo – which emerges in the course of the fable's metaphysical play. It is a pattern intrinsic to fable – master and slave – and, together with his obvious familiarity with fables and fabulists, particularly L'Estrange, argues a case for Swift as a fabulist still consistently in the central tradition, rather than as 'orthodox'. But as with Gay, there is a high degree of apparent accommodation to the orthodox: parsons may read 'Baucis and Philemon' as complacently as the Countess of Berkeley listened to the 'Meditation upon a Broomstick', and with less prospect of the ground shifting beneath them. Where Mandeville energizes the fabulist metaphysics of class, or the wit of class, through subversive rhetorical play and shifts of tone, Swift sets them in motion through play with imagery and illustrative wit which have a more durable patina of innocuousness.

That this pattern of play with class is native to Swift's fables is suggested by its appearance in the early *Battel of the Books*, which reworks The Spider and the Bee as radically as Mandeville reworked the Hive. Where it was a question of Ancients *versus* Moderns, the Bee was usually the busy Modern scientist (see above, p. 20), and the Spider the Ancient. Swift's Bentleyan Spider seems to grasp this, and tries to reverse, or re-reverse, Swift's figure, by fulminating about his own family, stock, and inheritance, but the Bee's elegant banter dissolves his claims to superior class-status.

This discursive power of Swiftian fable-authorities is always counterbalanced by the wider context of loss or reduction of power already noted in 'Atlas'. The Bee flies off. Aesop's subsequent attempt to deflect the tone of the Battel from the '*large Vein of Wrangling and Satyr*' (Swift 1939–75: I, 151) characteristic of Modern discourse is as well-meant and as fruitless as the attempt of the father, in the fable of *A Tale of A Tub*, to use his legacy of the three coats as an encouragement to family unity, or Swift's attempt in 1713 to reconcile the Tory ministers, who were 'at variance' (I, 188), to each other with the fable of 'The Faggot', the admonitory pre-*fascisti* Aesopian image of political unity as a bundle of sticks. Aesop vanishes from the *Battel*, having precipitated rather than forestalled the conflict of the authors; the father dies, leaving his sons to the appalling bedlam and schism which is Swift's vision of the history of the Christian churches; the government falls in less than two years, and Swift is thrown into the political wilderness of Ireland. From which, for ten years, he writes hardly any fables, a 'land of slaves' (2, 421) not being a good place from, or in, which to address intelligent masters. The exceptions are *The Bubble* and the poems of 1724–5 against Wood's debased coinage, of which the finest is 'Prometheus' (1724). Here the paradoxically unifying and factionalizing power of fable is, for once, brilliantly relevant to the Irish context, as is made clear by the quirky ironies that will develop into the illustrative story of Prometheus's stealing of Jove's cosmic golden chain and substituting a brass one:

> A strange Event! whom *Gold* incites
> To Blood and Quarrels, *Brass* unites:
> So Goldsmiths say, the coursest Stuff,
> Will serve for *Sodder* well enuff.
> So, by the *Kettles* loud Allarm,
> The *Bees* are gather'd to a *Swarm*:
> So by the *Brazen* Trumpets bluster,
> Troops of all Tongues and Nations muster:
> And so the *Harp* of *Ireland* brings
> Whole Crouds about its Brazen Strings. (1, 345)

The comedy of this passage lifts it well above 'limited and unequivocal application', as the brass of Wood's half-pence clearly does not have the same intention, of unifying the [Irish] nation, as do the other examples: Swift's wit discovers an irony and then sarcastically pretends to drop it. Nor does the moral take precedence over the story, the fable. There is no moral. The poem simply returns to its point of departure, 'the '*Squire*, and *Tinker Wood*' (1, 344), and makes a small mocking show of discovering the application which has been perfectly obvious throughout:

> Ye Pow'rs of *Grub-street* make me able
> Discreetly to apply this *Fable*.
> Say, who is to be understood,
> By that old thief Prometheus? WOOD
> For *Jove*, it is not hard to guess him,
> I mean *His M-----, God bless him.* (1, 346)

The fable and the passage of mock-similes illustrate the political story well, but disrupt it slightly. Swift cannot simply go back to praying for the return of the king's golden chain from England, as that would imply a return to 'Blood and Quarrels', so the moral has to exchange the brazen chain once more, this time for a '*Rope*; / With which *Prometheus* shall be ty'd, / And high in Air for ever ride' (1, 347). Swift, the Irish, His M----- (God bless him!) are all harmoniously reconciled, with just Wood excluded, Malvolio-like, from the happy comic ending. In fact Swift's fables are distinguished by *not* ending with a moral: the poem on Marlborough which resorts to aggressive pseudo-Christian moralizing at the end is not a fable but a forceful and unequivocal 'SATIRICAL ELEGY' (1, 295), with Swift tempted, as he is not tempted in fable, into the simple role of sermonizing rascal:

> Let pride be taught by this rebuke
> How very mean a thing's a Duke;
> From all his ill-got honours flung,
> Turn'd to that dirt from which he sprung. (1, 297)

A similar distinction could be made between the force of Swift's more aggressively scatological poems and the strangely socialized talking turds of fable, in this case the charming if egregious Horse-turd, lifted from L'Estrange, of the poem 'On the Words—Brother Protestants, and Fellow Christians' (1733). This is the final fable in a sequence which runs from '*Tim* and the *Fables*' in 1728, after *Gulliver's Travels* and the first series of Gay's *Fables* the previous year, and which includes *The Beasts Confession to the Priest* (1738: written 1732) and the introduction to the brilliant mini-*Dunciad* called *On Poetry: A Rapsody* (1733). In this later sequence – which includes *Gulliver* – the new, wider, common theme or motif is that of misreading or mistaking, either class, or nature, or the fable. Swift's Horse-turd is thrown into the 'flood' that has carried off the farmer's crops and the surrounding 'litter',

> Uniting all, to show their Amity,
> As in a general Calamity.
> A Ball of new-dropt Horse's Dung,
> Mingling with Apples in the Throng,
> Said to the Pippin, plump, and prim,
> *See, Brother, how we Apples swim.*
>
> THUS *Lamb*, renowned for cutting corns,
> An offer'd Fee from *Radcliff* scorns;
> *Not for the world---we Doctors, Brother,*
> *Must take no Fee of one another.* (3, 811)

And so on, rising, or falling, to the 'Lice' and 'Maggots', the 'Fanatic Saints' who must be addressed as 'Brother Protestants' (3, 812) by those who argue for repeal of the Test Act. The Horse-turd misreads himself as an Apple; the poet pretends to misread the situation as one appropriate to fabulist politeness, until recalled to his scurrilous satirical (rather than just moral) self by recalling that his hero is a turd.

Other lesser examples of misreading would include '*Tim* and the *Fables*', where Tim (alias the violently Whig Irish member, Richard Tighe) reads himself in Tonson's plate of the beau-monkey illustrating Gay's 'The *Monkey*, who had seen the World', and the charmingly odd 'Death and Daphne', in which Daphne (the 'extremely lean' (3, 902) Lady Acheson) manages to mistake the equally skeletal Death as a fit subject for her romantic advances. But three longer and more important late poems complicate this stress on 'misreading' considerably, developing a very full aura of Swiftian duplicity and bamboozlement.

In the *Answer to Dr. Delany's Fable of the Pheasant and the Lark* it is the reader who must misread the fable, because this is (or is very probably) the disguised 'Scrubb [low-class] libel' that Swift decided to write against himself in the manner of the 'scoundrels' (Swift 1963–5: 3, 418) his opponents (see Woolley 1981, and Williams 1981, *passim*). Imitating the manner of scoundrel opponents means addressing himself as 'the Worst of disaffected Deans', making dull, 'orthodox' complaints about the wholly unexceptionable mixing of men, beasts, and birds in Delany's fable, and griping about how fable-animals really should conform to set characters, 'The Ass . . . dull, the Lion brave', and so on. Lions in fable are usually anything but straightforwardly brave, as Swift would know, but the level of the poem, with the wit confined to the slightly showy but engaging low-Hudibrastic style from which he usually restrains himself lends a conspiratorial gloss of plausibility to the opinions proferred:

> A Pigeon would, if shown by *Aesop*,
> Fly from the Hawk, or pick his Pease up . . .
> Did ever mortal see a Peacock
> Attempt a flight above a Haycock? (2, 512, 513)

It is as though a dullish normative critic had suddenly acquired the Swiftian manner: for example Joseph Warton grumbling about the lack of probability in Gay's 'The *Elephant* and the *Bookseller*' – 'an elephant can have nothing to do in a bookseller's shop' (Warton 1782: 245). From this, critics unaware of the poem's deliciously duplicitous status continue to misread Swift as an orthodox verse fabulist in Rodino's fashion, whereas the truth is somewhere near the reverse. Swift may be the slave-fabulist, but he is the organ-grinder, not the monkey. The monkey here is the reader, misreading the poem as a contemptuous libel against Swift and joining in with the bumbling orthodoxy of the criticisms of fable. Everyone their own *Tim*, flattering themselves complacently with their dull reading.

In the introduction to *On Poetry*, humanity in general is felt to misread itself, mistake its own talents, unlike the beasts: a premise familiar to readers from works such as *The Praise of Folly*:

> All Human Race wou'd fain be *Wits*,
> And Millions miss, for one that hits. . .
> What Reason can there be assign'd
> For this Perverseness in the Mind?
> *Brutes* find out where their Talents lie:
> A *Bear* will not attempt to fly . . .
> A *Dog* by Instinct turns aside,
> Who sees the Ditch too deep and wide.
> But *Man* we find the only Creature,
> Who, led by *Folly*, fights with *Nature* . . .
> And, where his *Genius* least inclines,
> Absurdly bends his whole Designs. (2, 640–1)

An opening gambit which is then ironized or clouded – given a different handle – by the poem's becoming a '*Rapsody*' against poets whom, to quote the sarcastic end of a short paragraph full of rhetorical bite, '*Phebus* in his Ire / Hath *blasted* with poetic Fire'. Poets who are thus (as Swift in Ireland felt *he* was) 'disqualified by Fate / To rise in *Church*, or *Law*, or *State*' (*ibid.*).

Does the poet include himself, as poet, in his reading of humanity as mad, absurd, and below the animals, or does he proudly stand above it? Boisterous doggerel is hardly the right class of form in which to claim a satirist's superiority to *poets*. It might be objected that 'poetic Fire' is merely dismissive in its irony, but Swift's own metaphysical play is often troublingly heady and sparky. His poetry may be written primarily, as Auden says all real poetry is, 'to disenchant and disintoxicate' (Auden 1963: 27), but *On Poetry*, like *A Tale of A Tub*, depends for its full effect on the reader's unwitting absorption into the brilliantly demonic illustrative analogies (five in six couplets, at one point) which pepper the poem and the reader. So, as with Peachum's lawyers and thieves, this poem is for poets and against 'em.

These lesser examples, particularly the last, bring the discussion to the extraordinary fable – so compellingly and chillingly devious that one hesitates to call it a poem – *The Beasts Confession to the Priest, on Observing how most Men mistake their own Talents*. This is a masterpiece of which almost all Swift scholars fight strikingly shy. Four major books on Swift's poetry (Jaffe, England, Schakel, Fischer), plus Vieth's *Essential Articles*, yield just one quotation and six lines of comment between them. Rodino's perceptions that the *Confession* 'is motivated by a desire to "vex" the reader', and that it deploys 'rather staggering duplicity' (Rodino 1985: 95), look promisingly pertinent, but he unfortunately goes on to group the *Confession* with *An Answer to . . . the Pheasant and the Lark* as being concerned to deride conventional fables – in this case, to deride the offered version of the fable known in L'Estrange (1699, No. 217) as 'A Plague Among the Beasts', which occupies the first part of Swift's poem. This is less to the point: the *Answer* perversely derides supposedly *un*conventional fables, and the derision in *The Beasts Confession* will turn out to be similarly perverse. And the moral of Colin Horne's reading of the *Confession* is the moral that one would arrive at if one read *On Poetry* while ignoring or suppressing the ironizing of the opening paragraph by later ones: 'the one final truth for Swift is that man, proud man, by the corruption of his talents has set himself below the beasts' (Horne 1968: 204). Swiftian fables against pride are never so straightforward.

The Beasts Confession takes up the venerable and polymorphous fable known in La Fontaine's mordant offering as 'Les Animaux Malades de la Peste', in the medieval tradition usually as Lion, Fox, and Wolf, or Ass, Fox, and Wolf Confessing to Each Other, and by the names of more exotic animals such as Camel, Tiger, and Jackal in the many secular-satirical oriental versions – the *Pañcatantra*, the *Hitopadesa*, Bidpai's *Book of Calila and Dimna*, etc. – from which the medieval English and French versions derive. Received opinion is that Swift is adapting L'Estrange, but this is probably not so. Although L'Estrange has an incongruous oriental Tiger he broadly follows La Fontaine and the medieval fables, in which the list of animals confessing their sins in the hope of escaping what they take to be the collective divine retribution of the plague ends with the Ass, who confesses merely that he has eaten some grass on a field belonging to monks. The others promptly decide that this is sacrilege, and eat the Ass. Swift's Wolf and Ass are followed by Swine, Ape, and Goat, and the fable quickly forgets its religious origins – there is no visible priest, despite the title – with all the animals 'confessing' not to sins but to characteristics which are the opposites of those they really possess. The Ass confesses to wit, the Goat to chastity.

The next stage ironically applies this process to human life, with the various professions claiming virtuous qualities – the Lawyer conscience, the Chaplain humility, the Statesman sincerity. But this part of the fable is not under full rhetorical control, because some of the portraits are much more clearly ironical than others. The poetic tone is kept so plain and dour throughout that without overt verbal signs, irony effectively lapses: the reader needs an *aide-memoire* to misanthropy. In particular, the portrait of the Doctor grows into what appears to be a straightforward appreciation, and even returns briefly to the religious context which the fable at large has forgotten:

> He cannot help it for his Heart
> Sometimes to act the Parson's Part:
> Quotes from the Bible many a Sentence
> That moves his Patients to Repentance:
> And, when his Med'cines do no good,
> Supports their Minds with heav'nly Food . . .
> In his own Church he keeps a Seat;
> Says Grace before, and after Meat . . .
> He shuns Apothecary's Shops;
> And hates to cram the Sick with Slops:
> He scorns to make his Art a Trade;
> Nor bribes my Lady's fav'rite Maid. (2, 605)

The 'truth' of the picture, the painstaking and involving descriptive work which might even be taken as a portrait of Swift's beloved Arbuthnot, sits oddly with the insistence that the portrait be taken sneeringly or satirically. Even more bemusing, this is a perfect picture of the 'moral doctor' or good physician of the mind, one of the main figures for the function of the fabulist: yet it is offered with apparent derogatory intent inside a fable. Whoever is writing this is unaware of the metaphors for the function of fable, and not properly in control of irony. Can this be Swift? Then in the final lines things grow exponentially stranger, with the writer dismissing the original fable in 'an admission of inveracity [which] seems calculated to estrange and dislocate rather than to enlighten' (Rodino 1981: 95):

> I OWN, the Moral not exact;
> Besides, the Tale is false in Fact;
> And, so absurd, that could I raise up
> From fields *Elyzian*, fabling *Esop*,
> I would accuse him to his Face
> For libelling the *Four-foot* Race.
> Creatures of ev'ry Kind but ours
> Well comprehend their nat'ral Powers;
> While we, whom *Reason* ought to Sway,
> Mistake our Talents ev'ry Day:
> The Ass was never known so stupid

To act the Part of *Tray*, or *Cupid*;
Nor leaps upon his Master's Lap,
There to be stroak'd and fed with Pap;
As *Esop* would the World perswade;
He better understands his Trade:
Nor comes whene'er his Lady whistles;
But carries Loads, and feeds on Thistles;
Our Author's Meaning, I presume, is
A Creature *bipes et implumis*;
Wherein the Moralist design'd
A Compliment on Human-kind:
For, here he owns, that now and then
Beasts may *degen'rate* into Men. (2, 607–8)

This seems akin to a post-Rochester *Satire on Reason and Mankind*, but it is itself unreasonable. Why should the writer deride the falsity and absurdity of his own fable so bluntly, when absurdity and impossibility are fundamental features of the form? What fable is true 'in Fact'? Why does he think that Aesop wants to 'perswade' the world that asses really do imitate lap-dogs, as in the fable? Would he also think that Aesop wants to persuade us that a Horse-turd, or rather a horse-turd, could really talk to an apple? Classically, literary fables disavow this kind of direct rhetorical function precisely by being absurd; true and false at once.

This impossibly plain, literal, superior, satirical mind cannot, despite the good if misanthropic paradox in the final line, be 'Swift', but who is it? Who has such a pathological concern for the truth that he would be unable to grant or credit that his fable is a fiction? Who tends to forget religion in the course of his narratives, or to apply it oddly? Whose experience has taught him such a concern for the equine world that he must think of horses as equal or superior to humanity, and must therefore read and apply the Ass as *a Man*? – the Ass stands on his back legs to embrace his master, in The Ass and the Lap-dog, and is thus *bipes et implumis*, Plato's 'unfeathered biped', '*A Definition of Man, disapproved by all Logicians*' (2, 608), according to the defensive footnote. The writer may not be skilled in fable, but he assumes that his audience is easily able to conjure up for itself the picture which he is misreading.

It should by now be clear that this is the fable that the formidable but mad satirist Lemuel Gulliver would write, if he could write a fable. The estrangement and dislocation are genuine, though not simply properties of the direct relationship between Swift and his reader.

There are many small signals or clues to Gulliver's presence, once the lens is adjusted. *The Beasts Confession* is the only Swift poem with an apparatus of more than a page: Preface, Advertisement, and three footnotes, the last of which, to the final line, says '*Vide* Gulliver *in his Account of the* Houyhnhnms' (*ibid.*): a remark which may be read as meaning 'this is what Gulliver would say, and I would agree with him', or as something a little wider. The judicious moderation of the title ('*most Men mistake their own Talents*') gives way to the more dogmatic tones of the Preface ('*there is not a more general and greater Mistake*') and then the Advertisement ('*the universal Folly in Mankind of mistaking their Talents*') in a mimicking of Gulliver's gradual loss of perspective in Book 4. '*How many pretenders to Learning expose themselves by chusing to discourse on those very Parts of Science wherewith they are least acquainted?*' asks this curiously unskilful fabulist. The Preface is full of Gulliver's characteristic diction of observing, measuring, estimating: '*there must be at least five hundred poets in . . .* London . . . *I compute, that* London *hath eleven native Fools of the Beau and Puppy-Kind, for one among us in* Dublin' (2, 599, 600, 601, 600). And it hardly takes '*Logicians*' to disprove Plato's definition of man: Diogenes thought of poultry; Montaigne went out into his garden and plucked the nearest capon. But all these clues are baffling, almost unreadable, because of the overriding rhetorical demand that the orthodox eighteenth-century reader should believe in the orthodoxy of the fable and the fabulist. Swift seems to be aware that this is now the main readership of fable: *The Beasts Confession*, like Sterne's Cock and Bull and other late fables, is a little like caviare to the general; or, in Swift's case, Pearls before swine.

So the misreading or mistaking is of several interrelated kinds. Mankind mistakes its talents; the fabulist has misread or misused fable; the modern, orthodox reader misreads *this* fable, thinking, with the fabulist, that fable is sincere, virtuous, and satirical, rather than playful, vexing, and bamboozling. Which, strangely enough, proves Gulliver's point (or is it Swift's?): mankind mistakes its talents. If every writer (including Gulliver) may now be their own Aesop, every reader may be their own Gulliver. The last horror of this fable is that, to date, *every* modern reader of it seems to have been made by the devil Swift to choose to be the person that the reader of the fable should absolutely not be.

In *Gulliver's Travels*, the Yahoos should be the fabulists. They are the deformed slaves, and they have the dung and the Pearls, the shining stones, and the good sense to prefer the gems to the dung, which they give away for reasons which (depending on your reading) range between sheer filthiness (Gulliver) and the fact that they worship a god called

Dung, which makes their distribution of Him over Gulliver a form of missionary zeal (Borges's *Dr Brodie's Report*). This is a fine reading, for it effectively makes the dung the Pearl. It also reminds us that the Houyhnhnms apparently neither defecate nor worship any god. But having no capacity to read, the Yahoos, like the Cock in his fable, must miss the figure which, in their pre-Adamic *naïveté*, they perform, and so remain trapped in fabulist limbo. In this, though, they share a situation with all the other actors in Book 4, because this is the one part of the story where there is *nothing to read.* Gulliver's '*Journal Book*' (Swift 1986: 226) is the only possible exception, and that is written, not read. Gulliver is as happy to do without reading as he is to do without salt.

The ending of *Gulliver's Travels* is essentially a fable against pride, perhaps the most dominant topic of orthodox eighteenth-century fables, but it is, as William Rose Wray once pointed out, a 'fable in reverse' (Wray 1950: 77). It is based on, or developed from, Gulliver's misreading the figure of his own fable, in much the same way that Tim, Daphne, the Horse-turd, the poet, the reader, misread theirs by seeing themselves in what surrounds them; Monkeys, leanness, Apples, orthodox fable, orthodox fabulists. If satire is '*a sort of* Glass, *wherein Beholders do generally discover every body's Face but their Own*' (Swift 1939–75: 1, 140), late Swiftian fable is the complementary mirror in which the reader/beholder must always discover *a face which looks very like my own*; and this is also what happens to Gulliver. Swift's Horse-turd sees only Apples; Tim sees only Monkeys; Daphne, leanness; the orthodox reader, only orthodox fables. If Gulliver is with giants, he thinks he is himself a giant, when he returns home. If he is with little people, their honours seem as real to him as those of his own kind. If he is with scientific projectors they seem quite like himself, and he is 'highly pleased' (Swift 1986: 172) with schemes to use pigs for ploughing, despite the expense and lack of crop. He is always happy to read himself in what he sees; to become, eventually, what he beholds.

But in Book 4 Swift faces him with both nothing to read, and too much to read: in a double mirror, he sees Yahoos *and* Houyhnhnms. That this might be a unified poetic figure for two sides of humanity, animal and rational, and that he himself might be neither of these but rather a paradoxical synthesis, a being darkly wise, not just a gentle Yahoo, is quite beyond him. A fable is always a metaphor, but he is no good at metaphysics or figures of speech, particularly oxymorons. Things are either true or false, and this is his true history, not an absurd fable. As in *Emma*, though for different reasons, there are practically no metaphors in his narrative, apart perhaps from his innocent rendering of 'My *Tongue is in the Mouth of my Friend*' (*ibid.*: 198). His style is 'very plain and simple', with 'an Air of Truth' (*ibid.*: xxxvii), and of course 'the Truth immediately strikes every Reader with Conviction' (*ibid.*: xxxvi). In this he, or his style, is very like the Houyhnhnms, who, having no rhetoric and so no word for *arguing* – and so being unable to 'argue with Plausibility on both Sides of a Question' – can, unlike Moses or Aesop or Ogilby, reason so as to 'strike . . . you with immediate Conviction' (*ibid.*: 259) without apparent persuasion. Gulliver tells us that the horses have no word for lying and we struck readers believe him, even though he immediately gives us their perfectly good *phrase* for it.

But in an impossible equivocation, both Yahoo and Houyhnhnm are true, because they are both there. Having first read the degenerated Yahoos as possessing 'a perfect human Figure' (*ibid.*: 232) like his own (which they do not), he must then read the Houyhnhnms as possessing Reason and all the humane virtues, which they do not. But as we are often forced to read with Gulliver, our travelling perspective or mirror – we have nothing else to 'read', so we must see our face in Gulliver's – we think they do. So we return schizophrenically to Redriff with him, inveighing violently against the terrible smell, the incorrigibility, and especially the *pride* of humankind, and entreating 'those who have any Tincture of this absurd Vice, that they will not presume to appear in [our] Sight', for in this particular we may now 'pretend to some superiority' over 'Mankind' (*ibid.*: 288, 285).

The Yahoos and Houyhnhnms are presumably still happy enough, in their different ways, but Gulliver is deeply alienated, in a world of his own, except that he has readers. But he is left as our main example of humanity, our mirror, and he still seems to have a disturbingly representative quality to him, despite, and even because of, his *angst*. 'What monstrous Animal is this, that is a horrour to himself, to whom his Delights are grievous, and who weds himself to Misfortunes!' (Montaigne 1693: 3, 154).

JOHN GAY: READING 'THE PRINCE'S FABLES'

A note on reading politically and biographically

The mirror of the *face which looks very like one's own* is a device common to Swift and to Gay's 1727 *Fables*. In '*Tim* and the *Fables*', Tim's initial misreading of the plate to 'The *Monkey*, who had Seen the World' – perceiving his own supposedly elegant features in the picture of the

Monkey – recalls, for example, that of the sitter in Gay's 'The *Painter* who pleased No body and Every body', staring at his ridiculously flattering portrait, which is modelled on the bust of Apollo that the painter has decided to use for all his male clients: 'My lord examin'd it anew; / No looking-glass seem'd half so true' (Gay 1974: 2, 326; subsequent references will be to this edition and will cite volume and page numbers only). Gay's sitter accepts absurd flattery, imagining it to be truth. Tim, admiring the plate, assumes a compliment until he reads the fable, when flattery turns suddenly into libel. Swift's dubious compliment in adapting 'The *Monkey*' for more clearly political ends is achieved by superimposing on one of Gay's fables interests which are common to many of the 1727 collection. In 'The Jugglers', Vice begins her attack by making her audience think well of themselves:

> This magick looking-glass, she cries,
> (There, hand it round) will charm your eyes:
> Each eager eye the sight desir'd,
> And ev'ry man himself admir'd. (2, 358)

But in turn, both Swift and Gay are reworking or sublimating devices and motifs – misreading or misrepresentation, innuendo, flattery, panegyric, slander, libel – which were also pressing topics in the political literature and journalism of the 1720s. The basic fable-principle behind the device of the *face that looks very like one's own*, for example, which is that 'application makes the Ass', is enunciated by a 1731 *Craftsman* pamphlet on the conditions of '*The Liberty of the Press*' under Walpole (Anon. 1974: 6, titlepage). The conditions of political discourse were such that the often-raided opposition *Craftsman*, more especially in its poetry but also some of its prose articles, felt the need to renew and take upon itself some of the traditional political functions of fable as a form of both attack and defence against the potential effects of ministerial odium. 'As long as I confine myself to *general Expression* or wrap up my Invectives against Vice *in Dreams, Fables, Parallels, and Allegories*', says an article on 9 March 1727/8, almost the exact date of publication of Gay's first series, 'I keep within the proper Bounds of a *Satirist*' (see Goldgar, 1976: 25). 'I draw from gen'ral nature', replies Gay mendaciously at the start of his second series, and 'write no libels on the state' (2, 382).

Given this diffusion of interest in fable and 'application' into political discourse at large, literary fables did not have to appear actively political, or even to use coded diction, to be read politically. If one takes from Gay's 1727 collection 'The *Painter* who pleased No body and Every body' and Fable 19, 'The *Lyon* and the *Cub*', as examples, a *Craftsman*-ish political reading of their silent morals would go as follows.

Gay's 'lord' is mature in years – he thinks at first that the portrait is 'far too young' (2, 326) for him – but he is patronizing a painter who, because he has always previously painted exact copies, warts and all, has no business nor reputation. This argues that the lord has as little expertise in selecting an artist as he has taste. And he likes to be flattered verbally by the painter, as well as in the absurd portrait. Walpole, who was over fifty, was notorious for having no artistic taste, for selecting second-rate writers to defend his policies, and for rewarding sycophants who wrote outrageously flattering poetic eulogies of him. Therefore the lord is Walpole, and the fable is a political satire; which is to say, *a fable which looks like one of ours.*

Similarly, 'The *Lyon* and the *Cub*' reflects on another of Walpole's well-known social habits, which even appears in Boswell's *Life of Samuel Johnson* (1791): 'Sir Robert Walpole said, he always talked bawdy at his table, because in that all could join' (Boswell 1970: 756). Introduced by reflections on those who avoid superior company in the hope of being 'supream in wit' among fools, Gay's fable begins

> A Lyon-cub, of sordid mind,
> Avoided all the lyon kind;
> Fond of applause, he sought the feasts
> Of vulgar and ignoble beasts,
> With asses all his time he spent,
> Their club's perpetual president.
> He caught their manners, looks and airs:
> An ass, in ev'ry thing, but ears! (2, 327)

This is clearly a remonstrance and warning to the court to disdain the less attractive personal and social attributes of their premier minister of state.

That these highly plausible readings are also slightly perverse hardly lessens their attractions. Gay was more closely associated with Pulteney, Wyndham, and the *Craftsman* group than with any other political grouping. But, as with Swift's late fables, these two perform in much wider cultural arenas than the simply political. In the case of 'The *Painter*', for example, the lord is merely the first of many who flock to this newly popular portraitist, whose flattering practice is almost certainly designed by Gay to call to mind the 'pontiff of . . . fashionable portraiture' Godfrey Kneller and his successors, whose prestigious portraits 'aimed at giving the sitters the looks they were supposed to like rather than those they possessed' (Williams 1962: 399). The application at the end of the fable is general rather than specific: 'each [client] found the likeness in his thought' (2, 327). Kneller had died in 1723, and his clientele had been captured by Jervas and by Jonathan Richardson father and son, who had so much work that they had to farm out the painting of everything except the faces to 'drapery men' and apprentices. Hence the 'bustos' of Gay's artist, who appears to be discovering a bright idea of his own but who is really choosing to paint flattering faces in the popular mode. And if 'The *Lyon* and the *Cub*' satirizes Walpole's dinner-table habits, it also satirizes Gay's friend Pope, who in the 1720s often dined with the great man. Johnson's remark as given by Boswell approves of Walpole's self-admitted practice as democratic, avoiding the possible contentions of serious conversation, and so likely to 'promote kindness' (Boswell 1970: 756) in the company.

So the fables float between operating as social satire with fairly specific points of reference; as potential political satire with a very specific point of reference; and as something which is neither of these, because there are no clear hints to either of the applications. There is no single reading: the fables are made unstable, open to readings. A fable must 'show without equivocation . . . what is intended' (*CR* 2 (Feb. 1761), 124), but Walpole, the sitter, and the reader are all faced with equivocal artistic objects. The presence of ideas and topics from fable in contemporary political discourse must be a large consideration in responding to Gay's fables, but this does not restrict his methods. The fables might be political satires, but they could equally be satires on the habit of reading politically, of seeing in them *a face or a fable like one's own.*

These pervasive qualities of ambiguity and incongruity in Gay's 1727 *Fables* have almost always been referred back to aspects of Gay's biography operating in tandem with his political situation. It has proved difficult to find a satisfactory alternative context that would argue for enough psychic distance to provide full artistic control in the collection, rather than for forms of compromised emotional investment or hypocrisy. William Empson started or aggravated this problem, with his striking sentence which finishes by pointing out that Gay attacked political bribery and parasitism, but wanted a place at court and 'succeeded in living as a parasite on the nobility' (Empson 1966: 166). He then partly solves the problem by implying that Gay thought that life *chez* Queensberry was actually *more* independent than living on his own income like a model New Whig or like poor old Swift, who was dependent on Gay for the management of most of his finances.

Unfortunately, subsequent writers tend not to take the point of this subtler paradox. Even Nokes, who is extremely appreciative of the attractions of the *Fables*, is eventually tempted back into the coarse ironies that appear when they are considered next to Gay's known personal and social habits: 'he adopted the rhetoric of the industrious bee, but he lived the life of an idle drone . . . The more he strove, vainly, to affect the style of a social butterfly, the more he revealed the instincts of a discontented snail' (Nokes 1995: 388, 510). Spacks specifies 'the idea of work' as 'of primary importance' in *Rural Sports* and *The Shepherd's Week* (Spacks 1965: 34) and moves on from this to consider the fables in the light of possible psychic tensions about the value of work and success in Gay himself. Joan Owen similarly ascribes the 'ethical tensions inherent in the persona' of the narrator to 'emotional ambivalence concerning the value and meaning of success' (Owen 1969: 137). Seen biographically, the ambiguities of the fables must also relate to the supposed split between Gay's urge towards personal and professional kinship with Swift and Pope, and his desire to ingratiate himself with the court.

These psychological splits and tensions may or may not be there in Gay, but allowing them to rule the roost has always tended to deny the possibility of the fables' having an independent life – an active and deliberate 'double capacity' – of their own. Empson's second paradox, if pursued, would argue for a kind of psychic integrity, and Gay's friends, though sometimes puzzled by him, did not often see him as a troubled spirit. And the essential theme of both the collections is representation, not work or success; discourse, not policies. In this they are classic in their orientation. Ian Donaldson's account of Gay's play with 'double capacity' in *The Beggar's Opera* describes a method in which the work seems simultaneously parodic and genuinely sentimental, 'painful and ridiculous' at once, and in which the audience is led to create a corresponding 'double picture' (Donaldson 1970: 172, 167) of each character. Empson's audience of the play 'roared its applause both against and with the applause of Walpole' (Empson 1966: 162). The full effect of the *Fables* involves a similar, if more subtle, set of qualities.

The 1727 *Fables*

The final seeming paradox of Swift's career as a fabulist is the letter he sent to Gay in 1732, in which he repined that he *could not write* fables. It appears that Gay thought that Swift held a low opinion of the form, and that Swift was anxious to disabuse him:

you have misunderstood me, for there is no writing I esteem more than Fables, nor is anything more difficult to succeed in . . . I have frequently endeavoured . . . in vain . . . I remember, I acted as you seem to hint, I found a moral first, and then studyd for a Fable, but cou'd do nothing that pleased me, and so left off that scheme for ever. (Swift 1963–5: 4, 38–9)

It is a curious letter, its apologetic tones more reminiscent of Gay's compliant mode of social expression than of Swift, who is deferring to a writer who he admires, but who is almost twenty years younger than himself and much less assertive. Swift allows 'Fables' to mean 'fables more like yours', implying 'an integrated collection of supposedly original fables; modern "orthodox" fables'. His reassurances feel genuine, but the notion of Swift consciously complying with the post-Bossu orthodoxy that morals, preferably 'truths entirely new' (La Motte 1721: 11), should take precedence over the fables in which they are embodied, is not convincing. This orthodoxy is implicit in the remark Gay seems to have passed, and his collections conform, or rather defer, to it. His apparent novelty in his 'NEW FABLES' (2, 299), which, according to the sadly uninformed Dearing, 'runs counter to the demands of the genre' (2, 620), in fact consciously imitates that of La Motte's recent prestigious *New Court Fables*: 'all entirely new . . . I have a moral or two more which I wish to write upon' (Gay 1966: 52, 122). Wray correctly describes invention as part of the 'general evolutionary process away from the traditional classical genre' (Wray 1950: 80). This novelty is, though, to some extent a fiction in Gay's case, because, as Dearing's notes make clear, many of his fables are reworked from La Fontaine and Phaedrus: as indeed are La Motte's. And if new fables are old (Modern and Ancient), orthodox fables may also be something else.

Swift's implicit distinction between kinds of fables, his own and his friend's, might be accepted at face value, were it not that critical practice to date has insisted on identifying both Swift and Gay as 'orthodox' fabulists. Swift's orthodoxy is a trick of the light, but what of Gay's? His 1727 *Fables* were written for the court, at a point when he was hoping for preferment, and were patterned on a well-known, polite French model. They had a huge readership and currency through the eighteenth century and beyond – over three hundred and fifty editions of the first and second series printed together, most before 1890. A copy of the *Fables* was the first literary possession of William Cowper, and Cowper was translating 'The *Hare* and Many *Friends*' and others from the first series into Latin shortly before his death. It is a collection of great power, penetrating newly emerging markets successfully and swiftly; women, children, provincial, overseas. To do this, fables must at least seem to be more like *Moral Tales for Young People* and less like *Pretty Poems for the Amusement of Children Six Foot High* (Smart's 1757 collection of poems) or *Fables For Grown Gentlemen* (Hall-Stevenson 1770). Gay seems to have had some natural depth of feeling for or with these new audiences. His origins were provincial (Barnstaple Nonconformist); his friends tended to see him as rather childlike; when he signs himself into the 1727 collection, it is in a simile with the female Hare of the final fable.

But these *Fables* must initially have sold to Gay's original sophisticated metropolitan audience, which, after initial shock and astonishment, was to idolize *The Beggar's Opera*'s dizzying blend of the sardonically satirical and the good-naturedly tuneful the next year. There were persistent grumblings from orthodox critics such as Joseph Warton and James Beattie, about Gay's deliberate perversity in respect of probability, 'ascribing to different animals and objects . . . speeches and actions inconsistent with their several natures' (Warton 1782: 245) and thus creating a 'fiction wherein no regard is had to the nature of things' (Beattie 1783: 507). If a fable must show, without equivocation, what is intended, it will be clear that a fable like 'The *Painter*', which teases the reader with possible applications on different levels of reference without quite committing itself to one, will be in danger of being apprehended as that irritating creature, the Enigma. Other techniques will heighten this danger. There is also Johnson's very reasonable complaint – a representative one, and if anything an understatement – that it is 'difficult to extract any moral principle' (Johnson 1905: 2, 283) from the collection. This comment carries more force, or conveys a greater sense of perplexity, than the similar ones that Johnson passes elsewhere about the drama of Shakespeare, because fables are by 1760 a self-avowedly ethical medium where Shakespearean drama is not. And readers who just wanted 'pretty' fables often preferred Moore or others – 'pretty' being Catherine Talbot's epithet for *Fables for the Female Sex*, which she elevates over Gay's collection (*A Series of Letters between E. Carter and Catherine Talbot* (1809): 2, 68, quoted by Wray 1950: 137).

This argues that different audiences might have been able to admire Gay's *Fables* for different reasons. It also seems that they might be less safe and rather more classically double in their relationship with various 'masters' – the court and ministry, first and foremost, but moral and technical orthodoxies too – than is suggested by their polite manner of address, by the 'negligible' (Goldgar 1976: 45) direct satirical content, and by the conventional aspects of their poetic technique. One of Swift's tricks in the *Intelligencer* (No. 3) provides a quite different gloss on the *Fables* from that in his letter to Gay in 1732, and the two comments taken together suggest that Swift sensed their double nature. In the *Intelligencer*, he extends his habitual stress on the misreadability of fables into a sly suggestion that Gay had acted unwisely in not considering that 'the Malignity of some People might misinterpret what [Gay] said' in his fables 'to the Disadvantage of present Persons and Affairs' (Swift 1939–75: 12, 35).

This is a deadpan insinuation that the Walpole administration might make the mistake of overreading the satirical nature of the *Fables*, after Tim's manner – every minister his own *Tim*. Swift's method here is a refinement of a technique of the *Craftsman*, which would critique 'the tendency of the government to overread plays, poems, or the *Craftsman* itself' (Goldgar 1976: 70) by gravely parodying such readings. The *Craftsman* would, for instance, condemn *The Beggar's Opera* as a despicable allegorical libel on Walpole's ministry, while at the same time explaining in great and over-ingenious detail just how this reading could be achieved. But Swift's comment also acts as a brief inverted hint to any *underreading* Tims that the *Fables* were intended to have a satirical application, which they would be fools not to see. So it is a double tease: whichever of the two handles or applications is taken, the minister is effectively an Ass. At this point – in 1728, just after the production of *The Beggar's Opera* – the ministerial organs were trying to cover themselves by pretending that even that piece was an 'innocent' one which had been 'explained into a *Libel*' by opposition malcontents (*Senator*: see Goldgar, 1976: 72). Ass by underreading: *The Beggar's Opera* is only innocent in the sense that it is hard to prove it guilty unless you have a mind to, although proving it guilty has, here, apparently proven it innocent.

One might think that Swift was being unfair to the *Fables*, co-opting and overreading them for a political position as Pittis and others had earlier with L'Estrange's. But, again, both the *Craftsman* and pro-government organs had already begun to do this. The *Craftsman* was quick to pick up the figure of the courtier-transformed-to-Cameleon in Fable 2 and use it against Walpole and the administration (in No. 110, 10 August 1728). Edward Roome, who ran the pro-administration *Senator*, answered Gay's Fable 25, 'The Barley-Mow and the Dung-hill', which has a brief reflection against Bubble-profiteers and upstarts who cancel their obligations, with 'The Oak and the Dunghill', in which Walpole is the mighty Oak and the *Craftsman* the scurrilous Dunghill. This in turn was answered by the *Craftsman* (no. 123, 9 Nov. 1728) with 'A Sequel to the Fable of the Oak and the Dunghill', in which the Walpolean Oak is festooned with parasitic Mistletoe and blue ribbons.

Given the general conditions of literary-political discourse, Gay's fables had to become political in *a* reading, and Gay must have known that this would happen. In such a situation, his strategy is to produce fables which can become political satire in only one kind of reading. He writes fables which primarily ask to be underread as either general social satire or 'transparent . . . crystalline moralism' (Patterson 1991: 149). So Swift is not co-opting the fables, he is placing them in their proper position between two different kinds of reading, just as (say) Pamela will place her final fable between different reading responses deriving from opposed genres, romance and piety.

But in a wider, more social sense, a prickly response from higher echelons to a collection with such items as an ethically superior speaking Dung-hill would seem quite natural. This would be a sense which would depend on the reader's, or implied reader's, acknowledging the premise of courtly politeness in the Dedication and the orientation towards La Motte's *Court Fables*, and then finding that this did not cover the case. One wonders, for instance, whether little Prince William, the supposed point of address of the 1727 *Fables*, ever asked his mother, Queen Caroline, the precise meaning of lines three and four of 'The *Hare* and Many *Friends*', and what Mrs Morland thought, if anything, when her daughter lisped

> Friendship, like love, is but a name,
> Unless to one you stint the flame.
> The child, whom many fathers share,
> Hath seldom known a father's care. (2, 368)

How very different from the home life of our own dear queen; but the couplet slides genteelly past, with hardly anything but children and fathers in it. What of 'The *Gardener* and the *Hog*', with its distinctly unpastoral 'swain': how peculiar is peculiar?

> A gard'ner, of peculiar taste,
> On a young Hog his favour plac'd . . .
> Where'er he went, the grunting friend
> Ne'er failed his pleasure to attend . . .
>
> Who cherishes a brutal mate
> Shall mourn the folly soon or late. (2, 366, 367)

Tastefully avoiding the doctrine of innuendo suggested by 'pleasure', 'grunting', and 'mate', we explain this safely to our infant son as an orthodox allegorical injunction not to cross class-boundaries, well aware that it is no such thing. And who exactly are 'we', in the opening lines of 'The *Old Woman* and Her *Cats*'?

> Who friendship with a knave hath made
> Is judg'd a partner in the trade.
> The matron, who conducts abroad
> A willing nymph, is thought a bawd;
> And if a modest girl is seen
> With one who cures a lover's spleen,
> We guess her, not extreamly nice,
> And only wish to know her price. (2, 333)

This little passage exhibits all the poetical modesty and lightness of touch, done through discreet punctuation, enjambement, and simple words – only one longer than two syllables, in eight lines, and that one with a little ironic stress-curl to it – that Faber, Gay's 1926 Oxford editor, rightly specified as characteristic of the 1727 *Fables*. This technique allows, even creates, a genteel preVictorian underreading of the passage, as it does of much of the collection, and sustains a sensation of safety. Everyone has their price, after all. At the same time, there is a kind of work going on in the space between the directness of one class of diction – 'trade', 'price' – and the more upmarket and pseudo-discreet 'cures a lover's spleen' and 'not extreamly nice', which is not so far from Mandeville's trick of eliding 'reasonable Prices' and 'the Chastity of Women of Honour'. Gay's technique, though, is more conspiratorial, the mock-pastoral reversal of classes, and the possibilities for under- and overreading, pretending to hide within poetic technique.

But the 'we' is a self-irony, or self-mock. The poor girl is, after all, modest: 'we', a Mohock-like group, lounging loutishly on some mock-pastoral Covent-Garden corner to size up the passing shepherdesses, have overread her by association. 'Judg'd' slips to 'thought', and then dissolves into 'guess'. This is not someone sleeping with a pig in a gutter, where we might *know* a man by the company he keeps; this world of perception is much slipperier. Where Swift's Tim and the courtier-politicians responding to *The Beggar's Opera* make Asses of themselves by overreading what claim to be fables or general satires into personal libels, or by underreading satire, the court or implied (even *common*) readers are here credited with having the wit to read temperately, not to make a fuss about the odd post-Restoration piece of wit, and with having the skill to take the hint about dissociating themselves subtly from the 'we'.

But although the relationship with the reader is not so combative as in Swift, there is an important exception in the case – or the representation – of the crucial figure of the boy and young male heir. This unfortunate may be transsexualized, sardonically warned against flattery, and then flattered, in Fable 1, addressed to Prince William – Gay plays both Chaucer's Nun's Priest *and* his Fox, Russel:

> Princes, like Beautys, from their youth
> Are strangers to the voice of truth:
> Learn to contemn all praise betimes;
> For flattery's the nurse of crimes . . .
> Must I too flatter like the rest,
> And turn my morals to a jest?
> The muse disdains to steal from those,
> Who thrive in courts by fulsome prose.
> But shall I hide your real praise,
> Or tell you what a nation says?
> They in your infant bosom trace
> The virtues of your Royal race . . . (2, 302)

Or he may be described as a doting mother's 'booby' and 'a shocking aukward creature / That speaks a fool in ev'ry feature' in Fable 3; or surreptitiously compared to a Spaniel and sycophantic courtier in Fable 2:

> A SPANIEL, bred with all the care
> That waits upon a fav'rite heir,
> Ne'er felt correction's rigid hand;
> Indulg'd to disobey command,
> In pamper'd ease his hours were spent;
> He never knew what learning meant;
> Such forward airs, so pert, so smart . . . (2, 306, 305, 304)

Hardly the stress on educable juvenility that one would expect from the start of a series of fables ostensibly addressed to a little prince. Young dominant males must find Gay's *Fables* most unnerving. And what the heir inherits is never very pleasant, as in the case of the sons of the dying Fox in No. 29, who reflect to their father:

> Think, what our ancestors have done;
> A line of thieves from son to son;
> To us descends the long disgrace,
> And infamy hath mark'd our race. (2, 341)

'Seek you to train your fav'rite boy?' asks the opening of Fable 9. A more hopeful start, followed by comfortable middle-class diction in the induction, such as 'preceptor' and 'manners', but the story is that of another dog. A Mastiff whose 'eye-balls shot indignant fire' challenges a 'monarch' Bull, who is curious to know the motive for such unequal combat. How has the plebian Mastiff acquired or inherited this 'world-destroying wrath of Kings'? The Mastiff says that he fights, like those heroes 'of eternal name / whom poets sing', in order to obtain 'fame', and that he was taught to fight by his master, a butcher. Well, says the Bull before killing him with a flick of his horns, that explains it:

> thou (beneath a butcher train'd,
> Whose hands with cruelty are stain'd,
> His daily murders in thy view,)
> Must, like thy tutor, blood pursue. (2, 312, 313)

Proleptically ironic in view of Prince William's becoming the Butcher of Culloden in 1746, but also socially and artistically provoking. The bourgeois security of the opening has somehow dissolved in the unexpected split between the royal Bull and the unruly but aspiring apprentice Mastiff; a process which also anticipates, in miniature, a strategy of *The Beggar's Opera*. 'Train' in the first line means 'educate', but the Bull's reply would gloss the word as simply the encouragement and management of animal instincts – unless the butcher is also responsible for teaching the dog to read heroic poetry. In this linguistically pullulating world where anything, even a Rose or a Pin or a face may speak ('a fool in ev'ry feature'), Gay's animals are inveterate and usually accurate readers, but seemingly by nature rather than by education. As indeed is the Bull, who could have read the Mastiff's rage as being inspired by the incongruous reading of heroic poets, but who chooses a different socially superior moral.

But how does one educate a 'fav'rite boy' who is, by constitution, a Mastiff? Simply avoid butchers and heroic poets? These seem the wrong parameters for the initial problem, which is itself peculiar enough, given the point of address. The supposed addressee (William), a strongly implied reader and potential patron who should be being flattered by the deferential poet, is instead being teased and just possibly educated through complex ironic wit. This is no timorous Hare. The relationship is much more like that between Aesop or Phaedrus and his masters than it is like any conventional relationship between common poet and aristocratic or ministerial eighteenth-century patronage.

The possibility of the collection being open to different perspectives and readings invites the larger question of how fable was more widely understood at this point, outside partisan ripostes and the usually orthodox critical pronouncements in prefaces and reviews. Was there a recognizable middle ground between verse fable and comic or satirical-burlesque opera that would form the definite but flexible context of response to which these fables seem to be appealing, between the poles of political satire and complaisant morality? Could a fable, in 1727, display some of the satirical bite soon to appear in *The Beggar's Opera* and also appeal 'safely' to genteel audiences?

A useful pointer to an answer is the attractive example of *Momus Turn'd Fabulist: or, Vulcan's Wedding. An Opera: After the Manner of the Beggar's Opera* (1729). This adaptation by Ebenezer Forrest (an attorney friend of Hogarth) of Fuzelier's *Momus Fabuliste*, ran for a full fortnight at Lincoln's-Inn Fields. Where *The Beggar's Opera* plays with mock-pastoral inversions of class, Forrest's *Momus* degrades the Olympian gods to the pseudo-political characters of a comic operetta, singing ballad-airs and chatting. The piece is set in the court of Jupiter, but even he has to scuttle offstage when summoned by a 'Minister of Destiny' (Forrest 1729: 6). The story is that of the gods' fascination with the newly born Venus, with Jupiter anxious to have her married to the lowly Vulcan as a cover for his own seedy activities. Momus, the scurrilous god of ridicule, is banned by Jupiter from speaking satirically against the court, on pain of permanent expulsion. Momus soliloquizes as to how to devise a counter-strategy: what form is suitable to someone in the equivocal position of being inside and yet outside the court, excluded, yet with a corrective function which he is constitutionally bound to fulfil?

> Jupiter only forbids me talking Satyrically—he allows me to think. Let us think then—but how the dickens shall one bring out one's Thoughts without speaking? . . . I have it . . . I'll invent Fables [and] evade the cruel Law that's imposed on me. (*ibid.*: 8)

And so he does, singing his fables to popular tunes. But the gods against and to whom he tells them are all unable to make the application. Vulcan, for instance, is unwilling or unable to see that 'The Ass Married for a Cover', a fable in which an illicit equine couple devise a plan of marrying the Mare to the Ass in order to 'avoid impending Shame' (*ibid.*: shades of *The Way of the World*), might apply to the unsavoury triangle of himself, Venus, and Jupiter. Here, Vulcan's lack of application, his underreading, makes the Ass. Only the nymph Aeglé has the wit to appreciate Momus's point directly: so *girls* can read fables properly, politicians cannot. Momus reflects on the dullness of his main audience:

> These great rich Rogues, with being constantly tickl'd with Flattery and Champaign, grow so dull that they have no more taste for an Epigram, than they have for Burgundy: Nothing but mere Brandy-Satyr will make them feel— (*ibid.*: 21)

Fables are thus identified as a possible middle ground somewhere between flattery ('those / Who thrive in courts by fulsome prose') and downright satire. The introductory exchange between the Player and the Gentleman assures the audience that all this is only polite general satire, which it indeed is. But there is a silent satirical application ('without speaking'), signalled by the claim of kinship with Gay in the extended title. *Momus* was staged almost immediately after the provoked Walpole had had the Lord Chamberlain forbid the production of Gay's *Polly*, the sequel to *The Beggar's Opera*, at the end of 1728. Gay had been silenced by Walpole just as Momus has been silenced by Jupiter, and Gay was the best-known English verse fabulist. Walpole, like Jupiter, was known to pursue extra-marital activity. Destiny, comically, is George Augustus, George II. The claim of general satire – 'general Expression' – and the claim of kinship with *The Beggar's Opera* were recognized gambits of the *Craftsman*'s anti-Walpole lampoons and essays: Gay carefully inserted an italicized moral to one of his fables (No. 36) – *'petty rogues submit to fate / That great ones may enjoy their state'* (Gay 1974: 2, 350) – which would be closely akin to the Beggar's moral at the end of his *Opera*. But his pseudo-distracting footnote to the line refers the reader, quite properly, to an equivalent moment in Garth's *Dispensary*.

So the whole of *Momus* becomes an epigram, a fable, the 'reading' of which is made to act as just the same kind of double-tease as in Swift's comment in *Intelligencer* 3. If the political masters as implied audience fail to make the application, they will be underreading Asses, like Forrest's gods. If they take the application as fully satirical, slanderous and bannable, using what the opposition was wont to complain of (and exploit) as what the 1731 *Craftsman* pamphlet *The Doctrine of Innuendo's* called the ministers' 'Doctrines of *Parallels* and *Innuendoes*' (Anon. 1974: 10), they will be overreading, applying the moral in a spirit alien to that of the play. Only if they have 'taste' will they relish their position, and taste was what the administration was perceived to lack. Lampoons were open to the criticism that they suggested bile and jealousy in the writer: ludicrous or burlesque works could be condemned as frivolous. But Forrest's operetta is merely a tasteful comic imitation of a polite French model: again, exactly the same strategy as in Gay's *Fables*.

Although Forrest is clearly directing the audience back to Gay's *Fables* as a work with some oppositional satirical function, his own stage-fabulist, Momus, still operates inside the court. His fables provoke amusement, not retaliation. He and his masters come to an accommodation through fable, rather as the 'Tory Wits' in general wanted, according to some accounts, to 'reach an accommodation' (Goldgar 1976: 28) with the Walpole ministry. And the morals of Forrest's fable are only politically pointed in the classic sense of being directed against the political conditions of literary expression and discourse. Firstly there is censorship by great men, being booted off the stage, and the way one might respond to this. Secondly there is the difficult question of the proper manner of speech or representation in such a response, between the scurrility of satire and the servility of flattery.

Momus recognizes each of these, satire and flattery, as a condition to be avoided. The reasons for this attitude lie partly in Walpole's notorious use of hack-writers to defend his policies and attack the opposition. In particular, flattery or eulogy was a sore point with the opposition, who felt that Walpole's rewarding of very minor talents for the right tone of voice was destroying the old system of patronage in which the literary artist was allowed a degree of independence. *The Doctrine of Innuendo's* complains of the defenders 'constantly in pay' of 'a certain Great Man', who 'are not only to excuse his Blunders, but to magnify his Services, and extol his Measures, tho' at the expense of Truth and common Honesty' (Anon. 1974: 9). But where prose replies such as this are usually direct, the opposition's verse replies characteristically adopt the pose of the object being parodied. As with fable in Mandeville and Swift, the 'colours' of the enemy may become the implements of attack, because they are also the target. Edward Young's fulsome eulogy of Walpole, *The Instalment* (1726), extolled the great man's exploits in war and peace, by land and sea. In reply, the *Craftsman*, besides offering and arguing the opinion that Young's poem was in fact a lampoon of Walpole, printed a free translation of some 'LATIN VERSES' that had supposedly been found, '*inscribed to the glory of a certain great Man, at the Bottom of an Emblematical Device . . .* ' As with Swift's 'Atlas', there are two 'Herculean' figures, a higher and a lower, in the lines:

Let Bards with Honour old *Alcides* dub,
Who slew the *Hydra* with his Sword or—Club.
Our English *Hercules* is greater far;
Whose Toils for *Peace* exceed his Toils in *War*.
He slew one *Hydra*; ours hath many slain;
Preferring *publick Good* to *private Gain*.
Let Envy gnash her Teeth; let *Craftsmen* rail;
While *Pallas* is his Guide, he cannot Fail.
How great, O *England*, may thy Greatness be,
Whilst He's thy WALL by Land, thy POLE by Sea?

('D'Anvers' 1731: 75–6)

The 'POLE' and Hercules's '—Club' leave readers in possession of an association (see above, p. 47) which allows them to imagine the appropriate emblematical 'device'. Satire is done through apparent flattery, heroic eulogy which rises only to low pun (there is probably another in '*Pallas*'): the art of sinking at sea in poetry. The *Craftsman*'s 'Sequel to the Fable of the Oak and the Dunghill' is also concerned with expression more than with policy, being written primarily against the hyperbole of Roome's poem. Conversely, the *Craftsman* would sometimes defend itself by apparently attacking its own numbers as slanderous, which is to say slanderous in effect or in application: *The Doctrine of Innuendo's* opens with a mocking description of the *Craftsman*'s 'dangerous Positions, which they every *Saturday* disperse, to the no small terror and scandalizing of the tender Consciences of certain Persons, who are continually alarm'd by their Papers' (Anon. 1974: 3). Flattery and satire melt into each other, genres and meanings dissolving at the twitch of a tone of voice. Indeed, language itself is felt to be dissolving, the meanings and value of words straining and distorting. Several of the opposition lampoons half-mockingly stress the appropriation of the minute particulars of the English language by Walpole and his ministry. The most notable of these is the song called 'An Excellent New Ballad, called A BOB for the C---t', which is to be sung 'to the Tune of, *In the Days of my Youth—In the first Part of the Beggar's Opera*', and which appeared after the Congress of Soissons had strengthened Walpole's hand by vindicating his foreign policies: 'BOB' is of course Robert Walpole, as well as a taunt or scoff:

Ye Poets, take Heed how you trust to the Muse,
What Words to make Choice of, and what to Refuse . . .

If *Congress* is nam'd, you must mean it a Slap,
The City of *Soissons* blot out of your Map:

Offend is a Word of such doubtful Import,
Application cries out, *That's a* BOB *for the C---t.*

If *Macheath* you should name, in the midst of his *Gang,*
They'll say 'tis an Hint you would *Somebody* hang,
For *Macheath* is a Word of such evil Report,
Application cries out, *That's a* BOB *for the C---t.*

('D'Anvers' 1731: 57, 59, 58)

Words, dramatic representation, even cartography: all modes of representation are drawn by the ministry's habits of reading into the shadowy world of occult meanings, code and hieroglyph.

Several of the political *causes célèbres* of the 1720s were in effect battles over language, the most notorious being the ministry's fruitless attempt to decode Bishop Atterbury's correspondence with the Jacobites. Atterbury was later discovered to have been engaged in a genuinely treasonable plot, but the ministry at the time simply assumed that a correspondence in code proved guilt, and acted accordingly. The *Craftsman*'s responses included the mocking 'Crambo-Satyricon', in which all the letters of the alphabet have supposedly been appropriated for cryptic purposes by opposition satirists:

Great A stands for Army, *as* B *stands for* Bubble,
And C *points out* Craftsman, *or* Caleb *in Trouble* . . .
N *stands for a* Name, *which I dare not speak out,*
But O *is a* Cypher *will* explain it, no Doubt. (*ibid.*: 17–18)

A passage in Book 3 of *Gulliver's Travels* is very similar. Everything, even a single letter, may now speak darkly of something else: the function of language is spoken of as not to convey meaning, but to raise doubt (hopefully, comic doubt) about what is being conveyed. 'Scepticism's your profession', says Gay sternly to the Lawyer of Fable 1 of the second series, 'you hold there's doubt in all expression' (3, 381): but serio-jocose scepticism, duplicity, and relativity of meaning were properties of a whole mode or area of expression in the world that provoked Gay's 1727 series.

With the use of language now clearly becoming political in its basis, it is as well to remember for a moment the contention over language as a source of power in the Civil Wars. If Walpole is felt to be abusing the English language and common literary genres, and disallowing their use to others, then he must also be felt to be appropriating the English nation. One might also remember the nature of John Ogilby's response to that context, which is not to factionalize further, but to move beyond the bounds of the dissension to a more wideranging, if equally disturbed, level. On this level, Gay uses politically current topics only to extrapolate from them or sublimate them, and to appeal to audiences and patrons of different kinds.

The nature and grounds of political expression in the 1720s influence the 1727 *Fables* quite directly. The fables exhibit, for example, a constant flux between flattery and satire, or between representations which flatter the object and others which denigrate it. In almost all the fables, what at first appears to be moral and physical reality – action, fable, and pro- or epimythium – dissolves into this representational flux. As in the political journalism of the period, it is rarely a question of what things or people are in themselves, rather of how they may be seen or spoken of, how they may be represented or misrepresented. Things are as they are seen: as the fables slip between satire and general morality, so the representations of the actors themselves are in constant motion, producing comic insecurities of perception. The child in Fable 3 is 'fair and wise' in the eyes of its parents, but 'a shocking aukward creature' with a 'squinting leer' in the eyes of its Nurse (2, 305). What it is *really*, we do not know. The Prince is either flattered or mocked with flattery in Fable 1, or both together: it is hard to tell. The Cameleon in Fable 2 is a satirical 'emblem of the flatt'ring host' (2, 304). A portrait both flatters and satirizes the sitter: Hope flatters the dying miser in 'The Sick Man and the Angel' that he may live, but he does not. Diction flatters, or pretends to flatter ('one who cures a lover's spleen'), or slanders ('know her price').

Sometimes this confusion of perception and representation is delegated to the actors themselves. The socially mobile but empty-headed millinery Pin addresses the Needle scathingly as a 'taylor's tool', not realising that, as this is 'Gresham hall' (2, 323), this Needle is more likely to belong to a compass in one of the exhibits. If a Poet sings to a Rose which he is about to place in his beloved's bosom about the superior charms of his lady which will provoke the Rose to withering envy and despair, the well-read Rose will reply crossly that the mistaken Poet should not thus denigrate one of his main poetical props:

> In ev'ry love-song roses bloom;
> We lend you colour and perfume.
> Does it to Chloe's charms conduce,
> To found her praise on our abuse? (2, 365)

Praise and abuse, 'flatt'ry' and 'slander'; and songs have 'colours' just as flowers do. The wife in 'The *Scold* and the *Parrot*' is provoked, by her remonstrating husband, to complain that where he objects to the 'slander' of her 'vixen tongue', he admires the Parrot's 'squawling song'

> A parrot's privilege forbidden! . . .
>
> Now reputations flew in pieces
> Of mothers, daughters, aunts and nieces,
> She ran the parrot's language o'er,
> Bawd, hussy, drunkard, slattern, whore . . . (2, 335)

But this is itself a slander by the poet of the Parrot, whose language turns out to be moralistic, not abusive: the Parrot gives the general moral:

> She, who attacks another's honour,
> Draws ev'ry living thing upon her . . .
> One slander must ten thousand get,
> The world with int'rest pays the debt. (2, 336)

An entirely equivocal Parrot, a Parrot with two languages. The general moral of 'The *Old Woman* and Her *Cats*' invokes the question of how we are spoken of, represented, by others:

> 'Tis thus, that on the choice of friends,
> Our good or evil name depends. (2, 332)

A nicely sceptical thesis, practically Mandevillean. Our reputation for virtue or degeneracy depends not on intrinsic qualities but on wholly relative or perceived ones, and perception is always relative. If one is a Fox, one will be seen and bad-mouthed as a Fox, and it is simply no use practising honesty in feeding, 'like harmless sheep'. So the virtue itself would be – again the Mandevillean conclusion – perfectly useless:

> Whatever hen-roost is decreas'd,
> We shall be thought to share the feast.
> The change shall never be believ'd,
> A lost good-name is ne'er retrieved. (2, 341)

Gay's animals are sometimes endowed with the ability that Ogilby's Hands and Lions possess, of seeing (or reading) more in or into their fable than seemed likely in the action. Here, his clever little Foxes see that the apparently natural morality of their fable-world – that foxes are wicked and will always steal chickens – is in fact dependent on the cultural construct of their being seen and read as Foxes. In effect, they read their readers.

Clearly, Gay is doing much more with the topics of flattery and slander than he would if he were simply reflecting his immediate political context. He seems to have a longer perspective; again, to be able to play with 'political' topics in a wider arena, as Swift's late fables do.

Here it is worth recalling Brean Hammond's point that Gay's engagement with the theme of literary flattery and libel for political hire does not originate with the *Fables*, but goes back as far as the 'very early' (Hammond 1989: 34) *Epistle to . . . Paul Methuen* (1720), which predates the Walpole ministry. Gay here tells the aspiring poet that he must write either 'ranc'rous libels' or 'fulsome praise' for 'party quarrels' if he is to rise in the world. As in *Momus*, flattery and libel are not opposite poles but similar extremes. The *Epistle* finishes with a fable in which a Crow, flattering a Lark because of his voice and strength, is rebuked by the Lark. Larks may 'sing sweet, and on strong pinion rise', but are caged for their voice, and shot for their flesh. For the fowlers, though, 'to shoot at crows is powder flung away' (1, 216, 217).

There are several echoes of this *Epistle* in the *Fables*, which, for example, berate 'fulsome prose' (in Fable 1) rather than fulsome praise. In the induction to 'The *Persian*, the *Sun* and the *Cloud*', Gay's personified goddess of Envy reads the 'nervous lines' of poets of genius, and

> Her hissing snakes with venom swell,
> She calls her venal train from hell,
> The servile fiends her nod obey,
> And all Curl's authors are in pay.
> Fame calls up calumny and spite,
> Thus shadow owes its birth to light. (2, 339)

Where the Painter is paid for suitably artistic flattery, Curl's authors earn for slander: prostituted representation results in money. This passage, with the apparent slander of Curl's authors nicely shaded by the instant tonal transition from the overwrought consonantal rhetoric of myth to the open-vowelled mock-ease of the Augustan writer who sees his enemies living almost next door, is a reprise or reworking of lines 75–80 of the *Epistle*, a passage to which the illustrative fable of Lark and Crow stands as parable:

> Had *Pope* with groveling numbers fill'd his page,
> *Dennis* had never kindled into rage.
> 'Tis the sublime that hurts the Critic's ease;
> Write nonsense and he sleeps and reads in peace:
> Were *Prior, Congreve, Swift* and *Pope* unknown,
> Poor slander-selling *Curll* would be undone. (1, 217)

These parallels suggest that the *Fables* are a development of Gay's longstanding feelings about, and interests in, the conditions of literary discourse, without requiring the discursive framework of the *Epistle*. The most apparent difference is that the less 'sublime' *Fables* exhibit a very varied manner of address, rather than exuding the prim air of security that comes from addressing a sympathetic acquaintance who is also a wealthy connoisseur and patron – or perhaps one should say *implied* patron. 'Yet let me not of grievances complain', says Gay with a tug of the forelock in the *Epistle*, 'Who . . . Can boast subscriptions to my humble lays' (1, 216). But the *Fables* were not published by subscription. Written 'for a Prince', they were sold to the public.

Hammond continues his discussion of the *Epistle* by remarking on its 'ideological' importance, and by following up Dearing's cogent perception that 'dissatisfaction at the present state of patronage was part of [Gay's] normal state of mind' (2, 586):

> the changing conditions of literary patronage were an important determinant of his expression – both of what he was able to express and of what he could only express unsatisfactorily through contradiction. (Hammond 1989: 39)

This seems right, except that the contradictions and paradoxes of fable may be qualities which Gay to some extent manages, rather than simply submitting to them. The fable at the end of the *Epistle*, for example, contains a very vivid example of Empson's paradox about dependency-and-independence. The poet-as-Lark is both free to fly in the dangerous public air *and* caged by the patron. But whether this is managed or not is hard to say, because the paradox has not been anticipated in the discursive mode of the earlier parts of the *Epistle*.

Although the context of political discourse clearly provides a good deal of impetus to the post-sceptical relativity of multiple reading in the 1727 *Fables*, their wider socio-economic context, or moment of transition, is important as well. There is a striking sense in the *Fables* of the replacement of a single point of address, or point of patronage, by a fascination with a quasi-Mandevillean, quasi-Phaedrian set of new energies, multiple foci, social mixing – Gardeners and Hogs, Philosophers and Pheasants, Wolves, Lords, and Painters, Persians, Envy, and Curl's authors – multiple audiences, tones of voice, patrons, purchasers of artistic representations, kinds of reading, codes of morality: child and adult, prince and Mohock. Not that some of the fables – 'The *Father* and *Jupiter*', for instance – are not morally secure in their epimythia, able to act as legitimate rest or reassurance for the reading of the tender orthodox reader, who is an important part of this brave new world. Gay, to repeat, always provides some points of emotional reference for the honest, sententious, or sentimental audience, even in his wildest burlesques: parts of the audience were in tears at early performances of *The What D'Ye Call It*, and as Peter Lewis says, 'those who were genuinely moved cannot be dismissed as naïve' (Lewis 1989: 140).

But such restful examples are comparatively rare. Most of the fables spin outwards, extending the obsession with modes of representation past the topics of flattery and slander and into a linguistically transformational world full of hallucinations, visions, omens, prayers, rhetorical apostrophes, the sideshows at Southwark fair, and conjuring tricks both actual and poetic. Language promises meaning and stability and sometimes performs these, but more often dissolves into breathtaking displays of perceptual and linguistic flux, relativity and wit. The wonderful Juggler of Fable 42 and his audience stand as emblems to this process:

> The cards, obedient to his words,
> Are by a fillip turn'd to birds . . .
> He shakes his bag, he shows all fair,
> His fingers spread, and nothing there,
> Then bids it rain with showers of gold,
> And now his iv'ry eggs are told,
> But when from thence the hen he draws,
> Amaz'd spectators humm applause. (2, 357)

It is in equal measure a socially transformational process, and, in terms of the wider framework of courtiers, princes, philosophers, and swains, distinctly low, with talking dunghills, hogs, butchers, rustics, girls with prices, and colloquial first usages such as 'coffin' (2, 351) for ember. A world which should be devoted to Florizel and Orlando fills up instead with the spirits of Autolycus and Jacques – and perhaps of Colonel Jack, for the breadth and confidence of social address strongly suggest a literary artist engaging with the kinds of social transformation that would interest the new audiences of prose fiction.

The entry into this metamorphosing world comes with the Shepherd of the introductory fable, who not only flatters the prince while warning him against flattery but also argues, pastorally, for learning from the natural morality of animals, and against bookish written morality – in a book of poems. Ah yes, says the responding Philosopher, 'Pride often guides the author's pen, / Books as affected are as men' (2, 302). An Elephant arguing with a Bookseller about bestiaries and criticism in a London shop is not, for example, exactly natural morality.

The swain's brief skirmish with one of the central paradoxes of pastoral, learning about nature in an artificial construct, is accompanied by another from one of the fables of the Aesop of legend, as the Shepherd fills up lines 31–4 of his 46-line monologue, easily the longest in the collection, by remarking

> My tongue within my lips I rein,
> For who talks much must talk in vain;
> We from the wordy torrent fly:
> Who listens to the chatt'ring pye? (2, 301)

Another of the many instances where the nature of the *Fables* shifts subtly if they are treated as performance art, poems to be read out to a (possibly sceptical) audience, juvenile or otherwise. Gay, remember, is a dramatist. There are now three different paradoxes operating inside a fable which can still be read as orthodox.

The installation of double vision continues in the first fable proper, as the induction shades from the section against flattery, through flattery, to lines about the young prince's future manly virtues of courage, bravery, and mercy. How good to have a story which will illustrate heroic princely virtues! But the story, of the Traveller spared by the Lyon, turns out to be a reworking of the central fable of representation, The Lion and the Man. In this subtly reversed version, where the related art is not painting or sculpture but flattery and fair-speaking, the Lyon describes his solitary den and shows the Traveller bones that speak – *everything* speaks – plangently of his own brave mastery over 'the savage brood':

> These carcasses on either hand,
> Those bones that whiten all the land
> My former deeds and triumphs tell,
> Beneath these jaws what numbers fell. (2, 303)

Flattering bones, which both speak the deeds and 'whiten', purify, them. The Man responds by telling the Lyon that it is not savage power but clemency and justice such as he himself has just been shown that speak of the real 'virtue worthy of a throne', the divine power of mercy. This should be the moral, but the Lyon's reply throws everything up in the air by reverting to the fable's initial topic of representation, the flattery of great men. There are no real virtues in this collection:

> The case is plain, the Monarch said,
> False glory hath my youth mis-led,

For beasts of prey, a servile train,
Have been the flatt'rers of my reign.
You reason well. Yet tell me, friend,
Did ever you in courts attend?
For all my fawning rogues agree
That human heroes rule like me. (2, 303)

The Lyon's lack of attention to the moral qualities that the Man has specified, and his parallel between bestial and human courts, raise the suspicion that he has simply responded to the Man's moral comments as to a superior form of flattery: the Lyon flatters himself that whereas his reign used to be akin to that of a human monarch, it is now superior. And as with the Lion in Grandville's illustration, if less knowingly, this one demonstrates that he is just as good as the Man at the art in question. His final question to the Man is the crux, because the Man has, in effect, repeated to him what the poet said about the prince at the end of the induction, the lines on mercy; so this poet *has* attended, and flattered, in courts poetical – and, quite possibly, real. As so often before, this collection is 'for' courts and against 'em.

Other fables divert moral and emotional force into morals that return even more provokingly to the nature of representation. In 'The *Wild Boar* and the *Ram*', a butcher slaughters a sheep that he has tied to a tree, while the flock watches 'in silent fright'. The 'ancient Ram' responds to the Boar's accusation of cowardice and passivity by replying that though sheep are timid and defenceless, unlike the Boar, this does not mean that they are not revenged for these 'massacres'. 'Those who violence pursue / Give to themselves the vengeance due':

Our skin supplies the wrangling bar,
It wakes their slumbring sons to war,
And well revenge may rest contented,
Since drums and parchment were invented. (2, 308)

Like Momus, the animal-satirists of fable respond 'silently' but speak, this time in two or three senses. So much for the Shepherd's patronizing initial vision of the natural morality of animals: the animals respond with a vision of reciprocal violence which depends on their ability to speak being extended into an ability to imagine parts of their own body being used as artificial 'speaking' constructions in the unnatural human arts of systematized violence and contention. *Speaking the body*, with a vengeance. That the Ram has a vision of a world where even dead sheep can speak and invite men to destroy themselves should not seem too sophistical in this world, where a dead kite, nailed to a wall by a Peasant, can speak 'terror to his kind' (2, 349).

Gay's perennial theme of money has also been subsumed into the wider interest in representation, as in the cases of the Painter and Curl's authors. But yet again, this conflation is extended or dissolved into even wider comic contexts. In 'The Universal *Apparition*', the spectral Apparition is the personification of Care or anxiety, a being whose function (an interesting one inside a supposedly moralistic form) is to create emotional disturbance by moralizing endlessly. Care first reforms the rake from his vices by moralizing on their effects, and then dissuades him from his next project, to 'venture on' a wife – a fine phrase for a supposedly reformed rake's next gamble – by moralizing on the expensive frailties of woman, so that to the now trembling rake,

> In other hours she represents
> His household charge, his annual rents,
> Encreasing debts, perplexing duns,
> And nothing for his younger sons. (2, 343)

The poor rake is *so* emotionally disturbed that he populates his reflections with the legitimate heirs which he will not be able to sire without the imagined wife who will deprive them of their inheritances. Poor son and male heir, too, his future identity threatened by the demonic glint in his 'father's' eye. Money usually represents, stands as sign for, work and/or property, but in this semiotic and perceptual kaleidoscope an imaginary wife may stand as a sign for both money and its lack.

This sceptical pressure of comic relativism and metamorphosis in so many of the fables also allows Gay to flirt with and tease moral and technical orthodoxies, with potential Wartons, Beatties, Dennises, and Johnsons forming another of the several implied audiences. The 'morality' of the fables is often thrown into relief by juggling shifts of tone or tricks with language. In the superb '*Fox* at the Point of Death', the 'weak, sick, and faint, expiring' Fox alarms his sons with a forceful, sonorous, Richard-III-like vision of the haunting ghosts of his murdered victims among the poultry, delivered in lines which, comically, he is said to deliver in a 'whining', 'mumbling', and 'feeble tone' – do try it –

> See, see, the murder'd geese appear!
> Why are those bleeding turkeys there?
> Why all around this cackling train,
> Who haunt my ears for chickens slain? (2, 340)

The sons, convinced by the tone and entranced by the apparent 'promis'd feast', lick their lips and stare about them: where is this tasty treat?

> O gluttons, said the drooping sire;
> Restrain inordinate desire. (*ibid.*)

– an orotund moral sentiment which really needs the bold American 'r' for its best effect, but one which the little Foxes have no difficulty in countering with one of their own – 'A lost good-name is ne'er retriev'd' – which is, conventionally, not the property of children meditating sceptically on the way they are seen by others, but of moralistic parents or poets. Both sire and sons then agree that Foxes should behave like 'mod'rate' (2, 340, 341) Foxes and eat chickens when they present themselves, and there seems to be one clucking outside just now. The old Fox then confirms the suspicions generated by his style by remarking that even he might benefit from one.

Gay's deployment of aphoristic sentiments, sometimes with parallels in major poems such as Pope's *Essay on Man* six years later, is recognized as a main feature of his technique, but the overall effect is often to place the supposed moral in a comic sidelight of this kind. The Flea in 'The *Man* and the *Flea*' addresses his rhapsodizing and ridiculously complacent human host – 'Of what vast consequence am I!' – from the end of his nose. He produces what appears to be a miniaturized version of the general conventional moral against pride – 'Know then thyself, presume not God to scan' (Pope 1968: 516).

> Be humble, learn thyself to scan;
> Know, pride was never made for man.
> 'Tis vanity that swells thy mind. (2, 368)

But this, it transpires, is simply a remonstrance from another being who, like all the others in the fable, crab, snail, Man – and poet, who is rather more rhapsodic than moralistic in his energies – feels intense pleasure and gratification at the bounty of creation. And the Flea undoes the force of his own moral by reserving pride and consequence as the prerogatives only of the biting kind:

> What, heav'n and earth for thee design'd!
> For thee! made only for our need;
> That more important fleas might feed. (*ibid.*)

The world is certainly full of vain creatures, as the first couplet promised, but it is also full of a range of creatures who take poetic delight in their surroundings, and this quality, like the rhetoric of the 'dying' Fox, provides a context in which morality pales – in this case, beside the robust vision of a world where animal and human energies are in reassuring emotional unity. If a Crab may take pleasure in the golden sands of Tagus which seem to have been made just for him, it is only natural for a Man to feel the same about the sunset. That a Crab in the Tagus is almost as unlikely as an Elephant in a Bookseller's is not a point which arises naturally from the fable.

Elsewhere, morals suffer as Gay plays fast and loose with language. In 'The *Farmer's Wife* and the *Raven*', he first dramatizes the Farmer's Wife's superstitious fears of domestic omens such as spilt salt and leaping embers, and then rhetorically calms her with the promise of a post-prandial fable:

> Eat now, and weep when dinner's ended,
> And when the butler clears the table,
> For thy dissert I'll read my fable. (2, 351)

'A pun is perhaps intended between dessert and dissertation' (Gay 1926: 263) remarks Faber: in fact, as Wray sagely notices (1950: 121), the pun is triple, including also the sense 'because you deserve it, as your just deserts'. Puns, as the Craftsman's WALL and POLE testify, are not seemly in polite genres, especially multiple puns which reduce morality to a part of a meal. Gay even includes a pun in the form of a genuine enigma or riddle (a tactic calculated to provoke the odium of orthodox critics) at the end of 'The Universal *Apparition*'. The rake, who has now retired to farm pastoral groves, is still pursued by the spectre of Care, which torments him with hair-raising visions of snails and droughts. But at last the rake is allowed a suitably disturbed epimythium:

> At length he thus the ghost addrest.
> Since thou must be my constant guest,
> Be kind, and follow me no more,
> For Care by right should go before. (2, 344)

The puzzled reader may try to moralize this in time, so to speak – Care should precede actions and decisions – or as a play on words – one should be careful, with the care coming first, rather than full of care. The result is the same, but the moral itself is caught between three worlds, physical, moral, and linguistic: and anyone attempting to moralize it in space rather than time, the most natural first thought, will simply be puzzled and frustrated – as the rake has been, in the fable.

Several of the better doctoral theses on fable remark on the teasing nature of Gay's morals and aphorisms, without finding a wider context in which to place this quality. Joan Owen, for example, after noticing the pun above, points out that 'The *Pin* and the *Needle*', which raises expectations of a conventional labour/luxury ethical debate, resolves itself into narrative and social points-scoring rather than ethics: 'the confrontation . . . never materializes, and the reader is left without a clear pattern of the moral life' (Owen 1969: 174). John Shea (1967: 185–7) provides an astute reading of the supple Fontainean shifts of tone in 'The Old *Hen* and the *Cock*', with its brief introduction which appears to promise a moral story about the necessity for proper curbs on the behaviour of female children: 'Restrain your child; you'll soon believe / The text, which says, we sprung from *Eve*' (2, 328). But in the story the Cock, warned by his female parent not to jump down the well, is provoked by the 'foolish law' to do just that, and drowns, lamenting 'I ne'er had been in this condition / But for my mother's prohibition' (2, 329). So the introduction, now revealed as an ellipsis rather than an imperative, carries the sense of 'if mothers try to give their children moral advice, they will find that all of them, male and female, will yield to temptation and defy authority'. The fable proves the tragicomic inefficacy of domestic morality, in a form which will soon be conventionally understood to consist of lectures of moral and domestic wisdom. 'Believe / the text' at your peril.

Most provokingly of all, probability itself, the system of decorum upon which the notion of an orthodox moral fable, whether in verse, prose, or dramatic narrative, is predicated, becomes a specific target for fabulist banter. Gay begins 'The *Painter* who pleased No body and Every body', a fable in which success is achieved by idealizing and flattering the subject at the expense of artistic truth, by reminding tyro fabulists that, 'lest men suspect your tale untrue', they should 'keep probability in view'. But this does not mean that they should practice probability, merely that they should reflect on what they might be able to slip in by way of hyperbole. Flattery, for instance, 'never seems absurd . . . Impossibilities seem just' (2, 325). 'Flattery, then, is . . . one sort of improbability that the artist may safely indulge' (Shea 1967: 211), and fable, especially a fable with such multiple frames of reference as this one, is another. And finally, Gay chooses his most maddeningly unprobabilistic fable, 'The *Elephant* and the *Bookseller*', to tease orthodox minds with an introductory caution against travellers who write bamboozling and improbable fictions. This introduction then magically dissolves into what it appears to criticize, in a dexterous version of fable's basic truth/fiction paradox:

> We read, and in description view
> Creatures which Adam never knew;
> For when we risque no contradiction,
> It prompts the tongue to deal in fiction.
> Those things that startle me or you,
> I grant are strange; yet may be true.
> Who doubts that elephants are found
> For science and for sense renown'd?
> Borri records their strength of parts,
> Extent of thought, and skill in arts . . .
> And how by travel understand
> The language of another land.
> Let those who question this report,
> To Pliny's ancient page resort.
> How learn'd was that sagacious breed!
> Who now (like them) the *Greek* can read. (2, 314)

What in one line is definitely the 'fiction' of travellers in space is elided in the following lines to apparent truth, as the fable, via an unanswerable rhetorical question, becomes a 'report' based on classical and Renaissance authorities, travellers in time – the word 'report' transferring itself by a soft-shoe-shuffle of syntactical vagueness from Borri to the main discourse. This truth is almost as secure or 'probable' as Gulliver's first-hand account of his adventures, because

> for many, probability itself simply meant backing by authority . . . the Renaissance paradigm for explaining probability comes from rhetoric, and more directly from . . . proofs which come from the testimony of more or less authoritative (and hence probable) witnesses. (Patey 1984: 4)

Pliny and Borri are enlisted as *probable doctors*: no one can possibly quarrel with antiquity and serious Italian chemists, though they may quarrel with the tales of adventuring travellers or the evidence of their own senses. Gay bounces one kind of probability (truth to nature and the actual world) off another (authoritative discourse), in a mockingly inefficacious attempt to forestall the entirely anticipated 'contradiction' of dull moral-probabilistic critics. At the same time he teases the *mere English* moralistic reader with the reminder that the Elephant, 'like them' – again, 'them' half-transferring itself in juggling syntax from the doctors to 'those who question' – can read Greek.

Not content with this exhibition of superior juggling, Gay promptly disrupts literary probability again by installing a double time-scheme. The 'now' of the last line of the introduction turns out to be a 'reading-time now', as the first lines of the story switch to 'As one of these, in days of yore, / Rummaged a shop of learning o'er' (2, 314). And not content with *that*, Gay then has the nerve to reverse the time-scheme yet again by having the impressed Bookseller ask the contemptuous Elephant whether he would like to pen something in Greek 'against the Trinity', or 'write the history of *Siam*' (2, 315) for him, which renders the scene rather more contemporary than 'of yore'. There are four pages of notes on Siam in *Purchas His Pilgrimage* (1613) and four in Sir Thomas Herbert's *Relation of Some Yeares Travaile* . . . (1634), but the 1688 translation of Nicolas Gervaise's *Histoire Naturelle et Politique* . . . *de Siam* and Simon de La Loubère's *New Historical Relation of Siam* (1693: the OED gives this as the first usage) are the only English works of reference on Siam, in 1727.

The fable-Elephant might seem to be a highly suitable author for this subject, as the '*Siamese* History is full of Fables' (La Loubère 1693: 8) as well as of elephants, but this is an Elephant (probably an Asian one) who is very concerned with accuracy of representation and data, and he does not bother to reply to the Bookseller's suggestion. Leafing through a bestiary in which all birds and beasts are 'portray'd' (2, 315) – probably Topsell's, which has illustrations – the Elephant expresses disgust at Man's false representations of the animals, which he likens to the distortions of critical battles, and also to the misrepresentations of flattery. Equally, he would be very sceptical of Sir Thomas Herbert's story about the Queen of Siam who tried to introduce sexual morality into her sodomitically inclined male subjects by commanding that they should all be fitted with a small metal bell attached to a rod fitted through the two opposing sides of their foreskin, with 'a dried adder's tongue' for a dissuasive clapper. The ingenious contortionist counter-measures of the virgin Siamese females (virgins 'of virgin years', who, by these measures, are become almost as rare as is a 'black swan' – Herbert 1634: 196) would likewise fill him with incredulity. So a Siamese history full of fables, which is to say full of implausible stories about men, gods, and beasts (like Gay's stories), would hold as little attraction for the Elephant as would the opportunity to write carping criticisms against the improbability of such performances. The fable turns out to be a very sophisticated reverse version of The Cockerel and the Pearl, with the Bookseller misreading the Elephant and the Elephant obliquely 'reading' the fables themselves. As with Swift, the complex, comic interweaving of so many different kinds of 'misreading' – ministerial-political, royal, orthodox-critical, fable-actor, reader – is a spider's web spun from the most basic materials of fable.

Gay's 1727 collection carries such densely packed forms of sophisticated wit that it takes some effort to remember that they are also almost orthodox fables, written for the new audiences. They carry their double nature extremely easily, managing their relationships with a varied readership with great aplomb. This collection is the last occasion on which verse fables could perform such complex tricks, because English fable was about to suffer its final set of transformations. All critical accounts of this process to date assume that it is uninteresting, and that fable after 1740 is either an egregious orthodox form of moral and domestic wisdom or a marginal 'fading form' of unspecified 'surreptitious conversation' (Lewis 1996: 185) with readers which exists in a climate hostile to fable itself. This cannot be wholly true, though fabulist conversation is always surreptitious. The willingness of very different canonical novelists to credit readers with a capacity for reading structurally deployed fables in an Augustan manner, the presence of fabulist wits such as Smart, Hall-Stevenson, and others after 1750, partly explored above, the many forms of literary activity which are related to fables, and the teasing quality of some of William Cowper's uses of fable, suggest a different case.

It is tempting to invoke large shifts in cultural sensibility in order to account for the changes in fable, but it may be more appropriate to try to stay within the terms of the discourse so far established, of the relationships between fable and the different kinds of voice or manner of address which characterize different 'masters'. In Jayne Lewis's version of the history of post-1740 fable, for instance, the spectralizing of cultural information and 'the demotion of the sensory image' (*ibid.*: 186) characteristic of the period are made to account for the decline of fable. One must concur; but at first view there is no reason why fable should not have been able to adapt or re-apply itself to changed cultural circumstances such as those of the later parts of the century. Langhorne's fables of the 1770s, for example, take fable through sentimental elegy into a sub-Gothic territory somewhere between *The Bard* and Radcliffe's Schedoni; the *Fables of Flora* are populated by murderous druids with 'crimson-streaming hand' and tempers evinced by 'the haggard eyeball's hollow glare' (Langhorne 1772: 43).

The problem may best be investigated by first focusing briefly on some of the characteristics of Gay's second series and noting the ways in which these presage qualities of two of the subsequent branches of the fabulist tradition, the orthodox, and the related areas into which fable eventually dissolved. It is hard to *like* Gay's second series, but one must admire their conscious anticipation of a new and different poetical universe. Secondly, the perspective will be reversed to illustrate the persistence of post-Augustan habits of fable in Cowper.

CHAPTER 8

Gay, Cowper, and the diaspora of fable

Gay's second series of *Fables*, published in 1738, six years after his death, is as different from his first series as Dryden's *The Hind and the Panther* was from his *Religio Laici*, though in reverse: it is the second series which advertises itself as the plain reader's fables. Gay's 1738 collection is, quite simply, a determined wrecking job on the central tradition of fable as represented and indeed defined by his first series. This may appear shocking, but it was characteristic of Gay (who was as sceptical about his own works as he was about those of other people) to use 'high-risk strategies' (Nokes 1995: 248) which sometimes amounted to a self-destruct button. His comedy-cum-farce *Three Hours After Marriage* (1717), for example, did not survive the performance at which Cibber, who had been persuaded to take the part of Plotwell, finally realized that this part was designed to travesty his own acting eccentricities.

But Gay's two series were, thenceforward, usually printed, read, and commented on together, as if there were no intrinsic difference between them. His second series was almost always preferred to the first: many of the later conservative 'ethical' fabulist-poets – Moore, Marryott, Langhorne, Hawkesworth – consciously echo examples from the 1738 collection in their own work, and normative critical opinion was often puzzled by the first. The only poet to find the first series more compelling was the most influential and widely respected poet of the period immediately before the Romantics, William Cowper, who also has a claim to be regarded as the last of the great Augustan writers. Cowper's imitations and translations of Gay's fables are all from the first series: to speak more widely, Cowper displays a curious temperamental parallel with Gay. Both poets were much exercised by the question of the value of work or *works* (their own and others'). Both were fascinated by the figure of Hercules (Gay's translations from the *Metamorphoses* centre on the career and death of Hercules in Book 9; Cowper's only translation of Virgil is of Evander inspiring Aeneas with an account of the labours of Hercules, in Book 8 of the *Aeneid*). Both were fascinated by the hero in feminine eclipse, Gay dramatizing the young Achilles in female disguise and himself as female Hare, Cowper dramatizing (in a letter to William Unwin, Jan. 1783) his pastime of winding thread with the ladies on Sunday afternoons as Hercules captive and subjected in the court of Queen Omphale. In perhaps the most complex and least utterable of all 'Herculean' messages, Cowper gave his early-beloved Theadora 'a seal ring of carnelian engraved with the figure of Omphale in the lion skin of Hercules' (Owen 1969: 209). All this suggests that the second series was a late attempt at a new departure, for Gay.

The most important difference between Gay's first and second series is his decision to revert from the openness of address characteristic of the first to the self-complacency found in the single point of address of the earlier *Epistle to . . . Paul Methuen.* In all the fables of the second series, a dominant persona now uses an intrusive first-person mode of 'rhetorical bravado' (Nokes 1995: 526) to secure an effect of authoritative moral perception. The action of the fable occurs after or parenthetically within the address given by this persona, so the only function of the animal actors is to illustrate the points being confidently made by their master. Nowhere are these curious effects more marked than in the first fable, offered as promythium, 'The *Dog* and the *Fox*', which is addressed 'To a *Lawyer*'.

In the induction, language and expression are immediately specified as the central subjects, but now the fabulist-narrator has nothing but contempt for the conspiratorial play of language that led Peachum to make his mocking comparison between himself and the lawyer. Indeed, Gay begins by interrogating the notion of 'double capacity' from the point of view of a reformed, moralistic Peachum, someone now concerned to stress the post-Shaftesburyan virtue of single reading against the characteristic 'ease' of a duplicitous post-Mandevillean wit:

> I know you Lawyers can, with ease,
> Twist words and meanings as you please;
> That language, by your skill made pliant,
> Will bend to favour ev'ry client; . . .
> When you peruse the clearest case,
> You see it with a double face;
> For scepticism's your profession;
> You hold there's doubt in all expression. (2, 381)

Any possibility for play with Augustan practices of irony, self-contradiction, or teasing multiple audiences with each other, is emphatically ruled out. Ambiguity is now taken to be 'the outer expression of moral duplicity' (Owen 1969: 178).

The narrator continues in the same mode. My words are clear and unequivocal: I only draw from 'gen'ral nature', I loathe 'private slander', and if anyone thinks that the fable applies to him, ' 'Tis his own conscience holds the glass' (2, 382). No magic mirrors here.

In the fable's illustrative story, a Fox talking to his friend, a shepherd's Dog, unwittingly reveals his own crimes by responding angrily to the Dog's insouciant intrusion of the words 'poultry' and 'lamb' into the conversation. The Fox protests his own innocence, but in so doing happens to specify the correct number of the shepherd's lambs that were killed on a particular night. The Dog kills him. Language, we are invited to agree, is neutral and innocent, so that to misread or misapply words as personal slander, as the Fox does, must be evidence of guilt and self-conviction.

The little Foxes from Gay's first series would, of course, have had the wit to point out while being cross-examined by the Dog that 'poultry' and 'lamb' are hardly neutral words when you are in conversation with a Fox, and that the Dog may in turn be overreading a word ('three') as corroboration, where it could be a coincidence. But this Fox is so dull as not merely to misread the Dog's words, but to read the wrong sign entirely – 'Your meaning in your looks I see' (2, 383). And this Fox's name is specified to us early on as 'Renard', which is not the name for a fox, but for a duplicitous Fox who steals chickens and tells lies: so the right reading of the moral action is available to the reader, via a not-very-innocent word, before it takes place. Hence we assume that the word that the Fox uses for the number of lambs lost, 'three', speaks in the way that the Dog implies it does by his killing the Fox. The interests in doubleness, in the loading of language and in 'reading' are still very much present, but in the second series the presumption is that the reader requires easy access to a single, communal moral which overrides or contextualizes these interests.

The collection is then full of robust protestations of pastoral virtue and innocence from the narrator; disclaimers of topicality, disdain for party, for libel, for bribes ('Be virtue mine: be theirs the bribe'), for hypocritical public life, for 'screening fraud' (2, 385), for a 'pension' (2, 386), and so on. Often the protestations of truth and the lies of others are placed side by side, with the notion of doubleness clearly still exercising Gay:

> The man of pure and simple heart
> Through life disdains a double part;
> He never needs the screen of lyes
> His inward bosom to disguise. (2, 398)

But the pure and simple nature of the words is (as anyone who recalls the opposition keywords for Walpole will already have guessed) a pure and simple fiction. 'Should we state-mysteries disclose, / 'Twould lay us open to our foes' says the officious Ant in Fable 4: all his vast expense was for 'the swarm's defence' (2, 393). '"State-mysteries" was one of Walpole's favourite excuses for refusing to explain his policies to his Tory critics, and "the swarm's defence" was his reason for maintaining a standing army in peacetime' (Armens 1954: 196; Walpole had clearly taken the moral of *The Grumbling Hive*). Such words are, again, neither innocent nor general; they are specific coded diction designed to articulate a politically oppositional stance.

So the frequent protestations of general nature, general satire, and honest truth without personal or topical political application, are lies. Addressed to a knowing opposition audience, these would be mockingly and self-mockingly transparent lies. Addressed to an honest, moral audience unexpert in reading politically, they are simply invisible. Pope and Queensberry presumably published the *Fables* for the first of these – 1738 also marks the coming-out of Pope as a committed opposition writer – but the audience of fable was shifting rapidly towards the second. Opposition literature was so much more direct by 1738 that where the collection would have been explosive in 1730, it 'went virtually unnoticed by the political press' (Goldgar 1976: 166).

Gay has created an impossibly destructive position. It is not merely a question of the values of 'industrious zeal . . . toil', and 'gen'ral use' (2, 410, 408) specified in Fable 8 being ludicrously inappropriate to Gay's residence in Burlington Gardens, nor of the images of pastoral retreat being equally unapt to his genteel hunting excursions with the Queensburys on the downs at Amesbury. The whole enterprise of the second series is built on an astonishing inversion of fable's usual premise that *the truth is moral, though the tale a lie*. Gay's premise is that *though the tale is moral, the truth is a lie*. As well as bamboozling the administration's ministers, Gay bamboozles the new, honest audience of fable, people who think that fable really is abstracted from all party considerations and that it is concerned with the transmission of transparent, crystalline moralism. Mocking the classic mode of fable, the collection also mocks the 'orthodox' audiences even as it appeals to them and effectively creates a blueprint of fable for future generations. Joan Owen remarks that the later audience of fable was so ready to overlook ethical strains and oddities in Gay that the *Fables* 'inadvertently became a model of ethical fortitude' (Owen 1969: 145), but in the case of the second series this process can be understood as a natural effect of the apparent moral and technical security of the collection.

There *is*, in short, a 'double-handed' capacity about it, a magic glass held up to the reader which is not simply that of conscience, but at such a deeply concealed level that the strategy appears Swiftian in its reserve and duplicity. This seems unlike Gay: one is forced to remember that he apparently chose not to publish these fables. The only possible alternative explanation is to notice that the division of the audiences described above is really an argument after the fact, from knowledge of what happened after Gay's death in 1732. Gay may have had a vision of the ideal or hypothetical reader of the second series as someone like Samuel Croxall – and by extension, the readers of fables more like Croxall's – someone who had a foot in both 'reading' camps, who could both engage with the metropolitan opposition code and feel the need to present or to attend to a plain moral case directly and unambiguously, after the manner of a sermon.

Almost all the other techniques of the 1738 collection support its identity as orthodox rather than classical fable. There is nothing risqué: there are no extremes or provocative varieties of diction: in an Iago-like moral democracy, the audience is assumed to be as 'honest' as the fabulist. Instead of being matter for paradox and celebration, incongruity of kind and action is avoided or condemned. Where, in the first series, an Elephant in a Bookseller's shop may win the moral argument, here, if a Bear gets into a Boat, as in Fable 5, such incongruity must lead to wreck, communal derision, and beating. Know your place. The paradoxes of fable are still used, but in the service of what is made to appear general moralism.

Only the extraordinary final fable, 'The *Ravens*, the *Sexton*, and the *Earth-Worm*', addressed 'To *Laura*', moves past this, with its sardonic final flourish. Gay begins the poem by imitating the urbane mode of late-Restoration female address of a poet such as Prior, moves on to sonorous general pronouncements on the common clay, and then illustrates the whole with a disconcerting fable in which two Ravens interrogate a giant Earth-Worm on the relative gourmet qualities inherent in the currently quietly decomposing local squire and his horse. At the last possible moment Gay allows his Earth-Worm to provide the epimythium, the other half of the frame, by making him drop his moralistic tone ('Virtue distinguishes mankind', not superior flavour) and judge the case of horse *versus* squire 'with a double face'. The Earth-Worm concludes the fable:

> So good-man Sexton, since the case
> Appears with such a dubious face;
> To neither I the cause determine,
> For different tastes please different vermine. (2, 438)

Scepticism is, it seems, the Earth-Worm's final profession: the legalistic tone and the mockingly knowing allusion to the first fable make it hard to take his Epicurean flourishing of *de gustibus non est disputandum* [there is no disputing about taste] as relating to the brute creation alone. The hierarchy of moral values vanishes: the hierarchy of wit briefly reappears, established by the 'lowest' creature in the collection.

The rhetorical self-confidence and singleness of address of Gay's second series was to be a main characteristic of orthodox verse fable until the end of the century. In effect, Gay is the unacknowledged legislator or moral godfather of this kind of fable, co-opted in the same way (though silently) as Dryden and L'Estrange had been by more radical parts of the conservative tradition. The hidden irony of the Earth-Worm's final profession was never noticed: the vermin who would be happy with the taste of this kind of fable are not credited with a taste or a capacity for the other: as so often, what appears to be a moral moral is also a moral about readers and reading.

The initial point of transmission or transfer of Gay's mode is the example of Moore and Brooke's popular and well-respected *Fables for the Female Sex* (1744). This collection's 'arch and condescending' attempts to mix 'advice and gallantry' (Wray 1950: 136) in their address to the weaker vessel have a main point of origin in their debasement of Gay's address 'To *Laura*' in his final fable, which is the first example of a specifically sexed or gendered address in verse fable (though some of Anne Finch's approach it). The feminization of the audience is given a very promising start in Gay. The poet's address begins by responding to Laura's rational refusal to accept conventional poetic praise on the grounds of its tone, its closeness to mere flattery – Laura is, one imagines, the well-adjusted bluestocking daughter of some opposition politician, well aware of the wider political implications of literary flattery embodied in the first series. Hence she will quite probably be capable of reading her fable properly, so the poet must concoct a moral fable rather than writing flattering 'lays', a situation to which he responds with self-deprecating wit:

> If you the tribute due disdain,
> The muse's mortifying strain
> Shall, like a woman, in mere spite,
> Set beauty in a moral light. (2, 434)

If Laura is capable of understanding the dynamics of fable and its contexts, she would also understand the stereotype of the spiteful (female) Muse: it is the poor male poet who is mortified by the muse's control and the wit of the girl. But mortification (Horse and Squire) is the subject of the illustrative fable, so the word also acquires a Volpone-like jest ('mortifying of a Fox': Jonson 1977: 182). As well as composing, the poet is dis- or decomposed; an unnerving joke to find in a posthumously published fable.

Moore and Brooke's second fable, by contrast, though written to a very similar pattern, achieves the dubious distinction of mixing the glutinously rakish with the pseudo-avuncular:

> Trust me, my girl, with greater ease
> Your taste for flatt'ry I could please,
> And similes in each dull line,
> Like glow-worms in the dark, should shine.
> What if I say your lips disclose
> The freshness of the op'ning rose?
> Or that your cheeks are beds of flowers,
> Enripen'd by refreshing show'rs?
> Yet certain as these flowers shall fade,
> Time ev'ry beauty will invade . . . (Moore 1749: 10–11)

To which Gay's Laura would probably respond by asking for the vote. After a history in which it has generally been assumed that women read fables more competently than men, when the comparison occurs, verse fable now assumes that women are part of an audience to which the fabulist may safely talk down, the audience which will accept that fables may be read safely because they are domestic lectures: *Moral Tales for Young Ladies*.

There were, though, repeated caveats about using fables in this way, from writers who still had a fuller sense of fable and who wished to disrupt such complacent relations. In his *Émile* (1762), Rousseau objects strongly to fables being used as an educational medium, his brilliant extended analysis of 'The Crow and the Fox' from La Fontaine illustrating the case that the moral in La Fontaine's fables is only capable of being apprehended by Children Six Foot High. Fable

> is so mixed and so disproportionate to their age that it would lead them more to vice than to virtue. These again, you will say, are paradoxes. So be it; but let us see whether they are truths. (Rousseau 1979: 113)

An attitude which was anticipated in English by Lord Kames in the year before *Émile*, in his *Introduction to the Art of Thinking* (1761): 'to disguise men under the guise of goats and bulls, leads to little other purpose than to obscure the moral instruction' (Home 1810: vi); and Vicesimus Knox repeats and enlarges on Rousseau's objections in his *Winter Evenings* (1788), in Evening 51, 'On the Aesopian Fables as a School-book for very young Children'.

Later 'ethical debate' fables often echoed Gay's second series very closely. Marryott's Fable 22, for instance, stresses innate or natural rather than nominal and inherited gentility in its attempt to reveal fable as the vessel of the plain man's morality –

> With due respect, unroll'd I see,
> His lordship's antient pedigree;
> Yet am not clear that he inherits
> His great, great, great, great, grandsire's merits.
> I read *their* virtues on record,
> In *him* can only find – my lord. (Marryott 1771: 169–70)

Gay's lines in Fable 3 of his second series are more thoughtful, more subtly inflected, and less concerned to establish the address as being from a securely single point. He begins from the democratic premise that both author and reader can be allowed to misread –

> With partial eye we're apt to see
> The man of noble pedigree.
> We're prepossest my lord inherits
> In some degree his grandsire's merits;
> For those we find upon record,
> But find him nothing but my lord. (2, 387)

The bravado of much of the rest of the second series makes it hard to rescue delicate effects such as this in a general reading. And the 'knowing' nature of the opening lines of 'The *Dog* and the *Fox*' might be paralleled by many later examples, including the first-person proto-Wordsworthian insistence of the close of the tenth fable of Langhorne's *Fables of Flora*:

Whatever charms the ear or eye,
All beauty and all harmony,
If sweet sensations these produce,
I know they have their moral use.
I know that NATURE's charms can move
The springs that strike to VIRTUE's love.

(Langhorne 1772: 41)

In later instances such as these, *the fabulist becomes his own master*: there is no longer any relation between the voice of the fabulist and any determinate source of power. Where Gay's Muse is mortifying, bitchy, or quirky, these are complacent and strident. Fabulists purify their collections of vermin, and announce proudly in their prefaces that they have done so. Satirical fables now begin to depend on the establishment by the fabulist of a secure unorthodox persona, a rhetorically stable eccentric voice, prior to the writing of fables. Hall-Stevenson publishes his fables on the back of his *Crazy Tales*; Smart's 'Mother Midnight' persona modulates into his eccentric occasional fables; John Wolcot establishes 'Peter Pindar' as his voice before writing his charming fable-like satires.

But after 1730 the energies, interests, and figures of fable began to be absorbed by, or into, other poetic forms (as well as novels) in which the point of address was similarly secure and single, because the writer was concerned to foster a sense of community between the utterance and the reader. Panegyrics and odes came to be considered as moral poems or fables in their own right, and poets took to adapting ode quite consciously to fable, working from earlier Augustan examples such as Addison's wonderful ode in *Spectator* 465 paraphrasing Psalms 19:1–4 on the confirmation of faith. Addison's stars fulfil a classic function of fable in a highly original manner, by 'answering' the scepticism of materialistic reason as they rejoice silently but articulately:

What though in solemn Silence, all
Move round the dark terrestrial Ball?
What though nor real Voice nor Sound
Amid their radiant Orbs be found?
In Reason's Ear they all rejoice,
And utter forth a glorious Voice,
For ever singing, as they shine
'The hand that made us is divine.' (Addison 1965: 4, 145)

Fable's basic conceit of the moral voice of the mute creation, the speaking voices of nature, is absorbed by forms interested in more sublime and numinous manifestations of power and relationship than those of fable. The meditative voices of man's 'fellow-creatures' strike 'th'abstracted ear / Of Fancy' (Thomson 1981: 86) in Thomson's *Summer* (1727) in the same year as the animal-voices of Gay's first series are striking ears which are not told how they are to be tuned. It might be true to say that fable so denatured is not fable at all; but it may equally be right to say that such figures and voices all depend on the writer's premise that their readers are still conversant with fable and will recognize the implicit kinship of their new forms with the old tradition.

This process of inflating fable into ode and blank verse did not pass off without comment, most notably and directly from Thomas Gray, whose mischievous 'Ode on the Death of a Favourite Cat, Drowned in a Tub of Gold Fishes' (written 1747) produces a continuous series of tiny 'translations' between the classes of diction appropriate to the two forms in order to achieve its effects. The 'Tub' of the title is mysteriously elevated to a 'vase' in the first line, the water in it to a 'lake'; but the self-complacent 'applause' of the Cat viewing itself is merely 'purr'd' – the speaking voice of nature, instead of needing interpretation, merely makes a noise. Even 'favourite' suffers class-metamorphosis from the 'Favourite Cat' of the title to the reflective 'a Fav'rite has no friend'. Common folk may have favourite cats; princes have *favourites.*

Gray's pious echo of the moral of Gay's little Foxes – 'a lost good-name is ne'er retriev'd' rendered as 'one false step is ne'er retriev'd' (Gray 1977: 27, 28) – acquires an equally delicate absurdity. Young ladies are not often in danger of falling into pots of water, though they are, conventionally, in danger of being deserted by their former friends if they suffer a moral lapse. The heroine of 'The Female Seducers' (the last and longest of the *Fables for the Female Sex*), a virgin female Hercules abroad in a moral landscape, makes a drastically wrong choice of female figure and passes a night in implicit lesbian bliss. Returning home the next morning, she finds she is no longer in good odour among her previous juvenile acquaintance. Gray's dalliance with Gay-like effects may well have been directed against this specific and inviting target.

Other functions of fable are similarly absorbed by publicly acceptable genres which establish themselves in their own right. Fable's capacity to act as a provoking, reflexive form of epitaph, visible in examples from the death of Socrates through Dryden's *Fables* to the antipenultimate letter of *Evelina*, is lessened as epitaph becomes the practice of 'sepulchral inscriptions' which must preclude (according to Johnson's 1740 *Essay on Epitaphs*) 'the admission of all lighter or gayer ornaments' (quoted in Devlin 1980: 129, 131–2) such as conscious wit. Epitaph is elevated from simple speaking stones to entries in the *Gentleman's Magazine* and *London Chronicle*: Viscountess Downe's epitaph in York Minster goes so far as to refer the inquisitive reader to the *Gentleman's Magazine* for May 1812 'for her character and other particulars' (see Tidy 1974: 85, which also provides a graphic illustrative comment).

Instead of allowing the good reader free play to 'come in for half the performance' as in the literary examples of fable-as-epitaph, the speech of epitaph is now interpreted by an external reader-interpreter who must tune the ears and prescribe the reaction; from Arbuthnot's 'O indignant reader!' to the Johnsonian-Wordsworthian insistence that the reader be moved. Crucially, epitaph can no longer be a form of conversation; it is now writing. 'Approach and read', says the 'swain', the poetically-spoken but illiterate rural peasant, to the reader-poet in Gray's *Lines Wrote in a Country Church-Yard* (1751: the *Elegy*), as they both view the writer-poet's epitaph on the now-silent speaking stone, 'Approach and read (for thou can'st read) the lay' (Gray 1977: 390). Epitaphs and fables are now less the property of discursive slave-fabulists than of masters whose sensibilities and education give them the power to enforce emotional compliance. And emperors, to repeat, cannot write fables.

This was not William Cowper's vision of the role of speaking stones.

> Reader, behold a Monument
> That asks no sigh or tear
> Though it perpetuate the event
> Of a great burial here. (Cowper 1980–95: 3, 61)

A reader could only begin to 'read' this stone by looking around it: Cowper wrote the lines on the occasion of the sowing of a grove of oaks at Chillington in 1791. The scenery, not the inscription, speaks the moral: the reader is invited to work, to enter into conversation, not merely to read. To Cowper almost everything was song or conversation, achieved or missed. The lonely satisfaction of substitute conversations is made clear by his inward version of the Phaedrian *arbores loquantur* dramatized more succinctly in the lines above:

> The man to solitude accustomed long
> Perceives in ev'ry thing that lives a tongue,
> Not animals alone, but shrubs and trees
> Have speech for Him and understood with ease . . .
> Birds of all feather, beasts of ev'ry name

> That serve mankind or shun them, wild or tame,
> The looks and gestures of their griefs and fears
> Have, all, articulation in his ears,
> He spells them true by intuition's light,
> And needs no glossary to set him right. (*ibid.*: 3, 47)

The literary fabulist has no need for literacy. This being so, it is not surprising to find that his poems sometimes hold quiet conversations between each other. A translation of Horace on 'the golden mean' will be answered by a Christian 'Reflection' which disdains and edits out the 'unmanly fears' of the pagan moralist in favour of the confidence in 'duty' (*ibid.*: 1, 419, 421) and plain trust in God which Cowper never felt. But the conversation of the fables with other forms is usually in the reverse direction.

Cowper's fables illustrate or respond to the tendency of eighteenth-century fable to move towards looser forms. The 'traditional form of the animal fable' is easily capable of extension into his favourite mode of dramatizing and moralizing 'the natural incident taken from life' (Trickett 1983: 479). 'Adapting the ethical tale to the personal lyric of loss and estrangement . . . often they are not fables altogether, but thinly veiled fictional renderings of intensely personal experience' (Owen 1969: 195, 272). But in doing this, they also fulfil fable's classic function of 'answering' other forms of discourse, standing beside or behind Cowper's less private modes of hymn, satire, and domestic epic as a commentary in a minor key. They form a backdrop-by-contrast to 'the idyll of the satires' with their 'attempted postulation of fruitful labor and suffering in the mask of the Herculean civiliser', employing instead 'the alternate myth of captivity, decadent idleness, and failure' (*ibid.*: 230). More even than that, perhaps: where *The Task* (1785) elegantly praises the cultivation of the many exotic fruits of the greenhouse, the fable of 'The Pine Apple and the Bee' (1782) applies the vain attempt of the Bee to penetrate the glass frame of the pinery as the 'sin and madness' of mankind's 'vain desires' for forbidden fruits natural and artificial. And the Bee is not only 'unsuccessful' and 'silly' in the action, he (workers are not male, but they are in Cowper) has his fabulist identity removed too, in the ending:

> We long for pine apples in frames,
> With hopeless wish one looks and lingers,
> One breaks the glass, and cuts his fingers,
> But they whom truth and wisdom lead,
> Can gather honey from a weed. (Cowper 1980–95: 1, 419)

The fable doubles: our informed reader will now recognize the allusion – as of course Cowper might have expected his reader to – to The Spider and the Bee; but it is the Bee who should be able to gather honey from weeds. If the Bee cannot gather honey, perhaps readers fond of more artificial poetry can no longer gather morals from low fables by recognizing allusions; so the moralizing of the writer (who has been moralizing luxuriously expensive pineapples, not pastorally-low-and-hence-valuable weeds) is as fruitless as the attempts of the Bee. A triple mutual exclusion as complex and as forceful as that in Gray's *Elegy*.

Reversing the perspective, some of Cowper's fables contain, control, or render comic energies present in his larger poems. As an example, one might take the terrifying sense of exclusion and incarceration in 'Hatred and Vengeance, my Eternal Portion' (written *c.* 1774) with its 'sentence / Worse than Abiram's'

> Him the vindictive rod of angry Justice
> Sent quick and howling to the centre headlong;
> I, fed with judgment, in a fleshly tomb, am
> Buried above ground. (*ibid.*: I, 210)

This will eventually have a reverse-counterpart in a fable-poem, 'The Retired Cat' (*c.* 1788), about a cat which is entombed in a chest of drawers by a chambermaid devoid of any malignity, and which is eventually rescued when her mewing comes to the poetic ears of the poet.

Most strikingly, fable may answer hymn. Joan Owen has a fascinating passage on the connections between the hymn 'Light Shining out of Darkness', and 'A Fable' (from Gay's 'The *Farmer's Wife* and the *Raven*'). Both of these poems are from the 1770s, the fable later than the hymn. The fable tells the story of a Raven who counts her chicks prematurely, while they are still in the shell; the nest survives a storm only to be plundered by the yokel, Hodge. This is the fable's reflective epimythium:

> 'Tis Providence alone secures,
> In ev'ry change, but mine and your's.
> Safety consists not in escape
> From dangers of a dreadful shape,
> An earthquake may be bid to spare
> The man that's strangled by a hair.
> Fate steals along with silent tread,
> Found oft'nest in what least we dread,
> Frowns in the storm with angry brow,
> But in the sunshine strikes the blow. (*ibid.*: I, 401)

Owen compares this with

> God moves in a mysterious way,
> His wonders to perform,
> He plants his footsteps in the Sea,
> And rides upon the storm . . .
>
> Judge not the Lord by feeble sense,
> But trust him for his Grace,
> Behind a frowning Providence
> He hides a Smiling face . . .
>
> Blind unbelief is sure to err,
> And scan his work in vain,
> God is his own Interpreter,
> And he will make it plain. (*ibid.*: I, 174–5)

'In this poem', says Owen of the fable, 'finally, the country landscape, the garden, has ceded in the final section to the amorphous sublime of hymn, and Cowper's terminal passage on Providence is nicely comparable to perhaps his most well known' (Owen 1969: 267).

But this is sentimentalizing the uncanny power of the hymn, which comes from its standing on the verge of fear. To trust mere face when you are alarmed by Providence would be faith indeed, and Cowper's God was never any more articulate than he is here. The subtle synaesthesia of the final stanza similarly negotiates silently with unease: would blind unbelief be able to hear God interpreting himself; and can He be at once both Himself and an agent of Himself? So 'A Fable' may articulate a terror which remains repressed or subliminal in the hymn (and which is what makes the hymn so compelling) by moving on from 'Providence' to 'Fate', always reserved as the very highest power in fable (compare 'Destiny' in *Momus Turn'd Fabulist*), and hence removing or outflanking what should be the highest authority in Cowper's cosmos. The hint of the fatal thread in 'strangled by a hair' adds poetic credence. Here the blow is not from the divine frown, but from the sunny smile.

But such applications of fable are clearly very different in Cowper from all the earlier Augustan examples, because the links are more tenuous. They *seem* to be there, especially to a reader habituated to fable – which is why Joan Owen has been quoted to such a large extent, as corroboration – but they invite the reader's strenuous speculation in a much looser way than does classic fable. One has to have an idea about Cowper – probably involving biographical speculation – before the links between the fables and other modes become fully visible. The 'reading' has to be done from outside the fables themselves, and this promotes an uneasy sensation that one may be simply imagining what is there, rather than applying the fable properly – a risk one runs to some extent with all fables, of course. This may be the pointer to why fable was marginalized as a literary form in the nineteenth century: writers no longer credited the existence (or the purchasing power) of good, energetic readers who could 'come in for half the performance' or 'bring half the entertainment along with them'. Queenie Leavis's magisterial word for Scott's prose read against Smollett's, 'fatigued' (Leavis 1932: 139), perhaps indicates the wider context of the problem. Readers who might help to create their own imaginative and intellectual literary constructs would not flourish in an atmosphere where imaginative creation was characteristically imaged, as Cowper himself began to image it, as a cross between solipsism and reverie, and as beyond the power of thought:

> Me oft has fancy, ludicrous and wild,
> Soothed with a waking dream of houses, towers,
> Trees, churches, and strange visages expressed
> In the red cinders, while with poring eye
> I gazed, myself creating what I saw. (Cowper 1980–95: 2, 194)

Figures involving the central strategies of fable, the negotiations between speech and print, speech and silence, changed so radically from fabulist uses towards internalized unheard music or sounding cataracts that haunt like passions that they became almost unreclaimable: post-Augustan strategies of reading and writing were no longer viable. The audience of fable was probably still very much there – Cowper, who wrote and used fables, was an extremely popular poet; Wordsworth, who could not write fables, always felt the lack of an audience among the folk of whom he wrote – but the writers who now thought of themselves as being above fable presumably assumed that their readers felt they were too.

There *are* many fully Augustan uses of fable in the nineteenth century – the creature's extraordinarily pregnant murmuring-to-himself of 'it was as the ass and the lapdog' (Shelley 1982: 110) in Shelley's *Frankenstein* (1818), for instance, as he prepares to recount to his master-creator the episode of his conversation with the blind De Lacey and his subsequent beating by the cottagers. Gay's strategy of addressing a readership which is nominally five years old but actually adult – Children Six Foot High – is still available to Charles Kingsley in 1863, in *The Water-Babies.*

Randolph Caldecott's absorbing Aesopian illustrations all 'read' fable, and encourage reading, in the classic manner. One of the most eccentric of nineteenth-century composers, Alkan (Charles-Valentin Mohrange), has a nine-minute set of comic variations on a nursery-rhyme tune entitled 'Le Festin d'Esope' (opus 39, no. 12). Diaspora, but no dilution: though the processes through which fable had passed in the late eighteenth century apparently meant that it was no longer available as a full mode in itself.

However, every time one observer feels that fable died out, or died away, there will be another who feels that fable flourished. The efflorescence of the derivatives of the related *conte philosophique*, the prose tale which says more than it seems to say, is perhaps the most notable achievement of fiction in the twentieth century. *Ulysses*, for example, with its multiple silent applications and its stress on the restraint of Bloom's speech against the ranting and rhetoric of so many of the book's other voices, might remind us that John Ogilby spent his middle years in Dublin. As, in the ancient fable of The Sun and the Wind, the Wind becomes the Ranters, so the Cyclops becomes the ranting Citizen, or Aeolus the headlines of the newspaper. Epic was not different from Augustan fable, but a kindred form. But this, though it may perhaps be part of the same generic tradition, is another story.

References

The bibliographies in the dissertations of Wray, Pritchard, and Bush below form a composite bibliography of verse fable in the period 1650–1800 which would fill about one-third of the present volume.

Anonymous *Aesops* are listed chronologically under their title: the collections almost certainly compiled by William Pittis have been given honorary 'anonymous' status. Place of publication is London unless otherwise noted. Date of first publication of primary sources, if different from below, is given parenthetically near the first reference in the main text. Following the hint provided by the description of collections of fables as 'translations', some translators in the period 1650–1800 (Ozell, Creech, Toland, Lockman) have been credited with honorary 'authorial' status, but where a modern translation has also been used (as with Cotton's *Montaigne*) reference is to the original author.

Addison, Joseph, and Richard Steele. 1965. *The Spectator*. 5 vols. Donald F. Bond ed. Oxford

Aesop Improved, or, Above Three Hundred and Fifty Fables, mostly Aesop's, with their Morals, Paraphrased in English Verse. 1673

Aesop Naturaliz'd and Expos'd to the Public View in his own Shape and Dress. By Way of Essay on a Hundred Fables. 1697. Cambridge

Aesop at Tunbridge, or a Few Select Fables in Verse, by No Person of Quality. 1698[a]

Aesop at Amsterdam. 1698[b]

Aesop at Bathe. 1698[c]

Aesop at Epsom. 1698[d]

Aesop Return'd from Tunbridge; or, Aesop Out of his Wits. In a Few Select Fables, in Verse. 1698[e]

Old Aesop at Whitehal. 1698[f]

Aesop in Select Fables, [probably ed. Edward Ward. 1698[g]: contains the six 1698 pamphlets above]

Aesop at Islington. 1698[h]

Aesop at Richmond, Recovered of his Late Illness. A Poem in Burlesque. 1698[i]

The Life of Aesop of Tunbridge, Written by the Ass. 1698[j]

Aesop in Spain. 1701

Aesop at Oxford. 1708: expanded [by William Pittis] as *Bickerstaffe's Aesop* below

Bickerstaffe's Aesop: or, the Humours of the Times Digested into Fables. 1709

Aesop at the Bell-Tavern in Westminster, or A Present from the October-Club. In a Few Select Fables from Sir Roger L'Estrange. 1711

Aesop an Alarmist. 1794

Amory, Hugh. 1971. '*Shamela* as Aesopic Satire'. *ELH* 38.2, 239–53

Anon. 1687. *The REVOLTER: A Trage-Comedy Acted between the Hind and Panther, and Religio Laici, &c.*

1701. *Canterbury Tales Rendred into Familiar Verse*

1966. 'Looking for Secrets in the Bayeux Tapestry'. *The Times* (London), 15 April 1966, 14

1974. *The Doctrine of INNUENDO's Discuss'd; or, The Liberty of the Press Maintained.* In *The Craftsman: Four Tracts.* Stephen Parks ed. New York and London

Armens, Sven M. 1954. *John Gay, Social Critic.* New York

Arwaker, Edmund. 1708. *Truth in Fiction, or, Morality in Masquerade*

Auden, W. H. 1963. *The Dyer's Hand*

Audin, Prieur de Thermes. 1648. *Fables héroïques comprenans les véritables maximes de la politique chrétienne et de la morale . . . avec des Discours enrichés de plusieurs histoires tant anciennes que modernes sur le sujet de chaque fable . . .* Paris

Austen, Jane. 1926. *Northanger Abbey* and *Persuasion.* R.W. Chapman ed. Oxford. 2nd ed.

Bacon, Francis. 1915. *The Advancement of Learning.* London and New York

Bakhtin, M. M. 1984. *Problems of Dostoevsky's Poetics.* Caryl Emerson ed. Manchester

Baldwin, T. W. 1944. *Shakespeare's Small Latine and Lesse Greeke.* 2 vols. Urbana, IL

Barlow, Francis. 1703. *Aesop's Fables, with his Life: in English, French and Latin, the English by Tho. Philipott Esq., the French and Latin by Rob. Codrington, MA. Illustrated with One Hundred and Twelve Sculptures by Francis Barlow*

Bath, Michael. 1994. *Speaking Pictures: English Emblem Books and Renaissance Culture.* London and New York

Baudoin, Jean [i.e. Pierre de Boissat the younger]. 1660. *Les Fables d'Esope Phrygien. Illustrées de Discours Moraux, Philosophiques et Politiques.* Paris. As *Les Fables d'Esope Phrygien traduites et moralisées.* Rouen. 1701

Beattie, James. 1783. *Dissertations Moral and Critical*

Beer, Gillian. 1989. 'Rethinking *Arcadia*'. In Doody and Sabor, pp. 23–39

Behn, Aphra. 1990. *Five Plays.* Maureen Duffy ed.

Bell, Ian A. 1994. *Henry Fielding: Authorship and Authority.* London and New York

Bender, John. 1987. 'Prison Reform and the Sentence of Narration in *The Vicar of Wakefield*'. In *The New Eighteenth Century: Theory, Politics, English Literature.* Felicity Nussbaum and Laura Brown eds.: pp. 168–88

Benson, Donald. 1982. 'Dryden's *The Hind and the Panther*: Transubstantiation and Figurative Language'. *JHI* 43, 195–208

Bentley, Richard. 1697. 'A Dissertation upon the Epistles of Phalaris, Themistocles, Socrates, Euripedes, and others, and the Fables of Aesop'. Appended to William Wotton's *Reflections upon Ancient and Modern Learning.* 2nd ed.

Bernstein, David J. 1986. *The Mystery of the Bayeux Tapestry.* Chicago and London

Blackham, Harold J. 1985. *The Fable as Literature.* London and Dover, NH

Boccaccio, Giovanni. 1620. *The Decameron: the Modell of Wit, Mirth, Eloquence and Conversation . . .*

Borkat, Robert F. Sarfatt. 1976. 'The Spider and the Bee: Jonathan Swift's Reversal of Tradition in *The Battel of the Books*'. *Eighteenth-Century Life* 3, 444–6

Boswell, James. 1970. *The Life of Samuel Johnson, LLD.* R.W. Chapman ed. 3rd ed.

Boursault, Edmé. 1693. *Les Fables d'Esope*. Paris. Played as *Esope à la Ville.* 1690

Brooks, Colin. 1984. 'The Country Persuasion and Political Responsibility in England in the 1690s'. *Parliament, Estates and Representations* 4, 135–46

Brown, Tom. 1690. *The Late Converts Exposed: or the Reasons of Mr. Bays's Changing his Religion . . . Part the Second . . . as also the Fable of the Bat and the Birds*

[or Durfey, Thomas]. 1691. *The Weesils; a Satirical Fable*

Brown, Shirley Ann. 1988. *The Bayeux Tapestry: History and Bibliography.* Woodbridge, Suffolk

Burrow, J. A. 'Henryson. "The Preiching of the Swallow"'. *EC* 25, 25–37

Burton, Richard or Robert, writing as 'Nathaniel Crouch'. 1691. *Delightful Fables in Prose and Verse. None of them to be Found in Aesop, but Collected from Divers Ancient and Modern Authors: with Pictures and Proper Morals to every Fable, some very Pertinent to the Present Times*

Bush, George E. 1965. 'The Fable in the English Periodical, 1660–1800'. Ph. D Diss., St John's University

Caldecott, Randolph, with Alfred Caldecott. 1883. *Some of Aesop's Fables, with Modern Instances, Shewn in Designs by Randolph Caldecott, from new Translations by Alfred Caldecott*

Carnes, Pack, ed. 1985. *Fable Scholarship: An Annotated Bibliography.* New York and London

Certeau, Michel de. 1992. *The Mystic Fable: Volume One, The Sixteenth and Seventeenth Centuries.* Michael B. Smith trans. Chicago and London

Chaucer, Geoffrey. 1973. *Complete Works.* W.W. Skeat ed. 1912. Rpt.

Chippendale, Thomas. 1762. *The Gentleman and Cabinet-Maker's Director.* 3rd ed.

Clark, George. 1965. *The Later Stuarts.* 2nd ed.

Clarke, M. L. 1959. *Classical Education in Britain, 1500–1900.* Cambridge

Cohen, Ralph. 1974. 'On the Interrelations of Eighteenth-Century Literary Forms'. In *New Approaches to Eighteenth-Century English Literature: Selected Papers from the English Institute.* Philip Harth ed. New York and London: pp. 33–78

Colie, Rosalie. 1976. *Paradoxica Epidemica: The Renaissance Tradition of Paradox.* Princeton, 1966. Rpt. Hamden, CN

Cotton, Charles. 1923. *Poems of Charles Cotton, 1630–87.* John Beresford ed.

Cowper, William. 1980–95. *The Poems of William Cowper.* 3 vols. John D. Baird and Charles Ryskamp eds. Oxford

1979, 1981. *The Letters and Prose Writings of William Cowper.* 2 vols. James King and Charles Ryskamp eds. Oxford

Creech, Thomas. 1684. *The Odes, Satyrs, and Epistles of Horace, Done into English.* Oxford and London

Croxall, Samuel. 1766. *Fables of Aesop and Others.* 8th ed.

1730. *A Sermon Preach'd before the Honourable House of Commons, at St. Margaret's Westminster on Friday January 30, 1729*

Daly, Peter M. 1979a. *Emblem Theory: Recent German Contributions to the Characterization of the Emblem Genre.* Liechtenstein

1979b. *Literature in the Light of the Emblem.* Toronto, Buffalo and London

Daly, Peter M. and Leslie T. Duer and Mary V. Silcox, eds. 1993. *The English Emblem Tradition.* 2 vols. Toronto

Daniel, Stephen H. 1982. 'Political and Philosophical Uses of Fables in Eighteenth-Century England'. *The Eighteenth Century* 23, 151–71

'D'Anvers, Caleb'. 1731. *A Collection of Poems on Several Occasions; Publish'd in the Craftsman. By C. D'Anvers.* [This pseudonym covers Nicholas Amherst, Bolingbroke, Pulteney and others.]

Darbishire, Helen, ed. 1932. *The Early Lives of John Milton.*

Day, Geoffrey. 1987. *From Fiction to the Novel.* London and New York. [Chapter 5 is an edited version of Beattie, 'On Fable and Romance', in his *Dissertations Moral and Critical.*]

Defoe, Daniel. 1732. *A New Family Instructor*

Dennis, John. 1693. *Miscellanies in Prose and Verse*

1939, 1943. *The Critical Works of John Dennis.* 2 vols. Edward Niles Hooker ed. Baltimore

1721. *Original Letters*

Devlin, D. D. 1980. *Wordsworth and the Poetry of Epitaphs*

'De Witt, Johan'. 1703. *Fables, Moral and Political with Large Explications. Translated from the Dutch.* 2 vols.

Dobson, Austin. 1896. 'Fielding's Library'. *Eighteenth Century Vignettes* 3, 164–78

Donaldson, Ian, 1970. *The World Upside-Down: Comedy from Jonson to Fielding.* Oxford

Doody, Margaret Anne. 1985. *The Daring Muse: Augustan Poetry Reconsidered.* Cambridge

Doody, Margaret Anne and P. Sabor eds. 1989. *Samuel Richardson: Tercentenary Essays.* Cambridge

Downie, J. A. 1988. 'Gay's Politics'. In Lewis and Wood, pp. 44–61

Dryden, John. 1942. *The Letters of John Dryden With Letters Addressed to Him.* Charles E. Ward ed. Durham, NC

1962. *The Poems and Fables of John Dryden.* J. Kinsley ed. Oxford

1956–92. *The Works of John Dryden.* 20 vols. Edward Niles Hooker, H. T. Swedenberg, et al. eds. Berkeley, CA

Dunton, John. 1707. *Athenian Sport: or, Two Thousand Paradoxes Merrily Argued, To Amuse and Divert the Age. By a Member of the Athenian Society* [i.e. John Dunton]

[Durfey, Tom]. 1698. *Pendragon, or, The Carpet Knight his Kalendar*

Durham, Willard Higley ed. 1915. *Critical Essays of the Eighteenth Century, 1700–25.* New Haven, CN and London

Eames, Marian. 1961. 'John Ogilby and his Aesop'. *BNYPL* 65, 73–88

Economou, George. 1990. 'Hercules in the Mind'. In *The Mythographic Art: Classical Fable and the Rise of the Vernacular in Early France and England.* Jane Chance ed. Gainesville, FA: pp. 246–56

Ellwood, Thomas. 1900. *The History of the Life of Thomas Ellwood.* C.G. Crump ed.

Erskine-Hill, Howard. 1983. *The Augustan Idea in English Literature.*

1995. 'On Historical Commentary: the Case of Milton and Dryden'. In *Presenting Poetry: Composition, Publication, Reception. Essays in Honour of Ian Jack.* Howard Erskine-Hill and Richard A. McCabe eds. Cambridge: pp. 52–74

Etherege, George. 1979. *The Man of Mode.* John Barnard ed. London and New York

Farquhar, George. 1988. *Works.* 2 vols. Shirley Strum Kenny ed. Oxford

Ferry, Anne Davidson. 1962. 'The Bird, the Blind Bard, and the Fortunate Fall'. In *Reason and the Imagination: Studies in the History of the Ideas, 1600–1800.* J. A. Mazzeo ed. New York and London: pp. 183–200

Fielding, Henry. 1967[a]. *The History of the Adventures of Joseph Andrews, and of his Friend Mr. Abraham Adams.* Martin Battestin ed.: Middletown, CN

1967[b]. *The Complete Works of Henry Fielding.* W.E. Henley intro., n.d. Rpt. New York

1971. *An Apology for the Life of Mrs Shamela Andrews.* Douglas Brooks ed. Oxford

1973. *Pasquin: A Dramatick Satire on the Times.* O. M. Brack, Jr., William Kupersmith and Curt A. Zimansky eds. Iowa City, IA

1974. *Tom Jones, or the History of a Foundling.* 2 vols. Fredson Bowers ed. Oxford

1982. *The Life of Mr. Jonathan Wild the Great.* David Nokes ed. Harmondsworth

1988. *The Covent-Garden Journal.* Bertrand Goldgar ed. Oxford

Forrest, Ebenezer. 1729. *Momus Turn'd Fabulist: or, Vulcan's Wedding, an Opera: After the Manner of the Beggar's Opera*

Frese, Dolores Warwick. 1991. *An* Ars Legendi *for Chaucer's* Canterbury Tales: *A Re-constructive Reading.* Gainesville, FA

Gay, John. 1926. *The Poetical Works of John Gay.* G. C. Faber ed.

1966. *The Letters of John Gay.* C. F. Burgess ed. Oxford

1973. *The Beggar's Opera.* Peter E. Lewis ed. Edinburgh

1974. *John Gay, Poetry and Prose.* 2 vols. Vinton A. Dearing and Charles E. Beckwith eds. Oxford

Gloag, John. 1968. 'English Furniture in the French Taste: Part One, The Mid-Eighteenth Century'. *Antiques* September 1968, 355–62

Goldgar, Bertrand A. 1976. *Walpole and the Wits: The Relation of Politics to Literature, 1722–1742.* Lincoln, NE and London

Goldsmith, Oliver. 1966. *The Vicar of Wakefield.* In *Collected Works.* 5 vols. Arthur Friedman ed. Oxford: 4, 13–185

Gould, Robert. 1693. *The Corruption of the Times by Money. A Satyr*

Graham, A. Edwin. 1960. 'John Gay's *Fables*: Edited with an Introduction on the Fable as an Eighteenth-Century Literary Genre'. Ph.D Diss., Princeton University

1969. 'John Gay's Second Series, the *Craftsman* in Fables'. *Papers on Language and Literature* 5, 17–25

Gray, Thomas. 1977. *Thomas Gray and William Collins: Poetical Works.* Roger Lonsdale ed.

Hale, David G. 'Aesop in Renaissance England'. *The Library*, 5th series, 27, 116–27.

Hall-Stevenson, John. 1761. *Fables for Grown Gentlemen: or, A Fable for Every Day in the Week* [there are eight of them]

1762. *Two Lyric Epistles: or, Margery the Cook-Maid to the Critical Reviewers*

1768. *Makarony Fables: with the New Fable of the Bees*

1770. *Fables for Grown Gentlemen . . . for the Year 1770*

Hammond, Brean. 1988. '"A Poet, and a Patron, and Ten Pound": John Gay and Patronage'. In Lewis and Wood, pp. 23–43

Hampton, Timothy. 1990. *Writing from History: the Rhetoric of Exemplarity.* Ithaca, NY

Hanazaki, Tomoko. 1993–4. 'A New Parliament of Birds: Aesop, Fiction, and Jacobite Rhetoric'. *ECS* 27. 2, 235–54

Harris, Benjamin. 1697. *The Fables of Young Aesop, with their Morals. Illustrated with 40 Curious Pictures Applicable to each Fable . . . written by B. H.*

Harrison, Bernard. 1993–4. 'Gaps and Stumbling-Blocks in Fielding: A Response to Çerny, Hammond and Hudson'. *Connotations* 3.2, 147–72

Hartley, Lodwick. 1971. 'Sterne's Eugenius as Indiscreet Author: the Literary Career of John Hall-Stevenson'. *PMLA* 86, 428–45

Hawkesworth, John [as 'H. Greville']. 1741. 'The Experimental Moralist, a Fable'. *GM* 11, 602–3

Heiserman, Arthur, 1977. *The Novel Before the Novel: Essays and Discussions about the Beginnings of Prose Fiction in the West.* Chicago and London

Henderson, Arnold Clayton. 1981. 'Animal Fables as Vehicles of Social Protest and Satire: Twelfth Century to Henderson'. In *Proceedings of the Third International Beast Epic, Fable and Fabliau Colloquium.* Jan Goosens and Timothy Sodmann eds. Köln: pp. 160–73

Hepwith, John. 1641. *The Calidonian Forrest*

Henryson, Robert. 1933. *The Poems and Fables of Robert Henryson, Schoolmaster of Dunfermline.* H. Harvey Wood ed. Edinburgh and London

Herbert, Sir Thomas. 1634. *A Relation of some Yeares Travaile begunne Anno 1626, into Afrique and the Greater Asia . . .*

Heyrick, Thomas. 1687. *The New Atalantis, a Poem . . . With some Reflections upon the Hind and the Panther*

Hirschkop, Ken. 1986. 'Bakhtin, Discourse and Democracy'. *New Left Review* 160, 92–111

Hobbes, Thomas. 1996. *Leviathan.* Richard Tuck ed. Cambridge

Home, Henry, Lord Kames. 1810. *An Introduction to the Art of Thinking.* Edinburgh. 5th ed.

1762. *Elements of Criticism*

Hopkins, Robert H. 1975. 'The Cant of Social Compromise: Some Observations on Mandeville's Satire'. In Primer, pp. 168–92

Horne, Colin J. 1968. '"From a Fable Form a Truth": A Consideration of the Fable in Swift's Poetry. In *Studies in the Eighteenth Century* 1. R. F. Brissenden ed. Canberra: pp. 193–205

Hornbeak, Katherine Gee. 1937. *Richardson's Familiar Letters and the Domestic Conduct Books: Richardson's Aesop*. Northampton, MA: pp. 30–50

Howard, Sir Robert. 1668. *The Duell of the Stags*

Howell, James. 1640. *Dodona's Grove, or the Vocall Forest*

1660. *The Parly of Beasts, or Morphandria, of the Enchanted Land*

1661. *Apologs, or Fables Mythologized*

Hunter, J. Paul. 1990. *Before Novels: The Cultural Contexts of English Fiction*. New York and London

Jacobs, Joseph, ed. 1889. *The History of the Aesopic Fable, The Fables of Aesop as First Printed by William Caxton in 1484 with those of Avian, Alfonso and Poggio.*

Johnson, Samuel. 1755, 1756. *A Dictionary of the English Language*. 2 vols. 2nd ed.

1905. *Lives of the English Poets*. 3 vols. George Birkbeck Hill ed. Oxford

1958–90. *The Yale Edition of the Works of Samuel Johnson*. 16 vols. Various hands eds. New Haven and London

Jonson, Ben. 1977. *Volpone, or The Fox*. David Cook ed. 1962. Rpt.

Josipovici, Gabriel. 1971. *The World and the Book: A Study of Modern Fiction*

Joyce, James. 1992. *Ulysses*. Annotated Students' Edition. Introduction and notes Declan Kiberd. Harmondsworth

Kettle, Arnold. 1967. *An Introduction to the English Novel*. Vol 1. 2nd ed.

Kinsley, James. 1953. 'Dryden's Bestiary'. *RES* ns 4, 331–6

Kishler, Thomas Charles. 1959. *The Satiric Moral Fable: A Study of an Augustan Genre with Particular Reference to Fielding*. Ph.D Diss., University of Wisconsin

Kramnick, Isaac. 1968. *Bolingbroke and His Circle: The Politics of Nostalgia in the Age of Walpole*. Cambridge, MA

La Fontaine, Jean de. 1962. *Fables choisies, mises en vers*. Georges Couton ed. Paris

1991. *Oeuvres Complètes*. Vol. 1: *Fables, Contes, et Nouvelles*. Jean-Pierre Collinet ed. Paris

La Loubère, Simon de. 1693. *A New Historical Relation of the Kingdom of Siam . . .* [translated] *by A. P. Gen. R. SS*

La Motte, Antoine Houdar de. 1721. *One Hundred New Court Fables Written for the Instruction of Princes, and a True Knowledge of the World . . . with a Discourse on Fable*. Robert Samber trans.

Langhorne, John. 1772. *Fables of Flora*. Dublin

Leavis, Q.D. 1932. *Fiction and the Reading Public*

Le Bossu, René. 1675. *Traité du Poëme Epique*. Paris

1697. *A Treatise of the Epick Poem*. 'W. J'. trans.

1970. *A Treatise of the Epick Poem*. 1697. Rpt. *Le Bossu and Voltaire on the Epic*. Stuart Curran intro. Gainesville, FA

Lennox, Charlotte. 1989. *The Female Quixote; or, The Adventures af Arabella*. Margaret Dalziel ed. Oxford

L'Estrange, Sir Roger. 1692. *Fables of Aesop and other Eminent Mythologists with Morals and Reflexions*

1699. *Fables and Storyes Moraliz'd. Being a Second Part of the Fables of Aesop*

1970. *Sir Roger L'Estrange: Selections from the Observator, 1681–1687*. Violet Jourdain ed. Los Angeles, CA

Levine, Joseph M. 1981–2. 'Ancients and Moderns Reconsidered'. *ECS* 15, 72–89

Lewis, Jayne E. 1996. *The English Fable: Aesop and Literary Culture, 1651–1740*. Cambridge

Lewis, Peter, and Nigel Wood eds. 1988. *John Gay and the Scriblerians*. London and New York

Locke, John, 1703. *Aesop's Fables in English and Latin, Interlineary, for the Benefit of Those Who Not Having a Master, Would Learn Either of These Tongues*

1989. *Some Thoughts Concerning Education*. Yolton, John W. and Jean S. eds. Oxford

1975. *An Essay Concerning Human Understanding*. P. H. Nidditch ed. Oxford

Lockman, John. 1744. *The Loves of Cupid and Psyche . . . from the French of La Fontaine . . . by Mr. Lockman*

Longley, Edna. 1986. *Poetry in the Wars*. Newcastle-upon-Tyne

Lord, George DeForest, with William J. Cameron, Frank H. Ellis, et al. eds. 1963–75. *Poems on Affairs of State: Augustan Satirical Verse, 1660–1714*. 7 vols. New Haven, CN

Loveridge, Mark. 1991. '*Northanger Abbey*; or, Nature and Probability'. *Nineteenth-Century Literature* 46, 1–29

1992. 'Stories of COCKS and BULLS: The Ending of *Tristram Shandy*'. *Eighteenth-Century Fiction* 5, 35–54

Lydgate, John. 1934. *The Minor Poems of John Lydgate: Part 2, Secular Poems*. Henry Noble MacCracken ed.

Mandeville, Bernard. 1703. *Some Fables after the Easie and Familiar Method of Monsieur de la Fontaine*

1924. *The Fable of the Bees: or, Private Vices Publick Benefits*. 2 vols. F. B. Kaye ed. Oxford

1966. *Aesop dress'd, or A Collection of Fables Writ in Familiar Verse*. J. S. Shea ed. Los Angeles, CA

1989. *The Fable of the Bees*. Philip Harth ed. Harmondsworth

Mann, Jill, 1991. *Geoffrey Chaucer*. Hemel Hempsted

Mannings, David. 1993–94. 'Reynolds, Garrick, and the Choice of Hercules'. *ECS* 17, 259–83

Marie [de France]. 1984. *The Fables of Marie de France*. Mary Lou Martin trans. and intro. Birmingham, AL

Marryott, Thomas. 1771. *Sentimental Fables Designed Chiefly for the Use of the Ladies*. Belfast

Marvell, Andrew. 1971. *The Poems and Letters of Andrew Marvell*. 2 vols. H. H. Margiolouth ed. Oxford. 3rd ed.

Mayo, Robert D. 1962. *The English Novel in the Magazines, 1740–1815, with a Catalogue of 1735 Magazine Novels and Novelettes*. Evanston, IL

McKendry, John J. 1964. *Aesop: Five Centuries of Illustrated Fables*. New York

McKeon, Michael. 1987. *The Origins of the English Novel, 1600–1740*. Baltimore, MD and London

Miller, Rachel Ann. 1984. 'Dryden's Fables in Seventeen Hundred'. Ph.D Diss., University of California at Los Angeles

Milton, John. 1952. *Paradise Lost*. Helen Darbishire ed. Oxford

Miner, Earl. 1967. 'Chaucer in Dryden's *Fables*'. In *Studies in Criticism and Aesthetics 1660–1800: Essays in Honour of Samuel Holt Monk*. Howard Anderson and John S. Shea eds. Minneapolis: pp. 58–72

1967. *Dryden's Poetry*. Bloomington, IN

Montaigne, Michel de. 1693. *Essays of Michael Seigneur de Montaigne . . . Made English by Charles Cotton, Esq.* 3 vols.

1958. *The Complete Essays of Montaigne*. Donald M. Frame trans. Stanford, CA

Moore, Edward, with Henry Brooke. 1749. *Fables for the Female Sex*. 3rd ed.

Morgan, John R. 1993. 'Make-Believe and Make Believe: The Fictionality of the Greek Novels'. In *Lies and Fiction in the Ancient World*. Christopher Gill and T. P. Wiseman eds. Exeter: pp. 175–229

New, Melvyn. 1976. ' "The Grease of God": The Form of Eighteenth-Century English Fiction'. *PMLA* 19.2, 235–44

Newbigging, Thomas. 1895. *Fables and Fabulists: Ancient and Modern*

Newton, Theodore F. M. 'William Pittis and Queen Anne Journalism: Part II'. *MP* 33, 279–302

Nichols, John. 1823. *The Progresses, and Public Processions, of Queen Elizabeth*. 2nd ed.

Noel, Thomas Lawrence. 1975. *Theories of the Fable in the Eighteenth Century*. New York

Nokes, David. 1995. *John Gay: A Profession of Friendship*

North, Roger. 1959. *Roger North on Music: Being a Selection of his Essays Written During the Years c. 1695–1728*. John Wilson ed.

Ogilby, John. 1651. *Fables of Aesop, Paraphras'd in Verse, Adorned with Sculpture and Illustrated with Annotations*

1668[a]. *Fables of Aesop* . . . Revised ed. [References in the text are mostly to this edition, as this is the one most likely to be available to readers, courtesy of the Augustan Society reprint (intro. Earl Miner. Los Angeles, CA. 1965). Numbering the editions is problematic: the 1668 is a revision of an edition of 1665, together with superior illustrations.]

1668[b]. *Aesopics: or A Second Collection of Fables, Paraphras'd in Verse*

1670. *Africa*

1672. *The Holland Nightingale, or the Sweet Singers of Amsterdam: Being a Paraphrase upon the Fable of the Frogs Fearing the Sun would Marry*

Owen, Joan Hildreth. 1969. 'The Choice of Hercules and the Eighteenth-Century Fabulists'. Ph.D Diss., University of New York

Ozell, John. 1708. *Boileau's* Lutrin . . . *render'd into English Verse* [by John Ozell]

Patey, Douglas Lane. 1984. *Probability and Literary Form: Philosophic Theory and Literary Practice in Augustan England*. Cambridge

Patterson, Annabel. 1987. 'Fables of Power'. In *The Politics of Discourse*. Kevin Sharpe and Steven N. Zwicker eds. Berkeley, CA: pp. 271–96

1991. *Fables of Power: Aesopian Writing and Political History*. Durham, NC and London

Paulson, Ronald. 1974. 'The Simplicity of Hogarth's *Industry and Idleness*'. *ELH* 41, 291–320

Pearson, Roger. 1993. *The Fables of Reason: A Study of Voltaire's* Contes Philosophiques. Oxford

Perry, Ben E. 1965. *Babrius and Phaedrus.* London and Cambridge, MA

Phillips, Edward. 1675. *Theatrum Poetarum Anglicanorum or a Compleat Collection of the Poets*

Pinkus, Philip. 1959. 'Swift and the Ancients-Moderns Controversy'. *UTQ* 29, 46–58

1975. 'Mandeville's Paradox'. In Primer, pp. 193–211

Pittis, William. See under *Aesop at Oxford* and *Bickerstaffe's Aesop.*

Plato. 1986. *Phaedrus.* C. J. Rowe ed. Warminster. 2nd ed.

Pope, Alexander. 1968. *The Poems of Alexander Pope: A One-Volume Edition of the Twickenham Pope.* 1963. John Butt ed. Rpt.

Potter, Lois. 1989. *Secret Rites and Secret Writing: Royalist Literature, 1641–1660.* Cambridge

Powell, Marianne. 1983. *Fabula Docet: Studies in the Background and Interpretation of Henryson's Morall Fabillis.* Odense

Pratt, Robert A. 1972. 'Three Old French Sources of the Nonnes Preestes Tale'. *Speculum* 47, 422–44 and 646–68

Primer, Irwin, ed. 1981. *Mandeville Studies.* The Hague

Prior, Matthew. 1959. *Literary Works.* 2 vols. H. Bunker Wright and Monroe K. Spears eds. Oxford

Pritchard, Mary Henrietta. 1976. 'Fables Moral and Political: The Adaptation of the Aesopian Fable Collection to English Social and Political Life, 1651–1722'. Ph.D Diss., University of Western Ontario

Quarles, Francis. 1635. *Emblemes.*

Radcliffe, Ann. 1968. *The Italian; or, The Confessional of the Black Penitents.* Frederick Gerber ed.

Renoir, Alain. 1967. *The Poetry of John Lydgate*

Reverand, Cedric D. II. 1988. *Dryden's Final Poetic Mode: the Fables.* Philadelphia

Richardson, Samuel. 1739. *Aesop's Fables. With Instructive Morals and Reflections, Abstracted from all Party Considerations, Adapted to all Capacities; And Design'd to Promote Religion, Morality, and Universal Benevolence.... And the Life of Aesop Prefixed*

1967. *Pamela; or, Virtue Rewarded.* Part II. M. Kincaid-Weekes ed. 1962. Rpt.

1971. *Pamela; or, Virtue Rewarded.* T.C. Duncan Eaves and Ben D. Kimpel eds. Boston

1972. *Clarissa, or, The History of a Young Lady.* Angus Ross ed. Harmondsworth

Rodino, Richard H. 1981. 'Notes on the Developing Motives and Structures of Swift's Poetry'. In *Contemporary Studies of Swift's Poetry.* John Irwin Fischer and Donald C. Mell, Jr. eds. Newark, NJ: pp. 87–100

Rogers, William E. 1986. *Upon the Ways: The Structure of* The Canterbury Tales. Victoria, British Columbia

Rothstein, Eric. 1981. *Restoration and Eighteenth-Century Poetry 1660–1780*. Boston, London, and Henley

Rowland, Beryl. 1971. *Blind Beasts: Chaucer's Animal World*. Kent, OH

Rousseau, Jean-Jacques. 1973. *The Social Contract* and *Discourses*. G. D. H. Cole trans. London and Melbourne

1979. *Emile, ou L'Education*. Allan Bloom trans. Harmondsworth

Russell, William. 1772. *Fables Moral and Sentimental*

Rymer, Thomas. 1678. *The Tragedies of the Last Age Consider'd and Examin'd . . .*

Sands, Donald B., ed. 1960. *The History of Reynard the Fox, Translated and Printed by William Caxton*. Cambridge, MA and London

Shaftesbury, Antony Ashley Cooper, Third Earl of. 1914. 'A Historical Draught or Tablature of the Judgement of Hercules'. In *Second Characters or the Language of Forms*. Benjamin Rand ed. Cambridge: pp. 29–61

Shea, John S. 1967. 'Studies in the Verse Fable from La Fontaine to Gay'. Ph.D Diss., University of Minnesota

Shelley, Mary Wollstonecraft. 1982. *Frankenstein; or, The Modern Prometheus. The 1818 text.* James Rieger ed. Chicago and London

Sherlock, William, 1690. *A Vindication of the Case of the Allegiance due to Sovereign Powers*

Sloman, Judith. 1968. 'The Structure of Dryden's Fables'. Ph.D Diss., University of Minnesota

1970–71. 'An Interpretation of Dryden's Fables'. *ECS* 4, 191–211

1985. *Dryden: The Poetics of Translation*. Toronto

Smart, Christopher. 1980–96. *Poetical Works*. 6 vols. Marcus Walsh and Katrina Williamson eds. Oxford

Smith, Mahlon Ellwood. 1915. 'The Fable and Kindred Forms'. *JEGP* 14, 519–29

1931. 'Aesop, a Decayed Celebrity'. *PMLA* 46, 225–35

Spacks, Patricia Meyer. 1965. *John Gay*. New York

Spence, Joseph. 1966. *Observations, Anecdotes and Characters of Books and Men, Collected from Conversation*. 2 vols. James M. Osborn ed. Oxford

Spiers, John, 1971. *Poetry Towards Novel*

Stallybrass, Peter, and Allon White. 1986. *The Politics and Poetics of Transgression*. Ithaca, NY

Steele, Richard, with Joseph Addison. 1987. *The Tatler*. 2 vols. Donald F. Bond ed. Oxford

Sterne, Laurence. 1978. *The Life and Opinions of Tristram Shandy, Gentleman*. 2 vols. Melvyn New and Joan New eds. Gainesville, FA

1935. *Letters of Laurence Sterne*. L. P. Curtis. ed. Oxford

1996. *The Sermons of Laurence Sterne: the Text*. Melvyn New ed. Gainesville, FA

Swift, Jonathan. 1957. *Poems*. 3 vols. Harold Williams ed. Oxford

1963–5. *The Correspondence of Jonathan Swift*. 5 vols. Harold Williams ed. Oxford

1986. *Gulliver's Travels*. Paul Turner ed. Oxford, 1971. Rpt.

1939–75. *The Prose Works of Jonathan Swift*. 16 vols. Herbert Davis, et al. eds. Oxford

Taylor, Rupert. 1967. *The Political Prophecy in England.* New York, 1911. Rpt.
Theobald. 1928. *A Metrical Bestiary of Twelve Chapters by Bishop Theobald.* Alan Wood Rendell trans.
Thornbury, Ethel Margaret. 1966. *Henry Fielding's Theory of the Comic Prose Epic.* Univ. Wisconsin, 1931. Rpt. New York
Tidy, Bill, with Bevis Hillier. 1974. *Dead Funny*
Toland, John. 1704. *The Fables of Aesop. With the Moral Reflexions of Monsieur Baudoin. Translated from the French*
Topsell. Edmund. 1658. *The Historie of Foure-Footed Beastes and Serpents*
Trickett, Rachel. 1967. *The Honest Muse.* Oxford
1983. 'Cowper, Wordsworth, and the Animal Fable'. *RES* ns 34, 471–80
Vanbrugh, John. 1927. *The Complete Works of Sir John Vanbrugh.* 2 vols. Bonamy Dobree and Geoffrey Webb eds.
Varey, Simon, ed. 1982. *Lord Bolingbroke: Contributions to the* Craftsman. Oxford
Venning, Ralph. 1647. *Orthodoxe Paradoxes, or, A Believer Clearing Truth by Seeming Contradictions*
Voltaire, François Marie Arouet. 1972. *Le Monde Comme il Va*; and *Zadig, ou la Destinée.* Claude Blum ed. Paris
Wallace, John M. 1969. 'John Dryden and History: A Problem in Allegorical Reading'. *ELH* 36, 265–90
1974–5. '"Examples Are Best Precepts": Readers and Meaning in Seventeenth-Century Poetry'. *Critical Inquiry* 1, 273–90
Ward, Edward. 1692. *The Miracles Performed by Money.* [See also *Aesop in Select Fables.*]
1955. *The London Spy.* K. Fenwick ed.
Warton, Joseph. 1782. *An Essay on the Genius and Writings of Pope.* 4th ed.
Williams, Basil. 1962. *The Whig Supremacy, 1714–1760.* Oxford. 2nd ed.
Williamson, Audrey. 1974. *Wilkes: A Friend to Liberty*
Wilson, Richard M. 1952. *The Lost Literature of Medieval England*
Wind, Edgar. 1938–39. '"Hercules" and "Orpheus": Two Mock-Heroic Designs by Durer'. *Journal of the Warburg and Courtauld Institutes* 2, 206–18
Woodman, Tom. 1988. '"Vulgar Circumstance" and "Due Civilities": Gay's Art of Polite Living in Town'. In Lewis and Wood, pp. 83–93
Wray, William Rose. 1950. 'The English Fable, 1650–1800'. Ph.D Diss., Yale University
Wynne, John Huddlestone. 1773. *Fables of Flowers, for the Female Sex*
Yost, Calvin Daniel Jr. 1936. *The Poetry of the Gentleman's Magazine: A Study in Eighteenth Century Literary Taste.* Philadelphia
Zwicker, Steven N. 1984. *Politics and Language in Dryden's Poetry: the Arts of Disguise.* Princeton, NJ

Index

Four of the central fables, The Cockerel and the Pearl, The Lion and the Man, The Lion's Share, and The Swallow and Other Birds, have been indexed so as to allow readers to compare different 'applications'. Aesop is indexed as *Aesop*, i.e. as title only. 'Epitaph' is used in its wider sense of 'closure'.

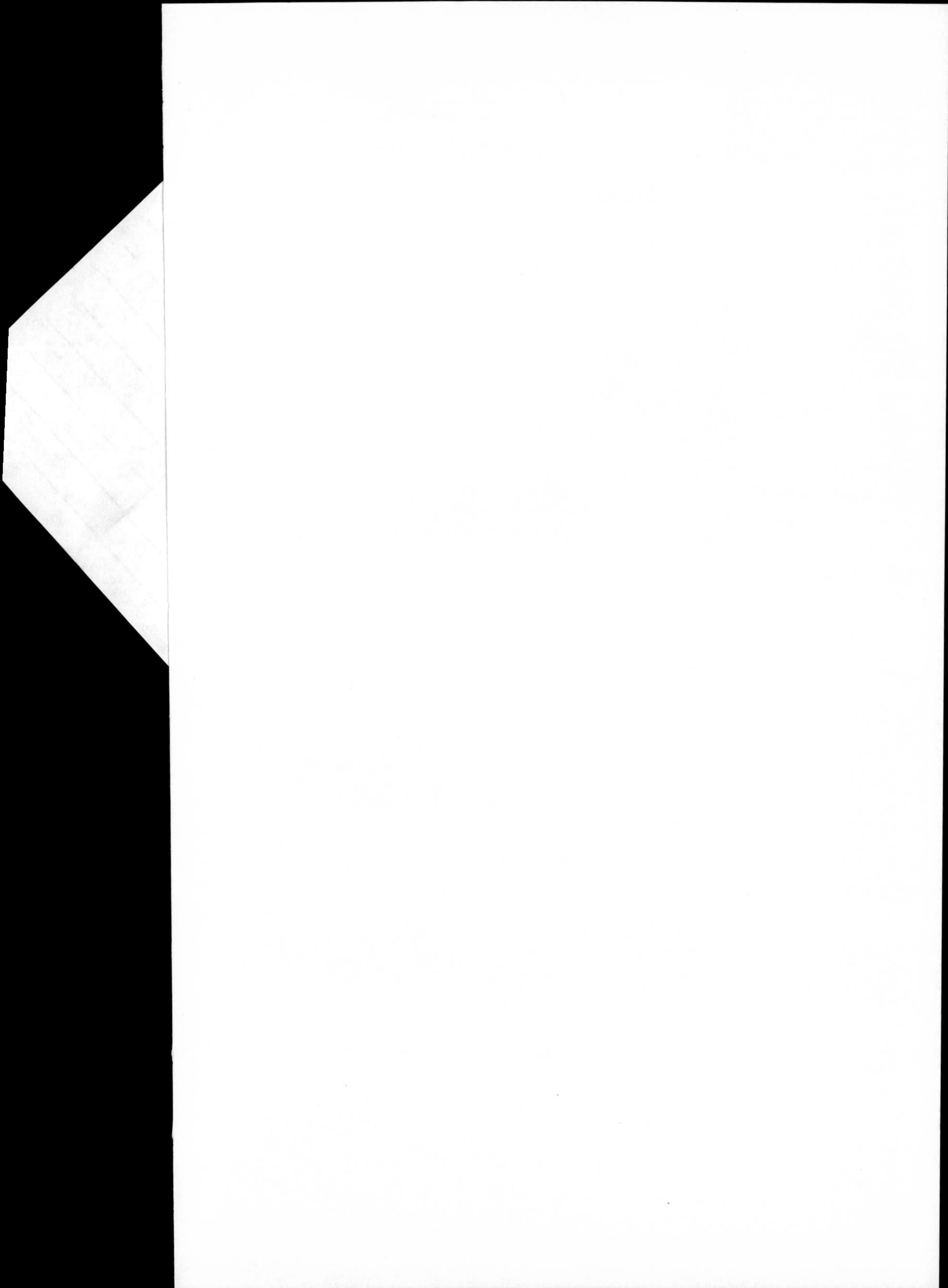

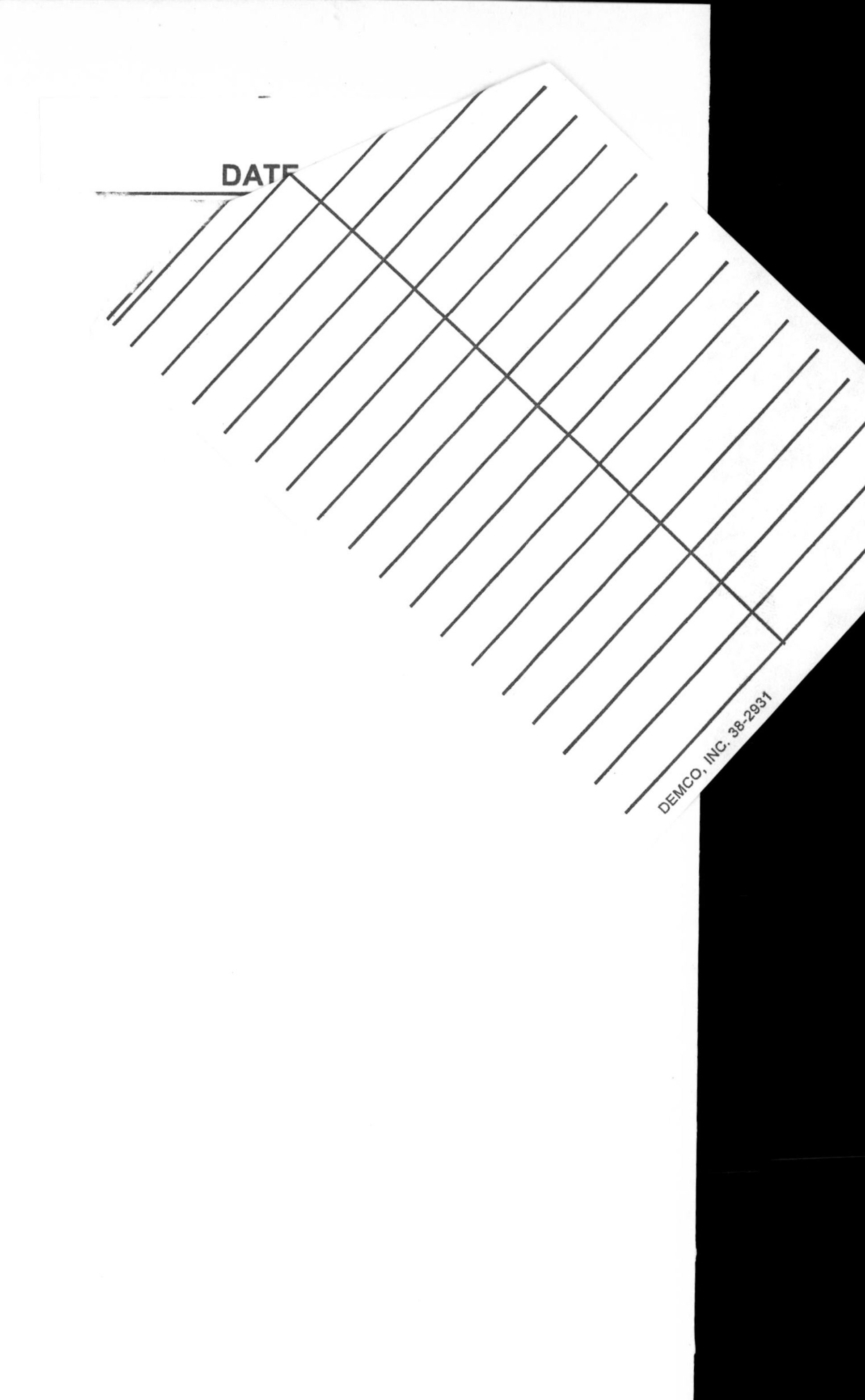
DATE
DEMCO, INC. 38-2931